DETROIT
and the
"Good War"

DETROIT
and the
"Good War"

The World War II Letters of
Mayor Edward Jeffries
and Friends

Dominic J. Capeci Jr., Editor

The University Press of Kentucky

Frontispiece: Mayor Edward J. Jeffries Jr. (right) with
Harold J. Scachern, 1940s, courtesy of Kathlyn Nies.

Scholarly publisher for the Commonwealth,
serving Bellarmine College, Berea College, Centre
College of Kentucky, Eastern Kentucky University,
The Filson Club, Georgetown College, Kentucky
Historical Society, Kentucky State University,
Morehead State University, Murray State University,
Northern Kentucky University, Transylvania University,
University of Kentucky, University of Louisville,
and Western Kentucky University.

Editorial and Sales Offices:
The University Press of Kentucky
663 South Limestone Street, Lexington, Kentucky 40508-4008

96 97 98 99 00   5 4 3 2 1

Library of Congress Cataloging-in-Publication Data

Jeffries, Edward, 1900-
    Detroit and the "Good War" : the World War II letters of Mayor
Edward Jeffries and friends / Dominic J. Capeci, Jr., editor.
        p.   cm.
    Correspondence between Mayor Edward Jeffries, journalists
Martin S. Hayden and John M. Carlisle, and former Detroit city
councilman George C. Edwards.
    Includes bibliographical references (p.   ) and index.
    ISBN 0-8131-1974-X
    1. Jeffries, Edward, 1900- –Correspondence.   2. World War,
1939-1945–Michigan–Detroit.   3. Mayors–Michigan–Detroit–
Correspondence.   4. Detroit (Mich.)–History.   I. Capeci, Dominic J.
II. Title.
F574.D453J44   1997
940.54'8173–dc20   96-2414

Manufactured in the United States of America

Per il mio mentore e amico

GERALD DAVID NASH

CONTENTS

ACKNOWLEDGMENTS

Preparing this manuscript would have been impossible without the assistance of numerous individuals and institutions. I first came across some of the letters in 1977 while researching the rich documents on Detroit history in the Burton Historical Collection and the Archives of Labor and Urban Affairs for a study of race relations during World War II. Into the 1980s and 1990s I uncovered more letters and received cooperation from Burton chiefs Alice C. Dalligan (now retired) and Noel Van Gorden and their staffs, especially Mary M. Karshner, John Gibson, and Judy Barmatoski. Similar support came from Archives assistant director Warner Pflug (now retired), Margaret Raucher, Pat Bartkowski, and Raymond Boryczka. Former director Philp P. Mason assisted with a Henry J. Kaiser Family Foundation Research Travel Grant in 1990. William K. McElhone, curator of research at the Dearborn Historical Museum, sought out letter writers, their heirs, and photographs for me. And the friendship and research of Mike Smith, curator of the Detroit Historical Museum, who also located the book jacket photograph, has been indispensable.

I have benefited also from the talents of several others, including Willa J. Garrett, Carol Lynne Freeman, Frances K. Wolff, and Jim Coombs of the Duane G. Meyer Library; Mark A. Oglesby and Paul Lines of Computer Services; Lyn Young and Margie von der Heide of the secretarial staff, Southwest Missouri State University. Professor Matthew J. Mancini, chair of my department, supported this research most enthusiastically. The late Betty Hindman typed the original draft of each letter, which Holly Bowdidge transposed to computer disk. Judy Barrett Litoff of Bryant College and David C. Smith of the University of Maine, renowned historians of wartime letters and readers for the University of Kentucky Press, advanced many useful suggestions, while Pat Sterling copyedited superbly.

Friends and colleagues also aided me in numerous ways. Professors Robert V. Haynes of Western Kentucky University, Frederick J. Blue of

Youngstown State University, and James N. Giglio of Southwest Missouri State University encouraged this study, as they have all of my previous scholarship. So did George J. Selement. Professors David W. Gutzke and William G. Piston of Southwest Missouri State University and Colonel Daniel D. Murphy of the U.S. Army provided extensive background information, while Teresa L. Layton commented thoughtfully on the initial introduction. Professor Jack C. Knight of Southwest Missouri State University assisted me in preparing the manuscript for publication and, for five months, served as researcher and co-editor; he made its completion possible. I am deeply appreciative of his ability, creativity, and self-sacrifice—and ever grateful for his friendship. Few of us are so gifted and giving.

Nor can I thank enough the letter writers and their families. Eleanor Pedersen granted permission to publish the letters of her uncle, Edward J. Jeffries, Jr., and provided information about him and his family. Before their deaths, George C. Edwards and Martin S. Hayden gave permission for the use of their letters and diary, respectively, and gave several interviews. Their families, as well as those of John M. Carlisle, Harold J. Schachern, and Walton Stoddard White—as the text notes specify—also consented to publication, granted interviews, located photographs, and shared additional materials that enhanced the manuscript. To Margaret McConnell Edwards, James M. Edwards, Betty Hayden, Martin S. Hayden Jr., Anita Ellinger Carlisle, William O. Carlisle, Florence Schachern Smith, Mark Schachern, Kathlyn E. Nies, and Peter S. White I am deeply in debt. Similarly, James P. Simpson released his letters and shed much light on military terms and operations of a bygone era. Glouster B. Current, Louis E. Martin, and George Schermer contributed one or two letters, as did Trude Lash for her husband Joseph and Marie M. Gilbert for her brother, John J. McElhone.

Warmly, I dedicate this manuscript to Gerald David Nash, Emeritus Distinguished Professor of History at the University of New Mexico, who, through his teaching, scholarship, and example, has taught the lessons of life. Few mentors have affected so many and even fewer have been less appreciated, doubtless because his commitment to objectivity and civic duty has seemed incomprehensible and ancient, indeed Periclean to ideologues who turn more on scripted theory than on human spirit. But for those he has touched over the past thirty-seven years, he remains a student's professor and a historian's historian who shared his heartfelt caring and enormous talents, making us better individuals and producing ground-breaking scholarship in twentieth-century administrative, economic, and especially western history.

ABBREVIATIONS

AFL	American Federation of Labor
ALUA	Archives of Labor and Urban Affairs, Walter P. Reuther Library, Detroit
AWOL	Absent without Leave
BHC	Burton Historical Collection, Detroit Public Library
Chronicle	*Michigan Chronicle*
CIO	Congress of Industrial Organizations
DPW	Department of Public Works
DSR	Detroit Street Railways
FDRL	Franklin D. Roosevelt Library, Hyde Park, N.Y.
FFI	Free French Interior
Free Press	*Detroit Free Press*
IRTC	Infantry Replacement Training Center
NARS	National Archives and Records Service, Washington, D.C.
NAACP	National Association for the Advancement of Colored People
News	*Detroit News*
OCD	Office of Civilian Defense
OCS	Officer Candidate School
OPA	Office of Price Administration
PAC	Political Action Committee
Times	*Detroit Times*
SOL	Standard Operation Letter (Edwards)
UAW	United Automobile Workers

NAMES

Ballenger, John F.: police commissioner, 1944–46

Carlisle, Gladys "Peggy" O'Neil: wife of John M. Carlisle

Carlisle, John M.: reporter and war correspondent for the *Detroit News*

Cobo, Albert: city treasurer

Current, Gloster B.: executive secretary, Detroit NAACP

Donovan, Leo: reporter and columnist for the *Detroit Free Press*

Dowling, William E.: Wayne County prosecutor (1942–44); Detroit corporation counsel (1945–46)

Edgecomb, Charles F.: director-secretary of the Detroit Housing Commission

Edwards, George C.: serviceman, U.S. Army (World War II); member of the Detroit Common Council

Edwards, Margaret "Peggy" McConnell: wife of George C. Edwards

Ford, Mabel Nancy: personal secretary to Edward J. Jeffries Jr.

Hayden, Betty Dodds: wife of Martin S. Hayden

Hayden, Jay G.: father of Martin S. Hayden; Washington correspondent for the *Detroit News*

Hayden, Loret Taylor: second wife of Jay G. Hayden

Hayden, Martin S.: serviceman, U.S. Army (World War II), former reporter for the *Detroit News*

Jeffries, Edward J. Jr.: mayor of Detroit (1939–47)

Jeffries, Florence O. Bell: wife of Edward J. Jeffries Jr.

Jeffries, Gary: son of Florence and Edward J. Jeffries Jr.

Krause, Paul E.: corporation counsel (1942–45); Recorder's Court judge (1945–46)

Lamson, William D.: serviceman, U.S. Army (World War II); former secretary of Wayne County CIO Council

Lash, Joseph P.: serviceman, U.S. Army (World War II)

Lodge, John Christian: longtime member of the Detroit Common Council; former mayor (1928–29)

McElhone, John J.: serviceman, Royal Canadian Air Force (World War II); former editor of the *West-Side Conveyor* (UAW Local 174)

Martel, Frank X.: president of Detroit and Wayne County AFL

Martin, Louis E.: publisher and editor of the *Michigan Chronicle*

Moody, Blair: Washington and war correspondent for the *Detroit News*

O'Brien, Gerald K.: Wayne County prosecutor (1945–46)

Oakman, Charles G.: secretary to Edward J. Jeffries Jr.; member of the Detroit Common Council (1945–46)

Schachern, Florence O'Leary: wife of Harold J. Schachern

Schachern, Harold J.: serviceman, U.S. Marine Corps (World War II); former reporter for the *Detroit Times*

Schermer, George: regional representative of the Federal Public Housing Authority

Seiffert, Karl: reporter for the *Detroit News*

Simpson, Anna Beth Lee: wife of James P. Simpson

Simpson, James P.: serviceman, U.S. Army (World War II); former attorney in Corpus Christi, Texas

Slutz, Donald: Detroit city controller

White, Margaret "Peg" Phalan: wife of Walton Stoddard White

White, Walton Stoddard: serviceman, U.S. Army (World War II); former rewrite journalist for the *Detroit News*

Witherspoon, John H.: police commissioner (1942-43)

DETROIT
and the
"Good War"

INTRODUCTION

Written during the "Good War" by close friends who shared a love for the city in which they worked and played, these letters reveal much about personal relationships in an era of dynamic change. They provide insights into the operation of city government and, equally, the city pride that first drew these politicos and newsmen together in the late 1930s. They also indicate the enormous socioeconomic impact of World War II on Detroit as it shifted from a depressed automobile-producing center to the Arsenal of Democracy accountable for fully 70 percent of Michigan's and 35 percent of the nation's war production.[1]

Even more than the changes or plans at home, however, the letters tell the story of military life–basic training and promotion, combat and tragedy, victory and demobilization–and the deep caring between very talented men who jousted and joked, sometimes even competed, but always respected and loved one another. Theirs was more than simple friendship, though it bore many of the same traits: equality, "visceral intimacy," mutual protection or "wildness," respect, esteem, deep caring, and "a holding in the heart."[2] Indeed, these letter writers created a kinship by association that bound them to one another and to civic values.

Detroiters[3] in more than residency, they drew their energy from Edward J. Jeffries Jr., the city's four-term mayor, and shared his commitment to public citizenship. Twelve to fourteen years older and more accomplished than most of the others when they first met in the late 1930s, he enjoyed the greatest authority and, however indirectly or unconsciously, assumed responsibility for their well-being.[4] His reverence for the city as a center of active life impressed the letter writers, who genuinely shared a Greek civic virtue that required laws in place of "personal whims," principles of duty to "the socially disadvantaged," and enhancements for "the grace of living." His hope–and theirs–was to see Detroit as a "single body, highly diversified in detail" but unified in "all matters which concerned the good of the city."[5] Jeffries, like the Athenian Pericles, seemed to fear his mistakes more than his enemy's

1

strategies, while his friends endeavored to harmonize their individual lives and personal thought and understood that the essential quality for community building, if not for humanity, was politics and "political character."[6] These Detroiters approached their municipality as a living organism and considered their relationship to it and to themselves in terms of commitment and loyalty.

Jeffries combined class, education, and public citizenship to emerge as the group's exemplar and Detroit's leader during World War II. Born to Minnie J. Stotts and Edward J. Jeffries on April 3, 1900, he and his sisters, Grace and Lola, grew up in a loving, socially aware, and politically active family. His Detroit-born parents often spoke about "municipal problems" and infused in their son a love of the city and a sense of civic obligation.[7] His father had been an alderman, police justice, and—for twenty-four years—Recorder's Court judge. Elected by blacks, ethnics, and laborers, he envisioned himself "the personal body guard of the downtrodden."[8] A maverick who had recruited for Coxey's Army, identified with various parties, and sought the mayoralty several times, "Ole Jeff" had taught his son political independence and constitutional rights, and instilled in him ambition for public office. Young Jeffries's mother, in contrast, appeared less ideological and more practical than the judge and thankful (after years of making ends meet while he represented poor clients) for the steady income of his judgeship; her son's sense of fiscal responsibility began with her example and continued under his sister Lola's influence. Small wonder that Jeffries considered his participation in public life inevitable and combined "liberal instincts with a pragmatic streak."[9]

Young Jeff embraced his father's respectability instead of his radicalism. He had been exposed to both, for the judge's brilliant legal mind, irreproachable honesty, and ability to separate politics from friendship appealed to Detroit's elite. Hence the elder Jeffries held membership in the Maccabees (the fraternal insurance society), helped organize the Detroit Hunt and Fish Club, and hob-nobbed with millionaires such as Henry Ford.[10] Because of his father's status, his mother's influence, and his own identity needs, Jeffries embraced the middle class, although he believed that it was losing ground to both the lower class that had elected his father to office and the upper class that had embraced him socially. He rejected his father's commitment to the new urban politics that had resulted in the competition by special interest groups for municipal favors; he confided that others, particularly lawyers like himself, deserved "more consideration" than they had been getting.[11]

Nonetheless, Jeffries both followed in and walked beyond his father's footsteps. After attending Detroit public schools, he graduated from the

Figure 1. Edward J. Jeffries Jr. and his wife, Florence, late 1930s or early 1940s. Courtesy of Eleanor H. Pedersen.

University of Michigan with a Bachelor of Arts degree (1920) and, like his father, a law degree (1923). He then studied Roman and British common law at Lincoln's Inn in London and visited much of post–World War I Europe. Upon returning to Detroit the following year, he opened a legal practice. In 1930 he married Florence O. Bell. Meanwhile, in 1929 he had become the Maccabees' general counsel, a position that he held until his death in 1950 and that enabled him to remain an independent and honest public official. Benefiting from the "natural inheritance" of his father's popularity and teamster following, he won a seat on the Detroit Common Council from 1932 to 1938 and its presidency for 1938-39.[12]

Ironically, during Jeffries's councilmanic service, he combined his father's nonpartisanship with the progressive creed of those who had desired the judge's political demise. He knew that the Detroit Citizens League sought to unseat the judge. Founded in 1912 as a Protestant crusade for moral uplift that evolved into a political reform movement for good government—successfully revising the city charter along lines of nonpartisan, at-large elections and business-efficient municipal operations five years later—the league then endeavored to influence law enforcement. Led by secretary William P. Lovett, it charged liberal judges such as the elder Jeffries with coddling lower- and working-class offenders, and associating with "a political 'gang' allied with the 'underworld.'" The judges countered that the league, no longer representing true reform, sought to control the Recorder's Court by replacing independent justices with its bloc of "Big Four" candidates.[13] Judge Jeffries and his liberal colleagues survived one of the bitterest municipal campaigns ever to hand the Citizens League its first serious defeat, largely because the *Times* and, especially, first-time judicial office-seeker Frank Murphy flailed away at "The Danger of Bloc Controlled Justice." They scored big among black and ethnic voters who resented the league's so-called court reform as a program to impose social control over their lives, a point reiterated by league candidates receiving support from native-born whites. Only Murphy appealed across class, ethnic, and race lines to finish first, while Jeffries finished third, and two of the Big Four survived in the fourth and fifth positions.[14]

That had occurred in 1923, while the younger Jeffries was studying abroad yet supporting his father's political ordeal, if not all his left-leaning beliefs. In fact, ultimately, he embraced a neo-progressive philosophy that stemmed from turn-of-the-century endeavors of organizations and individuals such as the Citizens League and Lovett. Thus, he believed that Detroit suffered "growing pains of tremendous social changes," requiring urgent though not radical action; he considered its government system "unexcelled" among major cities and most "thoroughly democratic," needing only to increase middle-class input and find competent men—"good men" in the league's words—to serve. In addition, he emphasized independence and efficiency. Less caught up in the politics of morality than were many league members, he nevertheless acted like many progressives—the so-called instrumentalists—in deciding what needed to be done and figuring out "some morally acceptable way of doing it."[15]

Jeffries's neo-progressivism was also influenced by the Great Depression, in part from the philosophy of President Herbert C. Hoover and in part from his own membership on the Common Council. Like Hoover, he emphasized independence above all and equated its loss with federal intervention; unlike Hoover, he seemed less concerned about individual citizens "selling their traditional freedoms for government subsidies" than fearful of state and local officials losing their rights of governance.[16] As a councilman during the height of economic crises, however, Jeffries realized that federal assistance was imperative for the city because its financial burdens were beyond local solution and were being addressed inadequately by the state officials who controlled much-needed revenues. He learned from Mayor Frank Murphy the lesson of organizing unprecedented coalitions with other mayors across Michigan and, via the United States Conference of Mayors, throughout the nation as a means to advance their interests in order to resolve urban problems.[17]

Jeffries also came under the wing of John C. Lodge, who had been reelected to the Common Council every year since 1909, had won the mayoralty with Detroit Citizens League backing in 1927, and had befriended "Junior" in council throughout the 1930s. The elder statesman's moderate political philosophy and dignified public demeanor reinforced his own. No doubt as a "boon" companion to John Christian Lodge, one of the league's most prominent original supporters, Jeffries also became increasingly attractive to the "power structure"; like his father he was articulate and honest but, unlike him, he stayed within the "conventional bounds" of socioeconomic theory and personal style.[18] He understood social justice but lacked his father's passionate commitment to it. Furthermore, he disagreed outright with his father's radical economics, despite having followed Ole Jeff's urging to experience the world of the working class by toiling on the assembly line at Ford's Rouge plant before its unionization. Sympathetic with workers yet advocating a "middle-of-the-road" position in industrial problems, young Jeff envisioned himself an arbiter for labor-management negotiations.[19] Ironically indeed, the league and its constituents, who had worked for the judge's political demise, would actively promote his son's mayoralty (endorsing it four times and emerging as one of its major supporters).

On the eve of his first mayoral campaign (1939), Jeffries meshed his upbringing and Lodge's friendship with his own experiences to create a Periclean idiom. Speaking confidentially about his candidacy to William P. Lovett of the Detroit Citizens League, he contended that the city was "in crying need of civic leadership." His version of it, he said, would be unafraid, without political ambition, and characterized by practical economics and "rigid independence of opinion and action" without favor to anyone or any group. Jeffries committed himself to keeping "organized pressure groups" in perspective while seeking to unify the entire community.[20] Clearly, he promoted the "middle-class ethos" that created his father's progressive opponents and considered the "immigrant ethos" of the judge's constituency problematic or even threatening, though not wholly intolerable; as a modern orator and legislator—a statesman in classical terms—he envisioned himself building coalitions for the common good, and his supporters envisioned him as a personality capable of individual, independent leadership.[21] Significantly, he remained his father's son while also being his own man, reconciling the judge's radical politics, irrepressible personality, and civic responsibility with his own moderate beliefs, personal impulses, and obligation to all citizens. Full of hope and confidence in himself and in his city, he sounded very much a reformer of the day: an apolitically democratic, economically conservative, and socially responsible "civic mechanic" who understood the city's operations and loved its people.[22]

Small wonder that Jeffries seemed the ideal candidate to end the corrupt tenure of Mayor Richard W. Reading and begin the reform of city government. In 1937 Reading had campaigned on his long-term position as city clerk and presented his opponent's liberal and union supporters as Communists seeking to control the municipality. Once elected, he invoked mayoral powers and, with his son as executive secretary, engaged in graft, selling protection for policy games and promotions to police officers. His corruption, which ultimately resulted in the indictment of 135 persons, first came to light as he prepared for reelection in August 1939. Given this revelation and the ongoing labor strife in the automobile industry, his charges that Jeffries's backers, like those of his previous opponent, represented radicals bent on controlling city hall fell on deaf ears.[23]

Indeed, Jeffries crushed Reading: he received more than twice as many ballots—226,185 to 108,973—and carried 731 of 961 voting precincts, including many of those working-class ethnic and black neighborhoods that had supported his father and that also sought changes in a police department known for its brutality and bigotry. Jeffries presented himself as the candidate of all people, promising every citizen and every group full participation in a truly representative government. He privately criticized Reading for an administration "shot through with politics" and inept in economic and budgetary matters; he publicly pledged himself to appoint a new police commissioner, negotiate labor-management conflict, and impose fiscal responsibility.[24]

Jeffries moved quickly to make good his promises of reform and civic leadership. He did appoint a new police commissioner and supported his efforts to clean up the department and improve its tarnished image. He named Italian-American James V. Bellanca as civil service commissioner and Rev. Horace A. White of Plymouth Congregational Church as the first black housing commissioner, thereby delivering on his pledge to open the government to all groups and on his debt to black voters. In time, he also investigated racial conflicts at Northwestern High School and Belle Isle, hired numerous blacks in municipal jobs, and remained neutral enough on labor relations throughout the city to retain black and union support for his reelection in 1941 over Recorder's Court Judge Joseph A. Gillis.[25]

During that first mayoral term, Jeffries introduced the electorate to new people, new jargon, and new dreams. In fact, his most important appointments were noteworthy for their youth. He selected banking attorney Frank D. Eaman as police commissioner, *News* reporter Donald Slutz as city controller, and his law partner–college roommate Paul E. Krause as corporation counsel. A councilman at thirty-one, council president at thirty-seven, and mayor at thirty-nine, Jeffries surrounded himself with "new brooms turned loose on a dirtied city," only one of which—Eaman—had reached his forty-first birthday.

Not surprisingly, insiders referred to themselves as "the boys in the movement" and warmed to their boss's colorful references to himself as "Pop," as in "Pop is going to get things done"; to themselves as "Great" Slutz, "Hermie" Krause, and similar sobriquets; and to the electorate as "the folks out front." He spoke inspirationally of the need for a public servant to be "intellectually honest—not just money honest." He boldly dreamed "big dreams" for the municipality, everything from zoning codes to expressways.[26]

Perhaps most characteristic of Jeffries's mayoralty, in his commitment to "fishbowl" government, were his relations with newsmen, particularly those who covered city hall. He knew that the press shaped public opinion and contributed to a candidate's election or defeat and to an elected official's success or failure. Beyond these political realities, he believed that voters were entitled to understand the operation of government and, subsequently, approve or change it. His political sense, government philosophy, and no-nonsense personality fit well with an era that permitted journalists to sit at the same table as council members or to occupy city offices, including the mayor's, with the familiarity of relatives. Sometimes he criticized a specific reporter or story for misinterpreting him or his administration; generally, he responded to journalistic queries and endeavored to get his point before the public. Unlike his father, who had feuded with reporters, he befriended them.[27]

In part, this occurred because Jeffries shared their life-style. Like them, he worked long hours and played hard afterward, sometimes beyond midnight. Like them, he smoked heavily, drank moderately, and gambled often, particularly in their running card games of gin rummy and poker. Like them, he enjoyed sports, watching the Detroit Tigers play baseball and Andy Varipapa bowl; he too bowled and, above all, played golf regularly and well. Like them, he found in all these activities genuine camaraderie, friendly competition, and momentary relaxation— a respite from mayoral responsibilities, and, given his father's renown, perhaps an identity of his own and a liberation of sorts. Like them, he enjoyed life and asked, quite rhetorically, "Do you want to live forever?" Neither an alcoholic nor a Lothario, he was never seen drunk or with a woman other than his wife; and when they adopted three-year-old Gary in 1940, he found time for their son.[28]

Jeffries also consorted with newsmen because they shared similar philosophies and commitments. His moderate politics and pragmatism reflected theirs, no one being an ideologue of the right or left. His open-government philosophy dovetailed with their belief in a free press, both of which emanated from the Bill of Rights, which his father had espoused. His desire to serve the public and "do good things for the people of Detroit"—albeit with greater impact than that of reporters—mirrored their sense of civic duty.[29] So did his job, which allowed him "to mind other people's business" and brought him great pleasure.[30]

Simply put, Jeffries and newsmen liked one another. He was outgoing: "quick talk, quick think, quick everything." He was also "a smart aleck" and a caring friend, a proven ally and a feisty rival, or the sternest of critics.[31] Sometimes brutally frank and other times absolutely sensitive, Jeffries never gave the impression of "sitting on his throne." Exciting to be around, he loved a good argument and exchanged verbal thrashings without bearing a grudge.[32] A friend forever, he could be counted on for a good news story or a reference letter. To reporters close to him, he was one of them.

Of those who covered city hall, Martin S. Hayden first met Jeffries in early 1938 and became one of his closest friends. Born in 1912, the son of Marguerite Scholl and Jay G. Hayden (who became the *News*'s national correspondent thirteen years later and served in that capacity for half a century), Hayden spent most of his youth in Washington, D.C. He was twelve when his mother died; subsequently, his father married Loret Taylor, whom Martin respectfully called "Aunt Loret." Shortly thereafter, Hayden entered the Culver Military Academy in Indiana and worked on its newspaper before graduating in 1929. Admonished by his father to get a job at the age of seventeen because of his lack of interest in academics, he worked for eight months as a cub reporter on the *Kansas City Star*. That summer of 1930, Hayden enrolled at the University of Michigan, and—with his father's assistance—hired on as the News correspondent in Ann Arbor.[33]

Like Jeffries, Hayden was influenced by his father. Despite very early aspirations to become a policeman or a soldier, he turned to journalism; he also embraced the politics of his father, a liberal Republican who had handled the campaign for municipal ownership of the street railway system. Indeed, the elder Hayden had possessed "a hell roaring enthusiasm for Theodore Roosevelt" in the presidential election of 1912 and supported Robert M. La Follette twelve years later—both Progressive Party candidates who were, like Jeffries, in search of order.[34] Hence, when the younger Hayden was encouraged by the noted Civil War historian Dwight L. Dumond to pursue a doctorate at the University of Michigan, he thought about it "for twenty-four hours"—and then entered his father's profession, hopeful of becoming, like him, a correspondent in Washington. After eloping with Elizabeth Dodds in mid-1938, he honored his father by naming their first child for him: Jay George (1940). Their second son, born the following year, carries the name of his maternal grandfather, John Daniel.[35]

Following graduation from college, Hayden became a member of the *News* staff in Detroit and served in various capacities until his assignment to city hall during Jeffries's term as president of the Common Council. Their friendship was forged in the mayoral campaign, when Hayden rode with Jeffries "every night" and they shared personal thoughts. Hayden served as a confidant and sounding board for some of Jeffries's most important decisions, including the appointment of Eaman as police commissioner. Over time their relationship deepened, prompting a normally very stoic Jeffries to admit during the war: "I thought an awful lot about you in the last couple of weeks and worried some."[36]

Jeffries also thought highly of John M. Carlisle, star reporter for the *News*. Born in 1905 to Catherine Louise West and John MacGregor Carlisle, he experienced a somewhat rocky childhood. His father, a very good chef and baker, drank heavily, brandished a temper, and lost jobs regularly; his mother, also a talented cook and a devout Lutheran, held the family together as it moved around Michigan. Indeed, Carlisle's mother provided his "only security," seeing to it that he completed grammar school in Detroit and high school in Lapeer, where at sixteen he worked as a "printer's devil" and reporter for the *County Press*. In 1927, again with his mother's support and after working on the college paper, he graduated from the University of Detroit. That same year he married Gladys O'Neil—daughter of William O'Neil, the president of Dodge Motor Company—and joined the staff of the *News*. Thereafter, he and Peggy, as he called his wife, settled in Highland Park and reared John (1933), William (1936), and Susan (1941). He also loomed large as the city's hardest-driving journalist, covering the trials of gangster Al Capone and child-killer Alphonse Vlemminck, the kidnapping of Charles Lindbergh's baby, and the underworld of the Purple Gang.[37]

Lacking the paternal influence enjoyed by Jeffries and Hayden, Carlisle acquired his mother's persistence—which in him became a relentlessly competitive spirit. As a youngster he loved sports, especially football, and as an adult he pursued a story like "a runaway horse" and trampled anyone in his path, including fellow reporters on his own newspaper.[38] Short and husky, aggressive and blunt, sometimes profane and guileful, he was capable of placing "out of order signs" on public telephones to prevent competing journalists from calling in stories ahead of him; he also proved to be dependable, resourceful, and talented, a professional true to his sources.[39] He believed that "the world belongs to the bull" and that "there is no such thing as a 9 to 5 reporter." A hard-working, hard-drinking Scot, Carlisle considered himself politically nonpartisan, moderate, and independent. Small wonder that he and Jeffries understood each other, or that their friendship grew as Jeffries rose in Detroit politics.[40]

Among newsmen with whom Jeffries was close but less intimate, the most important were Walton Stoddard White and Harold Schachern. In some ways White resembled Hayden. He was born in 1913, the son of Florence E. Baker and Lee A. White, cofounders of the Cranbrook Institutions (a complex of privately supported cultural centers). His father was renowned as a journalist, lecturer, and official for the *News,* as well as one of the originators of La Choy Food Products.[41] White and his sister Elizabeth grew up in Birmingham, outside Detroit. He became an apprentice for the weekly *Birmingham Eccentric* and, while still in his teens, its managing editor. He attended the University of Michigan, as had his father before him. There he met and married Margaret Phalan, "Peg," though they waited until after the war to begin a family.

He graduated in 1934 and went to work for the *News,* doubtless with his father's assistance, where he excelled as a rewrite man. White was known by his middle name or its abbreviation, "Stod." Slight in build, less voluble and less assertive than most of Jeffries's friends, he was gracious and urbane. Nor was he "a political animal," though he stood to the left of Jeffries and unsuccessfully endeavored to establish a guild for editorial writers at the *News.* He always supported Jeffries, whose path he crossed increasingly once assigned to city hall in 1939, and he became a favorite of the mayor's secretary, Mabel Nancy Ford.[42]

Harold J. Schachern also covered city hall and became a good friend of Jeffries. Like White in demeanor, his working-class and ethnic background came closer to resembling that of Carlisle. Born in 1913 to Blanche Mateer and James Schachern, German-Irish grocers from western Pennsylvania, he grew up in Pontiac with older brother Keith and younger sister Kathlyn. He on saxophone and clarinet, Keith on piano, and a friend on drums, they earned money as part-time musicians. Six feet tall and of medium build, he also played football well enough to receive an athletic scholarship to Assumption College in Windsor, Ontario, which enabled him to attend Western Ontario University in London and St. Michael's College in Toronto. After graduating in 1938, as the son of devout Roman Catholics and the product of parochial education, he seriously considered entering the priesthood. Instead, Schachern joined the *Washenaw Post Tribune* and then the *Pontiac Daily Press* before signing on with the *Times.* Doubtless he did so because of equally devout Florence O'Leary, a nurse he had met the year of his graduation and married a year later. They settled in Pontiac, he commuted to work in Detroit, and in 1940 she gave birth to Kathlyn.[43]

Like White, Schachern possessed a keen, encyclopedic mind and a warm personality. Witty and perceptive, he related well to everyone, a characteristic that enabled him to express an "ecumenical spirit" as an internationally known religious writer later in life.[44] Like many in Jeffries's circle, he enjoyed a drink and sports. Yet he neither gambled nor bore a combative personality, and his liberal politics on race relations and union policy placed him to the left of most newsmen at city hall. Perhaps as significantly, his daily commute, budding family, and religious commitment preempted late evenings in Detroit. He covered the Jeffries beat and became a "good friend," but he neither advised nor ran with the mayor. Their friendship, like that of Jeffries and White, rested on each one's admiration for the other's ability and willingness to advance the other's efforts as far as possible.[45]

Very different in background and upbringing from the newsmen, George C. Edwards became almost as close to Jeffries as Hayden. A

Texan, born in 1914, he enjoyed a loving upbringing in Dallas. Because his parents suffered from tuberculosis, he and and older sister Nicky had lived with aunts during the first four years of his life, but thereafter the family united and proved inseparable. George and his sister bore the names of their father and mother, George C. Edwards and Octavia Nichols, public school teachers who also played a role in founding the Episcopalian Church of the Incarnation in Dallas. Their mother stressed religion, while their father, already disenchanted with it, became a lawyer who represented cotton mill workers, unionists, and blacks. He enrolled his infant son in the Socialist Party; emerged as the local labor, American Civil Liberties Union, and NAACP lawyer; supported La Follette in 1924; grieved for Sacco and Vanzetti in 1927; and opposed the Ku Klux Klan throughout his life. His commitment to social justice—like his motto, "*Toujours l'audace*," courage always—greatly influenced young George.[46] So did Octavia Edwards's willingness to give individuals a chance, for ironically her husband "loved humanity" but "wasn't that fond of people." From different perspectives they taught that "love is the single most important principle in the universe."[47]

The college-bred Edwardses educated their children as well. Nicky attended Southern Methodist University and won a scholarship to the Sorbonne, her studies never limited because of gender. George, in turn, graduated from SMU in three years and completed a Harvard University master's degree in literature in one year. In 1934, not yet twenty, he left academe "to make some contribution toward a society where sanity and reason could dominate brute force and passion." He headed for New York City, roomed with Joseph Lash (a later confidant and prize-winning biographer of Eleanor Roosevelt), and worked for Norman Thomas's League for Industrial Democracy.[48]

Two years later he arrived in Detroit with the hope of writing a novel about autoworkers. Instead, he took a job at the Kelsey Wheel Company, joined the United Automobile Workers, and became an organizer assigned to Walter P. Reuther's Local 174. Assisting female workers at the Yale & Towne Manufacturing Company in a sit-down of 1937, he defied a court injunction and challenged a judge; refusing to apologize for his actions, he served thirty days in jail. He emerged as director of the UAW Welfare Department the following year, and came to know several reporters and officials as his work brought him to city hall. During this period he also befriended Bill Lamson, secretary of the Wayne County CIO Council, and John J. McElhone, editor and educational director of UAW West Side Local 174.[49]

In 1939 Edwards married Margaret McConnell, well-educated daughter of Lillian Florence (Morganson) and Rollin "Cap" McConnell, a prominent stockbroker. He and Peg began a family with the birth of "Andy," né George C. Edwards III, in 1940. That year Edwards also became Jeffries's director of the Detroit Housing Commission, assuming his first public office at age twenty-five.[50]

Surely, Edwards and Jeffries seemed an odd couple: one a young, little-known outsider, a liberal, and a unionist, a man who both studied law at the University of Detroit and enjoyed home life in the evenings; the other a somewhat older, prominent native son, a moderate, a publicly elected official, and a sports enthusiast who lived hard by night. And yet they shared much: as sons who sought both to emulate and to become independent of their accomplished fathers; as highly educated, well-traveled, public figures who endeavored to make their world a better place in which to live; as highly intelligent, very personable individuals who respected each other. Their paths crossed in the Common Council, where Edwards debated Jeffries over labor issues and where the mayor realized that the UAW welfare director, although loyal to the union, was (as later described by columnist W. K. Kelsey) more than "a stooge for a special group."[51] In all likelihood, Edwards appeared to the mayor as his Periclean self, one decade removed.

From the beginning, Edwards and Jeffries realized that they could achieve common goals together. Like most unionists, Edwards had worked for Jeffries's election and afterward, as housing director, fulfilled his commitment to represent all Detroiters. Edwards so impressed Jeffries that in 1941 the mayor urged him to run for a council seat and used his personal influence and political machinery to help elect this youngest councilman. Beyond their friendship, Jeffries also understood the reality that labor was a permanent political force requiring representation in the city government and that he—and the privileged sections of Detroit that he had opened to Edwards—preferred to deal with a personable, educated unionist. Once in office, Edwards aligned with liberal forces but, like Jeffries, served "the community as a whole."[52]

While becoming a true Detroiter, Edwards still kept in touch with Dallas friends, including James P. Simpson, one of three or four fraternity brothers at Southern Methodist University who appreciated in one another an inquisitiveness and "an interest in argumentation."[53] Simpson, born in 1914, the son of Nellie Lee and James P. Simpson, a pioneer in movie advertisement, came from an upper-middle-class family. He enrolled in Culver Military Academy but soon felt out of place with the "country club set." Then in 1930, he received word of his father's suicide (one of many triggered by fiscal disaster in the Great Depression). With his mother's assistance, he endured that shock, graduated from military school, and attended SMU. There he became friends with Edwards, a "fascinating" and intellectually stimulating upper classman, and his family. He borrowed books from the Edwardses' library, and in the summer of 1932 he, George, and two other fraternity brothers traveled south of the border. It was his first contact with a foreign nationality, and that experience with the "naturally polite and civil" Mexican peasants greatly influenced his positive view of the Filipinos a decade later. After graduation in 1937, Simpson practiced law in Corpus Christi. He corresponded with Edwards throughout the 1930s and the two visited whenever Edwards came to Dallas. Simpson married Anna Beth Merritt in 1941, and they vacationed in Mexico with George and Peg Edwards. Within a year, he entered the service.[54]

As the 1940s opened, then, Jeffries and friends were entering the most exciting time of their lives—and of both Detroit's and the world's history. The previous decade had been difficult; the city had sunk lower during the Depression than most other large urban centers, its banks among the first to close and its industry among the hardest hit. In the early 1930s, automobile workers experienced large-scale unemployment or, for those fortunate enough to hold their jobs, lower wages and the speed-up of production lines that increased underemployment. Indeed, the industrial employment index dropped to 41.8 percent in March 1933 as 350,000 Detroiters stood like "hostages" in idle lines. Black residents, having never been fully accepted into car manufacturing or any other part of the municipality, constituted nearly a third of the relief rolls during the same period. And even as the city's total population initially declined, their numbers had increased by the end of decade—as had the abject housing conditions in which many Detroiters lived and the labor-management strife, which was ultimately won by the UAW.[55]

Jeffries took office amid these socioeconomic conditions and ongoing conflicts. Detroiters numbered 1,623,452 and, more than ever, were overtaxing the already limited housing and recreation facilities. Many of them—particularly among the nearly 150,000 blacks who made up 9.2 percent of the population—remained on the edges of economic recovery and beyond the continuing labor wars, though union and management increasingly fought for their allegiance. Given ten years of bust, the onset of war abroad, and ongoing economic uncertainty at home, few of the city's residents expressed confidence about the future.[56]

The Second World War heralded the change to come. After cleaning up the corruption left by Reading, Jeffries faced a myriad of problems as Detroit became the "Arsenal of Democracy." Automobile magnates hesitated to accept federal contracts until the summer of 1940 and refused to halt car production completely for another twenty months–long after the nation's official entry into the war. UAW leaders criticized this hesitancy, even though converting from peacetime to wartime output led to temporary unemployment. By the end of 1942, however, despite hundreds of wildcat strikes, industrialists and laborers closed ranks long enough to produce war materiel at the rate of over $8 billion a year. Their output–and their strikes–increased steadily (as did job security and wages) and peaked in October 1943 at the incredible annual pace of $12 billion. Indeed, Detroiters produced "the tools of victory."[57]

As war production brought economic prosperity, it changed Jeffries's city into "a frontier town of the gold rush period."[58] Job-seeking migrants–numbering over 190,000 between April 1940 and March 1943–inundated the metropolitan area.[59] Unloaded from "every train, bus and jalopy" and representing all parts of the nation, they found plenty of work but inadequate shelter. They filled every conceivable structure: shacks, stores, stables, abandoned buildings, and garages.[60] Black newcomers, numbering 35,000 by the war's end and facing widespread discrimination, encountered especially difficult circumstances. Most of them packed into "Paradise Valley"–the already overcrowded, dilapidated eastside ghetto–and, as their numbers steadily increased after mid-1942, spilled over into previously all-white neighborhoods. Their presence, as well as that of recently arrived southern whites, the so-called "hillbillies," intensified an already tense racial situation.[61] In fact, well before the arrival of newcomers, long-standing black and white residents had been competing for the city's wartime resources and occasionally drew one another's blood–as they did in February 1942, when black workers and Polish homeowners fought over the federally built Sojourner Truth Homes.[62]

That riot exemplified the impact of war on both traditional problems and federal-city relations. Jeffries found himself and his municipality caught between a policy of segregation in public housing and a war for democratic aims. He smarted as housing officials in Washington disregarded his opposition to their site selection and, worse still, they vacillated between assigning the Sojourner Truth project first to blacks, then to whites, and back again to blacks. He blamed government agents for the outburst and afterward installed blacks in the homes. In the spring of 1943 he opposed placing future black units in neighborhoods where they would alter existing racial characteristics, a position that virtually guaranteed the end of federally built projects for black Detroiters throughout the war. Essentially, the mayor had begun to realize that he could not represent all the people and that the war had accentuated and expanded perennial issues beyond narrow local confines. Fearing greater racial violence and, no doubt, political repercussions, he sided with the white majority. He acted not as a hateful bigot but as a leader under siege, endeavoring to stem intergroup hostilities while simultaneously searching for the solution to a problem that he did not fully understand.[63]

Jeffries's strategy and progressive philosophy failed him, nonetheless, for he endured a race riot in June 1943 and political backlash in August. He lamented the destruction wrought by what was at that point the worst upheaval in national history: thirty-four dead, 765 injured, $2 million in property losses, and a million hours of absenteeism by defense workers.[64] Like most officials, he wrongly held black leaders, black "hoodlums," and white "hillbillies" responsible for the bloodshed. In reality, black leaders had protested inequalities but hardly incited outburst; and rioters of both races tended to be fully employed persons without previous records, and Detroit residents for over a decade.[65] Jeffries expected blacks and white liberals to oppose him in the mayoral primary that August, but he never imagined losing that race to CIO-backed Circuit Court commissioner Frank FitzGerald.

Having lost former black and union allies, Jeffries set out to win the runoff election in November by deliberately playing to threatened, prejudiced, and anti-labor whites. He realized that many moderate and conservative voters had opposed him in the primary for his irresolute handling of the housing issue, which they believed was responsible for black assertiveness and, ultimately, the riot. "Getting murdered in the black wards and in the racist white wards," he told Edwards, "I might lose this election, but I am not going to lose it both ways."[66]

Therefore, he sided with whites and openly charged black militants and union leaders with trying to force integrated housing and take over the city in a time of a national crisis. He played up, as his father had against the Detroit Citizens League (1923) and as Reading had against him (1939), the fear of bloc-controlled government by a small, radical, special interest group; and in what many considered racist terms he forced FitzGerald to oppose biracial housing. Jeffries's relentless campaign attracted the support of the News, Times, and numerous neighborhood weeklies and shrewdly divided the rank-and-file unionists from their liberal leaders. He defeated the isolated and equivocal FitzGerald by 32,000 ballots.[67]

Jeffries succeeded in part because of the assistance he received from some of the boys in the movement, evidence again of their brotherhood and loyalty. Most notably, he benefited from the journalistic talents of Slutz and Carlisle, who, along with other members of the press, especially those from the News, prepared his radio broadcasts and advanced his candidacy in various ways. They formed, in Carlisle's words, "the greatest God-damned underwater swimming team" ever, aiding Jeffries clandestinely as they were covering the contest for their newspapers. Even Schachern, who was not one of the frogmen, accompanied the candidate's every step and wrote favorable, supposedly objective stories for the *Times.* Hayden and White would have done the same, had they been in Detroit rather than in army camps. Much more than good friends who assisted the mayor in return for exclusive copy, Carlisle, Hayden, Schachern, and White believed in Jeffries and his leadership.[68]

Only Edwards, who ran for reelection to the council in the same campaign and—alone among local officials—advocated equality in present-day terms, opposed Jeffries's tactics. Still, he and Jeffries, pursuing different offices and appreciative of their friendship, neither spoke out publicly against each other nor questioned privately the unconditional nature of their relationship.[69] One of Edwards's staunchest promoters, however, tore into Jeffries for dragging his campaign through racial hatred. "Egotistical impulses," editorialized Louis E. Martin of the *Chronicle,* led the mayor to believe "that he is some municipal god out of Greek legend who has been wronged by the rabble populace."[70]

Jeffries knew, of course, that housing limitations alone had neither caused the riot nor exhausted the city's problems. He considered blacks as citizens who deserved "the concern of the city government," but he and his advisers had come into the mayoralty as novices in race relations and, for all their well-meaning intentions, failed to respond effectively to the "ninety-miles-an-hour" pace of wartime change.[71] Still, once reelected, he continued to search for locations—such as those at Eight Mile Road near Wyoming Street and in surrounding communities—where additional black homes could be built. Jeffries's efforts proved unsuccessful for the most part, largely because of his reluctance to press "democratic idealism" upon a hostile constituency.[72] In such volatile times he chose to risk neither political defeat nor another racial explosion.

Perhaps this was Jeffries's rationale for having failed as a statesman in one of the most important areas: community unity. In blaming black and white toughs for the riot, he drew from both the progressives and classical leaders who imposed social control in the name of public order; in appealing to white voters he revealed the progressive's fear of heterogeneity and the Greek insistence on unconditional allegiance. In other words, he claimed moral superiority over his enemies and denied politically reprehensible ambition. Similarly, he sought reconciliation following his re-election to a third mayoral term because, if a civic leader was required to control members of an unruly mob, he was also required to hearten them afterward. To see himself as egotistical and opportunistic—as Louis E. Martin saw him—meant to see himself filled with arrogant pride or hubris: gravest of leadership failings. Instead, Jeffries envisioned himself as a responsible central authority, though the product more of the centralizing forces of progressivism and the twentieth century than of classical history.[73]

That Jeffries was unprepared for the riot—as were many in government, including Edwards—seems less culpable than his response to it. Perhaps he experienced personal misgivings about his behavior in the election campaign—certainly some of his closest friends believed that he did—yet as early as his primary loss, Jeffries appeared to deem the race issue insoluble during the war. Thereafter, intentionally or otherwise, he sought to manage rather than be overwhelmed by it. Leaving any permanent resolution of race-related questions for the postwar era, he grappled creatively with other matters.[74] Doing so enabled him to continue his quest to build rather than simply govern Detroit.

Population pressures also affected education, recreation, and particularly transportation. Periodically, friction surfaced in overcrowded public schools and municipal parks, areas already hard pressed by years of depressed budgets and limited planning.[75] Conflict occurred most frequently on the Detroit Street Railways. Edgy, overworked passengers, drivers, and conductors jostled and berated each other daily, increasingly so as migrants entered the city in large numbers and, after 1 December 1942, all car owners faced gasoline rationing.[76] As the number of DSR fares rose astronomically—from 30,811,660 in early 1940 to a peak of 57,209,805 in late 1944—so did the frequency and seriousness of arguments and fights on buses and trolleys. Personal frustrations and resentments sparked aggressive behavior on the impersonal conveyances, particularly against strangers of another race and increasingly after the summer of 1942. Indeed, black-white altercations continued and intensified even after the 1943 riot.[77]

Rationing posed another problem, but one that neither fomented much conflict nor necessitated much mayoral attention. In order to conserve military resources and control wartime inflation, federal officials instituted the Office of Price Administration and by May 1942 had issued coupon books for the purchase of rationed items. Besides tires (1941) and gasoline (1942), OPA agents also required coupons for sugar and coffee (1942), meat, canned goods, butter, and the like, as well as shoes (1943). Despite some hoarding and black market activity and considerable grumbling, OPA apportionments generally succeeded, perhaps because they seemed necessary and for the most part equitable.[78]

In contrast, Jeffries benefited from another set of war circumstances to turn the city's finances around completely and restore faith in its government. Full employment and meaningful salaries increased the number of taxpayers and the amount of money they paid to the federal government, which—along with the sale of war bonds and deficit spending generally—financed the war. Similarly, sales, corporation, and an array of excise taxes filled the coffers of the state, while real estate taxes provided most of the revenue for the city, enabling Jeffries to refinance Detroit's long-standing debt at more favorable interest rates. He crowed, in early 1944, that the municipality was "in the best financial shape it has enjoyed in a quarter of a century." Still, he constantly sought new revenues from local utility and occupational taxes, as well as an excise on parimutuel betting at the State Fair Grounds. Recalling the administration of Frank Murphy, he joined other mayors in pressing Governor Harry F. Kelly for part of the state sales tax, but as the war wound down, he settled for an allocation from higher levies on beer and whiskey.[79]

Most significantly, Jeffries endeavored to rebuild the city in the face of mounting demographic pressures. Beyond funds from the United States Housing Authority, he applied to several federal agencies for additional grants and loans. Through the Lanham Act, for instance, he sought monies from the Federal Works Agency for public works, and stewed when federal officials took eight months to approve his request.[80] Despite government largesse, Jeffries disdained the arrogance of many federal officials and their ignorance of local problems. His early experiences with housing officials who dominated supposedly "joint undertakings" recurred throughout the war and reinforced his skepticism of federal power. Only "broad gauged planning" by municipalities could check this "appetite for greater control," he said, and "preserve the strength and virility of local governments."[81]

Thus, as the tide of war turned, Jeffries began his third term with an ambitious plan for peacetime Detroit. The city, he proclaimed in January 1944, stood at "the crossroads in a highly competitive struggle between metropolitan areas." Ever mindful of the race riots and, no doubt, uncomfortable about his divisive campaign against FitzGerald, the mayor spoke of the community working together to overcome "frictions" and solve problems. He described Detroit as "socially alert, economically advanced and industrially developed," and he advanced a program to ensure its lead over "all other cities" in the greatest of industrial eras that lay ahead. This would require attracting skilled workers, providing satisfactory government services, and modernizing the physical facilities in which everyone worked and lived. More specifically, Jeffries called for cooperation between the government and the

automobile industry; for vocational training, housing and zoning, health
and recreation programs; for "a network of express highways," expanded air transportation, and capital improvements in public buildings and water supply facilities. Above all, he raised anew the need for
additional sources of revenue and when necessary, as in the case of road
building, lobbied for federal monies to underwrite postwar plans. He
again emulated Mayor Murphy and promoted the needs of cities nationally—for example, representing the American Municipal Association
before the House Committee on Roads.[82]

Jeffries's initiative laid the basis for ultimate change. Later that
year the Detroit Postwar Improvement Committee identified long-range
plans for public housing, recreation areas, and expressways, as well as
a new airport, a civic center, and (as part of an expanded Wayne University) a medical center.[83] These efforts notwithstanding, he again faced
the perennial opposition of blacks and union leaders in his run for a
fourth term as mayor.

In 1945, in a replay of the previous election, Jeffries and Richard
Frankensteen engaged in a "nasty" campaign of mudslinging and in-
nuendo. Jeffries won as he had in 1943, by combining support from
affluent white districts that had opposed his father with that of working
and ethnic white districts that had supported the judge; he lost "huge
majorities" only in black areas. He beat the UAW official by 57,000 ballots, dividing his own father's constituency and the union's membership
over what had become the impasse of racial housing and the third CIO
effort "to capture City Hall."[84] Though Jeffries appeared less than Periclean to the vanquished, he considered himself a fair-minded ruler,
protecting black citizens and white laborers alike from their own "usually self-ordained" and hypocritical leaders. Believing that many black
leaders demanded unequivocal support of their agenda, while some of
their white union counterparts refused to employ blacks in local or
international positions, he—and they—sought votes in a highly charged,
self-serving, and unforgiving political context.[85]

Whatever his self-image as a politician, however, Jeffries quickly returned to his ideal for Detroit. He and his planners, determined that a
"super–limited access highway" would best serve public and private
transportation, disregarded alternatives that would have diversified or
eased the city's car culture. Hence, in 1946 their Detroit Plan ignored
the question of improving the public transportation system. Jeffries also
believed that slum clearance and housing for low-income people could
best be achieved by having the city act as a broker to condemn, acquire,
clear, and sell to private builders, at drastically reduced prices, land
marked for redevelopment. Instead, though his plan removed slums it

failed to provide homes for their residents, as developers and others opposed public housing. Ironically, the Detroit Plan, which waited until 1948 for council approval and until 1951 for publication in its final form, accelerated the shift from an era of city building to one of suburbanization. Its slum clearance provisions pushed blacks beyond ghetto boundaries in search of shelter and threatened whites with the possibility of more low-income projects in their midst; its expressways provided the arterial for white flight to surrounding communities, where automobile manufacturers began building their new plants. As these developments played themselves out, they contributed to Detroit's peak in the 1950s—and its decline in the 1960s.[86]

Of course, neither Jeffries nor his policymakers envisioned—much less intended—such consequences. Like Detroiters serving abroad, they saw the war as pushing the city beyond the Depression and into a new era of growth and progress. World War II, in Martin S. Hayden's opinion (which represented that of all letter writers), produced the most exciting and significant of times for Detroit, "the Arsenal of America."[87]

Entering the Army Air Corps as a second lieutenant in July 1942, Hayden became the first of Jeffries's friends to leave Detroit. He spent sixty days at Officers Training School in Miami Beach before joining the Forty-ninth Aviation Squadron briefly at Fort Wight, Spokane, Washington, and then for eight months in Salina, Kansas. There he rose to first lieutenant. While on leave in Washington, D.C., where his wife, sons, father, and stepmother lived during the war, Hayden learned from his wife's uncle, Colonel William H. Dodds, that the Transportation Corps was seeking officers for the personnel on ships carrying cargo into Europe. That assignment "sounded a helluva a lot better than spending the war in Salina," so in May 1943, at Colonel Dodds's request, he was transferred to the Boston Port of Embarkation, promoted to captain, and, because of his journalistic experience covering labor stories, made an industrial relations officer. Within four months, however, he clashed with his superior, Brig. Gen. Clarence Kell. Hayden had been instructed—against his own advice—to inform the longshoremen that they would no longer receive additional pay for unloading explosives, known as "dirty cargo." When the dock workers balked and, through Congressman John McCormick, forced the War Department to rescind the policy, Kell blamed Hayden for the fiasco. Hayden confronted his superior, whose action made him "useless" in any future labor negotiations, and found himself reassigned as an executive officer to the 502d Port Battalion—a unit of black stevedores stationed at Camp Myles Standish in Taunton, Massachusetts, and shortly thereafter selected for overseas duty.[88]

In October 1943, Hayden and the 502d sailed for Scotland, where they trained through the following spring and were chosen to take part in the invasion of Normandy. As part of the Fifth Engineer Brigade, Hayden's unit landed two days after the "Big Show" began on 6 June 1944, its schedule delayed by German resistance that turned more than one Navy vessel into "a floating butcher shop." Once on the beach, Hayden and his men witnessed immobilized tanks, demolished jeeps, burned landing craft, and dead bodies. Their commanding officer, Col. James Pierce, stepped on a mine and lost his foot. "Only chance saved me," Hayden wrote in his diary, along with a caring but grotesque description of applying a tourniquet to Pierce's leg and "dumping sulpha powder on the stump." After three days of unloading ships under combat conditions, Hayden's battalion worked twelve-hour shifts seven days a week for the next month, and outperformed the brigade's other port battalion—a white unit.[89] Promoted to major, Hayden led the 502d until it prepared to leave for Le Havre in November. He did not get along with the new commanding officer, who lacked leadership qualities and experienced speech and hearing difficulties. Hayden, no doubt wondering why he was not given permanent command after proving himself an effective officer during the invasion and its five-month aftermath, sought a transfer. Still, he came away from the experience more than ever convinced of the worth of black soldiers; before and after the invasion he praised their performance and realized the need for them—and all veterans—to be given a rightful "place in the postwar world."[90]

On leave in Paris, Hayden met Col. Samuel L. A. Marshall, a former *News* staffer and then executive officer of the European Theater of Operations Historical Section. He requested and, in late December, received a transfer to the Fifth Information & Historical Section in Paris. He soon joined the fifteenth Army headquarters in Suippes, collected documents, engaged in public relations and, eventually, administrative duties. He also traveled in Belgium and Germany, befriended Californian William Knowland, and met Gen. Dwight D. Eisenhower. After V-E Day, 7 May 1945, he hoped to return home but instead found himself assigned to the Public Relations Division of the U.S. occupying forces. He served in Paris and Wiesbaden until mid-September before finally heading for Le Havre, as *News* higher-ups requested his release to take an executive position with the newspaper. Following an Atlantic voyage as "Commander of Troops" on board, Hayden reported to Fort Meade and, on October 3, was placed on terminal leave. He returned to civilian life as a lieutenant colonel on the reserve list.[91]

Like Hayden, John M. Carlisle experienced the war first-hand, serving as a thirty-seven-year-old correspondent for the News in Europe. Before doing so, he replaced Hayden on the city hall beat in September of 1942 and covered it periodically thereafter. Despite Jeffries's doubt that he could take Hayden's place, Carlisle proved to be a solid journalist and a fun-loving, frequent companion. He also wrote numerous features, including a story on the race riot report of the Governor's Fact-Finding Committee and a series on the police graft under Mayor Reading.[92] From early February to early June 1944, Carlisle covered Washington as national correspondent for the *News*, filling in for Blair Moody, who was interviewing Detroit servicemen during a "whirlwind tour" of Iran and England.[93] Then he and Moody essentially reversed positions, Carlisle departing for Europe three days before the Normandy invasion began.

Carlisle caught up with the action in early July with the First Army. Subsequently, he traveled with Lt. Gen. George S. Patton Jr.'s Third Army, giving special recognition to Michigan soldiers in hometown, human interest stories. Whether writing about the heroism of "the Bazooka Kid," Private John F. Ballenger Jr.–son and namesake of Detroit's police commissioner–who destroyed a Nazi tank single-handedly in Normandy, or the lives of "Detroit Lads" and Michigan boys of lesser-known parents who drove toward Paris and helped win the battle of France, he considered every GI significant.[94]

Carlisle, in fact, lived the life of a GI, eating field rations, washing out of his helmet, sleeping fitfully in full gear, dodging bullets, playing cards, and–with Ernest Hemingway–liberating wine cellars.[95] He also impressed and was impressed by Patton, with whom he rode on several occasions, always crouched down in the seat behind the general, "half scared to death" of being hit by cannon fire. He marveled at the General's never-flinching courage, no matter how close a shell fell, and devotion to his soldiers. At first skeptical of Patton's reputation as a showman, Carlisle returned to Detroit in October 1944 believing him an indomitable leader who inspired his troops to be tough, fearless, and great. When George C. Scott won an academy award for the film *Patton* years later, Carlisle refused to see some "snooping actor portray the greatest general in the history of the world and fuck the whole thing up."[96]

Back in Detroit for approximately six months, Carlisle returned to *News* reporting and city hall camaraderie, but by early spring 1945 he was in the Philippines, again covering war experiences of Michigan soldiers. Soon he accompanied the Thirty-second Division of the Sixth Army, already in combat ninety days, along the Villa Verde trail, high in the Caraballo Mountains of northern Luzon. His stories of the "Red Arrow Men"–building a road and pushing back the enemy yard by bloody yard–were published in book form before the year ended.[97]

Thereafter, Carlisle covered the Forty-first Field Hospital, the Michigan Red Cross workers, the 868th "Black Snoopers" Squadron of the Thirteenth Army Air Force, and other units. He described in moving prose the devastation of Hiroshima, which resembled "a vast dumping ground"; the bombing of Nagasaki, which "smashed this vast war industrial center into nothingness"; the silence of Tokyo, standing "scorched to a crisp"; and the surrender aboard the U.S.S. *Missouri*, which brought the world "aglow in the bright sunlight of complete peace."[98]

Before reporting his last story, an interview with Admiral William F. Halsey aboard the U.S.S. *South Dakota* as it led the third Fleet into San Francisco Bay, Carlisle filed several stories on GI life in postwar Japan.[99] Privately, he considered Gen. Douglas McArthur an outstanding military leader, though he thought that unlike Patton the Pacific commander suffered from "an overblown image of himself" and cared little for his men.[100]

During his six months in the Pacific, Carlisle again lived and worked tirelessly like the servicemen and civilians about whom he wrote. He badgered miliary officials constantly for permission to accompany combat units, even arranging for a dangerous submarine cruise in the Japan Sea. Neither that adventure nor the invasion he sorely desired to accompany came to pass because of the Japenese surrender, which placed him out of harm's way for the first time in months—and on board the *Missouri*.[101]

Others, such as Walton S. White, prepared for such historic moments but never witnessed them. White reported to Fort Custer for duty in September 1943 and soon found himself training at Camp Van Dorn, Mississippi, as a member of the Sixty-third Infantry Division. He returned home the following month for his mother's funeral and was greeted by Jeffries's heartfelt condolences.[102] Assigned to public relations upon rejoining his unit, he prepared its newspaper, doing "exactly what he did as a civilian." Unlike most draftees, he was joined in early 1944 by his wife, who found civil service employment on the base and a trailer home in nearby Centreville. He enjoyed his work and relished Peg's presence until his division was sent to Europe on the eve of Germany's surrender—more than a year and a half after his induction.[103] Transferred shortly thereafter to *Stars and Stripes*, White became the managing editor of its German edition. He covered the early proceedings of the Nuremberg trials for that official military newspaper, the Army News Service, and the Armed Forces Radio Network. In 1946 he left the service as a technical sergeant and returned to Detroit and the *News*.[104]

Harold J. Schachern served with the U.S. Marines in the Pacific. He enlisted in 1944, and trained as an air ground officer. His wife, Florence, and daughter Kathlyn attended his commissioning ceremonies at Quantico, Virginia, but their visit was interrupted by the death of his mother-in-law, and he did not see his wife again until June 1945, in Tacoma, Washington, at the commissioning of the U.S.S. *Puget Sound.* He then embarked for the South Pacific as a fighter director officer aboard that aircraft carrier, expecting to be part of the force gathering to invade Japan. Much to his—and his comrades'—relief, the atomic bomb ended the war and preempted the invasion, which government officials believed would have cost an estimated one million American and Japanese lives. Schachern spent several months in and around Japan before returning home in early 1946, a first lieutenant on active reserve.[105]

George C. Edwards also entered the service later in the war. Since 1941 he had spent numerous hours as a member of the Common Council and, as the war progressed, Detroit's chief air raid warden. He resigned the latter position to become deputy chief in the spring of 1943, a self-imposed "demotion" that allowed him time to work as an assembler on the afternoon shift at the Timken-Detroit Axle Company. He took this job because he realized that every able-bodied person was needed in defense work and that Peggy and their son would require additional income when husbands and fathers like him were called for military service.[106] That autumn, however, he returned full time to his council work and political campaign. By the year's end he had received a reclassification of draft status and, despite his recent reelection to the council, reported for induction on 10 January 1944 and then to the Infantry Training Replacement Center at Camp Wheeler, Georgia—retaining his council seat but turning back his salary to the City of Detroit.[107]

Perhaps more than those who preceded him, Edwards carefully considered his decision to enter the army. Clearly, he was providing much-needed leadership in the municipal government and in its defense activities, for which he received commendation.[108] Edwards also possessed political ambitions and, more significantly, genuine concerns about the war. His background of pacifism aside, he understood that "no peaceful means" existed in the face of totalitarian aggression. His efforts, with Jeffries's assistance, for naval officer candidacy in early 1943 proved futile, in part because of his defiance of Judge Arthur Webster's injunction five years earlier and in part because of his imperfect eyesight. That rejection gave him more time to consider his status, but by late spring he had decided to serve in whatever capacity he was called to.[109] "The political angle on the army question seems important," summarized his sister, Nicky, but so did her brother's ever present desire "to be in the thick of things," do more than his share, and act on his beliefs.[110]

The year 1944 proved eventful for Edwards. Breaking a knuckle playing football set back his training and prevented his being shipped as a replacement to the Ninety-ninth Division in Europe.[111] In early summer he passed the Michigan state bar exam and held his son James McConnell (born on 7 April) for the first time. And in late autumn he was assigned at last to Officer's Candidate School, at Fort Benning, Georgia.[112]

In March 1945, Edwards—the "Detroit philosopher"—graduated and returned to his native state as a member of Company B, Eighty-third Battalion, Twenty-first Regiment at Camp Maxey, Texas. There the new second lieutenant sharpened his skills as a platoon leader, fully expecting to be part of the Japanese invasion force when he was ordered to the West Coast in August and, as part of a replacement unit, sailed to the Philippine Islands aboard "a foul-smelling Dutch ship." Given Japan's surrender and his legal training, however, he became an investigator for the War Crimes Division before returning to civilian life in January 1946 as the recently elected president of Common Council.[113]

That victory the previous November, in which the council candidate with the most votes also became president, demonstrated Edwards's political acumen and popularity. In absentia, he won a stunning reelection and a historic upset of long-time council member and mentor John C. Lodge to become the youngest council president ever. He followed his father's advice for victory in a previous election: neglect not "a single point in your campaign." Throughout 1944 and 1945 he had kept in contact with numerous campaign workers and prominent backers through lengthy, sprightly mimeographed missives that he called "Standard Operation Letters."[114] They, in turn, distributed copies to office workers, who read them to their friends and families, in one case as a lesson for a teenage boy about "what soldiers must endure."[115] Portions of the SOLs were reprinted in office bulletins and the daily press, most frequently by influential and admiring columnist W.K. Kelsey.[116] In addition, Edwards received informal reports and printed materials on municipal issues from city officials and interested parties and, when on furlough, participated in council meetings.[117] He also kept in contact with Jeffries, dashing off shorter letters and notes, sometimes on the copy of a SOL sent to city hall.

Aware of his commitment to labor and its political clout, Edwards raised the question of his candidacy with Walter P. Reuther. He received word by early 1945 that the union leadership supported him and, suggested UAW president R.J. Thomas, "might have to go out and put on a campaign for you." Unionists certainly played an important role in Edwards's bid for a third term, as did Jeffries, but no one did so much to organize the campaign or deliver the victory than Peg Edwards and a group of friends.[118]

Very close in everything they undertook, George and Peg Edwards relied heavily on each other, and in 1945 Peg did what came "naturally."[119] She, Frank Winn, "Doc" Mueller, John Penczak, Ernest Jones, Richard Sullivan, Karl Seiffert, Victor Reuther, Gloster B. Current, and numerous others from Edwards's previous councilmanic campaigns formed the Re-elect Councilman George Edwards campaign. They divided into committees covering every aspect of electioneering–from finances to foreign language, veteran, and church groups–and established headquarters in the Transportation Building.[120]

"It was no accident that skyrocketed Edwards to the top of the heap," wrote *Times* reporter James Inglis in the aftermath of the November election. Edwards, he elaborated, benefited from CIO Political Action Committee, mayoral support (necessarily passive), and "the endorsement of all the good government leagues, plus the status of a soldier on active duty." His excellent councilmanic record and his absence from "the partisan-tinged mayoral embroglio" also accounted for his leading twenty candidates "with just under 50 percent of the vote," added Jay Hayden of the *News*.[121] Significantly, Edwards's overwhelming victory, which surprised many, came about because his voter support, like his committee, cut across every segment of Detroit.

He would likely have received James P. Simpson's vote as well, had the latter been a Detroiter. From 1942 until 1946, however, Edwards's close friend from Texas served in the army. As a draftee, Simpson completed basic training at Camp Wallace, Texas, and then Officer Candidate School at Camp Davis, North Carolina. Back in Texas at Camp Hulen, the new second lieutenant became an adjutant–an administrative officer–for the 202d Antiaircraft Artillery Battalion. At Camps Cooke and Irwin, California, in 1943 the unit underwent intense firing practice in the desert before shipping out. In the Pacific Simpson experienced combat; once his ship was sunk. He noted that the army secured beaches before landing administrative personnel, whereas the Marines simply expected them to make it on their own. The danger notwithstanding, he enjoyed the 202d and its commanding officer, Major Karl Eggen, who chose Simpson because of his law background in 1942 and recommended his promotion to first lieutenant the following year. They remained together until July 1945, when Simpson reported to the Military Government School at Charlottesville, Virginia, and then went on to Korea. In April 1946 he returned home because his wife, Anna Beth, who had worked in Corpus Christi during the war, was ill with her first pregnancy. After Lee was born, Simpson remained at home, having accumulated enough points for discharge, and mustered out of the service three months later. He became a reservist for five years and rose to the rank of captain.[122]

Simpson and his Detroit counterparts wrote their wartime letters for several reasons. Jeffries and Hayden, representative of all correspondents, expressed genuine interest in each other's welfare and in "the nitty gritty of politics in Detroit." The correspondence brought one closer to home and the other closer to the war zone, allowing each friend to share his personal thoughts and confidential information without fear of judgment or discovery. Their letters, Hayden later recalled, carried no "deeper purpose."[123]

Edwards's Standard Operational Letters, however, transcended the personal. Finding "a considerable amount of dead time" on his hands and uninterested in most of the recreation activities available to trainees, he reached out not only to those he cared about and who cared about him but also to powerful and prominent acquaintances, doubtless aware of his councilmanic standing and political future. Although Edwards ascribed no historical worth to his letters, they enabled him to keep in touch with numerous people, inspired others to write, and spread the news of mutual friends.[124]

In fact, however, the servicemen provided historically significant, firsthand, graphic accounts of training camp, combat conditions, and postwar developments in Europe and Asia; and Jeffries charted an equally historical record of personalities and politics in wartime Detroit. Together, they described the flesh and blood—the humanity—that lay behind the headlines of both battlefronts and, possibly, the paramount home front.[125]

Amazingly, Jeffries exchanged letters with more individuals than anyone else and yet sent an identical letter to different persons only once. He provided sincere references for the commissions of White and Schachern, among others, and they supported his bid for reelection in 1943 and 1945.[126] He carried on special relationships with Hayden, Carlisle, and Edwards.

Edwards also received numerous letters from other Detroiters concerned about municipal policy and politics, such as Charles Edgecomb, housing director; George Schermer, Federal Public Housing Authority area representative; Gloster B. Current, NAACP executive director; Louis E. Martin, *Chronicle* editor. His enormous personal ability and political acumen attracted conservatives and liberals such as Edgecomb and Schermer; his "friendship" and "intelligence" appealed to black leaders such as Current and Martin, who appreciated his ability to understand both practical and principled reasons for "playing fair."[127] Accordingly, they worked in his councilmanic campaigns and responded to his SOLs.

Edwards got letters as well from his very close friends Bill Lamson and Jack McElhone. Before the war, Lamson had served as secretary of the Wayne County CIO Council and as a major operative in Edwards's political campaigns. He entered the army in early 1944, trained in a "heavy weapons" infantry unit at Ft. McClellan, Alabama, fought as a machine gunner in Germany, and died of combat wounds incurred there in November.[128] Less than three months later, former UAW editor McElhone was reported missing in action. A pilot in the Royal Canadian Air Force, he had volunteered for service early in the war. By 1944 he found himself marking time in England without "serious duties," but in the new year he began flying missions over Europe. He never returned from a February raid.[129] His death, like Lamson's, left close friends stunned and saddened. Their sudden and violent passing, juxtaposed to the camaraderie and humor of correspondents trying to make the best of a frightening and unpredictable era, brought home the reality of war. Clearly representative of others, Sgt. William F. Dufty told Edwards that he endured the traumatic news of Lamson's and McElhone's fate "on spite and spleen and alcohol."[130] Later, their friends established the Lamson-McElhone Fund "to help young liberals go to law school."[131]

Collectively, then, the letter writers provide insights into wartime Detroit and its residents, the military centers at home, the theaters abroad, and the servicemen in all those areas. They signified—through "Quiet Doing"—faith in themselves, in the city, and in the nation. They never doubted the war's outcome or democracy's triumph in Berlin, Tokyo, or—despite its race and class divisions—Detroit.[132] Their views bear added weight because their letters covered almost the entire period of American involvement in the war and its immediate aftermath, represented middle-class leaders and newsmen deeply committed to the Motor City, and were written with professional clarity and personal feeling. Simpson's contribution signifies the relationships that extended beyond "Boys Town" and provides a broader perspective from which to view the Detroiters and the war.

All the correspondents were college educated and—except for Simpson—relatively well connected through family or marriage. They loved the English language, read widely, and wrote very well, in some cases for a living. In addition to their letters, Hayden kept a diary of his military experience, Carlisle published a collection of his columns in *Red Arrow Men,* and Edwards touched on parts of his war years in *Pioneer-at-Law.*[133] Some of them revealed the influence of their achieving fathers. Few seemed affected by deep religious beliefs, Schachern being the most devout and Carlisle—ultimately an avowed agnostic—the least.[134] Still, they endured the ordeal of war with a sense of belonging that transcended patriotism and family and emanated from a circle of close-knit friends who drew strength and meaning from their commitment to the city and their love of the man most responsible for its welfare.

Jeffries's longtime secretary, Mabel Nancy Ford, reinforced the kinship that permeated the mayor's office. Nancy, as she was known, kept track of the correspondents' whereabouts, took down Jeffries's letters to them in shorthand, then typed and posted them. As much a friend of the newsmen as was Jeffries, she occasionally wrote to them herself, informing Edwards of official business or praising Hayden for his promotion and Carlisle for his stories; and she teamed with Slutz to send Stod White a birthday greeting, and with Schachern to congratulate Edwards on the birth of his son.[135] Similarly, secretary Gwynn Davis and switchboard operator Elsie Mills befriended the letter writers and their families. Indeed, along with the mayor, they greeted wives who visited city hall and gave their children the run of the office.[136] These were the "girls in the movement" to whom Hayden referred.[137]

Nancy Ford especially was the important link between Jeffries, figuratively and literally "the boss," and the boys in the movement.[138] Thus, she enjoyed access to letters which, for the most part, were intended for the eyes of male friends. The letter writers related to their spouses in various ways: Edwards shared everything, military and otherwise, with Peggy in loving letters that were written four and five times a week; Hayden exchanged letters regularly with Betty, including some material that he shared with Jeffries, such as the execution of three Germans civilians for having killed a U.S. pilot who parachuted into their midst. Schachern, however, revealed little about the ordeal of war to Florence, who was never aware of his "Dear Friends" missives.[139] And Carlisle, who came close to having his "bean blown off a number of times" in Europe and the Pacific, never wrote much about brushes with death to Peggy; he "didn't want The Sweetest Gal in the World to worry."[140]

Neither Carlisle nor his friends envisioned the war as "a healthy adventure" or in any way "good for them," as had American soldiers in the Great War, but once in it they desired to act manly.[141] Edwards never experienced combat but prepared arduously for it and recognized the special status of those "who have been there and done the job." White felt it necessary to explain his administrative assignment so that his male friends would understand why "a lot of guys" drafted later probably would serve overseas long before he did, "if ever."[142] Those who did fight reinforced concerns about their personal performance. Hayden suspected that he might retreat and, when he stood tall, downplayed his heroism in true warrior fashion.[143] Carlisle expressed both insecurity and manly pride, simultaneously describing himself as "the worst goddamn coward in the army" and (quoting one colonel) "the only goddamn war correspondent who had guts enuff to go with our outfit."[144] He revealed a near-obsession, repeatedly badgering military authorities for front-line clearance and throwing himself in the face of fire to report the war and, one suspects, to prove himself.[145]

Jeffries, too, demonstrated himself a soldier on the home front mounting the political barricades repeatedly in 1943 and 1945. His wars in Detroit were driven by concepts of local commitment and public statesmanship similar to those of national patriotism and individual performance that drove the training camp and battlefield efforts of his friends. Jeffries, of course, risked less (a career rather than his life), but he provided—despite his devisive political campaigns—examples of civic and masculine duty for those who remained at home.

Essentially, Jeffries, the boys in the movement, and by inference their wartime generation of white, middle-class males were transitory figures in the changing concept of manhood. In contrast to their fathers' Victorian precepts of male individualism, energy, and aggression, they defined themselves in more modern terms of "achievement, reason, and inner strength." They stood midway between "self-discipline and self-expression," though nowhere approaching the later ideals of an "existential hero" who suspects authority, distrusts women, and considers civilization corrupt; a "spiritual warrior" who searches for supposedly lost male passions and camaraderie; a "pleasure seeker" who works hard for the sole purpose of playing hard. They seemed team players in channeling their aggressiveness into this century's competitive organizations, though in civic duty and political endeavors rather than economic enterprises; they seemed team players in positing a society where women experienced "difficulty surviving" as competitors in the workplace, but they thought little about an issue that came to fruition in a later generation.

In part, they believed their spouses possessed (in Carlisle's neo-Romantic phrasing) "that sweetness and spirituality" of "eternal femininity so precious to guys like us." In part, they respected their loved ones as modern wives, mothers, and—in the case of Peggy Edwards and Peggy White, respectively—political operative and working mate. That they loved their spouses deeply (in traditional and contemporary terms) was jubilantly expressed by Hayden as he prepared to reunite, after two years of overseas duty, with Betty: "My sweet, get that long-time sitter, pack your bag and stay within telephone range because the big day is coming."

Importantly, then, unlike contemporary team players or pursuers of other manhood ideals, the boys in the movement scarcely felt "personal isolation and a withered sense of community."[146] Instead they experienced a meaningful and supportive association, recognizing one another as ambitious individuals bound to themselves and a higher purpose. Their rites of passage had occurred during progressivism and economic crises, and their masculinity was shaped further by the influence of Jeffries and the context of World War II. Like the mayor and the era itself, they lived as men of hope who struggled at home and abroad to improve life for themselves as individuals and as families, and for their city as a community.

In their prime, the letter writers entered the postwar era ready to get on with their personal and professional lives. The Detroiters were determined to build a better city. Jeffries's bid for a record fifth straight mayoral term in 1947 fell short before the challenge of councilman Eugene Van Antwerp. "You know," Jeffries told Hayden, "you say no to people long enough and each one you say no to remembers"; the effect "finally becomes cumulative."[147] No doubt his failed effort to capture the Republican Party gubernatorial candidacy during the previous year had soured him with supporters who expected him to deliver on his commitment to finish his two-year term.[148] Perhaps, as significantly, Jeffries experienced the discontent of voters increasingly aware of the socioeconomic changes wrought by war and their desire to ignore or quickly move beyond them, pushing aside those officeholders who addressed controversial issues seriously.[149] Jeffries continued his life of public service, nevertheless, winning a councilmanic seat two years later. Vacationing in Miami Beach the following year, he suffered a heart attack on 18 March 1950 and died on the eve of his fiftieth birthday.[150]

Hayden returned to pound his old city hall beat for the *News* until January 1948. Then he fulfilled his boyhood dream and followed in his father's footsteps as *News* correspondent in Washington, D.C., where his third son and namesake was born the following year. He, Elizabeth Dodds Hayden, and their family lived in the capital for the next decade. They returned to Detroit in 1959 when he became the associate editor of the *News* and within one year its editor. Hayden retired in 1977 after forty-seven years with the newspaper, during which time it became the largest afternoon daily in the nation. Over the years he had become "the last of a breed—a power broker as well as an editor" and, in the opinion of liberal journalists covering the socially and politically explosive decades of the 1960s and 1970s, a conservative.[151] He probably did not see himself on the right, however, much as Jeffries never envisioned himself at that end of the political spectrum. Significantly, when speaking about Jeffries and, one senses, himself, he contended that the mayor had not shifted from his nonpartisan beliefs after 1942: "The times changed." So had Detroit by the time Hayden died there on 17 September 1991.[152]

Carlisle too returned to the *News,* the only civilian correspondent awarded the Bronze Star (for his coverage of the Philippines). A reporter whose "greatest love" was the story, he wrote features and later the column "A Reporter about Town."[153] He tried his hand in the newsroom but always retreated to the beat; unlike most journalists who wrote for a living, he lived to write. He and Peggy O'Neil Carlisle raised their four children (Jennifer was born in 1946); several years after Peggy's death in 1963 he married Anita Ellinger, a Chrysler Corporation executive secretary. Later in life Carlisle founded the Hundred Club, a group of businessmen who aided "the families of policemen, fire fighters, and FBI agents killed on duty." He also assembled the Crisis Club, which engaged in numerous philanthropic acts. Upon retiring in 1970 he became a public relations consultant, advised labor leaders and politicos, and edited a union publication. He died in Detroit on 4 November 1986, following a long illness.[154]

White also continued as a *News* employee, first as a rewrite man and later as an authoritative reporter on Great Lakes shipping. He wrote the "Port and Marine" column weekly, covered major stories such as the sinking of the *Andrea Doria* (1956), and served briefly as a state advisory commissioner on export trade. He and Margaret Phalan White bought a home in Birmingham and became the parents of Peter in 1947. Margaret died thirteen years later; shortly thereafter Stod married Virginia Wegmann–a widow and former *News* replacement for him during the war–and became the stepfather of her daughter, Patricia. Following a bout with cancer, he died on 13 September 1972.[155]

Schachern's career, more circuitous than White's, ended with the *News.* He moved into Detroit, served as financial editor of the *Times* and, in 1949 he and Florence O'Leary Schachern added Mark to their family. Somewhat earlier he had become public relations director for the DSR and chairman of the Mayor's War Memorial Committee (which commemorated the city's war heroes by naming recreation areas in their honor). It was after short stints with the *Times* and the *Free Press* in 1950-51 that Schachern signed on with the *News.* He became its religion editor five years later and a nationally known writer who "helped to build bridges of understanding between all faiths and denominations." A president of Religion Writers of America, Schachern also served on the advisory board of the weekly *Michigan Catholic* and of the parochial girls school, Vista Maria. On 5 May 1969 he died unexpectedly of a heart attack following a visit to the Vatican for Detroiter John C. Dearden's elevation to Cardinal.[156]

Edwards too played a major role in postwar Detroit. Following his Common Council presidency, he lost the 1949 mayoral election to former city treasurer Albert Cobo. Even more than Jeffries, he endured the wrath of white voters who opposed public housing, increased taxes, and racial challenges. He became active in revitalizing the state Democratic Party and supporting G. Mennen Williams for governor; between 1951 and 1956 he received gubernatorial appointments to Wayne County Juvenile Court, the state circuit court, and state supreme court. Incredibly, to some, Edwards resigned from Michigan's highest court in 1962 to become Detroit's police commissioner under Mayor Jerome Cavanaugh. Perhaps he did so in part because political circumstances worked against his desire to be appointed chief justice.[157] As likely, he was expressing personal concern for the upheaval of 1943 and could not "live with having Detroit blow up in another race riot" when he had been asked "to take a whirl at ameliorating the problem."[158] Edwards ran the department without political interference, and before leaving at the end of 1963 he began the slow process of black promotions.[159] That same year he accepted a seat on the United States Sixth Circuit Court, rising to chief judge in the 1970s and senior judge in the 1980s. He entered semi-retirement in 1985. Thereafter, his health deteriorated, and he died of complications from Parkinson's disease on 8 April 1995 in Cincinnati.[160]

As Edwards and the others returned to Detroit after the war, Simpson headed for Texas. He and Anna Beth Lee Simpson increased their family beyond Lee to include Andrew (1948), Sara (1950), Edward (1952), and Ellen (1954). Over the same period he moved from a bank job in Corpus Christi to a Veteran's Administration position in Dallas. He then worked for the Texas and Pacific Railroad, until his retirement in 1979.[161] He still resides in Dallas.

Before 7 December 1941, none of these friends could have imagined the disruption that awaited their lives. On that day Hayden was just taking his son for a bike ride when his wife alerted him to the Japanese attack on Pearl Harbor. He rushed into the house to listen to the radio with her, while young Jay endured the "unbelievable experience" of being forgotten outside for more than an hour. That evening, thinking of his wife and family, Hayden "speculated as to what, if anything, the war would mean to us."[162] Doubtless all the other letter writers engaged in similar speculation. What follows, in their eloquent words, reveals the significance and true meaning of World War II for each of them—and for America.

NOTES

1. Studs Terkel, *"The Good War": An Oral History of World War Two* (New York: Oxford Univ. Press, 1984).

2. Stuart Miller, *Men and Friendship* (Los Angeles: Tarcher, 1983), 1, 10, 15.

3. John P. Simpson of Dallas, Texas, was the exception.

4. Daniel J. Levinson et al., *The Seasons of a Man's Life* (New York: Knopf, 1978), 27-30. As the other letter writers experienced young adulthood (initiation), Jeffries was entering middle adulthood (dominance) in a position of influence, if not outright leadership.

5. C.M. Bowra, *Periclean Athens* (New York: Dial Press, 1971), 122, 124, 130.

6. Werner Jaeger, *Paideia: The Ideals of Greek Culture* (New York: Oxford Univ. Press, 1970), 1:xxi, xxvi.

7. Alan Clive, *State of War: Michigan in World War II* (Ann Arbor: Univ. of Michigan Press, 1979), 34; Robert Conot, *American Odyssey* (New York: William Morrow, 1974), 378.

8. Alfred Stolinski to Paul Vaught, 3 March 1943, Box 6, Mayor's Papers, BHC; Edward J. Jeffries Jr. (hereafter EJJ) to D.M. Ruth, 3 Oct. 1944, Box 7, Mayor's Papers.

9. *News,* 3 April 1950, 1; *News,* 25 June 1967, Reading Room Files, BHC; telephone conversation with Eleanor Pedersen (Dearborn), 22 May 1995. Lola had been secretary-treasurer of the First Mortgage Bond Company and was married to banker Edmond M. Hanavan.

10. EJJ to D.M. Ruth, 3 Oct. 1944; interview with Martin S. Hayden (hereafter MSH), Detroit, 9 Aug. 1990.

11. *News,* 14 Sept. 1939, 18, 28; Malcolm Bingay, "Good Morning," *Free Press,* 13 Sept. 1939, 6; Howard Bowman, "Tribute Paid to Jeffries," *News,* 14 Sept. 1939, 18; *Free Press,* 28 Feb. 1940, 10; William P. Lovett, Memo re. EJJ, 31 Aug. 1939, Box 16, Candidate Files, Detroit Citizens League Papers, BHC 9 (hereafter Lovett Memo re. EJJ); Sidney Fine, *Frank Murphy: The Detroit Years* (Ann Arbor: Univ. of Michigan, 1975), 115-16.

12. Lovett Memo re. EJJ; interview with George C. Edwards (hereafter GCE), Cincinnati, 8 April 1983.

13. Raymond R. Fragnoli, *The Transformation of Reform: Progressivism in Detroit—And After, 1912-1933* (New York: Garland, 1982), 234-79, 382-87. Thomas Cotter, William Heston, Harry B. Keidan, and Pliny Marsh constituted the Big Four.

14. Fine, *Frank Murphy* (Detroit), 102-14, 116-18; Fragnoli, *The Transformation of Reform,* 276-79. The election order: Murphy, John Faust, Jeffries, Keidan, Cotter, and Christopher Stein. Heston and Marsh lost in places seven and eight.

15. Lovett Memo to EJJ; Thomas K. McCraw, "The Progressive Legacy," in *The Progressive Era,* ed. Lewis Gould (Syracuse, N.Y.: Syracuse Univ. Press, 1974), 182; William L. O'Neill, *The Progressive Years: America Comes of Age* (New York: Dodd, Mead, 1975), 104.

16. Joan Hoff Wilson, *Herbert Hoover: Forgotten Progressive* (Boston: Little, Brown, 1975), 211-31, 269-82.

17. Fine, *Frank Murphy* (Detroit), 340-87. Murphy was elected mayor in September 1930 in a special election after Detroit voters recalled Mayor Charles Bowles; he was reelected in November 1931. In 1933 he resigned after Roosevelt appointed him governor-general of the Philippine Islands. See ibid., 206-23, 432-39, 452.

18. Fragnoli, *The Transformation of Reform,* 323-24; interview with MSH, Detroit, 9 Aug. 1990; interview with GCE, 8 April 1983.

19. Interview with GCE, 8 April 1983.

20. Lovett Memo re. EJJ.

21. Fine, *Frank Murphy* (Detroit), 115-16; Jaeger, *Paideia,* xxvii; Wilbur C. Rich, *Coleman Young and Detroit Politics: From Social Activist to Power Broker* (Detroit: Wayne State Univ. Press, 1989), 31-32.

22. *News,* 3 April 1950, 31.

23. Conot, *American Odyssey,* 366-67.

24. Dominic J. Capeci Jr., *Race Relations in Wartime Detroit: The Sojourner Truth Housing Controversy of 1942* (Philadelphia: Temple Univ. Press, 1984), 15; Lovett Memo to EJJ.

25. Capeci, *Race Relations in Wartime Detroit,* 17-27.

26. Hayden "Tribute to Edward J. Jeffries Jr.," 20 Nov. 1960, Box 1, Jeffries Family Papers, BHC; *News,* 10 Dec. 1944, pt. 2, 9 (Krause was called Hermie after his older brother Herman, who preceded him at the University of Michigan).

27. *News,* 3 April 1950, 31; EJJ to D.M. Ruth, 3 Oct. 1944; interview with MSH, 9 Aug. 1990.

28. Interview with GCE, 8 April 1983; interview with MSH, Detroit, 26 Aug. 1985; EJJ to MSH, 11 Oct. 1944, Box 5, Mayor's Papers; EJJ to John M. Carlisle (hereafter JMC), 8 June 1945, Box 3, Mayor's Papers.

29. Interview with GCE, 8 April 1983.

30. Interview with MSH, 7 April 1988.

31. Interview with GCE, 8 April 1943; Joseph Coles, Oral History, Blacks in the Labor Movement, ALUA, 27.

32. Interview with Anita E. Carlisle (hereafter AEC), Detroit, 31 Aug. 1990.

33. Interview with MSH, 26 Aug. 1985; telephone conversation with MSH (Detroit), 19 Jan. 1991. Loret Taylor had a son by a previous marriage, Campbell Plicher, whom Hayden never knew well.

34. Interview with MSH, 26 Aug. 1985.

35. Interview with MSH, 7 April 1988.

36. Interview with MSH, 26 Aug. 1985; EJJ to MSH, 22 June 1944, Box 5, Mayor's Papers.

37. Interview with AEC, 31 Aug. 1990; AEC to author, 20 Dec. 1990 (postmark); JMC, *News* Information Sheet, n.d. (author's possession, courtesy of AEC); Stoddard White, "Our Man Carlisle," *News,* 30 Aug. 1970, 7D; *Free Press,* 6 Nov. 1986, 21A. On small newspapers a "printer's devil" assisted in the composing room and cleaned the type.

38. Interview with AEC, 31 Aug. 1990; *News,* 6 Nov. 1986, 11B.

39. Editorial, "Jack Carlisle," *News* 7 Nov. 1986, 12A.

40. Interview with AEC, 31 Aug. 1990; Al Blanchard, "Jack, A Master of His Trade," *News,* 22 Oct. 1970 (clipping in author's possession, courtesy of AEC); JMC, *News* Information Sheet.

41. *News,* 30 Sept. 1971, 14C; *Free Press,* 1 Oct. 1971, 1B.

42. Peter S. White to author, 2 Jan. 1991; *News,* 14 Sept. 1992, 20A; interview with MSH, 26 Aug. 1985; conversation with MSH, 19 Jan. 1991; interview with GCE, 8 April 1983.

43. *News,* 5 May 1969, 1, 8A; *Free Press,* 6 May 1969, 1B; telephone conversation with Florence Smith (Clearwater, Fla.), 27 Nov. 1990; telephone conversation with Kathlyn Nies (Spring, Tex.), 1 Dec. 1990; telephone conversation with Mark Schachern (San Francisco), 26 Nov. 1990.

44. *News,* 5 May 1969, 10A.

45. Conversations with Smith (27 Nov. 1990) and Nies (1 Dec. 1990); interview with MSH, 26 Aug. 1985.

46. George Edwards, *Pioneer-at-Law: A Legacy in the Pursuit of Justice* (New York: Norton, 1974), 20, 22, 24-25, 36-38, 43, 48, 55, 113-20.

47. Interview with GCE, Cincinnati, 9 Aug. 1979.

48. Edwards, *Pioneer-at-Law,* 137-38, 140, 156; George C. Edwards, "Journal, 1933-34," 23 Dec. 1933 entry, Box 7, pt. 2, Edwards Collection, ALUA; interview with GCE, 8 April 1983.

49. Edwards, *Pioneer-at-Law,* 159, 177-81; Carlisle, "Edwards of the CIO," *News,* 21 Nov. 1943, clipping in Box 2, pt. 1, Edwards Collection; interviews with GCE, 9 Aug. 1979 and 8 April 1983; interview with MSH, 7 April 1988.

50. Edwards, *Pioneer-at-Law,* 21, 185, 198; interview with GCE, 8 April 1983. Edwards was called "Andy" by his father in honor of Sewanee College Professor William P. Trent, who had influenced the elder Edwards more than any other person.

51. "The Commentator," *News,* n.d., clipping in Box 2, pt. 1, Edwards Collection.

52. Interview with GCE, 9 Aug. 1979; Karl Seiffert, "Era Closes for Council," *News,* n.d., clipping in Box 2, pt. 1, Edwards Collection.

53. Edwards, *Pioneer-at-Law,* 123.

54. Telephone conversations with James P. Simpson (hereafter JPS), Dallas, 11 Nov. 1990 and 24 Nov. 1990.

55. "Detroit Is Dynamite," *Life,* 17 Aug. 1942, 15; Clive, *State of War,* 12; Fine, *Frank Murphy* (Detroit), 246-53, 250, 376; Helen Hall, "When Detroit's Out of Gear," Survey, 1 April 1930, 54; Capeci, *Race Relations in Wartime Detroit,* 9-12; August Meier and Elliot Rudwick, *Black Detroit and the Rise of the UAW* (New York: Oxford Univ. Press, 1979), 3-82.

56. Harry Grayson to Leroy Peterson, 21 Sept. 1944, Box 52, Record Group 212, NARS; Meier and Rudwick, *Black Detroit and the Rise of the UAW,* 82-107; Clive, *State of War,* 15-16.

57. Clive, *State of War,* 29; Blair Moody, "Detroit Is Dynamite, and Don't Forget It!" *News,* [29 Aug. 1942], clipping in Box 4, Mayor's Papers.

58. William P. Lovett to Oswald Garrison Villard, 20 Jan. 1943, Box 40, Correspondence Files, Detroit Citizens League Papers, BHC.

59. President's Committee for Congested Production Areas, "Report: Detroit, Michigan," 1 Dec. 1943, Record Group 212, NARS.

60. Walter Davenport, "Detroit Strains at the Federal Leash," *Collier's,* 31 Oct. 1942, 37; anonymous UAW interoffice communication, n.d., Box 15, UAW Research Department Collection, ALUA.

61. Harry Grayson to Leroy Peterson, 21 Sept. 1944.

62. Capeci, *Race Relations in Wartime Detroit,* 75-99.

63. EJJ to MSH, 18 May 1943, Box 4, Mayor's Papers; interview with MSH, 26 Aug. 1985; interview with GCE, 9 Aug. 1979.

64. Harvard Sitkoff, "The Detroit Race Riot of 1943," *Michigan History* 53 (Fall 1969): 183-206; Robert Shogan and Tom Craig, *The Detroit Race Riot: A Study in Violence* (New York: Chilton, 1964).

65. Herbert J. Rushton, William E. Dowling, Oscar Olander, and John H. Witherspoon, "Factual Report of the Governor's Committee to Investigate the Riot Occurring in Detroit on June 21, 1943," 11 Aug. 1943, BHC; Dominic J. Capeci Jr. and Martha Wilkerson, *Layered Violence: The Detroit Rioters of 1943* (Jackson: Univ. Press of Mississippi, 1991), 32-86; Capeci and Wilkerson, "The Detroit Rioters of 1943: A Reinterpretation," *Michigan Historical Review* 16 (Spring 1990): 49-72.

66. Interview with GCE, 9 Aug. 1979.

67. Clive, *State of War,* 162-64; Meier and Rudwick, *Black Detroit and the Rise of the UAW,* 200-206.

68. EJJ to MSH, 27 Dec. 1943 (author's possession, courtesy of Martin S. Hayden Jr.); interview with GCE, 9 Aug. 1979.

69. Interview with GCE, 9 Aug. 1979.

70. Editorial, "Jeffries Jumps Overboard," *Chronicle,* 23 Oct. 1943, 6. Clearly, aspects of Jeffries's campaign were blatantly racist. Though he never knew or con-

trolled all that was said or done in his behalf, he set the tenor and direction of his re-election bid, which opened the way for the reactionaries who relentlessly and offensively pressed the race issue. That he ignored these activities exposed his leadership limitations and forever shadowed his otherwise impressive mayoralty. EJJ to MSH, 27 Dec. 1943, shows Jeffries's limited control of the campaign beyond the confines of city hall and an example of the role played by outsiders.

71. Interview with GCE, 9 Aug. 1979; interview with MSH, 26 Aug. 1985.

72. Interview with Louis E. Martin, Washington, D.C., 9 July 1979.

73. O'Neill, *The Progressive Years,* 96-97; McCraw, "The Progressive Legacy," 193-95; Jaeger, *Paideia,* 406.

74. Interview with GCE, 9 Aug. 1979. EJJ to MSH, 25 May 1945 (author's possession courtesy of Martin S. Hayden Jr.), reflects Jeffries's realization that many socioeconomic issues would be suppressed until the peace. The interpretation is the author's.

75. Federal Bureau of Investigation, "Survey of Racial Conditions in the United States," 1944, 16, 65-66, Box 44, OF 10-B, FDRL; George W. Beatty, "The Background and Causes of the 1943 Detroit Race Riot" (senior thesis, Princeton University, 1954), 55-59.

76. Richard R. Lingeman, *Don't You Know There's a War On? The American Home Front, 1941-1945* (New York: Putnam, 1970), 238-43; Clive, *State of War,* 112-14.

77. DSR Company, "Operating Statistics," n.d., Box 10, Mayor's Papers (1941), and Box 4, Mayor's Papers (1944); John H. Witherspoon to EJJ, 17 Dec. 1943, Box 7, Mayor's Papers.

78. Henry B. Parkes and Vincent P. Carosso, *Recent America: A History* (New York: Crowell, 1963), 2:238-39; Lingeman, *Don't You Know There's a War On?,* 234-48, 253; Clive, *State of War,* 93.

79. William E. Leuchtenburg, ed., *The Unfinished Century: America since 1900* (Boston: Little, Brown, 1973), 435-39; EJJ to JMC, 26 Oct. 1945, Box 3, Mayor's Papers; EJJ to Common Council, 4 Jan. 1944, Box 3, Mayor's Papers. Taxes covered 40 percent of the war costs.

80. Philip J. Funigiello, *The Challenge to Urban Liberalism: Federal-City Relations during World War II* (Knoxville: Univ. of Tennessee Press, 1978), 44-45; for more on the federal housing agencies, see ibid., p. 106; Clive, *State of War,* 101.

81. Interview with GCE, 8 April 1983; *News,* 11 June 1943, 12. Mark I. Gelfand, *A Nation of Cities: The Federal Government and Urban America, 1933-1945* (New York: Oxford Univ. Press, 1975), 30-39, 65-66, understates the skepticism about federal activity on the part of mayors such as Jeffries.

82. EJJ to Common Council, 4 Jan. 1944, Box 3, Mayor's Papers; *News,* 5 Jan. 1944, 6; 20 March 1944, 4; and 27 March 1944, 5.

83. Robert I. Vexler, comp. and ed., *Detroit: A Chronological and Documentary History, 1701-1976* (Dobbs Ferry, N.Y.: Oceana, 1977), 128-31.

84. *News,* 7 Nov. 1945, 1-2. The first CIO effort in mayoral politics occurred in 1937, when Patrick H. O'Brien lost to Reading.

85. Interview with MSH, 26 Aug. 1985; Meier and Rudwick, *Black Detroit and the Rise of the UAW,* 42n.

86. EJJ to JMC, 26 Oct. 1945, Box 3, Mayor's Papers; Conot, *American Odyssey,* 400-405; Joe T. Darden et al., *Detroit: Race and Uneven Development* (Philadelphia: Temple Univ. Press, 1987), 15-20, 62-65, 155-58.

87. Interview with MSH, 9 Aug. 1990.

88. "Diary of Martin S. Hayden: October 1943-August 1945" (author's possession, courtesy of MSH), 1; interview with MSH, 7 April 1988.

89. "Diary of Martin S. Hayden," 98, 100; interview with MSH, 7 April 1988; MSH private conversations with the author.

90. Blair Moody, "Detroit Captain Running a Crack Port Battalion," *News*, 6 May 1944, 9; "Diary of Martin S. Hayden," 175-76, 179.

91. "Diary of Martin S. Hayden," 186, 190, 237, 247, 255-56. Knowland mustered out somewhat sooner, having been appointed by Governor Earl Warren to fill the U.S. Senate seat vacated by the death of Hiram Johnson.

92. EJJ to MSH, 17 Sept. 1942, Box 4, Mayor's Papers; Carlisle, "Dowling Group Hits Leaders," *News*, 11 Aug. 1943, 1-2, and "The Inside Story of Detroit's Police Graft," *News*, 3 Jan. 1944, 1-2 (the first of over twenty stories).

93. MSH to GCE, 23 May 1944, Box 5, pt. 2, Edwards Collection.

94. JMC to EJJ, 6 June 1944, Box 5, Mayor's Papers; John M. Carlisle, "World War II: June 1944-October 1945" (author's possession, courtesy of AEC), 32-33, 38, 56. This compilation of Carlisle's stories as war correspondent was presented to him at his retirement.

95. Carlisle, "World War II," pp. 31-32; telephone conversation with William Carlisle (Running Springs, Calif.), 1 Sept. 1990.

96. Carlisle, "World War II," 81, 91-92, 94-95; conversation with William Carlisle, 1 Sept. 1990.

97. Carlisle, "World War II," 97-104; John M. Carlisle, *Red Arrow Men: Stories about the 32nd Division on the Villa Verde* (Detroit: Arnold-Powers, 1945).

98. Carlisle, "World War II," 154-56, 158, 164-85.

99. Ibid., 208-15, 217.

100. Interview with AEC, 31 Aug. 1990.

101. JMC to W.S. Gilmore, 4 and 22 Aug. 1945 (author's possession, courtesy of AEC).

102. EJJ to Walton S. White (hereafter WSW), 5 Oct. 1943, Box 4, Mayor's Papers.

103. WSW to Select Little Band, 8 Dec. 1944, Box 5, pt. 2, Edwards Collection; Peter S. White to the author, 2 Jan. 1991.

104. *News*, 14 Sept. 1972, 20A. White left Germany before the completion of the Nuremberg trials, which were held from 20 Nov. 1945 to 1 Oct. 1946.

105. Conversations with Smith (27 Nov. 1990) and Nies (1 Dec. 1990); *News*, 5 May 1969, 8A; Robert H. Ferrell, *Harry S. Truman and the Modern American Presidency* (Boston: Little, Brown, 1983), 55-56.

106. Carlisle, "Edwards Shuns Politicians," *News*, 19 May 1943, clipping in Box 2, pt. 1, Edwards Collection; Edwards, *Pioneer-at-Law*, 198-99.

107. Employee's Release/Transfer Form, 15 Oct. 1943, Box 2, pt. 1, Edwards Collection; "Edwards Ordered Inducted Dec. 20," n.d., clipping in Box 2, pt. 1, Edwards Collection.

108. "Award for Service," 1 Feb. 1944, clipping in Box 14, Edwards Collection.

109. Edwards, *Pioneer-at-Law*, 191; GCE, "Personal Data Sheet," 19 Feb. 1943, Box 4, pt. 3, Edwards Collection; Edwards to H.H. Perry, 5 Aug. 1943, Box 4, Mayor's Papers; interview with GCE, 8 April 1983. Edwards had aspired to be a radar plot officer, which required perfect vision.

110. Octavia Edwards to GCE, 5 May 1943, Box 4, pt. 3, Edwards Collection.

111. GCE, SOL I, 21 Feb. 1944, Box 14, pt. 1, Edwards Collection (hereafter the location of all SOLs unless cited otherwise); interview with GCE, 8 April 1983.

112. Edwards, *Pioneer-at-Law*, 199; GCE to EJJ, 24 July 1944, Box 3, Mayor's Papers. The Michigan legislature permitted law students within half a year of graduation to take the bar exam.

113. Graduation Program, Officer Candidate Class Fifth Co., Third Student Training Regiment, The Infantry School, Ft. Benning, Ga., 19 March 1945, 20, Box 4, pt. 3, Edwards Collection; GCE to Carl A. Foster, 25 Feb. 1947, Box 14, pt. 1, Edwards Collection; GCE, SOL X, 12 Dec. 1945, Box 2 (1946), Mayor's Papers.

114. George C. Edwards Sr. to GCE, 20 Oct. 1943, Box 4, pt. 3; Victor Reuther to GCE, 23 March 1944, Box 4, pt. 3; Eugene I. Van Antwerp to George C. Edwards, 19 April 1944, Box 5, pt. 2, all in Edwards Collection.

115. Peg Schouman to GCE, 27 March 1944, Box 4, pt. 3, Edwards Collection. Schouman worked in the Detroit Housing Commission office.

116. Donald J. Sublette to GCE, 30 March 1944, Box 4, pt. 3, and W.K. Kelsey to GCE, 4 Oct. 1944, Box 5, pt. 2, Edwards Collection; "The Commentator," *News,* 15 March 1944, and "The City Hall Was Never Like This," *Free Press,* clippings in Box 2, pt. 1, Edwards Collection.

117. Glen C. Richards (DPW Superintendent) to GCE, 23 June 1944; Benjamin Tobin (Detroit Auditor General) to GCE, 9 Feb. 1945; and David D. Henry (Wayne University President) to GCE, 17 Oct. 1944, all in Box 5, pt. 2, Edwards Collection. "Pvt. Edwards Resumes Council Post on Furlough," *News,* 21 Oct. 1944, clipping in Box 2, pt. 1, Edwards Collection.

118. Walter P. Reuther to GCE, 27 Nov. 1944; R.J. Thomas to GCE, 8 Jan. 1945, all in Box 5, pt. 2, Edwards Collection.

119. Interview with GCE, 8 April 1983.

120. Minutes, Re-Elect Councilman George Edwards Campaign, n.d.; Ethan Edloff and Irene Urban to Dear Friends, 8 June 1945; Richard Sullivan to George and Peg Edwards, 5 June 1945; Doc Mueller to George and Peg Edwards, 5 June 1945, all in Box 5, pt. 2, Edwards Collection. Winn, UAW official; Norvel Mueller, Detroit civil servant; Penczak, automobile worker active in the UAW; Jones, Detroit Department of Purchases and Supplies Commissioner; Sullivan, Detroit corporation counsel; Seiffert, *News* reporter; Reuther, UAW official; Current, Detroit NAACP executive secretary.

121. "Oakman Gets Seat Vacated by Sweeny," *Times,* clipping, Box 2, pt. 1, Edwards Collection; "CIO Helps Democrats Win but Own Candidate Loses," *News,* 8 Nov. 1945, clippings in Box 2, pt. 1, Edwards Collection.

122. Conversations with JPS, 11 and 24 Nov. 1990; JPS to author, 24 Nov. 1990.

123. Interview with MSH, 7 April 1988.

124. Interview with GCE, 8 April 1983; phone conversation with Margaret McConnell Edwards, 9 Dec. 1995. Overwhelmed with letters from family and friends yet unable to respond to all of them, Edwards wrote the first SOL as a practical way of catching up with his correspondence; he enjoyed writing it and, realizing its popularity and political worth, continued the practice throughout the war. He wrote the original draft and sent it to Peg; she passed it on to John N. Lenz, secretary of the Common Council, who had it typed, mimeographed, and returned to Edwards. Edwards then addressed and posted the SOL to over fifty persons.

125. EJJ to WSW, 5 Oct. 1943, Box 4, Mayor's Papers.

126. EJJ to Commandant, USMC, 21 Feb. 1944, Box 5, and Harold J. Schachern (hereafter HJS) telegram to EJJ, 12 Nov. 1945, Box 3, Mayor's Papers.

127. Interview with Louis E. Martin, 9 July 1979.

128. Bill Lamson to GCE, 4 Feb. 1944; Doc Mueller to GCE, 15 Nov. 1944 and 28 Feb. 1945, all in Box 5, pt. 2, Edwards Collection. *Free Press,* 1 Jan. 1945, 5.

129. John J. McElhone to Peggy Edwards, 24 Dec. 1944, Box 5, pt. 2, Edwards Collection; *United Automobile Worker* (West Side Local 174 Conveyor Edition), 15 March 1945, 6.

130. William F. Dufty postcard to GCE, 11 March 1945, Box 4, pt. 3, Edwards Collection.

131. GCE to author, 13 Sept. 1989.

132. Editorial, "One Flag, One Cause!" *News*, 8 Dec. 1941, 1.

133. Interview with MSH, 26 Aug. 1985. Hayden recorded his experiences in Europe from 13 Oct. 1943 to 21 Aug. 1945. While preparing for the Normandy invasion, he received orders that personal items should not be taken on the assault. Hence he passed his diary—via Blair Moody—to his father for safekeeping, with instructions not to read it. Nevertheless, the elder Hayden shared the manuscript with his son's wife. In retrospect, Hayden recognized that his innocent effort to save the diary posed "a most horrible breach of security."

134. Conversation with William Carlisle, 1 Sept. 1990, verified JMC's agnostic beliefs in later life; Nancy Ford (hereafter NF) to JMC, n.d., Box 5, Mayor's Papers (1944), reflects his Presbyterian faith, however nominal, during the war years.

135. Lee A. White to NF, 28 Dec. 1944, Box 3, Mayor's Papers (1945); NF to GCE, 21 Feb. 1944, Box 4, pt. 3, Edwards Collection; NF to MSH, attached to EJJ to MSH, 18 July 1944, Box 5, Mayor's Papers; NF to JMC, n.d., and NF and Don Slutz to WSW, 18 April 1944, Box 5, Mayor's Papers.

136. Conversation with Smith, 27 Nov. 1990.

137. MSH to EJJ, late July 1943, Box 4, Mayor's Papers.

138. NF to MSH, 28 March 1944 (author's possession, courtesy of Martin S. Hayden Jr.).

139. Conversation with Smith, 27 Nov. 1990.

140. JMC to W.S. Gilmore, 22 Aug. 1945 (author's possession, courtesy of AEC); JMC to EJJ, 17 July 1945, Box 3, Mayor's Papers. Whether White provided Peggy with his mimeographed dispatches is unknown.

141. Paul Fussell, *Wartime: Understanding and Behavior in the Second World War* (New York: Oxford Univ. Press, 1989), 129, 130.

142. GCE, SOL III-VI, [late July 1944]; WSW to GCE, 11 March 1944, Box 4, pt. 3, Edwards Collection.

143. MSH to EJJ, 1 July 1944, Box 5, Mayor's Papers.

144. JMC to EJJ, 11 Aug. 1944, Box 5, Mayor's Papers.

145. JMC to W.S. Gilmore, 22 Aug. 1945 (author's possession, courtesy of AEC).

146. E. Anthony Rotundo, *American Manhood: Transformations in Masculinity from the Revolution to the Modern Era* (New York: Basic Books, 1993), 284-93; JMC to EJJ, 17 July 1945, Box 3, Mayor's Papers; MSH to Betty Hayden, 5 Sept. 1945 (author's possession, courtesy of Martin S. Hayden Jr.).

147. Interview with MSH, 9 Aug. 1990.

148. Throughout the war he had become increasingly like Hoover and those progressives who opposed much of Roosevelt's New Deal, for reasons of its centralization and "collective solutions" to local and individual problems. In June 1944 his public opposition to a fourth term for Roosevelt brought him to the attention of Republican Party friends. But Jeffries placed third in the primary for governor, unable to overcome his reputation as an urban leader constantly at odds with the rural areas that controlled statewide elections. See *Civic Searchlight*, March 1947, 1-2; Otis L. Graham Jr., *An Encore for Reform: The Old Progressives and the New Deal* (New York: Oxford Univ. Press, 1967), 166-86; EJJ to MSH, 22 June 1944, Box 5, Mayor's Papers; NF to MSH, 19 June 1944 (author's possession, courtesy of Martin S. Hayden Jr.).

149. Conot, *American Odyssey*, 402-3.

150. *News*, 3 April 1950, 1, 31.

151. Nora Ephron, *Scribble, Scribble: Notes on the Media* (New York: Knopf, 1978), 123.

152. Interview with MSH, 26 Aug. 1985.

153. Conversation with William Carlisle, 1 Sept. 1990.

154. *News,* 6 Nov. 1986, 11B; interview with AEC, 31 Aug. 1990; AEC to author, 20 Dec. 1990 (postmark).

155. *News,* 14 Sept. 1972, 20A; Peter S. White to author, 2 Jan. 1991.

156. *News,* 5 May 1969, 1, 8A, 10A; conversation with Smith, 27 Nov. 1990.

157. Conot, *American Odyssey,* 403, 405, 451; Helen Washburn Berthelot, *Win Some, Lose Some: G. Mennen Williams and the New Democrats* (Detroit: Wayne State Univ. Press, 1995), 85-93.

158. Interview with GCE, 9 Aug. 1979.

159. Sidney Fine, *Violence in the Model City: The Cavanagh Administration, Race Relations, and the Detroit Riot of 1967* (Ann Arbor: Univ. of Michigan Press, 1989), 103-5.

160. *News,* 9 April 1995, 10A.

161. Conversations with JPS, 11 and 24 Nov. 1990.

162. "Diary of Martin S. Hayden," 178.

THE GREAT HAYDEN

(SEPTEMBER 1942–JANUARY 1944)

Just as those left behind thirsted for information about their loved ones in uniform, soldiers themselves craved news of the home front.[1] In addition to word of their families from parents, wives, and children, they relied on close friends for tidbits on the latest developments in their former workplaces. Indeed, Martin S. Hayden urged Councilman George C. Edwards to "unloose with the gossip." Quickly, however, he looked to Mayor Edward J. Jeffries Jr. for insider material on who was "in or coming out of the dog house" and what feuds were surfacing in and about city hall.[2]

In part, the Hayden-Jeffries correspondence evinced a very special friendship that included inquiries about each other's families. Thus Jeffries called Hayden's parents when on municipal business in Washington, D.C., and kept abreast of the condition of his friend's stepmother, Aunt Loret, who required hip surgery.[3] Hayden, in turn, regularly extended his love to Jeffries's wife, Florence, and the men shared family anecdotes: two-year-old John Hayden enjoying his grandmother's cast as his personal seat, Gary Jeffries forging—incorrectly—his father's name on a report card.[4]

Similarly, Hayden felt no compunction about making "a peculiar request": he wanted slot machines—which were legal on military property, if not in Detroit—in order to make money for the newly established officer's club on the Salina Army Air Base and wondered if the mayor "could dig any up."[5] In fact, Jeffries did locate at least one machine, but federal law prohibited its shipment across state lines.[6]

And both men enjoyed mocking the saga of Albert Cobo, the longtime city treasurer and mayoral hopeful. In October 1942 Jeffries forwarded to Hayden the story that everyone had expected the "financial wizard of Detroit" to use the occasion of his forty-ninth birthday party to announce his candidacy for city hall, a year in advance of the election. Instead, Jeffries and Cobo donned carnations, shook hands with well-

Figure 2. Martin S. Hayden, courtesy of Martin S. Hayden Jr.

wishers, praised each other in their speeches, and parted company
without anyone knowing what the treasurer intended to do about his political ambitions. To Jeffries's delight, a much-rumored event had proved
to be political shadow boxing.[7] Thereafter, he skewered Cobo whenever
possible, and Hayden followed suit, noting local editorials that ripped
the thin-skinned Cobo and, later, his predictable opposition to the

administration's tax plan, which gave him "a chance to sound off in the *Free Press.*"[8] In the fall primary of 1943, Jeffries was challenged by a crowded field of thirteen candidates—without Cobo.[9]

Cobo stayed on the sidelines, revealing much about Detroit politics and himself. He knew that in nonpartisan municipal elections—a political system of personalities rather than parties—voters shifted their support from one candidate to another from one election to another, and that the very liberals, blacks, and unionists who had played important roles in Jeffries's first two victories (against a corrupt mayor and an ambitious judge) were now engaged in a no-holds-barred campaign to defeat the mayor. Indeed, Cobo realized that influential black leaders and powerful UAW officials would endorse the candidacy of Circuit Court Commissioner Frank FitzGerald in a personal crusade sparked by Jeffries's housing policies and, especially, his handling of the riot.[10]

Cobo also knew the ideological spectrum of Detroit. In an era when sizable majorities of local voters supported Democratic candidates in partisan state and national campaigns, he sensed that his Republican conservatism was out of step with much of the electorate and many in his own party. For the moment, he preferred to avoid the volatile controversy that pitted a left-wing coalition against a rightward moving mayor, no doubt realizing that his own ideology was out of step with Jeffries's enemies yet in line with the mayor's constituents. He had nothing to offer either side and thus bided his time, ironically to reappear four years later as the successful heir to the racially divisive politics that pitted black against white and separated union leaders from rank-and-file workers.[11]

Jeffries won reelection to a third term following a bitter campaign and primary defeat. In the face of the racially explosive issues ignited by the Sojourner Truth housing controversy and climaxing in the riot fifteen months later, he evolved from coalition builder to a partisan of white voters.[12] He found unconditional support in Hayden, who reaffirmed his every move along the color line. In response to Jeffries's pre-riot musing of whether his policy of maintaining the "racial characteristics of neighborhoods" would improve the situation, Hayden quoted a black sergeant in his outfit: "It will either blow up or blow over"[13] In the aftermath of riot, when Jeffries defended his police department, charged the press with presenting a distorted picture of the upheaval, and blamed blacks for the violence, Hayden considered the official mayoral statement "excellent" and criticized the *Free Press* for "jumping on you and John Witherspoon" for an earlier "kid gloves" policy toward blacks.[14] Hayden's earlier reference to his black sergeant's contention—that the National Association for the Advancement of Colored People had

engaged in "rabble rousing" tactics elsewhere–probably reinforced Jeffries's public impatience with "those Negro leaders who insist that their
people do not and will not trust policemen."[15] When Jeffries placed
second in the primary vote, Hayden consoled him, hoping for "some
political mathematics" that would reverse the final outcome and wishing he could be there to assist rather than aboard the *Queen Elizabeth*
headed for a different kind of war zone.[16] Later, much relieved by Jeffries's victory in November, he jokingly assumed that the mayor had once
again become Detroit's "most picked on individual."[17]

In truth, Jeffries and Hayden possessed the enlightened, if political
and patronizing, racial views of their class and generation. Moderate
Republicans of the upper middle class, they stressed gradualism and
opportunity, personal pride and public decorum; public servants of a
racially prejudiced society in a war that accentuated democratic principles, they feared confrontational solutions and criticized those they
deemed most aggressive but least understood: black citizens. Thus Jeffries shifted from endeavoring to be the mayor of all Detroit in 1939–
honestly addressing black concerns of police brutality, for example–to
one who ran a race-baiting and labor-baiting campaign in 1943, following a primary defeat engineered by black and labor leaders. Between these years he found it more and more difficult to maneuver
through the racial minefields of defense housing and police-community
relations, misreading the urgency of blacks, the resistance of whites, and
his own ability to serve as arbiter or power broker in a rapidly changing
environment. Exactly because Jeffries–like many of the black leaders
who confronted him–did not envision himself a racist, he pressed his
campaign as necessary, if not righteous, politics.[18] For this reason he
became a partisan of white voters during his third mayoral campaign,
but once elected, he did not completely exclude black citizens from the
political process.[19]

Clearly, Jeffries understood Hayden's view of black servicemen,
doubtless believing it the solution for race relations. At Salina, Hayden
instituted a "race pride campaign," teaching black soldiers the lesson
that their behavior, good or bad, "would be used as bases for judgement
of their whole race." He was proud, for example, that they appeared off
base "far neater" than white service-men.[20] Occasionally, he referred to
blacks under his command as "Senegambians" or "on the dusky side"
and, once in command of his own squadron, labeled himself "de Mayor
of Smoky Hill's Harlem."[21] Yet Hayden genuinely believed black soldiers
capable; he was aware of their diversity, from "exceedingly intelligent"
to ignorant human beings; and his respect for Sergeant McCullough,
whose thinking, personality, and ideology matched his own, was very

real.[22] He contended that blacks performed best when, like those in uniform, they were given "a definite social standing and a chance to advance in accordance with . . . [their] merits." Good officers, presumably like good mayors, must "sell their men on the ideal that they are interested in them and desire to protect their welfare." Hayden indicated that a favorable environment and constructive leaders were necessary to offset both the "natural white antagonism" toward blacks and the "super race-consciousness" of some blacks, especially leaders.[23] Only in this way could housing controversies in Detroit or officer club confrontations in Salina be avoided; only in this way could blundering federal administrators or white officers be prevented from intensifying racial animosities.[24] Still, like Jeffries, he countenanced segregation when integration threatened violence, contending that blacks enjoyed themselves more alone than in a "white place." Yet both men realized that Jim Crow still rankled and knew—without saying so—that democracy demanded more.[25] Essentially, they held that blacks deserved a stake in citizenship and, once it was given, needed only to respond to it positively for progress to occur. How this was to be done in the face of white resistance and with only minimal government assistance they never explained.

Race was not the only topic that occupied the thinking of Jeffries and Hayden, who shared interests in national politics and newspaper coverage. Despite his own party affiliation, Hayden criticized Republicans for failing to appeal to servicemen everywhere and, consequently, "doing a swell job of campaigning for Brother Roosevelt."[26] Ever the insightful politician, Jeffries understood that the president's power derived largely from his monopoly of information and his authority as commander in chief of the armed forces and that wartime dissatisfactions "could be whipped into shape overnight if a glamorous demagogue appeared." In this as in other subjects, he charged Hayden's "late profession" with having confused the public.[27] On another occasion he lectured that the right to freedom of the press carries "the obligation of responsible citizenship to see that misinformation is not widely circulated."[28] That lambast notwithstanding, he generally found more support—as in the riot controversy—among his friend's former editors and co-journalists at the *News* than from the liberal staff of the *Free Press* or the conservative one of the *Times*.

Jeffries and Hayden also swapped tales of labor disputes and the role of unions in them. Linking labor and race, Hayden commented on the longshoremen's opposition to black soldiers appearing on the docks of Boston harbor because of past conflicts between Irish members of the segregated American Federation of Labor and black strikebreakers.

Union leaders "beefed" but finally moved to bring their rank and file into line.[29] Within weeks, however, Hayden reported that 1,500 long-shoremen had walked off the job over a withholding tax payment plan agreed to by AFL officials, who were attending a convention in New York City. He and other military conciliators failed to break the wildcat strike, so higher-ups brought in servicemen to load ships, and ulti-mately union leaders ordered their membership back to work for "patriotic" reasons. Though no racial violence occurred between long-shoremen and soldiers, many of whom were black, Hayden criticized pay scales, self-indulging union leaders, and their working-class, heavy-drinking constituents.[30] Jeffries reciprocated with the story of 23,500 Department of Public Works employees on strike for higher wages, whom he intended to replace within a matter of days if they did not report to work. Again, from Jeffries's perspective, AFL demands indi-cated the unreasonableness and greed of labor leaders and unions.[31] An earlier exponent of "high wages and good working conditions," Jeffries (and by inference, Hayden) seemed disturbed by civilian employees' constant drive for more money and a better environment at a time when war exigencies were already driving wages to record levels. He won-dered where it would end and what impact it would have on "the boys in the Army."[32]

Gradually, wartime issues fostered in Jeffries a defensive style and more conservative ideology. In late 1942 he acknowledged that World War II was "a very difficult time to be in government," and in the face of ongoing housing and labor conflicts, he began to worry about his beliefs.[33] Instances like the Sojourner Truth Homes riot reinforced his already skeptical view of big government, particularly federal in-trusion in municipal affairs by uninformed, single-minded officials.[34] He seemed increasingly overwhelmed by the myriad of municipal problems, the "rising tide" of racial animosity, the scrutiny of the press (which covered the mayor's life "so thoroughly" that he could add little to it),[35] and the steady criticism of his leadership from the housing disorder to the more devastating race riot the following year—all of which prompted Hayden to exclaim, somewhat seriously, that anyone "would be nuts to want to be mayor of Detroit."[36] Yet Jeffries pressed forward, determined to vindicate himself and thrust Detroit into post-war modernity.

Increasingly, the mayor—if not altogether lonely—walked alone. Hayden regularly mentioned "Boys Town" and "the boys and the girls of the movement," reminding him of the glory days when he and his youthful band of operatives and journalists inundated city hall in 1939. From then until the bombing of Pearl Harbor, they had shared a vision of what could be achieved in a truly nonpartisan, progressive government devoted to efficiency, order, and above all fairness; they had endeavored to include every citizen and every community in Detroit's rebirth, working hard by day and playing hard by night. Progress was made, only to be first slowed and then upended by war-related problems—too great a population, and too many demands, too few resources and too little patience—that taxed the abilities of most officials, including Jeffries, and emptied Detroit of many of his confidants. In this new, exciting, yet tumultuous and unpredictable era, Hayden understood—as most certainly did Jeffries, flush from his victory over FitzGerald—that the mayor reigned over "what used to be Boys Town."[37] Indeed, most of the "boys" who had served Jeffries and the city now served Roosevelt and the nation, but like Hayden, they all remained connected forever to the man, the municipality, and the movement that became identified as one.

NOTES

1. Judy Barrett Litoff et al., eds., *Miss You: The World War II Letters of Barbara Wooddall Taylor and Charles E. Taylor* (Athens: Univ. of Georgia Press, 1990), 137.

2. Martin S. Hayden (hereafter MSH) to George C. Edwards (GCE), [mid-Sept. 1942], Box 4, pt. 3, Edwards Collection, ALUA.

3. Edward J. Jeffries Jr. (hereafter EJJ) to MSH, 19 April 1943, Box 4, Mayor's Papers, BHC (hereafter all citations not otherwise specified refer to the Mayor's Papers, Box 4 of the year given).

4. MSH to EJJ, 2 July 1943; EJJ to MSH, 18 May 1943; MSH to EJJ, 27 May 1943.

5. MSH to EJJ, 16 Oct. 1942.

6. EJJ to MSH, 22 Oct. 1942; MSH to EJJ, 22 Oct. 1942; interview with MSH, Detroit, 19 Jan. 1991.

7. EJJ to MSH, 14 Oct. 1942, and Carlisle, "Birthday Party for Cobo Shuns Politics—Almost" (*News* clipping attached to this letter).

8. EJJ to MSH, 9 and 16 Dec. 1942, 8 Feb. 1943; MSH to EJJ, Jan. 1943, late July 1943.

9. *Civic Searchlight*, Sept. 1943, 2. The entrants were Patrolman Frederick P. Adams; former Mayor Charles Bowles; plumbing and heating engineer Edward A. Carey; restaurateur Charles J.T. Duggan; Circuit Court commissioner Frank Fitz-Gerald; retired businessman Andrew J. Gable; Chrysler employee Frank W. Holtz; former Mayor and Governor Frank Murphy; attorney Elmer G. Rice; physician Tom H. Robertson; attorney Frank Schwartz; mechanical engineer Roy C. Smith; state representative Adam W. Sumeracki.

10. August Meier and Elliott Rudwick, *Black Detroit and the Rise of the UAW* (New York: Oxford Univ. Press, 1979), 197-206. In 1939 Jeffries defeated Richard W. Reading 226,185 to 108,973, carrying 731 of 961 precincts; in 1941, he beat Recorder's Court Judge Joseph A. Gillis 218,967 to 71,874, winning all 1,015 precincts. See

Dominic J. Capeci Jr., *Race Relations in Wartime Detroit: The Sojourner Truth Controversy of 1942* (Philadelphia: Temple Univ. Press, 1984), 15, 27.

11. Robert Conot, *American Odyssey* (New York: William Morrow, 1974), 402–4, for Cobo's mayoral victory over George C. Edwards in 1949; Wilbur C. Rich, *Coleman Young and Detroit Politics: From Social Activist to Power Broker* (Detroit: Wayne State Univ. Press, 1989), 31, 74, for Cobo's public entrepreneurial style, 1949–57.

12. Rich, *Coleman Young and Detroit Politics*, 31–32, for the theories of political scientists James B. Cunningham and Charles Levine.

13. EJJ to MSH, 18 May 1943; MSH to EJJ, 27 May 1943.

14. MSH to EJJ, 2 July 1943; EJJ to MSH, 12 Feb. 1943; *News*, 30 June 1943, 1, 4, 33.

15. MHS to EJJ, 27 May 1943, and 2 July 1943; EJJ to Common Council, 29 June 1943, *Journal of the Common Council* (Detroit: Inland Press, 1944), 1829.

16. MSH to EJJ, 14 Oct. 1943.

17. MSH to EJJ, 8 Dec. 1943.

18. Interview with Louis E. Martin, Washington, D.C., 9 July 1979.

19. Rich, *Coleman Young and Detroit Politics*, 32, for the theory of Charles Levine.

20. MSH to GCE, [mid-Sept. 1942], Edwards Collection.

21. MSH to EJJ, Jan. 1943; MSH to EJJ, 27 May 1943.

22. MSH to GCE, [mid-Sept. 1942]; MHS to EJJ, 27 May 1943, Box 7, pt. 2, Edwards Collection.

23. MSH to EJJ, 2 July 1943; MSH to GCE, [mid-Sept. 1942], Edwards Collection.

24. MSH to EJJ, 24 Feb. 1943; MSH to EJJ, 27 May 1943.

25. MSH to EJJ, 27 May 1943.

26. MSH to EJJ, late Nov. 1943.

27. EJJ to MSH, 31 Jan. 1944, Mayor's Papers, Box 4 (1943).

28. EJJ to MSH, 22 July 1943.

29. MSH to EJJ, 2 July 1943.

30. MSH to EJJ, late July 1943.

31. EJJ to MSH, 22 July 1943.

32. EJJ to MSH, 16 Dec. 1942.

33. EJJ to MSH, 9 Dec. 1942.

34. Capeci, *Race Relations in Wartime Detroit*, 157, 218 n.97.

35. EJJ to MSH, 19 April 1943.

36. MSH to EJJ, 2 July 1943.

37. MSH to EJJ, 8 Dec. 1943.

LETTERS:
SEPTEMBER 1942–JANUARY 1944

Detroit. September 17, 1942

Dear Martin: *Edward J. Jeffries Jr. to Martin S. Hayden*

My conscience really troubles me for not having dropped you a note before this time. But as a brother hanger-around the City Hall you can appreciate the maelstrom we get into. What between work and play I just haven't taken time.

Your successor came on the job yesterday. John Carlisle is now the *News* No. 1 boy here. I feel certain that he will not fill your place. However, the machinations of men and mice go on inevitably and, while I am sure the *News* suffered a severe shock, I regret to announce they are still doing business. So are we, under raps [*sic*], of course, but we are struggling yet.

I have seen your Dad[1] a couple of times since you have been away, on my visits to Washington and, as you well know, he seemed very well. I haven't seen Betty since you left, except the same evening when they opened the Hall-Dodds Bowling Alley. I have talked to her over the 'phone in relation to leasing the house, but that's old stuff now. Everything was all right then. Brother Krause informs me that he took good care of her, and that she had a very good lease arrangement. . . .

I still haven't a D.S.R. commissioner. Up to the present I have asked four and they all have turned me down. You might be interested in knowing who they are: [Frank D.] Eaman, [Clarence W.] Avery, Lynn Pierson and Joe Dodge.[2] Incidentally, that situation is no better. . . .

[Glenn C.] Richards is now Superintendent D.P.W., qualifying under the Civil Service set-up. I just moved everybody in the Civilian Defense up one step. . . .

Perhaps now that I have started writing I can do a better job in the future. Believe me when I say my intentions are good, even if the flesh seems to be weak.

With the best of everything to you, I am   SINCERELY, JEFF

NOTES

1. Jay G. Hayden, then *News* correspondent in Washington, D.C.
2. Banking attorney and former police commissioner Eaman, who resigned that position over the federal government's handling of the Sojourner Truth housing controversy in 1942; Murray Corporation of America president Avery, industrialist Pierson, who headed the Michigan Works Progress Administration; and Detroit banker Dodge.

Army Air Base, Salina, Kansas. [mid-September 1942]
Dear George: *Martin S. Hayden to George C. Edwards*

Your newsy letter arrived this morning and the suggestion that a letter-bartering be put into effect is at once accepted. I had planned to write you sooner but, as you have noted, the army for me has so far been one long train ride and I really haven't gotten until now into a schedule where I could get to work on my correspondence.

Your report of the [Frank] Cody runaway in the primary was my first news of that race.[1] They ran it off in one of the periods when my subscription to the *News* and myself were headed in different directions. I agree with you that a younger gent would be much preferable. Under the present system you will still be the "Kid Councilman" when you are old enough for your social security pay.

The Army proceeds as usual. From letters to Miss Ford you of course know that I am one of the four Snow Whites in an outfit of 250 Negroes.[2] On the whole, they are very good boys and, with assurance that I am right, I can say that we have the best outfit on the base. Our captain is no ball of fire on social problems and when I came here I found an unofficial rule in effect that the subject of race should never be mentioned. I took a bite at that one and in a class on military courtesy which I was teaching last week I began to pound away at the idea that, as Negro troops, both their mistakes and their good jobs would be particularly conspicuous and would be used as bases for judgement of their whole race. It seems to have worked with perfection and we have gotten a number of comments on the fact that our men, when they appear on the streets of Salina, are far neater than their white colleagues and much more meticulous in their observation of rules as to saluting, etc.

Most of our men are from Pennsylvania and we have among others about five former employees of the Pittsburgh Courier.[3] Like their paper they are super–race conscious and I have been a little worried lest they may start campaigning among our rank and file who are of course of the cornfield variety. However, I think we are saved by the fact that we have five or six exceedingly intelligent and very level headed men who are keeping things on an even keel. So far there has been absolutely no trouble between white and black soldiers on this post. That, however, is one which can spring up over night and every now and then I have a nightmare when I dream of what it might lead to. In an effort to avert such a catastrophe we have our own M.P.'s and the Base Commander has ordered the white M.P.'s to call one of our men in case of trouble involving Negro troops. I think that will avert one of the chief causes of race riots on other posts—clashes between drunken Negro soldiers and white M.P.'s. Also our cops are much tougher than white ones would ever dare to be. When one of our boys gets out of line in town they just pitch him in a truck—with a bop on the head if necessary—and get him off the streets. Partially I think as a result of my race pride campaign, our M.P.'s get a world of reenforcement, when needed, from other men on pass who also seem to want the punks off the street.

And how is army life? Sometimes good and sometimes not so hot! The work is interesting as hell but there is constant aggravation from the fact that—competent or not—he who has an extra bar speaks as God when he opens his mouth. With the great expansion of the Air Corps we probably have a larger percentage of recent civilians as officers than have other branches. On the whole, the selection boards have done a very good job but, like [Fiorello H.] La Guardia,[4] when they make a mistake it is a "pip." As a Second Lieutenant I am of course fair game for almost anything with jewelry on its shoulder and the resultant training in self control has probably been most beneficial. I have every day or so one of those apoplectic seizures which used to take me over on the golf course but I have learned to keep them just under the surface. I find that the best way to handle a superior who is on the daffodil fringe is to accept and then forget about screwy orders. Ninety-nine times out of a hundred they forget them by the next trip around and, if they don't, it always pads their ego to have some second looie report that he "neglected to carry out the order and has no excuse sir." Usually they beam pontifically and strut off with a "take care of that matter lieutenant." To date I have never had a third call and if you hear I am in the jug you can deduce that I was unable to think of a new answer for the occasion. I repeat though that, as a whole, the officers are a good crowd, sincerely trying to do a good job.

How long I will stay here I do not know. This is a new outfit. Under the air corps system our type of organization is designed to build and maintain airports and bases and to act as the final line of defense in the event they are attacked. For that last purpose we will ultimately get a whole list of lethal weapons in the use of which we must train the men. We just got this week our first consignment of rifles and our boys are showing great interest in them. We will probably be here in Salina at least until the heavy work on this base is over and then be moved on to a new scene of action. The fact that most of the bases of the future will be built overseas seems to bode well for our ultimate departure on foreign service. At present I think about half of our men would prefer to remain road builders in Kansas for the duration but I think that will be altered as their training progresses and they have awakened within them the desire to actually use all of the killing equipment which will be issued them.

On the whole I think I was lucky to be assigned to troops. It is much more satisfying to work with men than to see your accomplishments portrayed in a neat pile of completed red tape wound around a desk somewhere. Promotion in this job may be slower or faster, depending on the breaks, than in a desk job. Of the four officers I rank third. If the two above me stay put and I stay put I will probably end the war as a second lieutenant. However, there can be lightening changes and if they start shuffling the deck, only two have to move to give me a Squadron Commander's assignment. The colonel who commands the post was over for lunch the other day and predicted over a piece of our super apple pie that "all three of you lieutenants will be captains and have squadrons within a year." But I've been in this long enough to recognize that as a latrine prediction to be believed when it happens.

This base is being built as a final training point and dispatch center for medium and heavy bombardment squadrons. Since it has been published in the local papers it is no secret that the Salina Air Base will be the third largest in North America. We already have here one runway, the concrete portion of which is 10,000 feet long and 500 feet wide. That is bordered by wide strips of asphalt and grass. The contractors tell me that it is the largest single slab of paving ever laid. Two others like it are in process of construction. Every now and then a flying fortress drops in to call and the whole base quits work to join in the cheers when it lands. The speed with which work is progressing indicates the sky around here will be lousy with them before very long.

Of course one thing that can happen to all officers attached to the base is that we will get a last minute order to join one of these bomber squadrons as it pulls out. All of us are busily learning the duties of ground officers with combat flying outfits in hopeful anticipation of the day when they may call us up with orders to get moving. It appears that it is a quite regular habit when an outfit which is short handed gets walking papers to draft some of the base personnel and take them along.

Betty and the children are down in Washington and seem to be both settled and happy. I know she would like to hear from Peg. Her address is 1 East Lenox Street, Chevy Chase, Maryland. Give my best to all of the gang and, for yourself, remember to write again soon. Particularly unloose with the gossip. Who is in or coming out of the dog house and what journalistic, political or combined feuds have popped to the surface?

With many regards,   MARTIN

NOTES

1. Former superintendent of Detroit Public Schools for twenty-three years, Cody led the primary for Common Council by a two-to-one margin over nearest runner-up, Fred C. Castator, bus driver nephew of the late city clerk and councilman Fred W. Castator. Cody went on to defeat Castator in the November election, 188,057 to 124,806, and to occupy the seat created by the death of John W. Smith earlier in the spring; in 1944, he became council president pro tempore. Castator, in turn, was elected to the council in 1943, seventh vote-getter in a field of eighteen, which ousted incumbent James H. Garlick. See *News*, 16 Sept. 1942, 1; 4 Nov. 1942, 1; and 2 Nov. 1943, 1.

2. Hayden's outfit was the Forty-ninth Aviation Squadron, one of several black units created in 1941–42 to perform routine labor and guard duties on army airfields. See Ulysses Lee, *The Employment of Negro Troops* (Washington, D.C.: Government Printing Office, 1966), 113-16; Alan M. Osur, *Blacks in the Army Air Forces during World War II* (Washington, D.C.: Government Printing Office, 1977), 25-28.

3. The *Pittsburgh Courier*, a militant black newspaper, coined the "Double V" phrase, calling for black Americans to fight for victory against undemocratic enemies and policies at home as well as abroad. See Lee Finkle, *Forum for Protest: The Black Press during World War II* (Rutherford, N.J.: Fairleigh Dickinson Univ. Press, 1975), 112-13.

4. The liberal mayor of New York City, 1934-45.

Detroit. October 14, 1942

Dear Martin: *Edward J. Jeffries Jr. to Martin S. Hayden*

It was good to hear from you. I talked to your father last Monday while I was in Washington being admitted to practice before the Supreme Court. He told me where you were and what you were doing. It runs in the family. He tells it well too. One nice thing about the army during war time at least, life doesn't seem to get too humdrum, does it. If you ever get to the novelist stage, you will have stored a lot of experiences.

Slutz and I collaborated on a speech to astound the world about Detroit and its war effort.[1] Slutz, Carlisle and I journeyed to Springfield, Illinois, last Thursday to deliver same. I can safely say it was a good speech because I wrote it and Slutz promptly rewrote it. I will have to admit that his was an improvement. We had a lot of fun, and I am sure that that was one thing you missed because you would have liked it, too.

I got a letter the other day from Bud Burnett, Guadalcanal, Solomon Islands, where he is a Lieutenant Colonel.[2] He started out by suggesting that if he had thought my budget sessions were hot, it was because he hadn't been aware of life in Guadalcanal. I suspect, from reading the newspapers, he is right literally and figuratively. In spite of his rank, I am not too envious.

Your Dad is well. Slutz certainly isn't losing weight—maybe gaining it and, by and large, everybody is about the same. [Albert] Cobo had a birthday party here about ten days ago that rumor had pegged as an announcement of his candidacy for mayor. At the last minute, apparently, the plans were changed and it didn't come off—that is, the announcement—the party did. Carlisle wrote a humorous piece on it, and I am enclosing it for your edification, if any.[3] Charlie Williams[4] stole the show. Every time he was presented the multitude tore the house down. I suspect that they were afraid if they applauded Cobo too much I would be resentful, and they compromised on Charlie. Maybe I am not fair to Charlie, but you can guess from Salina as accurately as I can. That's been the only funny spot around here in some time.

[William] Logan didn't do anything really except that Homer doesn't seem to like him, and I, needless to say, put no stone in the way of Homer's disposing of him.[5] Tommy McIntyre[6] is very anxious to have his job. He has asked everybody, except himself, to ask me.

Right now you are making me late for my bowling appointment, and I can just feel it that because I'll have to hurry and get all excited, I probably won't do well. If I don't I am sure there will be nobody to blame but Lieutenant Hayden, the erstwhile golfer. Incidentally, Slutz is interested in the game, and thinks he is pretty good now. He says his shots are good, as if they were.

The best of everything to you.   SINCERELY, JEFF

NOTES

1. Speaking before the Illinois Municipal League, Jeffries lambasted a national magazine story that portrayed the city's war production as crippled by labor and

racial strife. He considered the article "a keyhole glance at our town" and countered that Detroit was producing war materials "at a rate 32 per cent higher" than its peak in peacetime, in some cases even being ahead of production schedules by twelve months. Mocking the photo essay, he concluded: 'Detroit Is Dynamite—to the Axis!' See "Detroit Is Dynamite," *Life*, 17 Aug. 1942, 15-23; Carlisle, "Mayor Hails Miracles of War Plants," *News*, 17 May 1943, 1, 4.

2. Lt. Col. C.V. Burnett, USMC, former manager of the Detroit City Airport. In a series of stories he later recounted the Marine Air Wing defense of Guadalcanal. See *News*, 17 May 1943, 1, 4.

3. Carlisle, "Birthday Party for Cobo Shuns Politics—Almost," *News* clipping attached to letter.

4. Deputy city treasurer.

5. Logan was replaced as second deputy commissioner and secretary of the Detroit Police Department by Police Commissioner John H. Witherspoon, whom Jeffries sometimes called "Homer."

6. McIntyre, a *News* reporter, was passed over for Douglas R. Ginn.

Army Air Base, Salina, Kansas. [16 October 1942]

Dear Jeff: *Martin S. Hayden to Edward J. Jeffries Jr.*

Just a brief note and a peculiar request.

Here is my problem. We are shortly going to open the Officer's Club here and, as is the case on all new bases, the new organization will be short on cash. A standard and approved army way of remedying this situation is through installation of slot machines.

Our trouble comes from the fact that slot machines are no longer being manufactured and we cannot buy any. I wondered if by chance your gendarmes have any at the local clink that have not yet been destroyed or, if not, whether Don Leonard[1] might have some.

We would be perfectly willing to have it on record where they went as the use of slot machines on the army club property is not a violation of any law. If you could dig any up we would be glad to pay the freight and deeply appreciative. Incidentally if the Great Hayden could accomplish this miracle it would do him not a bit of [harm] with the local brass hats who have admitted that acquisition of the gambling machines are beyond their ability.

I would appreciate word as to what the possibilities are. We can use, incidentally, any number up to a dozen if you should find that the Witherspoon attic is bulging with them.

I'll write a longer letter soon.

Regards to all,   MARTIN

NOTE

1. Donald S. Leonard, captain, Michigan State Police.

Detroit. December 9, 1942
Edward J. Jeffries Jr. to Martin S. Hayden

Dear Martin:

I have just finished reading your letter to Miss Ford.

Hope you get the Christmas leave. It would be awfully nice if you traveled to Washington by way of Chicago and Detroit.

The Kansas farmers, incidentally, are not unlike Detroiters, native and adopted. Your former profession has so confused the general public as to what should be done, or even what will be done, that by the time the Government gets around to doing it, a sizeable percentage of the people have been convinced that it should not be done, and as a result, to quote a mutual friend of ours, multitudes of new Republicans are being made daily. I presume this is music to your ears.

I saw the Notre Dame-Michigan football game, and suffice it to say it was a great day for the Methodists.[1] You would have thoroughly enjoyed it. Our local boys played better than the score indicated, and with the exception of the first two or three minutes of the game, they were in complete charge at all times.

Our friend Al Cobo is getting madder, apparently, by the day at Charlie Oakman. Al finds himself again in the unenviable position of sinking to the level of City Treasurer. Tax collections are good, everybody has money and, therefore, it is necessary only to collect what the customers shove across the counter. The job is not glamorous and has but little, if any, news value. The strangest paradox of all is that the City has money and can't spend it and, more important than that, we are going to have a surplus in spite of everything we can do, I guess, and you know how little difficulty you have with money you can't spend. Therefore, the need for financial wizards is being curtailed by the war economy, and the routine operation of the City by law and by custom is in the hands of the Mayor, the Common Council, and the Controller's office. You can guess all the rest. I am not sure your bet is a good one. You know how little sense of humor the gentleman has, and he can be goaded and abetted into doing that thing.

Gasoline rationing has increased the problems of the D.S.R.[2] Our labor problems out there are as usual at fever heat, and the general overall demeanor of the runners of the D.S.R., I report, as usual. If you had suddenly appeared upon the scene this morning, you wouldn't have found a hair out of place from the last time you saw and talked to all of them.

Florence and Gary are well.

Slutz is patting his chest and telling everybody how important his job is, but gas rationing has knocked off about 20% of the traffic and will continue to do more. He will be like a bank receiver the first thing he knows—he will be liquidating a business.

Krause is the City's arbitrator in four D.S.R. arbitrations, plus the fact that he is trying to figure out whether a raise can be paid if granted. Confusion is the theme of the day too often.

We are trying to find quarters for the O.C.D. We think we have sold the Barlum Hotel for $550,000; $50,000 down.

My gin rummy has improved lately. Of course I know you always thought it was good.

By and large we are doing just about the same things as we did before. Few curtailments are being made here and there, and I can see in the not too distant future distinct changes in our living habits. It has been coming on slowly but it seems surely. This is a very interesting time but a very difficult time to be in the government.

I will try to do better with my correspondence.

Sincerely yours,   JEFF

NOTES

1. On 14 November, Michigan beat Notre Dame 32 to 20 in their first meeting since 1916. See *News,* 15 Nov. 1942, Sports Section, 1.

2. Gas rationing in Detroit began on 1 December, though it had been publicized several weeks earlier. See *News,* 17 Nov. 1942, 1.

Detroit. December 16, 1942
Edward J. Jeffries Jr. to Martin S. Hayden

Dear Martin:

Just shortly returned from a Board of Supervisors meeting called specially for the purpose of selecting three County Civil Service Commissioners. The Civil Service set-up for the County, as you may recall, was approved at the last general election. The successful candidates were Thomas V. LaCicero, William F. Von Moll, and Chester Martin.[1]

I had a candidate. In fact, I had three candidates and promised all three of them that I would vote for them. When I got to the meeting, in fact just a day or two days ago, I discovered that I would have to vote for one at a time, either one Democrat and two Republicans, or vice versa, and two from the city and one from out county, or vice versa. It was, therefore, necessary to eliminate one at a time and I did not, as a practical fact, have an opportunity to vote for all three.[2]

I put Monroe Lake[3] in for nomination. He was allegedly the CIO candidate. The first to be nominated was for the two-year term. Lake's name was in the hat. He did only fair. Needless to say I did not put his name in for the four-year term, but I did put it in for the six-year term. Then in Mr. Tracy Doll's[4] old inimitable way, he, in support of my motion to nominate, made a good old plea for a labor candidate on the Commission. The man sitting two seats from me promptly tore up his ballot on which Lake's name appeared. How many counterparts of that there were, I don't know. Anyway, Mr. Martel then took the floor and said that he wanted it distinctly understood that Mr. Lake was no representative of labor. The

fact of the matter is, he, Mr. Martel thought that he, Mr. Lake, was a rene-
gade of the first water, and that he was an enemy of labor. Well, I almost
laughed at that one, and then the balloting took place and Mr. Lake
ran third.

Mr. Martel promptly rose to his feet and suggested that the vote be
taken on the two high candidates who were Chester Martin and [State]
Senator [James A.] Burns. Incidentally, both of these gentlemen received
only two or three votes more than Lake in the nomination. No protest
was made, and the vote was taken. Jimmy Burns got 71 votes and Martin
got 60 votes, but because Burns did not get the required 81 votes or the
majority of members of the Board, rather than of members present, it
was necessary to ballot again, and then Mr. Tracy Doll again only as he
can do, got up and asked if those who knew anything about the qualifications of Chester Martin, knew that he was a stooge of the Wayne
County Road Commission. Nobody answered. Then [William A.] Comstock[5] who had placed the man's name in for nomination said that if
Mr. Doll's mind had been made up there was nothing to be done about
it, but that he knew Chester Martin was a good man, and proceeded to
tell why. Parenthetically I did not believe what he said because I know
better, but the ballot was taken and Chester Martin got 72 votes and
Jimmy Burns got 59.

Then, this probably seems incredulous to you, Brother Martel got
up and said that he had been authorized by Candidate Senator Burns to
state that Jimmy Burns *did not* have any fault to find with department
heads of the County, and that it was untrue that he couldn't be fair and
impartial with the department heads. And again, parenthetically, this
was the first intimation I had had that James Burns was Martel's candidate. And so, in the next vote Chester Martin was elected.

You talk about politics and politicos. Two allegedly veteran strategists,
Doll and Martel, did the best job of defeating their candidates that I have
seen demonstrated in many a long year. Literally, they seemed uncanny.
However, after three and three-quarters hours, we finished the task.

We are going to have a repetition of the Sojourner Truth affair[6] in
about thirty to sixty days or I am no judge of the future. This time it will
be centered around Wyoming and Eight Mile Road. Perhaps I am borrow-
ing trouble, but it is much better to think of the worst and be surprised
with a lesser amount of grief, than to underestimate. I don't think the city
can stand another one with the serious repercussions, and it looks to me
as though I would come out of this next one with cauliflower ears, man-
gled arms and legs. The fact of the matter is I am lucky if I can come out.

Believe me when I tell you there are worse things than fighting wars
by quite a bit.

Your description of your court martial experience leads me to believe
that you are very good either as a judge or a writer. Because I think you
are the latter I think your description is better than the actual experience, but I got a big kick out of it anyway, and I can't help thinking that

you are learning more and faster than you have in any other period of your life. And, Martin, I am not your father and, therefore, I probably shouldn't say this, but it is awfully good for you. I love to read your letters, and they are doing something to you, boy.

Monty Leonard[7] was in and explained how he missed seeing you and how disappointed he was in not having the opportunity to see you.

Carlisle got about half stiff the other day and almost got into a fight with [Brace] Beemer.[8] Carlisle mixes with people just as oil mixes with water and, of course, I can't say much more for the other fellow. And on the old assumption that when Greek meets Greek they start a restaurant, I can't understand why there wasn't a restaurant when Carlisle and Beemer got together.

There's never a dull moment in city business. Charlie Oakman, Tom Leadbetter[9] and I went to Chicago last Saturday to sign bonds. Mr. Cobo could not make it on Monday, and was not there until Tuesday. Depending upon whose story you take, someone was responsible for a delay which means the loss of a day's interest for the city. I don't know who it is who is so recklessly squandering the City's money. Two of our sterling guardians are now explaining why it takes so long to get bonds prepared for delivery, and because they couldn't have made a mistake, poor Charlie is to blame for making the schedule so tight. But his shoulders are broad, and when last seen, it didn't seem to be worrying him to an unusual amount.

Governor [Harold E.] Stassen of Minnesota[10] spoke at an old time Republican rally Monday, under the guise of the Economic Club of Detroit. Except for the fact that I have never seen so many Republicans together in Detroit, it was uneventful. Unfortunately even the Republicans had to press to do the occasion justice. I think that they will all admit secretly that they were a little let down. In fact, they seemed to be more let down than I was. He was not too bad and not too good either. I didn't agree with his philosophy very much, but I think he did pretty well with what he had. He is a nice looking chap and probably smart, but definitely cold and lacking the personality charm that Brother Roosevelt and Brother [Wendell L.] Willkie[11] have, and it is more or less necessary to have it to be successful in public life.

Your reaction to the philosophy of the Army is not different. In fact, I think it is a normal reaction. All these boys are working hard, long hours, small pay with a great deal of potential or real danger involved. To top it off, they are under rigid discipline. It is hard to be liberal under the rank of a major, if at all.

I am worried about myself. I have always been an exponent of high wages and good working conditions, but I have heard so much wailing, gnashing of teeth and shedding of crocodile tears lately about terrible working conditions, the rank pay, etc., as expounded by the Labor leaders and some people with more money than they have ever had in their history with the cost of living below the 1929 level, that I am wondering what the outcome will be. And when I hear the complaints and the horrible privation that our war workers have to deal with, and when I think of the boys in the Army, I at least understand better the reaction of the boys in the armed forces. However, I keep resorting to my friend [Reece B.] Oberteuffer's[12] philosophy–it will be all right. Something will happen–it always has happened. I hate to get down to that level, and really never thought I would, but it keeps cropping up in my mind more frequently, and certainly it seems to me that something ought to happen.

Here's hoping you will get that Christmas leave, and I repeat, it will be a lot of fun if either going to or from Washington you can drop off in Detroit.

Good Luck, and I presume that it is very appropriate to say, "Keep your powder dry."

Sincerely yours,   J E F F

NOTES

1. LaCicero, Republican and member of the Board of Supervisors, was selected (as chairman) for a two-year term; Moll, Republican and Monguagon Township supervisor, a four-year term; Martin, Democrat and former chairman of the Michigan Tax Commission, a six-year term. See *News*, 17 Dec. 1942, 41.

2. Of the 161-member Board of Supervisors, only 139 voted in the election, which required 81 ballots–a simple majority–for victory. Board bylaws also required that the Civil Service Commission be bipartisan–two Republicans and one Democrat, or vice versa–and that candidates for the commission resign as supervisors. See *News*, 16 Dec. 1942, 35; 17 Dec. 1942, 41.

3. Member of the DPW and regional executive of the UAW.

4. Head of the CIO Council.

5. Councilman and former governor of Michigan (1933-34).

6. On 28 February 1942, white residents from the surrounding area attacked black defense workers endeavoring to move into the federally built, racially designated Sojourner Truth Homes in northeast Detroit. They succeeded on that Sunday; however, following nearly eight weeks of negotiation between local, state, and federal officials, blacks moved into the project under armed guard and without incident. See Capeci, *Race Relations in Wartime Detroit*.

7. James Montrose Leonard, director of research, Detroit Bureau of Governmental Research.

8. A friend of Jeffries who played the Lone Ranger on radio and served on the Detroit Board of Health.

9. Thomas D. Leadbetter, city clerk.

10. A three-term Republican governor, lieutenant commander in the Naval Reserve, and presidential hopeful in the 1940s (and early 1950s), Stassen titled his speech "The Three-Fold Challenge of the Days Ahead": winning the war, preparing for postwar problems, and world affairs. He advocated federal assistance of free enterprise and establishment of the United Nations to deal with international travel, literacy, justice, trade, and police. Clearly, his concept of big government clashed with

Jeffries's commitment to decentralization and conflict with federal authority in local areas. See *News*, 14 Dec. 1942, 1, 2; 15 Dec. 1942, 9.

11. Republican presidential candidate who lost to FDR in 1940.

12. President and treasurer of the Super Dux Company, Inc.

Army Air Base, Salina, Kansas. [17 January 1943]

My Dear Jeff: *Martin S. Hayden to Edward J. Jeffries Jr.*

I received a long letter from you at Christmas time which was forwarded to me in Washington where I was basking in the glory of a ten day leave. I had meant to get off the answer before now but getting straightened out all the kinks which my absence had put into the army has kept me right busy.

I have been very amused at the screams of righteous if somewhat inexplicable indignation which Mssrs Carlisle and Company have been reporting as emanating from the Great Cobo. From what I can gather the whole affair must be most satisfying to such Cobo lovers as John Daley and Ken[neth J.] McCarren.[1] I would really have loved to have seen the Little Genius on the night last week after he had been rapped by both a *News* Editorial and Brother [W. K.] Kelsey.[2] Both I thought did right well and I presume that Cobo's thin skin was torn to shreds.

Getting home was of course the nuts. The family were all well and son Jay found cause in his father's return to stage a week long emotional jag. The younger one would give me no heed at all, much preferring his grandfather, a situation which caused the latter no small amount of delight.

Getting back here was not so good. We have acquired 111 new Senegambians[3] and it is reported that the Colonel has requested that we be given still another hundred. That will make us about the biggest outfit of our kind in the Air Force and is probably a prelude to splitting us into two squadrons which might mean some promotions, I have the feeling that they are getting one on the fire for me but to date I remain at my accustomed place on the lowest rung of this military ladder.

Shortly after my return we lost one of our officers and I was handed back my old job of being Mess Officer along with the newer one of supply. That means that I am signing, sealing and dispatching enough paper work so that if laid end to end, or something, it would in a year or so be sufficient to build a bridge that would make possible an invasion of Tokyo by foot. I fully expect that for the rest of my days I will be getting letters from the War Department asking for an accounting for the numerous odd items which are being checked out in my name.

Kansas continues to seethe with a growing hatred of all that is Democratic and New Dealish. Latest beef is over the fuel oil rationing which is a little harder to explain out here than is the gasoline ration. There is of course an abundance of fuel oil in this immediate area and neither rubber nor transportation are consumed getting it to the people's homes.

Still they are rationed and, what seems most regrettable, you hear no one out here doing any public relations for the rationing program. It seems strange to me that with all the hoopla that is being put behind some of the other war efforts, more is not done on the rationing.

There is considerable interest in Washington, incidentally, in what luck Prentiss [M.] Brown will have in [Leon] Henderson's[4] job. Dad says Brown is smart enough to dread it both because he realizes he has never done any big time administrating and because he knows that, at best, he will end up as a National SOB. He has the idea, however, that Henderson tried to go too much into detail on rationing and that the better answer is to push voluntary support of the program and let up on the issuance of multi-numbered, colored and shaped cards or tickets. It may work and, because I kind of like Brown, I hope so.

My Brother, Campbell [Plicher] was also home over the holiday enroute to a new assignment as a student for five months at the Navy War College in Newport. From there he will go to the staff of some admiral which is pretty much alright despite the fact that in this most unorthodox war admirals seem to be somewhat in the habit of getting killed.

During our visit Campbell had out to the house for dinner one of his Annapolis classmates who, after 14 months of sea duty as an observer on a British submarine, has just returned to Washington as a submarine expert on the staff of Admiral [Ernest J.] King.[5] He is the same youngster who used to delight my Dad about ten years ago when, as a midshipman out of the State of Iowa for the first time, he used to analyze Washington social life for Dad at the breakfast table. [He] . . . is now a much less naive young man, considerably hardened by his years under the sea. He celebrated December 7, 1941 and the sudden change of his status from neutral observer to combatant by being permitted to let go a torpedo which smacked a German destroyer somewhere off the coast of Norway. That probably entitled him to some sort of a "first" when someone writes an account of initial shots fired by us in this war.

[He] . . . did tell us one interesting story. You may recall that Admiral King, at a press conference just after our invasion of North Africa remarked that the invasion plans were "a very badly kept secret". [He] . . . said that the Navy learned a few days before the big convoys were to push off that the Germans had concentrated most of their submarine force at a point where they would intercept the convoy. The United Nations therefore got together a fake convoy made up of numerous old and empty ships with a lot of warship protection. The Germans jumped the fake convoy and, in the resulting melee sank 16 of the empty ships and lost a large number of their own craft. The remaining subs had to go home for fuel and ammunition and, before they could get back, the convoy got through the gap. He said that both British and American submarine officers were delighted when Hitler shortly thereafter removed the admiral commanding his undersea force. The busted admiral, he said, is recognized as the best in the business either on our side or theirs.

I do not believe the above constitutes any out of school talking but, while I have that thought in mind I enclose a piece of non-talk propaganda which might have been designed by one who had heard of the Jeffries' crack about need for "a zipper on my mouth."

Write when you get a chance and give my best to Nancy, Miss [Gwynn] Davis, Elsie [Mills] [6] and all of the Boys of the Movement.

MARTIN

NOTES

1. Daley, city controller under Mayor Richard W. Reading; McCarren, member, Detroit Board of Assessors.

2. The newsmen "rapped" Cobo for threatening to run against Jeffries unless the mayor apologized for releasing to the press a report of the budget director that supposedly contained a deliberate misrepresentation of something ascribed to the city treasurer. An affront, said the editor, seemed "a dubious qualification for getting elected mayor," while Kelsey wondered how "in the name of all that's wonderful" a private quarrel could concern the voters. See "Insufficient Reason," *News*, 5 Jan. 1943, 14; "A Matter of Punctilio," *News*, 7 Jan. 1943, 26.

3. Pejorative reference to black soldiers, alluding to the Senegal-Gambia area of West Africa.

4. Brown, Democrat and former U.S. senator from Michigan; Henderson, director, OPA, which was created on 11 April 1941 to fix price ceilings, control rents, and—on 27 December—establish rationing.

5. King, Chief of Naval Operations. Years later Hayden could not recall the name of Campbell's classmate.

6. Davis, mayoral secretary; Mills, switchboard operator.

Detroit. February 8, 1943
Dear Martin: *Edward J. Jeffries Jr. to Martin S. Hayden*

I am awfully sorry that I have been so slow in answering your letter, but the affairs of state when they wane for awhile, come on with a rush, to say nothing of my extra-curricular pursuits.

Today we start on the annual budget hearings. We have had no end of discussions relating to the financial affairs of the city. Mr. Cobo is telling everybody that the taxes should be reduced, and that the pay of the employees should be increased.

An interesting little sidelight that may intrigue you is that the annual custom of getting the city to make wage adjustments in the middle of the fiscal year has been on for some time. Mr. Lodge decided that the Council should have more information, and appointed a [labor] committee consisting of Mr. [George C.] Edwards as chairman, Mr. [William]

Comstock, Mr. [Frank] Cody, Mr. Krause, Mr. Oakman, Mr. Cobo and Mr. [George] Engel.[1] This committee has met a couple of times a week, and has been a great sounding board for the elected but non-voting public officials, together with the Union leaders. Mr. Cobo had a notion that the city should raise all the city employees 4.54% immediately, provided that the minimum of this increase be $136 per year. I haven't talked to Mr. Lodge about the situation, but I think he would feel that making a general pay raise in the middle of the year would be like creating a Frankenstein.

The committee split four to three in favor of the motion, and now the Council finds itself in the unenviable position of having to break an age-old precedent or refusing to follow the recommendation of the Council committee. The Council held a hearing last week on the situation. I asked if the matter could be deferred for a week so that in the meantime I could go over the budget.[2] Dave Addy[3] estimates that we will have a $5,000,000 surplus at the end of the fiscal year and, of course, everybody's mouth is watering to get his share of it. I suspect that some raking up will necessarily follow.

Everybody's health is good and life is about the same.

I'll try to write you at the wind-up of the above mentioned sessions in about a week or ten days.

With kind regards, I am
Sincerely yours,   JEFF

NOTES

1. Comstock and Cody, council members; Engel, auditor general. Lodge requested that the committee recommend to Common Council "wages, salaries, working hours, and classifications" for most city employees. See *News*, 6 Jan. 1943, 14.

2. Ultimately, councilmen approved the 4.54% pay increase for 30,900 employees, excluding all DSR workers; the city and DSR laborers had been in conflict for several months.

3. City budget director.

Army Air Force Base, Salina, Kansas. [24 February 1943]
Martin S. Hayden to Edward J. Jeffries Jr.
Dear Jeff and Nancy: *and Mabel Nancy Ford*

I am making this a double letter partially because my memory indicates I owe you each a letter and partially because it seems like a good idea—rating two letters for one output.

Things here in Harlem proceed about as usual. I have now recovered from the celebration attendant to my moving up from the bottom to the next-to-bottom step in the military hierarchy and have gotten right into the swing of figuring out now how to be a captain. As far as I can see getting promoted consumes most of one's energy in this army business and leads one to the speculations as to what an [Dwight D.] Eisenhower or [George C.] Marshall think about when they get four stars and there are no promotions left.

We still are awaiting actual news on some personnel shifts which promise to affect all of us one way or the other. Our captain is scheduled for a Majority and command of an outfit which is headed overseas. One of us first lieutenants will probably go along with him and the other will stay here in command for a couple of months more. The new outfits they are forming here to which we would probably be attached are very interesting. They call them Airdrome Squadrons and they have a sufficiently large complement of officers and men to set up in the field a complete airdrome with hangars, runways and shops for general repairs. I suspect that some at least of these squadrons will see quite a lot of travel if the war in the Orient develops into a gradual march through India and China where our side would have to carry their own air fields with them. Anyhow they keep telling us that we are all going somewhere shortly and that the WAACs[1] and cripples will take over here.

Saturday night we had another bad crash out in the countryside bordering the field and I was on duty as officer of The Day Monday when they hauled in, in three army trucks, the remains of the Flying Fortress in which nine crew members died. What happened no one seems to know. To look at it, it seemed unbelievable that the compact little piles of twisted debris had once been one of the big ships that go in and out of here. By some chance the tip of the nose was the one portion of the ship which was but slightly damaged. It hung from the back of the first salvage truck and there painted on it by some enthusiast of the crew was a blue and yellow drawing of Mickey Mouse in a hammock and the legend: "Rock a bye Baby".

Our boys are all in a stew about the Negro drive against alleged discrimination by the Air Corps against soldiers of their race. The Negro papers which are devoting most of the space to their campaign for their own kind of "freedom of the air" are full of it and devoured eagerly by our boys. Locally the thing has been fanned up a little because of the decision by the white corporals and sergeants on the field to "include our boys out" in the use and operation of the very super Non Commissioned Officers Club which is being built on the base. In a manner which qualified them for jobs as housing administrators in Washington they compounded the inevitable bad feeling by first inviting our ranking sergeants to a meeting at which, with our men voting, the club was formed and then sending around a committee to tell them the next day that they weren't to be permitted in. It looks to me like the making of a full grown army version of Sojourner Truth but the powers-that-be seem to think they have the situation well in hand. I hope they are right.

I have been following city hall events carefully as reported in the *News*. I note the budget sessions went off as usual with the same arguments and the same decisions. I presume, however, that this year, for a change, the absence of two of the principals caused omission of the annual debate over a pay raise for [Edward A.] Carey.[2] I also see that the union-busting Police Commissioner [Witherspoon] is now getting to be a pistol shot and that all of the policemen think he is wonderful. I suppose they will be giving him testimonial banquets right soon now and presenting him with shooting trophies after the manner of Mssrs [Fred W.] Frahm and [Wendell A.] Lochbiler[3] who, as I remember, used to wine and dine another police commissioner.

I still regret not being actually on hand to watch what was certainly the most colorful of the Cobo tussles with the electorate which so often clamors for his unwilling ascension to higher places. The little man gets funnier every year.

My court martial career continues with an almost unbroken line of losses for the defense. As an army defense counsel you have the unpleasant experience not shared by civilian lawyers of, during a tour as Officer of The Day, inspecting the guard house and finding it entirely peopled by clients. I got rid of one client by another route and with considerable relief. One of the gunners on a combat crew went AWOL just before his ship took off for more distant and less healthy lands. His commanding officer suspected (and I half believe he was right) that the young man had suddenly lost his stomach for going flying anywhere where the normal hazards were to be complicated by a little shooting. As a result he filed charges against the boy for Desertion In Face of Danger which potentially can carry a death penalty. Such a charge requires approval of the Second Air Force before it can be sent to trial and yesterday the answer came back from Spokane.[4] Instead of court martialing the prisoner they ordered him shipped under guard to Jefferson Barracks, Missouri where he will be assigned immediately to an outfit headed overseas. I don't think they could have made the desertion charge stick but I was nonetheless glad to get rid of it. Defending against a death penalty is a little rich for the blood of an "attorney" who, as . . . [it used to be said] of George Murphy, "learned his law out of the Saturday Evening Post."

As a result of my promotion I am now adjutant of the Squadron and spend my time trying to keep the accounts, records and correspondence in shape to meet the minute audits and inspections by the numerous officers assigned to the checkup job. I understand that when this war is over they are going to use all of the army files to build a bridge for picnic parties who wish to go from Frisco to Guadalcanal. In the past two weeks I think I have filled out or signed enough forms to build a span as far as Hawaii.

I heard from Betty yesterday at the conclusion of her Detroit visit and she reported that she had called the City Hall to check up on you all. She was due back in Washington this morning.

Write me, both of you, when you get a chance and give me all the latest news of feuds and other pleasant occupations in the halls of government.

MARTIN

NOTES

1. Women's Auxiliary Army Corps (later, Women's Army Corps, or WAC), created on May 15, 1942, to enlist volunteers for noncombat duties.

2. Plumbing and heating engineer employed by the city hospitals for nineteen years, and perennial candidate for Common Council (1935, 1939, 1941, 1943) and Congress (1934, 1936, 1940, 1942).

3. Frahm, first deputy commissioner and superintendent, and Lochbiler, district inspector, Detroit Police Department, served Police Commissioner Heinrich A. Pickert during the mayoralty of Richard W. Reading; both were among 125 persons, including the mayor, indicted for corruption by Circuit Court Judge Homer Ferguson in 1940. Lochbiler, for example, later received a two to five-year prison term for obstruction of justice (accepting bribes to permit the operation of illegal enterprises); he was sentenced in August 1942 and paroled in March 1944. See *News,* 17 March 1943, 13.

4. Fort George, Washington, headquarters of the Second Air Force.

Detroit. April 19, 1943

Dear Martin: *Edward J. Jeffries Jr. to Martin S. Hayden*

Just a line to revive our desultory correspondence. I will take the blame for the desultory part.

Business is as usual. Unfortunately the *News* covers the life of the mayor and its many ramifications so thoroughly that I presume there is little I can add. However, the weather has been lousy, and we are going directly from winter to summer—that is, if there is to be any change in the weather.

The DSR Commission is unchanged. Their problems are even more acute. By that I mean the clash of personalities is even sharper with the gentlemen of the press even less tolerant. However, in spite of everything the equipment keeps running and, while the public insists that it is being taken care of shabbily, I report that it is still being given care.

The Great Slutz is in his glory. Single-handed, he reports, the Detroit Traffic Association won for the City of Detroit first prize in the national competition. Occasionally to relieve the monotony of repetition, he mentions such minor agencies as the Police Department and the Traffic Engineer and, when he is especially beneficent, he refers casually to the general public.

When I was in Washington a couple of weeks ago I talked to your Dad and Mother over the telephone. They both sounded well. However, it was the day before your Mother had to go to the hospital for another operation, and I haven't heard as yet how she responded. The fact of the matter is, your Dad was at home when I called, and I could hear the Hayden grandchildren carrying on in the usual Hayden manner over the telephone. They certainly must take after their father rather than their mother. If volume is any indication, they are hale and hearty.

I enjoyed very much your observations during your experience as an advocate of justice. It should give you an insight as to why the unbroken line of victories of Brother [J.C.] Barnard excited the curiosity of some of his fellow-lawyers.

If you get any good ideas on how to handle the rising tide in relation to the racial question, send them by air mail. Unfortunately I feel that a bad situation is now on the program.

The budget is finished. The City is gradually going on a 48-hour week with time and a half for everybody over 40 hours.

The town is plowed from end to end in our usual flamboyant way, and we have taken up victory gardening with our usual gusto.[1] Somebody asked me how big my garden was, and I think I have a perfect description of it—as big as a wife and small child can handle. I hope that my luck holds out, and that I'll do my weeding on golf courses, excavating on traps, and avoiding the bending over and consequent crick in the back sensation at every opportunity.

Dave Hersh[2] has just returned from Miami. Apparently the same things in the same old way are transpiring at the Roney Plaza. He knows a young fellow who has just recently been commissioned as a second lieutenant, and is in charge of marching the boys to and from the Roney.

Stod White is back in the office at the *News*. The beat is now covered by the illustrious Carlisle and the hard-working Seiffert. The *Free Press* has added a man recently in Ken McCormick. [Leo] Donovan[3] has resurrected a chestnut in the Tenth Councilman, and he has been barbing everybody he can think of weekly.

Outside of a face-lifting, the physical appearance of the office bears little change. I will drop you a note again in a few days.

Sincerely,   JEFF

NOTES

1. Because of food shortages, civilians were encouraged to grow fruits and vegetables on personal or communal plots known as "victory gardens." See Allan Clive, *State of War: Michigan in World War II* (Ann Arbor: Univ. of Michigan Press, 1979), 118-19.

2. Detroit lawyer who replaced Jeffries as counsel for the Maccabees.

3. In his column, playing on the number of councilmen (nine), Donovan named himself number ten.

Detroit. May 18, 1943
Dear Martin: *Edward J. Jeffries Jr. to Martin S. Hayden*

This should reach you by your birthday. In any event, many happy returns of the day.

It's a shame that you haven't been here during the last two or three weeks to participate in the free discussion of Detroit as an air center.

With all your recent and up-to-date experience, I am sure that you could have qualified as an expert guesser too. In any event, I feel quite sure that the psychosis of the public has done a complete back-flip. So far as I am able to determine, your late employer [the *News*] is advocating the expenditure of something between $70,000,000 and $100,000,000 for airports alone. It is not exactly clear yet whether they mean to spend our money or Uncle Sam's money, but they think that we ought to have in the neighborhood of ten additional airports.

It is astounding how rapidly we can complete the cycle. Ten years ago now we were issuing our first scrip. Only since the first of this year has our assessed valuation exceeded the amount set by the Constitution as sufficient to warrant additional bonded indebtedness. Along this same line, three times within the past couple of weeks I have had employers of labor ask me if I could help them get employees. I think that completes the series. I have now seen and heard everything.

For an additional reason I am sorry that you are not here. I am about to embark, I think, on a program having to do with so-called blight areas which, I am sure, would warm the cockles of your heart. And, with your background, you, no doubt, would revel in it.

The Great Slutz and I are collaborating on a speech to be given in Albany before the New York Municipal League on June 10.[1] As usual, in fact more than usual, I wish I hadn't said yes. It is becoming increasingly difficult to know right from wrong in relation to public leadership. I presume, however, that we are about to go into an era in which men can easily make or break themselves and, therefore, life will be more exciting.

We had a recent aftermath of Sojourner Truth. The Negro groups, together with the Ford Local [600] of the CIO, the Council of Churches, and some other agencies coordinated their efforts to get the Housing Commission to declare mixed occupancy as the over-all policy to be followed in all defense housing projects.[2] Unfortunately all of the housing projects are poorly located for this purpose. By that I mean they are in exclusively Negro districts or exclusively white districts. I suggested to the Council that we direct the Housing Commission to adopt a policy to the effect that no action on their part be taken which would change the racial characteristics of the neighborhood. The Council concurred in my suggestion, and it was actually done. As an anti-climax a hearing was held before the Council. Needless to say the Council and the Housing Commission did not change this policy. I don't know whether the situation is better or worse as a result of it. I don't think it is worse, but because underneath the surface, emotions continue seething, it is hard to judge.[3]

The weather man around here has suddenly revived the biblical flood alleging rain for forty days and forty nights. It hasn't quite reached that point yet, but it is well on the way. If it doesn't stop raining soon, even the newspapers will be convinced that sewers are almost as necessary as are ten or twelve more airports.

The general health around here seems to keep at a high point. Whiskey and potatoes are both becoming scarce and, therefore, there is an outside chance that the new [human] race will be streamlined.

Sunday was our nicest day of so-called spring, and gasoline rationing seemed to be a matter of little concern. Everybody was out using up his four gallons of gas.

[Grant] Mickle is going to follow Don Kennedy[4] on a better job for more money, so he says—more money anyway. Am having some trouble getting anybody to take his place.

I know that you know Fred [A.] Nolan has left, and you probably know that Bill [William] Bullock[5] is now Acting General Manager. [Samuel] Gilbert[6] thinks that Bullock is a great improvement and is very promising. As an actual fact, I might observe in passing, he is always on the job, and when asked a question he doesn't have to go to the telephone to call somebody else to get the answer. But he hasn't been there long enough for us to determine his real worth. He does seem to look good.

Gary has been having a little trouble lately with his self-control and it culminated in his getting a U on an otherwise good report card at school. Because he was a little self-conscious as a result of this U standing out among all those more flattering letters, he decided that he wouldn't bring his report card home. His mother discovered, through one of the neighbors complaining how her daughter was doing in school, that the report cards had been sent out. When she questioned Gary about it he very nonchalantly said that he had left it at school. He was instructed under threat of death or worse to bring same home next day. I was home before his mother so I asked him where his report card was. He said that he had it, and started to produce it, explaining to me that he knew that neither his mother nor I would want to sign it and so he had written my name on it. He made one slight error in that he got the capital E turned around so that it looked like a 3. Aside from that he wrote very plainly Edward J. Jeffries, Jr. As the principal of the school said, never in the history of the school system had anybody in the B 2nd ever dared to do that before.

Of course when I saw it I committed, according to his mother, the unforgivable. I started to laugh. It probably was a good thing for Gary because his mother started to abuse me as though I had signed it instead of Gary. As the ancient doctors used to bleed people as a counter-irritant, I guess my laughing at the wrong moment stood Gary in good stead. I presented to his mother the counter-irritant. But to all outward appearances Master Gary is very contrite and he insists that he is trying very hard to improve his all around general behavior.

Miss Ford just reminded me that I didn't mention my golf. I didn't mention it primarily because it isn't worth it. The golf courses are flooded and much too long for me as a result of this condition. My enthusiasm is at a very low ebb.

Aside from that, things are about the same.

Sincerely,   JEFF

NOTES

1. Jeffries's speech before the thirty-fourth annual conference for the mayors of New York state criticized the federal government for exacerbating local problems (such as the Sojourner Truth housing controversy) and usurping municipal authority. It called upon fellow executives to protect their governments and plan for the future. See *News*, 11 June 1943, 12.

2. The biracial coalition was led by the local NAACP and included the Detroit Urban League, Ford Local 600 of the UAW, and the Detroit Council of Churches.

3. Fearing further racial violence and feeling pressure from white homeowners, Jeffries preempted action by the Detroit Housing Commission and persuaded the Common Council—over the protest of George C. Edwards—to recommend that neighborhood racial characteristics not be altered by housing projects under municipal jurisdiction. Following council action on April 29, the housing commissioners adopted the official policy of local control and residential segregation by a vote of seven to one—the lone black commissioner, Rev. Horace A. White, dissenting. Essentially, Jeffries sided with white conservatives and brought Detroit's policy in line with that of the federal government. See Capeci, *Race Relations in Wartime Detroit*, 144-45.

4. Mickle, city traffic engineer, resigned his $6,800 position for a similar job with the Automotive Safety Council in Washington, D.C., paying $10,000; Kennedy, deputy state highway commissioner. See *News*, 16 May 1943, 4G.

5. Nolan, general manager of the DSR before Bullock became general manager.

6. Gilbert, Jeffries's friend, local cigar manufacturer, and chairman of the DSR Commission.

Dear Jeff: *Army Air Force Base, Salina, Kansas. [27 May 1943]*
                    Martin S. Hayden to Edward J. Jeffries Jr.

Your letter arrived today to find the Great Hayden in the midst of important military developments.

Currently the *News*' ex No. 1 Man at the City Hall is the No. 1 Man, High Mogul and Commanding Officer of the 49th Aviation Squadron. The boys are a little on the dusky side, in some cases not too bright and in many cases not too military but they are mine-all-mine. The development came about when our C.O. for the past eight months, not-too-affectionately known by his officers as Capt. Boom Boom, was transferred to the Air Base at Kearney, Nebraska. The Colonel called me in to explain my new and great responsibilities and informed me that I am now de Mayor of Smoky Hill's Harlem. That happened yesterday. This morning I arrived at the glory of my new private office to find that after a long spell of good Squadron behavior four of my dark huskies had gotten their tanks full last night and more or less systematically broken all the rules in the book. On the suspicion that they may have been celebrating the arrival of a "soft touch" in the front office I dispatched them at once to start work on a small "fox hole" (10 feet deep, 10 feet wide and 10 feet long) in the soil of an adjoining wheat field. Give me time and I will work up to being an S.O.B. equal to my predecessor.

However, if things go right here I may not be long a C.O. or long in Kansas. I received a letter a few weeks ago from our old friend Col. [William H.] Dodds[1] who is now running the Port of Embarkation in Boston. He stated that the newly formed Transport Corps (which runs all rail and ship transportation) was in need of officers who would go to the Ports to work in administrative capacities while they learn the business and then be shipped out on transports as what are known as Transport Commanders. As I gather it their function is to handle the administration and discipline on troop ships as representatives of the Port Commanders who remain in charge of transit troops until they reach their destination. He asked me if I would be interested and I answered a hearty "yes." Two weeks ago a communication signed by the Major General who is in command in Boston finally found its way to the office of our Colonel here asking for my transfer. The colonel approved it providing he gets a replacement for me and it started its way back through what the army calls "channels." Most any day now it should be getting to whoever in Washington must make a final decision and then we shall see what we shall see. If things go right I may head Bostonward before long and, if so, I will send you a card with the new address. If you hear nothing you can rest assured that Kansas is safe in the hands of Hayden.

I was sorry to hear that racial affairs in Detroit remain in their usual state. God knows what the solution is. We have here in our outfit one remarkable Negro, a staff sergeant named McCullough[2] who has made the grade (a tough one for a Negro in the Air Corps) and is leaving shortly for Officer Candidate School. He is a University of Pittsburgh graduate, a former State employee in Pennsylvania and one of those rare Negroes who can talk dispassionately about the problems of their race. I read him the race paragraph from your letter. Previously he had shown me the "spreads" in the Pittsburgh Courier about the Negro job drive program in Detroit.

This morning he commented thusly: "Yes, the NAACP is getting ready to shake the boys down in another drive for funds and must do a little rabble rousing first. Tell the Mayor to just keep cool. It will either blow up or blow over and there is nothing he can do about it."

Incidentally this boy will be a gem for some political staff if and when this damned war ends and the boys come marching home. He has saved our lives a couple of times when trouble brewed up all around us. The most recent case involved the new Non Commissioned Officers club being built on the base complete with a beer garden, bowling alleys, etc. It is a government project but is to be turned over for management and use by the non coms. In an unfortunately typical manner the white noncoms invited our boys to send representatives to an organizational meeting and they did so, participating in the voting et al. The next day a committee of white non coms waited on our first sergeant and told him that Negroes would not be permitted in the club. You just think there was trouble about Sojourner Truth! McCullough got into the breach and stemmed the riot and with the cooperation of the Red Cross, the USO [United Service Organizations] and the Salina Chamber of Commerce we managed to get and furnish downtown an ex lodge hall which is now our own Non Coms Club. The boys actually are having more fun there then they would in the white palace but, as you may well realize, there is still a rankle which will probably burst out now that I am the official custodian of all headaches in this end of Harlem.

You mentioned Aunt Loret. She underwent her operation and everyone was pretty well bowled over a week later when, on examination prior to moving her from the hospital, they found that the damned hip had slipped apart again. They took her on her fourth trip to the operating room stuck it together again and put her in a cast which, Betty says, covers the whole lower part of her body. She is now home but is most uncomfortable and the Hayden family is about ready to abandon medics for Christian Science. The only one who enjoys the present situation is small John[3] who, according to Betty, has no end of fun sitting on the cast on Gag-Ga's stomach.

I have been no end amused by the antics of your DSR Commission. As the chief exponent of good public relations in public office you have a lulu in [Samuel] Gilbert & Co. Possibly a little outside intolerance enters the picture of their bad publicity but, to say the least, the boys are most cooperative in aiding those who would make them look ridiculous.

Incidentally, tell brother [Douglas R.] Ginn that an old school mate of his, a chap named Munn is now a lieutenant colonel on this field and by virtue thereof one of the big shots. Although very young like most of the Air Corps rankers he is a swell guy and entertained me no end the other night with an account of an afternoon during which he and brother Ginn teamed up to sell airplane rides at some County fair or other. Ask the Witherspoon aide about it and, if he tells the truth you will discover that in [William R.] Logan you had a con man who, by comparison, was only an amateur. . . .[4]

Give my best to the Gents of the Press and of course to my girl Nancy who will no doubt have read all of this before it gets to you. Write again soon. And my official signature—

MARTIN S. HAYDEN
1ST LT., AIR CORPS COMMANDING.

NOTES

1. Uncle of Betty Hayden.
2. Years later Hayden could not recall McCullough's first name.
3. Hayden's son.
4. Ginn succeeded Logan as second deputy commissioner and secretary of the Detroit Police Department; years later Hayden could not recall Munn's first name.

Boston Port of Embarkation. [2 July 1943]
Dear Jeff: *Martin S. Hayden to Edward J. Jeffries Jr.*

I would judge that, if the years have not taken care of the matter, the events of the past couple of weeks should have done considerable to add a little gray to the heads of the bosses of Boy's Town.

I yesterday received a copy of the *News* with the text of your statement as to the beginnings and events of the riot era.[1] I thought it was an excellent statement and should have some effect among the critics who must, I know, be beating a path to the City Hall door. I showed the statement to Col. [William H.] Dodds who was most interested in it. He expressed the opinion that there was something rotten in Denmark in the statement of ranking regular army officers involved that they did not know that direct Presidential authority was necessary to use Federal troops.[2] He contends that every regular army officer that he ever knew was perfectly aware of that.

In the statement I was particularly interested in your slap at irresponsible Negro leaders. It seems that they, probably more than any other group you can put your finger on, are to blame for making worse the bad situation which comes from the natural white antagonism to too close an association with Negroes. I believe I mentioned to you the comment along that line of my Sergt. McCullough out in Salina who complained most bitterly of Negro leaders. He had the theory that the Negro race had so few leaders who had any stable basis upon which to premise their position as leaders, that most of them had spent their entire lives trying to be just "leaders" while the white race, seeking leadership, could turn to men who had been outstandingly successful as business men, professional people or politicians. I think he was probably right. I do know that, in the Army, racial trouble can be kept at a minimum if white officers assigned to Negro troops can sell their men on the idea that they are interested in them and desire to protect their welfare. Also, I think, the Negro in the army is more likely to get along because he has a definite social standing and a chance to advance in accordance with his merits. It struck me in Salina how willing the Negro soldiers were to accept even the hated segregation if they had with it the same privileges and the same opportunities given white troops.

I got a certain amount of ironical amusement out of the very bitter *Free Press* editorial jumping on you and John Witherspoon for using a "kid glove" policy instead of doing something when the *Free Press* "pointed out" the Negro situation to you some months ago. Typical of such editorials it stuck to good safe generalities in deciding what it was that you should have done.

I really don't believe that the whole affair was so bad for Detroit as a publicity factor as you might think it was. It does not, for instance, compare as a destroyer of the town's reputation with what the sit down strikes did. I think that for the reason that every reasonably sane person in every other city is perfectly aware of the mess which the racial problem has created in his own back yard.

In my present job I run into the Boston ramification of the race problem. From time immemorial the docks of Boston have been worked by longshoremen who are almost 100 percent Irish. They are of course bigoted as only the Irish can be and particularly hate the Negroes because during several strikes in the past the ship operators have imported Negro strikebreakers. The AFL longshoremen's union of course allows no Negro members and, until the Army arrived, there just were no Negroes on the docks. Now, however, we are getting in some Negro Port battalions. The Port is in South Boston and the Negro outfits, like many of the white ones, are quartered in old school buildings throughout South Boston. There was naturally a terrible stink from the neighbors when they found that their neighborhood, already as bad a slum area as I have ever seen, was to be "polluted" by Negro soldiers. The Union leaders beefed about the Negroes being brought to the docks but have finally accepted it and are trying to keep their members in line. So far we have had no "incidents" but then Detroit didn't have much on-the-surface trouble either—for a while.

I have been watching the Detroit papers carefully in the expectancy that some hopeful would use the criticism of the riots to become a real candidate against you next fall. I think it is a compliment that so far no one has. On the other hand, it may be that the incident has been sufficient to convince them all that anyone would be nuts to want to be mayor of Detroit.

The big news around here today was the report that the White Father had decided to spare the life of Max Stephan.[5] Being in the army has probably blunted my political acumen but I can't see where the move can be very popular. Certainly there have been a lot of bitter remarks around here today.

Betty and the young Haydens continue to progress although getting along with the limited assistance of a high school kid on the afternoons when the young lady decides she wants to work is definitely wearing Mom down. Last Tuesday was scheduled as the unveiling day for Aunt Loret's hip. To date we have gotten no reports on the success of this latest stay in a cast.

I want you to thank Nancy for forwarding me the clippings which kept me informed when my *News* temporarily quit coming during the "hostilities." . . .

Give my love to Florence.

Sincerely,   MARTIN

NOTES

1. EJJ to Common Council, 29 June 1943, *Journal of the Common Council* (Detroit: Inland Press, 1944), 1826-29.

2. Late Sunday evening, on 20 June, the worst race riot to that date in urban history began in Detroit and continued for forty-eight hours before federal troops put an end to it; skirmishes and cleanup carried into the following week. First believing that local police units could suppress the riot, Jeffries realized on Monday at 9:00 A.M. that outside force would be needed and quickly requested assistance from Harry F. Kelly. The governor later called U.S. Army authorities, wrongly believing that his call set federal troops in motion. Realizing by midafternoon that local patrolmen and state police were unable to quell the escalating carnage, and that state guardsmen would not arrive until dawn, Jeffries pressed Kelly for federal help. The governor responded a second time, only to be informed by military spokespersons that he must declare martial law before President Roosevelt would order army regulars into the city. Jeffries urged Kelly to comply, but the Republican governor then hesitated to ask for assistance from the popular and powerful Democrat. Finally, in the face of mounting casualties and mayoral pressure, Kelly relented at 9:20 P.M., and shortly before midnight Roosevelt signed the proclamation authorizing deployment of soldiers, who—having arrived earlier from nearby locations in Michigan—took control of the streets within moments of the governor's latest request and long before the president's official signing. Clearly, the costly misunderstanding and political maneuvering prolonged the bloodshed by twelve hours and created a finger-pointing controversy among Jeffries, Kelly, and ranking army personnel, though the mayor was least responsible for the snafu and had been most insistent in demanding federal troops at whatever cost. See Dominic J. Capeci Jr. and Martha Wilkerson, *Layered Violence: The Detroit Rioters of 1943* (Jackson: Univ. Press of Mississippi, 1991), 9-16; Robert Shogan and Tom Craig, *The Detroit Race Riot: A Study in Violence* (Philadelphia: Chilton, 1964), 66-82; Harvard Sitkoff, "The Detroit Race Riot of 1943," *Michigan History* 53 (Fall 1969): 191-96.

3. On 1 July Roosevelt reduced the sentence of Detroit restaurateur Max Stephan, convicted of treason for assisting a German soldier who had escaped from Canada. The president was convinced by U.S. Supreme Court Justices Harlan F. Stone and Frank Murphy—the former Michigan governor (1937-38) and Detroit mayor (1930-33)—that the death penalty was too harsh because the crime lacked a preconceived plan; Stephan provided the escapee with food, shelter, and money for two days, which the judges compared to murder in the second degree. Roosevelt commuted Stephan's sentence to life in prison, a harsher punishment than the pardons that President George Washington issued to Whiskey Rebellion insurgents in 1795, the last persons previously sentenced to die for treason. *New York Times*, 2 July 1943, 1; Sidney Fine, *Frank Murphy: The Washington Years* (Ann Arbor: Univ. of Michigan Press, 1984), 405-6.

Detroit. July 12, 1943

Dear Martin: *Edward J. Jeffries Jr. to Martin S. Hayden*

Much water and some blood have run over the dam since I last dropped you a note.[1] Unfortunately nothing has been accomplished in soothing or solving the race problem, with this exception, there are always those in a community who advocate violence for the purpose of solving any problem. These, at least, are temporarily satiated. Those folks who advocate a less strenuous and, ofttimes more workable formula, are busy as bees trying to determine upon a program that will have an overall effectiveness. I am mindful, however, of the fact that the same old people are here with the same old problem.

We will be better prepared for a next time if for no other reason than we have had previous experience. I personally have been experiencing the usual overhead of public life. Everything good or bad that happens in the community, I get the credit. In the particular instance, the solution is so nebulous, and the blame so hard to allocate that I have had the exclusive credit for all the things that went wrong. I can't say that I have enjoyed it, but I must confess that I am still doing business at the same old stand, and I suspect that I can take it.

The subject matter is on the lips of everybody in the community. We have shoved the war off the front pages for a day or two, and we certainly shoved it off the minds of most of the people of the community for at least a temporary period.

The newspapers, either by accident or deliberately, did not handle the early stages well, in my humble opinion. No daily news reporter or photographer dared to enter the Negro section. Therefore, all the pictures were of white groups pursuing a single or two Negroes, and no pictures were taken where Negroes were the aggressors. It so happened that more whites were killed by Negro mobs than Negroes by white mobs; more whites were injured than Negroes. The Negroes started it. The Negroes stoned the first automobile and turned over the first automobile. They did all the window-smashing and looting. Thirteen or fourteen Negroes were shot by the police while either looting or shooting at the police. Apparently only the Negroes carried guns. I repeat, the newspaper accounts, especially those carried by newspapers in other communities and national magazines, pictures this happening as a persecution of the Negroes by the whites. The exact antithesis would be more accurate.[2]

Conditions generally in town are not wholesome. An honest-to-goodness manpower shortage is apparent on every hand. A friend of mine was in a restaurant the other night where there were twenty customers and he was the only man, not excepting the help in the establishment.

We are considerably short of manpower in practically every department of the city, and I don't know hardly a soul that runs any kind of business who isn't complaining about the inability to get sufficient help. The average weekly payroll of factory workers is estimated at $61 a week.

Shortages of all kinds of things are beginning to show up, and we have the unhealthy situation of a man with money in his pocket and not much to do with it. Consequently recreational pursuits are becoming more lavish, and harder, fundamentally, on the constitution.

By now I think that every family in the country has someone in the armed forces. Worry has increased. Everyone is getting into some stage of fighting mood and getting more difficult to get along with. As a result, people need but little of an excuse to fly at one another's throat.

The operation of city government is kind of a paradox. The detail of operation is much simpler, but our new problems are so difficult to solve, if not impossible to solve, that our public officials who are conscientiously serious, are worrying themselves to death rather than working themselves to death.

I'll bet it is very pleasant to have Betty and the youngsters with you. I hope sincerely that your Aunt Loret's hip has improved.

In strict confidence, brother Witherspoon is a great study in human behavior. For fifteen years he has enjoyed the unanimous commendation of the general public. All of a sudden he finds himself in a position of being severely and caustically criticized, in many instances unjustifiably, for his actions. I must say that, to his credit, to date he is taking it well. If he continues to, he will be a much better man for it. It is easy to be good when the sun shines, but sometimes it is difficult under fire.

There has been a distinct change in the beat. I received a letter from Doug[las D.] Martin[3] the other day, to the effect that the *Free Press* would no longer consent to any off-the-record news. Leo [Donovan] and I in conversation this morning, regarding the letter, mutually understand that from now on I am in the category of every defendant. I am on official notice that anything I say may be used against me. It presents a little problem for me because neither the *News* boys nor the *Times* boys are in the same category and, therefore, I can still be free and easy with them, but not with Donovan. Therefore, I am going to have difficulty in seeing that I am not quoted secondhanded. However, as I have told you many times, the one thing they will never be able to take away from me is my experience, and what I am learning bids fair to be a new and very interesting venture. From time to time you probably will be able to witness the results.

With wishes for the best of luck, I am

Sincerely,   JEFF

NOTES

1. Jeffries was referring to the race riot of June 20-21. The mayor and police commissioner were criticized for the police department's handling of the disorder, which they sought to parry by blaming the violence almost completely on blacks. See Capeci and Wilkerson, *Layered Violence*, 17-20, 22, 28-31, 88-89.

2. While correct about the absence of reporters and photographers in the black sections, Jeffries oversimplified the origins of the riot and its patterns. He also advanced erroneous impressions of perpetrators and victims. In fact, of twenty-five black fatalities, policemen killed seventeen, white civilians killed six; blacks killed one (a light-skinned black women mistaken for white); and unknown assailants killed one. Of nine white fatalities, blacks killed eight (including one lawman), and unknown persons killed one. During the most intense hours of the upheaval, 433 persons—222 whites and 211 blacks—were treated at Receiving Hospital, which handled

most of the rioters and their victims; hence blacks, constituting less than 10 percent of the city's population, accounted for nearly 50 percent of the injured; they also made up greater numbers and percentages of those hospitalized for gunshot wounds, stabbings, and beatings and of those who died from their injuries. In addition to Patrolmen Lawrence A. Adam, who was slain by a black sniper, forty-five bluecoats were assaulted by rioters from both races, and thirty more incurred accidental injuries (mostly tear gas irritation). Nor were blacks the only rioters to bear firearms, though whites tended to shoot only at black victims (as opposed to patrolmen). See Capeci and Wilkerson, *Layered Violence*, 87-94.

   3. *Free Press* managing editor.

Dear Jeff:

> *Boston Port of Embarkation. [late July 1943]*
> *Martin S. Hayden to Edward J. Jeffries Jr.*

   Thanks for your long if not particularly optimistic description of Detroit as it is today. I have been pleased to note from the *News* that the town is staying relatively quiet, at least on the surface, which must be some relief after the turmoil of the past month.

   Much of what you described as Detroit characteristics is also prevalent here. Boston also has its labor shortage, its absurd pay scales and a mad scramble on almost everyone's part to make as much hay as possible out of the war situation. We last week had our first real labor trouble since my arrival and my Major boss and I spent several anxious days trying to get the machine going again. As is usually the case, much of what happened seems amusing when regarded in retrospect. As are most Longshoreman affairs–this one was screwy. Since time immemorial Stevedores [ship operators] have paid off their longshoremen in Boston immediately upon the completion of a job or on every Saturday afternoon if a job, started before Saturday, was to continue on into the next week. That plan had to be partially amended with the coming of the Victory Tax which required enough payroll computation on the part of the Stevedores to necessitate a payoff 48 hours after completion of the work.

   Then came the withholding tax on July 1.[1] Numerous conferences between the Stevedores, Army accountants and union leaders made it plain that the complicated bookkeeping under the new tax could not be completed in 48 hours. The Union leaders agreed to a plan under which each Friday would be payday and the men would be paid at that time for all work completed up to 7 am the previous Monday. Having agreed to the program all of the union officials went off to New York for the TWO WEEK annual convention of delegates of the International Longshoreman's [sic] Association (AFL). (That was the convention that made Joe Ryan the ILA president–for life).

   The first Friday payday passed without incident although there was some grumbling. The following Tuesday it rained and it was necessary to stop loading to wait for the weather to clear. The men on one ship got niff nawing among themselves on the pay situation and decided–the Hell with it–they would quit. Word spread from ship to ship and within an hour all of the 1,500 Boston longshoremen were standing quietly outside the pier gates while streams of freight began to pile up on the docks.

The Stevedores were helpless and it fell upon the Army to try and settle the matter. Major [Robert] Kretschmar, my boss, and I spent literally hours making speeches. It was most discouraging. The longshoremen were and are very friendly to the Army. We would stand up and explain the tax bill from "A" to "Z" and throw in a little about the fox holes of Guadalcanal and the deserts of Africa. When we were through nobody would say anything. Then some cluck in the back of the crowd would say "but why can't we get our money now?" Meanwhile we were frantically calling New York to get the union leaders back—no soap because they were all drunk. At the same time we were being bombarded with phone calls from Washington and visitations from Jewish conciliators who wanted to move right in. Each conciliator would issue a new and more erroneous report to the newspapers on what was going on. Col. [William H.] Dodds at the time was Port Commander in the absence of the General. He left the matter to the Major and I which made us feel ten times worse because it is an old army custom to blame the commanding officer for everything. On the second day of the strike the Colonel ordered in several hundred troops from various parts of the State and they with the soldiers already stationed here resumed the loading of the ships. Finally after three days we got a telegram out of Mr. Ryan calling on the longshoremen to be "patriotic" and go back to work. They ultimately did and are still going primarily because we have not had another rain storm with the incidental opportunity to stand around and shoot the breeze.

The Boston longshoremen were averaging about $35 a week—when they could get work—prior to the war. They are now making approximately $100 per week. No one of them has of course in any way improved his or his family's standard of living but the bars are doing a land office business and the boys are literally dead broke by the end of each week.

I note with amusement that Brother Cobo is agin [sic] your tax plan. I presume that you neglected to make him a co-author which, coupled with a chance to sound off in the *Free Press* would naturally make him an opponent. Incidentally, I would be interested in seeing some of the *Free Press* blurbs. I hope they aren't getting under your skin. Unless they have improved since I left, they are so heavy handed in their technique that I don't believe they make much impression. They certainly must not be getting far if they haven't as yet been able to encourage some candidate of significance to make the run next fall.

I am expecting to get my extra bar on about the fifteenth of next month and am hoping that the promotion will result in some slightly more dramatic assignment. After all this labor relations is just like home—the old arguments, the same old faces and the same old answers. The only difference is that it is all dressed up with a few uniforms. The army has many strange labor policies of which I will tell you some day. One regulation states that labor relations officers must never do anything other than give out information in the event of labor trouble. That is what the book says. Actually they banish you to the hinterlands if you don't get out and get things settled—and quick. Of course, if you throw yourself around in the wrong directions, then they take the regulations literally and smack you for disobeying them.

Write again when you have time and meanwhile give my best to Nancy and the boys and girls of the movement.

MARTIN

NOTE

1. The Revenue Act of 1942 included a so-called victory tax of 5 percent on incomes, to be paid at the time of earning, thereby initiating the principle of tax withholding. In 1944 the tax was first reduced to 3 percent and then repealed entirely. The law and the war boom also brought most workers into the income tax system for the first time. Hence, longshoremen struck over the tax itself and for having to wait for their wages until the withholding taxes could be figured and deducted. Paul K. Conklin and David Burner, *A History of Recent America* (New York: Crowell, 1974), 376-77.

Detroit. July 22, 1943
Dear Martin: *Edward J. Jeffries Jr. to Martin S. Hayden*

I received your letter relating to labor problems at a very opportune moment. Of the 3200 employees of the Department of Public Works, only 700 are working now. To date the official demands of the A.F. of L. Union have not been received. Unofficially we are informed that the employees will go back to work only after the Council raises their pay. We have just ordered ads in all the daily papers to the effect that Monday morning it will be business as usual, and any employee of the D.P.W., who does not report to work at that time will be considered as having left the pay roll, and the position to be filled forthwith. (You know we will be a little slow in filling them because it is getting awfully hard to get people for jobs.)

So much good copy has been flowing from the City Hall that even the newsboys are beginning to complain a little. They are hoping for a quiet week-end sometime this summer. It is good to hear that merit is recognized in the Army, and that you are able to join a new stratum. You may get the opportunity for more dramatic work, but I honestly believe that you are experiencing the most important phases of this war. To my humble way of thinking, we are doing much worse on the home front in this war than we are on the armed front. I have heard it suggested that we can win the war on the fighting front and lose it on the home front. Every day I live I become more conscious of that possibility.

Your former profession, in my humble opinion, is missing its responsibility by a thousand miles. Dissemination of news print in the usual orthodox channels is either oblivious or careless in regard to its obligation to the general public. Many things are printed that are not true, in conjunction with the many things that they print which are true and, as a result, the general public is having a great deal of difficulty in separating one from the other. Having been in this discussion with you and your confreres before, I know that you will immediately say that someone says it and, therefore, we can print it. To my humble way of thinking this is the reply in the way of an alibi. The right to profit by the dissemination of news, the right to freedom of speech and press, carry with them the obligation of responsible citizenship to see that misinformation is not widely circulated.

The general public is so worried and emotionally aroused anyway, over the war, that it presents a fertile field for all ideas, crackpot, subversive and genuinely good. Therefore, it seems to me that the responsibilities of your late profession have increased manifold, at least in theory and, due to manpower shortage and a thousand and one other things, I sometimes doubt that actual practice has kept pace. Don't misunderstand me. I haven't anyone in particular in mind. I am thinking of that old saw, "He who is without sin, cast the first stone." But I am very conscious of the problem and, my boy, it is a real one. The alibi used so consistently, "O Hell, he said it, what was I to do," isn't sufficient to meet the needs of the time. I will drop you a note next week and tell you how our newest problem worked out.

Give my best to Betty and the family.   JEFF

Queen Elizabeth, Atlantic Ocean. [14 October 1943]
Dear Jeff: *Martin S. Hayden to Edward J. Jeffries Jr.*

A New York paper carrying the primary results[1] today found its way to this spot which the censor lets me describe only as "somewhere in the East."

Certainly I can't say that things look too good but I am, as you know, hoping that there is some political mathematics in the situation which I do not know and which will make things look better when November rolls around. If there isn't, I think I know you well enough to be sure you won't worry about it too much although frankly this first vote counting somewhat shakes my confidence in the perspicacity of our "folks out front." I am mindful, however, of the fact that any office holder who consistently tries to do things and do them honestly gradually builds up a collection of disgruntled minorities who will one day cause him trouble. Anyhow, Jeff, I wish I could be on hand to do a little helping for I suspect that you are as of this morning witnessing a sudden departure of some previously right vocal supporters.

As I say I can't mention where I am, nor can I comment on when I will move or where the next stop will be. The latter curbs are however purely technical because I know no more of the answers than do you. I like my new job and am enjoying being back with troops again even though they are on the dark side.[2] In that respect I have the feeling, perhaps only imaginary, that I can sense a difference in the attitude of these men as compared with that of my old outfit in the Air corps. I see considerable more evidence of racial straining which is, I guess, just symptomatic of the national trend.

As you will note on the envelope my current address is Hqts, 502nd Port Battalion, A.P.O. Number 4939, c/o Postmaster, City of New York. Anything sent there will either reach me here or ultimately catch me. When I get a permanent address I will write you again and I am going to be looking forward to hearing frequently from both you and our friend Nancy.

Give my best to the boys in the movement and to Florence who must be dithering all over the place in righteous indignation. I don't know where I'll be when the final votes are counted but I will be thinking of the fight and hoping that the "folks" are back in line.

Your friend,   MARTIN

NOTES

1. In the Detroit mayoral primary of October 5, Jeffries came in second, 38,003 votes behind Circuit Court Commissioner Frank FitzGerald. None of the other twelve candidates drew substantial support, thereby setting the stage for the intense Jeffries-FitzGerald campaign that culminated in the November election.

2. Following a dispute with Brig. Gen. Clarence Kell, Commander, Boston Port of Embarkation, Hayden had been reassigned to the all black 502d Port Battalion and at the time of this letter was heading for Camp Crookston, Paisley, Scotland.

Camp Crookston, Paisley, Scotland. 8 December 1943
Martin S. Hayden to Edward J. Jeffries Jr.

Dear Jeff:

I suppose that by now you have forgotten all about the recent campaign and gotten back into the old routine of being the most picked on individual in what used to be Boy's Town.[1] In that I haven't gotten any mail in something approaching 108 years, I am still following what are to you old developments. The local Red Cross has a fine and continuing stock of two-month-old *Time*s so I drop in every now and then to read up on the home town. I have at this date disposed of the primary election and am now among the FitzGerald campaign speeches in which I read some strange accounts of things that happened when I was still back in Detroit. In that the gentleman could not have been wrong my recollections must have erred somewhere. The worst of it is that from what I gather from the overseas edition of *Time* and other cheaper periodicals the campaign was not fought on those issues at all so probably, even though you won, most of the voters have an upside down picture of such matters as bus purchases and the DSR fight against the private bus interests. It was illuminating to learn that you were an all[y] of Manfred Burleigh.[2] That was probably at about the same time that Frank [Martel] was boosting your candidacy for President.

Things over here are [routine] as usual. We spend many hours training for something, somewhere, sometime. If Mr. Hitler picks up his tent and retires before we use all of this there will certainly have been a lot of shoe leather wasted and waist lines reduced for nothing.

I have been much interested in watching Democracy as translated by John Bull [England]. In some ways they do better than we and in some not as well, but in most things it is just like home with a broad "a." For one thing the ideal that Britain has legislated grand unionism and later peace is so much hog wash. I have been quite close to portions of the union labor situation over here and it is just like home away from home. You have the same unauthorized strikes, the same irresponsibility on the part of union leaders and the same using of the war efforts for shake-downs for more money.

Also interesting over here is the manner in which liberalism pops up in places where at home we would never find it. Typical are several top ranking civil servants whom I have come to know. They are the kind who at home would shy from the slightest change in the established order for fear that it might upset their security. Here they talk constantly of change, not so much political change as economic. They are very bitter over financial and opportunity control in trusts and hereditary estates. It would seem that they need a Teddy Roosevelt to do a little selling of trust busting and a Taft to follow along and do the job.[3]

Now that the shooting is all over, lets have some letters from the City Hall. Give my best to Hermie and the Greatest Police commissioner since Harold Emmons.[4] Also of course my love to Nancy and Florence.

MARTIN

NOTES

1. Hayden's outfit had arrived at Camp Crookston on October 19. On November 2, Jeffries won his third mayoral term, defeating Frank FitzGerald by almost 32,000 votes: 207,799-175,817. See *News,* 3 Nov. 1943, 1.

2. Manfred Burleigh was president and general manager of Great Lakes Greyhound (1941-47) and an officer of the Greater Detroit Board of Commerce.

3. Theodore Roosevelt (in office 1901-8) was known as the first trustbusting president; President William H. Taft (1909-12) enforced antitrust legislation more vigorously than all other chief executives.

4. Paul Krause and John H. Witherspoon, respectively. Harold H. Emmons was the police commissioner whose dismissal by Mayor Charles Bowles in 1930 sparked the recall of Bowles for reasons that also included questions of underworld associations and mounting unemployment. Bowles became the first mayor in the United States to be recalled successfully. See Sidney Fine, *Frank Murphy: The Detroit Years* (Ann Arbor: Univ. of Michigan Press, 1975, 206-9).

Detroit. December 27, 1943

Dear Martin: *Edward J. Jeffries Jr. to Martin S. Hayden*

I feel kind of like a snide for not having written to you in such a long while. I have no good alibi except to state that my mind has been a little chaotic.

I don't know how much you know about the recent campaign, but knowing you get the *News*, suffice it to say that the Daily Bugle blew all out. From the primary to the election day, Carl Muller,[1] Don Slutz, with the able assistance and at times resistance of Jack Carlisle, read proof, wrote and generally prepared my public utterances by way of the radio. These, incidentally, were quite numerous. All the boys verged on a nervous breakdown because, as usual, I was quite active on the Chautauqua circuit. They were always scared that I would get completely on my own and say the wrong thing in the wrong way in relation to the theme. How well it was done is unimportant, but it was well enough done to enable me to scramble back by a whisker finish.

Some of the weak links in the chain were apparent. After the primary only the most avid and enthusiastic, together with the wishful thinkers gave me a chance. As a consequence some of the goats have been distinguished from the sheep. I presume that in the course of months the public will gradually catch on to the division.[2]

Jack Carlisle coined a phrase that is more descriptive than any other I heard when he said, "It was the greatest God-damned underwater swimming team I have ever seen." It was really an election miracle, and not anybody can describe it in all its ramifications. In fact, nobody knows all of the things that were done and how they were done and, until the closing minutes, none of us were sure it had been done.

The *Free Press*, after 500 precincts were in at 11:30 in the evening, called me and wanted to have me concede defeat. In fact, their first edition said that FitzGerald was in. We all know better now.

. Right after the election Florence, Gary and I went to Florida. As soon as I got back Betty called me and congratulated me. I haven't seen her, but she said she was well.

Incidentally, Witherspoon resigned the other day and I appointed John Ballenger to his place.

There is a new era of government. The *Free Press* wants Gestapo after the Cossack variety, but I still think that police work is simply a phase of social work.[3] So I imagine the *Free Press* snipers will continue their work.

There is a bitter fight brewing under the surface between the news-papers–the *News* and *Times* on one side and the *Free Press* on the other.[4] Occasionally it breaks before the public. I am just hoping that I won't be the battleground. I can be, but I don't have to be, and I certainly hope that they will pick some other area to close in the now down and finish fight.

Of course I have participated sub rosa a little. Instead of going to the Maccabees first thing in the morning, I am at the City Hall at 8:00 A.M., or thereabouts, and going to the Maccabees in the afternoon. Carlisle and Schachern are wilting under the hours, but their bad dispositions are re-quited, to a certain extent, by their desire to have three full editions before the rewrite boys of the *Free Press* get a chance at the news.

When we got back from Florida, Leo Donovan and his photographer came out to the house to take pictures and get a statement from me. Flor-ence shoved Donovan out of the house. She tried to slam the door on him, but I caught it. Leo called me the next day to thank me for saving him. Even I was mortified.

One of my New Year's resolutions will be to the effect that I will write oftener.

The best of everything to you my boy.

With kind regards, I am

Sincerely yours, JEFF

NOTES

1. Former *Times* journalist, then writing for the *News*.
2. Simply put, Jeffries viewed the division as nonpartisan government versus spe-cial interest politics; his opponents perceived it as a struggle for racial equality and union influence.
3. The *Free Press* had criticized Jeffries for a kid-glove policy of policing, espe-cially after the riot; hence his reference to heavy-handed Gestapo and Cossack methods, while oversimplifying his own view of police work.
4. The press rivalry stemmed from economic competition and ideological differ-ences; in broad terms the *Times* tended to be conservative, the *News* conservative and moderate (depending on the issue), and the *Free Press* liberal.

Camp Crookston, Paisley, Scotland.
[17 January 1944][1]
Dear Jeff: *Martin S. Hayden to Edward J. Jeffries Jr.*

Your letter of the 27th [December] arrived several days ago and gave me considerable pleasure. The orderly handed it to me just as we as-sembled for Officers Call and I read it on the quiet while the colonel was going on at length on some dull subject. I nearly broke up the meeting and earned his merited disapproval by snorting loudly and with glee over the report of Friend Florence's door slamming act.

And over here things go pretty routinely. I have now become thoroughly accustomed to getting up three hours before sun rise but I still can't get used to the condition which exists during certain stages of the moon and under which it gets progressively *darker* for the first couple of hours of the day. We continue to train endlessly and the new fangled stunts which were fun when we first started to practice them are now exceedingly boring as we do them ad nauseam in an effort to make them second nature with our men.

We note with interest the newspaper reports indicating that the home front generally agrees that the war is practically over and that Hitler's tent will be folded and put away any time a couple of our boys have a few days free to run over and take care of it. Of course no one has explained how that ties in with the facts that Mr. Hitler still has enough sting to bump off 60 fortresses in a single night and that it took 80 per cent casualties to invade, not the European coast but a sand spit called Tarawa.[2] My impressions are that the home news is not sitting too well with either the pilots who are riding out over the continent each day or the boys who are being taught a lot of tricks and tactics which do not appear to them designed for a peaceful boat trip.[3]

I have been interested in the accounts of the political re-awakening in Washington. Again my own observations are a little colored by distance and my associations with gents whose bases of thought are completely different from those at home. However I get the impression that the Republicans still have not learned and are doing a swell job of campaigning for Brother Roosevelt. The average soldier is for instance convinced that the Republicans are deliberately trying to keep them from getting to vote. I may be entirely wrong but I think the overwhelming majority of them will vote for Roosevelt if given the chance. I don't believe you will attribute the opinion to my long time record as a New Dealer. Why the soldiers like Roosevelt is simple. Their one and only interest is getting home whole and quickly. Without exception the generals who are running the works are highly respected by the rank and file and they further recognize that their equipment is pleatiful [*sic*] and superb and that the general war plan is aimed at keeping casualties at a minimum. All of the above to them means that the war is being well run and from their point of view Roosevelt is running it. His stock went up greatly when [Gen. George C.] Marshal[l] slapped the labor unions and Roosevelt came out in his favor.[4]

Above all, however, I think the soldiers are beginning to regard the Republican Party as the home of all of those who are arguing that the war is over and doesn't merit much more worry. As I have said, the idea does not sit well when it filters over to men who have just spent a day at strenuous training based upon the theme that a well trained soldier will have a slightly better chance of keeping his name off casualty lists which the men are being frankly told will probably be pretty long.

I continue to try and learn what makes our racial problem tick but am getting no concrete ideas as to its solution even though living with it 24 hours a day. A lot of work and a lot of care has removed our earlier worries as to our own outfit and we are now riding the crest of a public commendation from the District Commander for having the lowest rates of AWOL's and MP arrests of any outfit in the district. Elsewhere Negro units are in many cases topping lists.

Our success can be attributed solely to the fact that we have constantly tried to show the men that their white officers are on their team and that they can get nowhere without racial pride. The same ideas would probably help if they could be drilled into the Negro civilian population but there is of course the difference that, in the Army, we can line them up and they have to keep quiet while we talk to them. Our big worry is of course the white soldiers, particularly the hill billies, who carry over here their theories of sanctity of white womanhood and, after a few drinks, decide to do something about the British gals who dance with American colored soldiers. We have beat into the heads of our men the idea that we have a local Provost Marshal with a brain in his head. He lined up his MP's and threatened the wrath of God if he caught any of them officially discriminating. He backed the idea up by slapping down the first violator he found among his own men. The result was that our soldiers are beginning to have a sneaking idea that maybe an MP can be a friend in time of need. Unfortunately I am afraid that little that we are trying to drill into the men will be carried by them into civilian life. They get our ideas but put . . . [them] on a purely local basis. As I say we have sold them that their own officers are on their team but they don't carry the idea on to a similar regard for all officers. This is indicated by their pointed distinction between "our officers" and "them other officers."

To wind up the racial report in this letter we have witnessed one interesting example of successful mixing. We have attached to us a half dozen white solders from a truck company and three from a hospital detachment. The drivers have a barracks alone but the medics are quartered with one of our own medics. All of them are messed with our men. We have never had an incident of strife. The drivers willingly accept orders from our non coms and the medics faithfully make phoney reports, in the approved army style, as to the late arrivals and degree of drunkenness of their colored patients. The climax was reached the other day when two of the medics came to the colonel and asked if they could not be permanently transferred to our organization. I don't know what it means other than that inter-mingling will work if it is started off right and after the initial shock is overcome.

Sincerely,   MARTIN.

NOTES

1. The original letter is mistakenly dated 1943, when Hayden was stationed in Kansas.

2. On 21 November, Admiral Chester W. Nimitz began his strategy of "kangaroo leaps" across the Central Pacific with the invasions of Makin and Tarawa in the Gilbert Islands. "Bloody Tarawa" was secured after four days of intense fighting that cost the U.S. Marines, Second Division, 913 lives and 2,037 casualties.

3. Bombing missions over German-occupied territory and training for the spring invasion of Normandy.

4. Chief of Staff, U.S. Army.

Detroit. January 31, 1944
Edward J. Jeffries Jr. to Martin S. Hayden

Dear Martin:

You will be surprised how quickly your new mannerisms will wear off when you return home. That's the voice of experience. About the only thing that you will really retain will be your ability to understand the cockney language, to the amazement of all your local friends. It took me six months to know for sure what elevator boys and waitresses were saying to me. Now on occasion I can astound my friends by translating it immediately. I practiced for years saying "thanks very much" like the British but I must confess that I have never learned how to get the right inflection. It is a great way they have of saying it on account of everybody knows when he hears it that it isn't meant either, and if you can master it, as they have, on occasions it comes in very handy together with the banker's cold fish eye. If you can couple the two it will be helpful.

I was very much interested in hearing your comment on national politics. I think the whole thing can be summed up relatively simply. The war is a secretive business and everybody is anxious to have it over and sincerely anxious for us to win it. None of the general public really knows what is going on, how we are progressing, if we are progressing. Your late profession, rightly or wrongly, has done such a good job of confusing the public that really I think it is safe and conservative to state that the general public is bewildered. From that point on it is elementary to state that we have no local leaders. We turn to President Roosevelt not necessarily because he is a leader or that we think he is, but we must admit that he is the only one we have, and if anybody knows anything about it he should. No one else, I repeat, has the information and can, therefore, present a counter program. Whenever anybody tries the administration promptly points out that he doesn't know what he is talking about, and all public confidence is lost. As long as that condition continues, Mr. Roosevelt will be the fair haired boy of the country and the opposition cannot get a foothold. I sense, however, that the work and worry on the home front, coupled with the dissatisfaction at little things, has caused a state of mind that could be whipped into shape overnight if a glamorous demagogue appeared on the horizon. The weakness of Republicans is primarily one of personalities. [Thomas E.] Dewey[1] is their only hope as an individual, and he is playing very coy and hard to get. Maybe that's good. This is too early to determine. Many things can happen between now and the big showdown.

Mrs. [Eleanor] Roosevelt was here last Wednesday for the sole and exclusive purpose of attending an inter-racial meeting at the Ebenezer
[A.]M.E. Church. That is the old synagogue located at Brush and Willis,
and now housing the Reverend [George W.] Baber and his flock. The
church ordinarily will hold between 2500 and 3000, and conservatively
10,000 or 15,000 people were on the outside. The new police commissioner [John F. Ballenger] took no chances, and the surrounding streets
looked like an army camp except that the boys were in blue instead
of khaki. It was very peaceful. I welcomed the lady to Detroit and she
talked for 55 minutes. She reminded me of the song of the man on the
flying trapeze. She wanted to say something and was afraid she'd say
the wrong thing. As a result she practically said nothing and it took her
ages to say it. I presume, however, that her presence was very stimulating to the Negro. I know it was very irritating to some of the fanatic
whites.

Week before last Slutz, Oakman, Carlisle all attended the Conference
of Mayors in Chicago. It was about the same old thing except for the fact
that they had more speeches than I ever heard at any one convention.
[Henry J.] Kaiser, [Robert P.] Patterson, [Donald] Nelson, [Sam] Rayburn,
[Bernard] Baruch, [Chester] Bowles and [Paul V.] McNutt were just a
few.[2] The theme was almost exclusively to the effect that the war was a
long way from over, and that the problems of post war were acute and
must be planned for. While I don't remember much about the last war, it
does seem to me that the most wholesome thing about the present war is
the constant drilling into the public of the need for planning for after this
war. So many people cannot talk as much about how we are going to
conduct ourselves after the war without some good ideas jelling. As per
the usual schedule, I worked while everybody else played.

Incidentally Willow Run[3] went on a five-day-week schedule, ostensibly
to combat absenteeism. The [UAW] union is screaming its head off. After
talking to representatives of both sides it seems that they have more men
working there than they need, and neither the management nor union
will admit it, and I am not sure exactly what the reason is for the five day
a week schedule. It is a little amazing.

Friday night I attended a testimonial banquet for R. J. Thomas, com-
memorating his fifth year as president of the union. I was the brunt of all
ribbing. Fortunately it was good natured. It probably was helpful to me.
Brother Martel, however, who was there, couldn't resist a chance to be
nasty and sincere in his harpooning. I think that even helped me because
it was so sharp and apparently so sincere that he aroused, I am sure, a
wave of sympathy toward me.

By and large the routine remained the same. Last week the linemen in
the Lighting Commission served an official strike notice. As usual I don't
think they meant it and apparently things are quiet on that front now. I
wouldn't think, though, that we had many dull moments coming.

Carlisle has just finished a long series on how [Raymond W.] Boettcher
distributed the money to the police department officials in the period

leading up to the grand jury revelations.[4] They were quite good except they ran them too long.

Incidentally the State has been investigating the Legislature. Twenty-six of the boys were indicted.[5] Some of the legislators pled guilty and said they would tell all. They haven't done it yet. Therefore everybody is standing around with bated breath wondering what they are going to say. I think the [trial] will be held beginning February 2. It looks as though we were going to be finally cleaned up around here, even if temporarily.

The flu epidemic is past. Everybody seems to be enjoying good health. The fact of the matter is, the weather has been unseasonably warm. It was 67 degrees last Wednesday.

Little Jeff[6] was home for ten days. He went back to California yesterday. He has been assigned to a frigate as a medical officer and he will be starting off to the South West Pacific pronto. Grace has said good bye to him for the third time, and you can even get used to saying good bye, I guess.

The best of luck to you.

With kind regards, I am   JEFF

NOTES

1. Then governor of New York.

2. Kaiser, shipbuilder; Patterson, undersecretary, War Department; Nelson, director, War Production Board; Rayburn, speaker, House of Representatives; Baruch, presidential adviser; Bowles, director, OPA; McNutt, director, War Manpower Commission.

3. The enormous bomber plant built by Henry Ford near Ypsilanti, thirty-five miles southwest of Detroit.

4. Police inspector Boettcher was indicted for corruption during the mayoralty of Richard W. Reading.

5. Twenty state lawmakers, past and present, and six finance officials were indicted for conspiring through bribery to enact three bills that favored automobile loan companies in the 1939 legislature. The accused included nine representatives and two senators from Detroit and Wayne County, one-third of its delegation. See *New York Times,* 23 Jan. 1944, 1.

6. Benjamin Jeffries, son of Jeffries's sister Grace Cogan and her first husband, Clayton Benjamin, was attached to the maritime public health service and had earlier been stationed at the Marine Hospital in Portland, Oregon. He had been christened Jeffries Benjamin, but realizing that no male descendants existed to carry on the Jeffries name, he officially reversed the order of his names; this occurred after his parents had divorced and before the mayor and Florence adopted Gary.

2

THE BIG SHOW

(JANUARY–JULY 1944)

Throughout the first seven months of 1944, Jeffries and the boys in the movement commented on numerous issues that would become, in mayoral words, "very interesting history."[1] Indeed, Walton S. White, Harold J. Schachern, and George C. Edwards wrote of their experiences in southern training camps; friends of Edwards, as well as John M. Carlisle and especially Martin S. Hayden, recounted the reality of war both in the Pacific and in Europe where the tide of battle was shifting in favor of the Allies. Their insights into military life covered far-ranging issues and personal emotions associated with their transformation from civilians to soldiers against the backdrop of Japan's and Germany's midyear retreats. Most poignantly, Hayden described firsthand the meaning of combat—its excitement and carnage, its humor and suffering—in Operation Overlord, which opened the second front in Europe at Normandy.[2] Meanwhile, Jeffries struggled with a less spectacular but hardly insignificant domestic second front as race relations and politics continued to make their impact on Detroit, aftershocks of the previous year's riot and mayoral election. In this crucible of individual pressure and historical turningpoints, the camaraderie, friendship, and love of "Jeff" and company for one another shone through, as pronounced as military victories abroad and political developments at home.

Jeffries constantly expressed concern for those beyond his reach, inquiring about their well-being, encouraging their efforts, and checking on their families. Clearly the headmaster of Boys Town, Jeffries assured Carlisle that his writing had impressed Hayden and, in turn, informed Hayden that Edwards, who returned to Michigan for the bar examination, looked "swell."[3]

Less often, some of the wives of Jeffries and friends contacted one another and passed along information to their spouses. When they met for

93

lunch, Peggy Carlisle revealed to Florence Jeffries that she occasionally played the horses as a way of dealing with John's absence, while Betty Hayden reacted sharply to the remarks of one local official on "the subject of deferments" at a time when Martin was prepared to sacrifice his life at Normandy.[4] In the States, Peggy White provided firsthand information when visiting her husband, who, like most of the letter writers, also devoured copies of the Detroit dailies for news of the home front. Even James P. Simpson in far-off New Guinea learned of close friend George C. Edwards's imminent enlistment from clippings supplied by a Michigan soldier.[5]

What occupied the thinking of mayoral correspondents was the war, of course. Those in training described in precise detail every facet of camp activity: billet, food, rifle practice, bayonet drill, marches, midnight maneuvers, even the terrain and weather. As an army private at Camp Wheeler, Georgia, Edwards found seventeen weeks of "strictly combat training" much tougher than expected, forcing recruits–replacements bound for units already fighting–to respond or fall by the wayside. Ironically, he broke a hand playing football rather than running the obstacle course, delaying his graduation and forcing him back into the training cycle.[6] In contrast, P.F.C. Stod White, serving in the army's Sixty-third Division headquarters at Camp Van Dorn, Mississippi, divided his time between office work and infantry training. Having "two jobs to do" proved difficult yet much less physically arduous than the experience of Edwards or of 2d Lt. Harold J. Schachern, stationed at Quantico, Virginia, who proudly echoed the contention that U.S. Marines Corps training produced "the best fighting man in the world."[7]

As indicated by this boast, trainees engaged in ongoing interservice as well as intraservice rivalry, but they also focused on the similarities of their experiences. Admitting that some men, in White's words, looked for "things to bitch about," they noted the regimentation of military life.[8] Schachern opined that forging history's "greatest fighting machine" required breaking "every ounce of individuality and morale you ever had."[9] Edwards also understood the personal anonymity required by "mass training," but he doubted that "spit and polish" was "absolutely essential to a combat solider" or that regimentation stripped one of his identity completely. He observed, too, the tendency of the military to create a hierarchy that both inverted and reinforced class and age distinctions: for example, a recent high school graduate flaunting his rank of corporal over an older, successful realtor; a college professor turned sergeant harassing a wealthy, spoiled undergraduate.[10]

Given the physical fatigue and psychological browbeating of camp life, trainees sought relief wherever and however possible. White relished the visits of his wife–a rare exception made possible by his assignment to division headquarters—and used off time to collect beer bottles for extra income. Edwards enjoyed the "free air" of short day furloughs into Macon, Georgia, and padded his salary by playing poker in the barracks.[11] In their letters they taunted one another, occasionally venting frustration: "Anyone who asks 'What did you do to get such a soft job?' is uttering strictly shit for the birds," admonished a defensive White, who had been assigned to public relations without having been given "the choice of being a rifleman."[12]

More often, Edwards, White, and Schachern provided information on a range of subjects and emotions, some dead serious. Comparing prisoners of war at Camp Wheeler, for instance, Edwards described Italian soldiers as "happy little people"; German inmates were well-uniformed, very spirited, and "hard as nails," unrepresentative of "a thoroughly beaten Army" and more realistically the specter of what awaited infantry replacements in Europe.[13] Similarly, for the South Pacific theater, Schachern verified that the unpreparedness of the Marine Air Force in its initial encounters with Japanese pilots had forced that proud service to "open up its commissioned ranks to civilians"—like the Detroit newsman—for the first time.[14]

Personal saga also abounded. White avoided poker games on the base, having learned his lesson "around the green cloth at the City Hall." Edwards heard, upon being turned down for a furlough to witness the birth of his son, James McConnell, that "the Father is essential to the laying of the Keel but not at all necessary to the launching of the ship." Their humor sometimes gave way to feelings of uncertainty, exemplified by Schachern's signing off "apprehensively yours."[15] Nonetheless, trainees expressed a belief in themselves, in their fellow soldiers, and in the nation's ability to prevail, desiring in the best of all worlds to be home with family and friends yet wanting to serve in the most militarily effective and personally rewarding capacity. Thus, for reasons that combined talent, patriotism, and ambition, Edwards sought admission to Officer Candidate School and White a field assignment with *Yank*, monthly magazine of the Information and Education Division: "That would be great professional experience and would make me feel I was doing a lot more than I am doing here." [16] In whatever capacity, however, all were committed to facing the ultimate of sacrifices.

Stateside trainees and civilians often received firsthand reports of the war from comrades fighting it. Writing to Edwards from New Guinea, 1st Lt. James P. Simpson described the simplicity of the people and the beauty of the South Pacific island, which Allied forces had secured early in 1944. He hoped the United States would "clomp on" to some of this "promised land" for its own. As for Japanese soldiers who continued to attack U.S. artillery positions by night, it was true that they were un-

Figure 3. George C. Edwards holding George III ("Andy") and his wife, Peggy, holding James, January 1943. Courtesy of James M. Edwards

afraid of death, "cunning like wild beasts," and personifying "the offensive spirit."[17] Another friend of Edwards, Sgt. Joseph Lash, who fought at Guadalcanal and elsewhere, disagreed with Simpson's assessment of the postwar worth of New Guinea but was hopeful about the end of the war. By the fall of 1944, he predicted, Berlin and Tokyo would realize that only surrender or "national suicide" lay ahead and, in Japan's case, only surrender would "stave off revolution at home"; accordingly, both enemies would capitulate early the following year.[18]

Lash's prediction was based on the status of military events in June 1944. Japan's empire was receding throughout the South and Central Pacific, as U.S. forces invaded key islands and established naval supremacy. Over the previous six months, American victories in the Marshall, Admiralty, and Mariana Islands led to the Battle of the Philippine Sea (June 19-20), which opened the way for air attacks on Japan's home islands. Meanwhile, Allied forces landed in central Italy and prepared to open a second front in France, bombing Germany and building an invasion force in England. British citizens were experiencing shortages of everything and seemed tired from four years of fighting, said RAF pilot Jack McElhone–a close friend of Edwards–although he hoped for "great things of England" in the postwar reconstruction. No doubt the future of most Europeans brightened when Americans liberated Rome on June 4 and the Allied Expeditionary Force landed in Normandy two days later.[19] In Capt. Martin S. Hayden's phrase, the "Big Show" had finally begun.

Stationed near Glasgow as part of the invasion force, Hayden's 502d Port Battalion had been training in Scotland for several months and sworn to a more rigid secrecy than self-censorship expected of combat soldiers elsewhere or trainees in the States.[20] He knew of the invasion plans for his own unit but hardly imagined the extensiveness of Operation Overlord, which grew out of the Arcadia Conference in late 1941 and in early 1944 placed Gen. Dwight D. Eisenhower in command of the largest amphibious operation in history. Nearly 200,000 Anglo-American troops crossed the English Channel in 600 ships and landed along forty miles of Normandy beach in 4,000 invasion craft, under the cover of heavy naval and aerial fire, as six regiments of paratroopers dropped behind enemy lines. In fact, Hayden was not informed of the initial landing date (D-Day) or hour (H-Hour), receiving orders only for his battalion to land at Omaha Beach and, within two weeks, unload 12,000 vehicles and 50,000 tons of cargo from naval vessels to amphibious carriers for transportation to shore.[21] Nearly a month after D-Day, Hayden reported his experience in a letter that filled Jeffries with "envy, and awe and thankfulness" that he was not there.[22] In graphic, sometimes tragic, sometimes humorous prose, he spoke of heroism, hardship, and humanity. He surprised himself by not cutting out when actually fired upon, joking that there was no place to run. He praised his black soldiers for performing as well as whites in combat and recounted several acts of courage by both races.

Back in Detroit, news of D-Day "quieted down" most of the area's strife, indicating to Jeffries the impact of war on the home front, which had been changing in attitude, if not issues, throughout much of 1944.[23] He had noted earlier in the year that things were "relatively quiet" and economically flush: he was endeavoring to extract a greater share of the state's surplus revenues for the city, and defense workers—once trained—were moving to better-paying jobs. He mentioned, too, that postwar planning—especially in transportation—became increasingly significant as victory seemed nearer.[24] In April, Jeffries reported having a light work load and less personal contact with constituents, as people worked incessantly and worried about loved ones in the service.[25] Still, race relations and political campaigns remained ever present mayoral concerns beyond the good news of D-Day.

Although Jeffries continued to struggle with the question of where to build housing projects for black defense workers, he recorded a reduction in racial tension. Both the Mayor's Interracial Committee and Police Commissioner John F. Ballenger appointed as a result of the previous year's deadly riot, seemed effective.[26] In contrast, Gloster B. Current, executive secretary of the local NAACP and friend of Edwards, emphasized inadequate black housing needs, Rev. Gerald L.K. Smith's reactionary presence, and Jeffries's rightward political swing; Detroit remained "the hot spot of reaction, the home of the Fascist and the center of liberal activity."[27]

Jeffries, of course, viewed Current and other black leaders as overly sensitive, though he knew of the ability and sacrifices of black soldiers. Doubtless he believed, like Hayden, that most black leaders let their belligerency surface at "every slight" and, unlike the chaplain in the 502d Port Battalion, lacked a "capacity for self criticism." Such he also learned from Hadyen posed the greatest threat to racial harmony in the service, where black soldiers rarely started trouble yet contributed to it by responding to every gesture as "a racial affront." Most often this occurred off base, as when a black recruit dating an English woman came into contact with a "Hill Billy white." If Jeffries and Hayden disapproved of interracial mingling, they never said so, and despite their class bias toward both races, they believed that blacks possessed the right to fight. Not surprisingly, Hayden was angered by racist officers and, in training and combat, praised his unit's clean record and heroism.[28]

Black activity at home was quite another matter, especially when combined with politics. Having survived his third mayoral bid the previous year, Jeffries now endeavored to assist William E. Dowling, one of his supporters, for reelection. He realized that the Wayne County prosecutor faced a tough fight in the Democratic primary against Gerald O'Brien, who drew the support of blacks, liberals, and union leaders

smarting from the race riot of 1943. Jeffries endorsed Dowling, domi-
nant member of the Governor's Committee to Investigate the Riot and
major author of its "Factual Report," which–like the mayor himself–
blamed blacks and their leaders for the upheaval.[29]

Essentially, the Democratic primary of 1944 replayed the mayoral
primary and election campaign of 1943, but this time the backlash
proved successful. Jeffries believed that Dowling had a chance for victory, despite the "great strength" of blacks and CIO unionists within the
Democratic Party.[30] But after he watched the June-July campaign warm
up and in the final days get "even hotter than the weather," he seemed
resigned to Dowling's overwhelming primary defeat and, ever the real-
ist, discouraged the prosecutor from running as an independent candidate in the fall election.[31]

Throughout the entire period Jeffries became increasingly associated
by journalists and enemies with the Republican Party–in part because
of his confrontations with blacks, liberals, and union leaders who dominated the state Democratic Party, in part because of his opposition to
Roosevelt's seeking a fourth term, and in part because of his criticism of
the national government's handling of federal-local relations. Most significantly, his June 9 speech before the Executives' Club of Chicago
combined all these concerns. Speaking as a moderate politician and independent mayor, Jeffries openly opposed the president's bid for yet
another term and criticized labor for abusing its "tremendous power."
No doubt his anger at FDR emanated from the Federal Housing Administration's placement of the Sojourner Truth Homes in a white
neighborhood "over the protest of the city," which he wrongly blamed
for the massive riot that followed a year later. And his war with labor
stemmed from the political fallout of that upheaval: the unsuccessful
black, liberal, union effort to defeat his election to a third term. Indeed,
since that time, and certainly by the date of the Chicago address, Jeffries
considered the CIO and the Democratic Party of Michigan "synonymous
terms."[32]

Although critics and liberal friends such as George Edwards disagreed with that assessment, Jeffries hardly revealed himself as a
member of Lincoln's party.[33] He complained to Hayden of having been
"branded a Republican"–among other things.[34] Though surely more
philosophically aligned with moderate Republicans than with New
Deal liberalism, his public criticism of Roosevelt and the CIO stemmed
more from his theories of government and experience as a municipal executive than from partisan party politics. Entering the last half of 1944,
he looked to the national elections with the union "red-hot after me."[35]
More "big shows" awaited him at home and the Boys in the Movement
abroad.

NOTES

1. Edward J. Jeffries Jr. (hereafter EJJ) to John M. Carlisle (JMC), 22 June 1944, Box 5, Mayor's Papers, BHC (hereafter all citations of the Mayor's Papers refer to Box 5 for the year given, unless stated otherwise).

2. "Diary of Martin S. Hayden: October 1943-August 1945," (in author's possession, courtesy of Hayden).

3. EJJ to John and Peggy Carlisle, 10 March 1944; EJJ to Martin S. Hayden (hereafter MSH), 7 July 1944, Mayor's Papers.

4. EJJ to JMC, 22 June 1944; MSH to EJJ, 18 May 1944, Mayor's Papers.

5. Walton Stoddard White (hereafter WSW) to GCE, 11 March 1944, Box 4, pt. 3, Edwards Collection, ALUA.

6. George C. Edwards (hereafter GCE), SOL II, 21 March 1944, Box 14, pt. 1, Edwards Collection (hereafter the location of all SOLs unless cited otherwise). Lee Kennett, *G.I.: The American Soldier in World War II* (New York: Scribner, 1987), 42-90, is an excellent overview of the operation of training camps and "the view from the barracks."

7. WSW to GCE, 23 Jan. 1944, Box 5, pt. 2, Edwards Collection; hereafter all citations of the Edwards Collection refer to Box 5 unless stated otherwise; WSW to GCE, 11 March 1944, Box 4, pt. 3, Edwards Collection; Harold J. Schachern (hereafter HJS) to Dear Friends, 11 June 1944, Mayor's Papers.

8. WSW to GCE, 23 Jan. 1944, Edwards Collection.

9. HJS to Dear Friends, 11 June, 1944, Mayor's Papers.

10. GCE, SOL I, 21 Feb. 1944; SOL 2, 21 March 1944.

11. WSW to GCE, 23 Jan. 1944, Edwards Collection; GCE, SOL II, 21 March 1944.

12. WSW to GCE, 11 March 1944, Box 4, pt. 3, Edwards Collection.

13. GCE, SOL I, 21 Feb. 1944.

14. HJS to Dear Friends, 11 June 1944, Mayor's Papers.

15. WSW to GCE, 11 March 1944, Edwards Collection. GCE, SLO II, 21 March 1944; HJS to Dear Friends, 11 June 1944, Mayor's Papers.

16. GCE to EJJ, 2 March 1944, Box 3, Mayor's Papers; WSW to GCE, 11 March 1944, Box 4, pt. 3, Edwards Collection. *Yank* began publication on 14 June 1942; see Geoffrey Perret, *There's a War to Be Won: The United States Army in World War II* (New York: Random House, 1991), 464.

17. Quoted in GCE, SOL II, 21 March 1944; James P. Simpson (hereafter JPS) to GCE, 31 May 1944, Edwards Collection.

18. Joseph P. Lash to GCE, 29 June 1944, Edwards Collection.

19. John J. McElhone to George and Peggy Edwards, 29 May 1944, Box 5, pt. 2, Edwards Collection.

20. MSH to EJJ, 18 May 1944, Mayor's Papers; JPS to George and Peggy Edwards, 25 Dec. 1943, Edwards Collection; WSW to GCE, 11 March 1944, Box 4, pt. 3, Edwards Collection.

21. Statistics from Richard B. Morris, ed., *Encyclopedia of American History* (New York: Harper, 1953), 377; for history, see Vincent J. Esposito, chief ed., *The West Point Atlas of American Wars*, vol. 2, *1900-1953,* 5th ed. (New York: Praeger, 1972), sec. 2, maps 46-50; "Diary of Martin S. Hayden," 91-93, for the battalion statistics.

22. EJJ to MSH, 18 July 1944, Mayor's Papers.

23. EJJ to HJS, 29 June 1944, Mayor's Papers.

24. EJJ to GCE, 8 March 1944 and 30 June 1944, Box 3, Mayor's Papers; EJJ to JMC, 7 July 1944, Mayor's Papers.

25. EJJ to MSH, 24 April 1944, Mayor's Papers.

26. EJJ to GCE, 8 March 1944, Box 3, Mayor's Papers; EJJ to JMC, 29 March 1944, Mayor's Papers; EJJ to GCE, 30 June 1944, Box 3, Mayor's Papers.

27. Gloster B. Current to GCE, 30 June 1944, Edwards Collection.

28. MSH to GCE, 23 May 1944, Edwards Collection; MSH to EJJ, 1 July 1944, Mayor's Papers.

29. EJJ to MSH and EJJ to JMC, both 22 June 1944, Mayor's Papers; Dominic J. Capeci Jr. and Martha Wilkerson, *Layered Violence: The Detroit Rioters of 1943* (Jackson: Univ. Press of Mississippi, 1991), 30-31, 33, 37, 42-44, 48-49, 51-52; August Meier and Elliott Rudwick, *Black Detroit and the Rise of the UAW* (New York: Oxford Univ. Press, 1979), 196-97. State Attorney General Herbert J. Rushton, State Police Commissioner Oscar Olander, and Detroit Police Commissioner Witherspoon made up the rest of the committee.

30. EJJ to HJS, 29 June 1944; EJJ to JMC, 7 July 1944, both in Mayor's Papers.

31. EJJ to GCE, 30 June 1944, Box 3, Mayor's Papers; EJJ to MSH, 7 July 1944, Mayor's Papers.

32. EJJ to MSH, 24 April 1944, Mayor's Papers; *Detroit Tribune*, 17 June 1944, 1.

33. GCE to EJJ, 24 July 1944, Box 3, Mayor's Papers (written in longhand on the back of the last two pages of SOL III-VI).

34. EJJ to MSH, 22 June 1944, Mayor's Papers.

35. EJJ to MSH, 7 and 18 July 1944, Mayor's Papers. Jeffries's political independence emanated from his father's example; from his own commitment to a nonpartisan mayoral system; and from his ongoing conflict with blacks, liberals, and unionists since the Sojourner Truth housing controversy of early 1942.

LETTERS: JANUARY–JULY 1944

New Guinea, South Pacific. 25 December 1943
James P. Simpson to George C.
Dear George and Peg: *and Peggy Edwards*

Christmas Greetings from somewhere in New Guinea. I know where but I can't tell you. This is the dry season here. It seldom rains more than once a day. These are mountainous jungles, and not bad places at all. The heat is terrific for about two hours in the day, but there are plenty of cool places in the shade along the cool mountain streams. The nights are beautiful, and the cultivated coconut groves are delightful. It's a hell of a task to clear out habitable places to live, get rid of the mosquitos, and get adjusted generally, but not nearly so bad as we had imagined it would be. We take atabrine six days a week, to suppress any malaria that we might get and turn us yellow so our little yellow brethren won't be sure. The army refuses to let beer or any intoxicants come in here—though some get here anyhow—and it didn't even let us see Australia before coming here. However, these islands are beautiful, and if I could just go on back home now, I would be well pleased with the travels provided by the army. But "Golden Gate in Forty-Eight" is the cheery little slogan that is circulating around here. A friend of mine here who hails from Michigan and has heard me speak of you received a clipping from his wife from a

Detroit paper stating that you were supposed to get your greetings from your friends and neighbors soon–January 10 was the date I believe. I'm surprised that you haven't prevailed on Uncle Sam to make you a Captain in the AMGOT [American Military Government of Occupied Territories] what with your experience in such matters. But be not discouraged if you get drafted. It's really nothing like dying. Anna Beth and I spent a very pleasant nine months in California.[1] I've been trying to learn a little Pidgin English, although I haven't seen any natives who used it. We might some day. Their inability to grasp even the simplest abstract ideas, such as time and space and complex grammar, apparently caused them to develop this peculiar language when trying to learn English. It is a screamingly funny language, but has very definite rules of grammar and syntax. I is ME, WE is ME PELLA, WE (two of us) is WE TWO PELLA, NATIVE WOMAN is MARY, WHITE WOMAN is MISSUS, all tenses are present, and time and distance are reckoned only in positions of the sun, or in Sundays or Christmases. I want to quote you from "Yankee Doctor in Paradise" a lecture in Pidgin English by a Rockefeller Foundation Doctor. I haven't room here to quote much. Here's Rockefeller: "Master belonga me him make im altogether kerosene, him make im altogether benzine. How he old feller, close up him he die finish. He got im plenty too much belong money. Money belong him allesame dirt. He look about. Him he tink, 'Me like make im one feller some ting (do one thing), he good feller belong altogether boy he buy im kerosene belonga me.' New Gubment he talk along (to) master belonga me. Master belonga me him he talk, 'You, you go killim altogether senake belong bell belong boy belong island.' (Larvae, worms, etc. in the island boy's belly)." I recommend the book–S.M. Lambert.[2]

I'm sorry about this damn typewriter, but it gets a lot of abuse the way we live. One of my clerks, a sort of Will Rogers from North Carolina named [John R.] Raines [Jr.], has erected a sign in front of his tent: "Raines Inn." Equipment takes a beating here from rain, dust, rust, dirt and plenty of hard knocks. Our boys are having to work awfully hard seven days a week, but we have acquired a good PA System, short wave radio, super-phonograph, 90 records, and a 16 mm sound on film motion picture projector so that they do get some entertainment. We're the best equipped organization I know of in that respect. Write me of your activities private and public, and of things in general.

JP SIMPSON

NOTES

1. Simpson had trained at Camp Cooke and Camp Irwin in California.

2. In *A Doctor in Paradise* (London: J.M. Dent, 1941), 94-96, Lambert used these "word pictures" to introduce his sponsor–John D. Rockefeller–to the natives of Melanesia: "My master is the one who makes all of the kerosene and benzine used in

these islands. He is quite old and extremely wealthy. After thinking about it he said to himself, 'I would like to do something special for the good people who buy my goods.' When the New Guinea government approached him for help, he directed me to come here and kill the worm that infects your stomachs."

Camp Van Dorn, Mississippi. 23 January 1944
Dear George: *Walton S. White to George C. Edwards*

I'm told, and not without justification, that old friends never write once they get into the service, but I'm hastening to write to prove it's not always true. I've had fairly good luck keeping up with my friends, even though we all find we reply more slowly than we would have at home.

As long as what you wanted was to be a foot soldier, probably an IRTC is the place for you, and I hope you like it as much as you anticipate. I'm told they're pretty rugged, but you wanted that sort of thing. I still don't know what my future is—there is a good deal of uproar here because some fellows are being shipped overseas as replacements, and some of my friends are volunteering. I haven't decided what I want—except that we finally have been told by the commanding general that our paper will be published in theaters of operations, which means maneuvers and maybe actual combat. We have been collecting material from the foreign theaters on the advantages of continuing to publish in combat zones, and maybe that will help our case. If I should remain with this division and if it should go overseas I'd like very much to have a hand in publishing its newspaper. Most of our other public relations work would be taken over as a function of G-2 [Military Intelligence], though we might act as G-2 agents ourselves; we're now attending a course in intelligence subjects.

Your AGCT [Army General Classification Test] score and your interview at Sheridan will help in the future, even though you think you may be earmarked for plain infantry. It may [militate], too, against the sort of thing you want to do. I don't know much about an IRTC compared with a division, for instance, but the tendency around here is to yank men such as you out of the companies and put them in charge of orientation and similar subjects, unless they protest vigorously. Probably, however, because an IRTC's job is to furnish replacements, there isn't the company organization that we have and that might wait until you join division.

Your description of the men looking for things to bitch about jibes with my experience. I think in general the fellows are satisfied, but don't want to appear so.

You're probably much more fortunate in being near Macon. We're a mile from the village of Centreville, which had nothing to offer the war and has less now. It is distinctly unattractive. Few Army camps are physically attractive, but the principal disadvantage of this one is that it is so far from towns to which the men can get for amusement. We're 40 miles from Baton Rouge, an equal distance from McComb and Natchez, and more than a hundred from a really big town. Naturally, being unable to do anything but drink beer or go to the post movies or dances, the men feel that the camp and the division both are stinkers. Everyone agrees about the camp, but I've come to the conclusion—veteran of four months in the Army that I am—that the division is a pretty good one. It will take the future course of the war, of course, to determine whether the division ever sees action as a whole, whether it becomes entirely a replacement outfit (at present, in addition to sending men out, we are bringing in a lot from Europe for a rest), or whether its regiments and artillery battalions are a split off to join other out fits. So my own future is uncertain, not that it bothers me.

I don't know how much I could tell you about Basic Training. I've just finished it, but a guy who is in a line company could give you a lot more intelligent pointers, because in Division Hq we had only 62 weeks (day on and day off, alternating office work with training) and occasionally were pulled off that. However, we got through the Corps tests which follow Basic without trouble, and were complimented by the commanding general because we have a difficult job in a way; we have two jobs to do, whereas the line soldier can concentrate on learning soldiering. So I don't feel bad. We are now in the Unit Training Period, the second of four phases which a division goes through. In this period the squads, platoons, companies, battalions, regiments and so on . . . get their training, the individual having had his in the first 13 weeks. Our offices in Div Hq will function as units, we doing in the field the jobs we would do in a garrison ordinarily. That is our way of getting unit training, and it should be very interesting.

The radio says Americans are only 16 miles from Rome at one point; that Swedish correspondents can hear American and British artillery and that we have air power 13 times that of the Nazis in the sector where the new landings have been made. Sounds good; if you and I must be in this Army, well and good, but let the whole thing be over with as soon as possible.

Meanwhile I have achieved a slight promotion [Private First Class]—a $4 raise, but not enough promotion to get off KP—and am now getting my mail at the office instead of Hq Co, so would you make a note of the new address and try to write me soon?

STOD

Camp Wheeler, Georgia. 21 February 1944
George C. Edwards to Assorted Friends

Standard Operation Letter I

Subject: Pvt. Edwards and The Battle of Camp Wheeler.

1. All due thanks . . . for the correspondence received—all due execrations for letters not received—and all due apologies for the somewhat impersonal form of this letter.

2. Since I am just about to start on the seventh week of my military career, it is certainly high time for me to write of my . . . experiences and my views on the Army. . . .

3. I shall skip the first week. . . . Much has been written of reception centers, and I am not eloquent enough to add much to the picture of the misery of the raw recruit, as he is stripped, examined, bedded down, called out, measured, uniformed, classified, quizzed, punched, put to bed, washed up, and bawled out. My personal reaction was that I now knew how a Ford Chassis felt as it went down the assembly line. Should I note that the current greetings . . . yelled by the 24 hour veterans, at the new arrivals, were "Yeah needle bait" (the hypo needles) and "You'll be sorry."

4. At Ft. Sheridan the much vaunted Army in efficiency was no where in evidence to me. We arrived Tuesday A.M. By Saturday noon . . . most of us . . . were classified, outfitted, assigned and entrained on troop sleepers passing through the famed Chicago stock yards and obviously headed South.

> "Oh I wish I was in the land of cotton
> Old tunes there are not forgotten."

5. On the train I was introduced to K.P. . . . Our car fed the train all the way down. I served as third assistant butcher. The army really brings out the best qualities in a man. I never before knew I could butcher. Shortly after we lost the smell of the stockyards, the rumor went around that we were headed for a place called Camp Wheeler, near Macon, Ga. I had never heard of Camp Wheeler.

6. I now know a great deal about Camp Wheeler. I even share the typical Wheeler attitude that its fame or infamy should be increased. Camp Wheeler is an Infantry Training Replacement Center "accommodating" 25,000 soldiers. . . . It is composed of countless . . . two story wooden Army barracks, a number of one story tar paper covered barracks . . . and bare red clay parade grounds. . . . The whole is located in hilly Georgia pine woods country—not displeasing to the eye—if you are looking for scenery.

7. To depict Camp Wheeler and life there, I start with its folklore. I guarantee the veracity of none of these. In fact I profoundly doubt them all. I give two versions of somewhat parallel stories.

A. *Officer Version*: Camp Wheeler is the toughest, Goddamnest spit & polish Infantry Camp in the country.

   G.I. Version: Camp Wheeler is the toughest, Goddamnest spit & polish Infantry Camp in the country.

B. *Officer Version*: There are two armies, that of the United States and that of Camp Wheeler.

   G.I. Version: Ditto.

C. *Officers*: When you get through here (if you get through), you'll be a Wheeler Infantryman, and one infantryman is as tough as any two Marines.

G.I.: When trainees get through at Wheeler, [General Douglas] Mc-Arthur won't accept them in the Pacific for replacements. Says they're so burned out they haven't got any fighting left.

D. *Officer:* Everything done here is for your own good and you'll know it when you get to combat. Any trained infantryman can lick a tank.

G.I.: (Happily) "Did you hear that . . . Walter Winchell, [H.V.] Kaltenborn, Gabriel Heatter, etc. said over the radio last night . . . that Camp Wheeler was reported to treat its trainees worse than prisoners in a Nazi Concentration Camp?"[1] Any how we're looking for a transfer to the tanks corps.

E. *Officer:* Macon is the loveliest Army town in the country. Its people glow with Southern hospitality. It is full of gracious and beautiful women.

G.I.: Macon is the lousiest Army town in the country. The inhabitants would steal the railroad fare from a G.I. going to see his dying Grandmother. There aren't any women in town and . . . those that you see remind you of the Army film on Sex Hygiene.

In all the folklore there is a certain pride (yep G.I.s included) that the Post is either the best (never a G.I. version) or the worst. I suppose it all has something to do with what they call morale.

8. Some may be interested to know my exact status in this auspicious setting. I am an infantry trainee–technically a private–frequently referred to here as a yard bird. At Ft. Sheridan, in classification I got off quite a bit of conversation about wanting field service with either artillery or infantry. My interviewer . . . assured me that "with your score and work record, the Army wouldn't want to waste your administrative experience," whereupon I saw visions of me filing papers for the rest of the war. . . . that fear proved distinctly unfounded. I now am sure that I was industriously engaged in making a virtue of a plain unvarnished necessity. I'd a got here with or without the talk.

9. Some may also be interested in what I think of the Infantry. . . . The Army word for it is . . . "rugged,"–that is an understatement for "Goddamn Tough." I had expected it to be tough–but my expectations were something more than realized. The first three weeks were a plain endurance contest. It was a battle just to keep up and to stay in line. They say that the first three weeks are the hardest. . . . I believe it. The training doesn't get easier or the discipline laxer. The trainee just gets tougher and more immune.

10. This is strictly combat training. It is based on the assumption that most of the trainees join units in combat zones in a matter of a few weeks after leaving here. As such it makes sense. Anyone who goes through the 17 weeks is bound to be better prepared for combat–physically and technically. Those who fall out enroute don't get into combat. The Air Raid Warden program[2] left me prepared for the idea that mass training could not be adjusted to the individual. (And I assure you this isn't.) Just before stating this I read Ralph Ingersoll's *The Battle Is the Payoff,*[3] . . . a treatise on how important endurance and training were in actual combat, both

for winning and for survival. . . . Wheeler seems convinced of the same thing.

11. The Army also has its lighter side. There is always K.P. I see that the *Times* columnist Private [Jack] Pickering notes with pride that he *volunteered* for K.P. One such sin may be excusable. A repetition of that in print would automatically start vivid comparisons of the author & the rear end of a horse in any G.I. reader's mind. K.P. is something to be endured—not gloated about. Shall I regale you with my first few hours of K.P. at Wheeler?

We were awakened at 5:30 and a few minutes later stumbled into the kitchen to hear the cook's opinion on how slow we were. We set tables and I was happily handing out bread to the yawning G.I.s when in comes my barrack's corporal with fire in both eyes. He wanted to know whether or not I knew how to make a Goddamn X * # ! bed. Then he inquired "Why the goddamn X * X # ? don't you do it the right way?" I murmured something about K.P. and not having time to do it right. That apparently wasn't the right answer. . . . I found myself remaking my bed—this time with care. It took me six minutes. When I got back to the mess hall, the Mess Sergeant was waiting. Inquires he, "Where's that guy that takes half an hour to make a bed?" I look around to see who this nefarious character is. Then I realize he's addressing me. The next hour and a half I spent scrubbing the garbage cans . . . 9 of them, each holding 32 gallons. It wasn't such a hard job to catch on to . . . for I had the Mess Sergeant's personal supervision. Oh yes—me and Pickering we'll volunteer for K.P. anytime.

12. We also learn some things which the Army regards as essential to an infantryman . . . an astonishing amount in an astonishing short time. In the first three weeks of basic we

(a) Learned to take the M1 (Garand) rifle[4] apart and reassemble it (& then . . . to make sure—did it at night in the field), learned to load and unload the M1 and started dry firing.

(b) Learned the manual of arms and close order drill—started extended order drill.

(c) Marched innumerable miles each day and made three official marches [two, five, and ten miles] with full field packs and rifles.

(d) Completed Army first aid—9 hours of wound dressing, fractures, tourniquets and [stretcher] carrys.

(e) Had six or eight hours of bayonet drill.

(f) Had grenade & throwing with dummy grenades.

(g) Gas mask training—shades of O.C.D.

(h) Had hours of instruction on interior guard duty. (Along with the story of the Wheeler G.I. on his first guard . . . who was approached by the Officer of the Guard: "What would you do if I just kept coming after you shouted 'Halt' the third time?" The G.I. replied, "I'd call the Corporal of the Guard Sir." (Wrong answer.) . . . the Officer of the Guard grated out "Oh you would . . . and why would you call the Corporal of the

Guard?" The G.I. then answered (correctly), "To haul your dead body away Sir." We were told all that as a Wheeler happening. This week I read it in *See Here, Private Hargrove*[5] about Ft. Bragg. I suppose it happened at Valley Forge.

(i) Have run the obstacle course twice.

(j) Have run the 2 mile cross country run twice.

(k) Have had hour after hour of military courtesy, orientation on "Why we fight," training films on tactics and camouflage.

(l) Learned to roll field packs, pitch tents, camouflage positions, police the camp, wash our clothes, shave in 3 minutes in cold water, scrub a latrine, etc.

13. . . . I liked the M1, the marches (I have good feet, thanks be), the obstacles & cross country runs, the hand grenade drill and camouflage. Bayonet drill is tough as hell, and I haven't managed to learn to growl convincingly. The lectures were sometimes dull–but restful. The training films mostly pretty good . . . the first time you see them. They don't wear well and that *Sex Hygiene* one we have already been shown six times without even the vaguest chance to put it to any practical use.

14. The food is good–plain, fairly plentiful and . . . pretty well cooked. I can report however that the rumor of steaks . . . is a myth. "Yank" has a lovely Sad Sack cartoon on a G.I. and his chow. . . . Sad Sack is pictured marching the last weary miles before chow–his mind dwelling on food. He arrives at the bivouac, goes down on his knees before the cook and presents both lids of his mess kit. Cook fills 'em. Sad Sack eats ravenously. . . . Holds up mess kit for more. Eats it all and rises while cook stands by . . . to hear S.S. compliments. Wiping his mouth Sad Sack pronounces . . . *PHOOEY!*[6]

15. If army life is all as busy as the above you may wonder how come this letter. Thereby hangs a tale.

16. You will doubtless be pleased to hear that your particular G.I. is currently recuperating in the Station Hospital. No–it is not due to the ever popular Georgia pneumonia, nor to march exhaustion, nor to obstacles course injuries. . . . I busted a bone in my right hand playing football.

Ex-Detroit Newsman P.F.C. Walton S. White is really to blame. . . . I had just received news of his brand new stripe and naturally was green with envy. Bright and early Monday, a week ago now, I started . . . bucking hard for a promotion from yardbird to rookie. It so happened that fate had decreed that the [Company] . . . should run the two mile cross country to help settle our breakfasts. The C.O. . . . promised that the first 20% to finish would be rewarded. Well I staggered up the last hill somewhat behind 18 high school track men and one professional ballet dancer–but I was in the 20%. Hooray–now for the reward. We were allowed to play football. . . .

17. The cure for this disease is very considerably worse than the original malady. They have my hand incased in an apparatus which is vari-

ously described here as "a booby trap," "The G.I. Walkie Talkie" and "America's Secret Weapon." It looks somewhat like this: [diagram of wire frame, rubber bands, nail through finger, and cast]

I should be honest and report that it is not at all painful at present and that it hurt surprisingly little to begin with. Also it is about healed now. Altho I still have the interesting jobs of shaving and eating left-handed, I at least can now write right-handed—or can I?

18. Now I am perturbed because . . . the Army doesn't award the Purple Heart for football injuries.

19. There are a number of other Detroit G.I.s reposing in this same institution for more dramatic reasons. Don't print the following or I am subject for court martial under the article of war which forbids any acts tending to . . . discredit . . . the Army. Three days after this battalion (not mine) started training . . . [it] assembled for a gas grenade demonstration. Quoth the Lieutenant . . . "First we will show you a phosphorus smoke bomb. Now don't worry, this is perfectly harmless. This is sort of a new type of phosphorus bomb to me, but we'll just light it any how." At which point a *phosphorus incendiary* exploded. 52 men and the Lieutenant are now here. None died. You . . . will be happy to hear that the above is not standard operating procedure.

20. Several of my friends have expressed a slight irritation over the 5th Army's delay in clearing the Germans out of Italy.[7] General and inside information . . . is a helluva lot more available at home than here. But you might be interested in what we hear at this camp from which the cycles are steadily going to combat zones. The stuff about under age, undertrained, badly supplied and disheartened Germans and Japs is regarded as pure wishful thinking. True enough we have some Italian prisoners who seem happy little people and are frequently the envy of local G.I.s.

21. But we also see a few Germans and they're a different story. Six of them were at the Hospital yesterday. . . . They were all under 25—looked hard as nails [in] . . . combat uniforms and accoutrements . . . as well designed and of as good materials as ours. They were obviously aware that they were . . . under the eyes of the enemy. The two [German] officers fairly strutted about while . . . the group showed quite sufficient esprit de corps to have made Hitler proud. If they are members of a thoroughly beaten Army, they hardly seem to prove it . . .

22. A cast . . . has certain advantages. Hospital doesn't ask me to do Army K.P. or clean up, but so far the Ward Corporal hasn't figured out anything that I could do with one hand. I could help him on the problem, but I'm afraid of the precedent.

23. The cast doesn't . . . interfere with poker-playing and I am endeavoring to teach some of the other . . . fracture cases the rudiments of Texas poker. So far fortune has smiled on me. . . . Financially I can hardly afford to get well, what with G.I. pay and allowances, plus a pre-induction accident policy . . . plus poker. Everything would be fine if it didn't get so damn boring.

But all things end and so will this, and I hope shortly to be back in the thick of the Battle of Camp Wheeler.

Sincerely,   GEORGE

NOTES

1. Winchell, Kaltenborn, and Heatter were radio newsmen known for their gossipy or editorial styles.
2. Edwards had served as chief and deputy chief air raid warden of Detroit before entering the service.
3. Ralph Ingeroll, *The Battle Is the Big Payoff* (New York: Harcourt, Brace, 1943).
4. The weapon of issue for the infantry.
5. Marion Hargrove, *See Here, Private Hargrove* (New York: Holt, 1942).
6. Sad Sack was the creation of Sgt. George Baker of *Yank*, a former artist for Walt Disney.
7. Allied forces invaded mainland Italy from Sicily on 2 September 1943. The Italian government surrendered three days later. German forces seized Rome on September 10, however, and soon assisted Benito Mussolini to escape Italian authorities and proclaim a Fascist Republic in areas under German control. On 22 January 1944, Allied units established the Nettuno-Anzio beachhead thirty miles south of Rome; on June 4, Rome fell to U.S. Gen. Mark Clark's Fifth Army. As Allied efforts shifted to the invasion of France, the war to rid Italy of all German troops continued until 2 May 1945.

Camp Wheeler, Georgia. 2 March 1944
George C. Edwards to Edward J. Jeffries Jr.

Dear Jeff:

This is a long overdue letter—but for the first month I literally didn't have a minute to write and for the past 3 weeks I haven't been able to.

Most of the news about me is contained in the attached opus[1] so I won't rewrite it in the hope that you will be able to wade through it.

I have followed City Hall news with great interest. It seems to me that Detroit and Wayne County did get a few crumbs from the table when the legislature met and doubtless that was due to your campaign.

One rumor from home bothers me—for heaven's sake, not Carl Smith[2] for the Housing commission. Any other commission OK—but not that one. But of course I am pretty remote now to be saying anything on any subject.

If you know any Generals or high cockalorums in the War Dept. who would be interested in helping my pending O.C.S. application along you might mention me. My hopes are quite remote since, among other things, O.C.S. is practically closed.

You may not believe it but you can develop a helluva nostalgia for City Hall.

NOTES

1. SOL 1, 21 Feb. 1944.
2. Karl H. Smith, a Detroit realtor, president of various taxpayers' and property owners' organizations who opposed both public and integrated housing and who ran unsuccessfully for the Common Council in 1943.

Detroit. March 8. 1944

Dear George: *Edward J. Jeffries Jr. to George C. Edwards*

It was good to hear from you. In a roundabout way I have heard several times. By that I mean I have read your letters to other people. Cap Mc-Connell[1] has kept me pretty well informed.

I enjoyed no end your operational letter.

Things are relatively quiet at the minute. I have finished my budget sessions. Next week the Council gets the budget. Not much change has been made except we expanded the operating and maintenance fund of the Parks and Recreation Department $500,000. I recommended an increase to $1,800 for the minimum wage, and we finally are going to pay double time for the six main holidays. By the Houdini type of financing, the budget is up only $519,000. What the Council will do or how they will do it, of course, remains to be seen.

I note in your letter that you thought the State had given us some crumbs. Your are right if your magnifying glass is big enough to see them. I tried to talk to Governor [Harry F.] Kelly and convince him that he could be the No. 1 Governor of the United States if he backed up some of that terrific surplus. I thought at one stage I had him convinced but he reverted to type and he is just one of the 48.

The worst thing they [state legislators] did was to pave the road for a new bill regulating racing for 4% increase in the take of the race track, and for one year allowing Detroit to take half of the proceeds. They were adamant on the one year provision.

In fact, their persistence in taking this position only added fuel to my suspicion that they are trying to buy us off with a one year contribution. Perhaps I am wrong, but I will be pleasantly surprised if I am. In the meantime the increased cut of the race track with anticipated business of the race track leaves them in better financial position than before, and now it specifically excludes the municipality from even assessing their personal property. In other words they are free from us forever. . . .

Five million dollars was set up for post-war planning by cities and counties within the State. From our point of view that was a complete find. We actually expect to take advantage to the tune of $1,170,000 which will give us with our own contribution $2,340,000 for planning this next year. We can draw plans now faster than we can hope to finance them. . . . I do think that we are in practical agreement with the Road Commission and Highway Commission on the Harper McGraw Highway.[2] I think we are about ready to execute a contract. Maybe I am unduly optimistic, but I don't think so, on the basis that you heard discussed before you left for the service.

The race question is smoldering a little again as it relates to the Wyoming Eight Mile Road section.[3] Nothing yet is exactly crystallized and, therefore, I will report to you at a little later time what happens.

Karl Smith is a threat but not yet a certainty [for the Detroit Housing Commission]. While there is life there is hope.

I am going to Washington this afternoon as a delegate to a conference on the Palestine situation.[4] My title is the Christian friend of the Jew. I have been told that I don't have to know anything or do anything. All I have to do is just listen. I think I can qualify.

I expect also to see Carlisle who is now covering [Blair] Moody's beat [in Washington, D.C.], while Moody regales us with the life of the doughboy in the European theaters.

I was at Willow Run the other day. The bomber quota is 375, and in February they manufactured 419. They expect to exceed their quota in March by fully 50 planes, the first month over September last when the quota was exceeded only to the extent of one plane. As could be expected, they are constantly improving and are on the up grade. It might be of interest to you to know that they have actually shipped 3,400 planes away from the plant. These figures were not told me in confidence but are part of a new program to publicize what they are doing. Consequently I am not giving away a military secret. Their big problem still is turnover. Just as they get a man well trained he gets a job somewhere else.

Good luck and let me hear from you more often.

Sincerely,   JEFF

P.S. I will try to get the Great Carlisle working on the O.C.S. matter. There is nothing like having a boy in the front office and if I am not mistaken, Washington still houses the front office.

NOTES

1. Edwards's father-in-law, Detroit stockbroker and conservative Republican Rollin M. McConnell.

2. The state highway department planned to extend the McGraw-Harper expressway into Macomb County and connect it with a new highway that would lead to a public beach proposed for 420 acres of Huron Point on Lake St. Clair. *News*, 22 Feb. 1944, 4; 24 Feb. 1944, 13.

3. The site for a prospective black housing project on the border of northwest Detroit, located in a predominantly black area. Over the previous two years, City Plan Commission and Common Council members had persuaded the State Land Office Board to withhold the property (842 lots obtained through tax default) from the open market until it could be redeveloped completely. The state board reversed its action,

however, in response to a Federal Housing Administration decision to insure mortgages for the construction of low-cost private homes in the area, which—in turn—caused the commission and its supporters to appeal to the mayor and councilmen to help them once again preserve the site for a black housing project. The commission-led coalition—comprising the local NAACP, the housing division of the UAW, the Detroit Citizens League, and the Engineering Society of Detroit—persuaded Jeffries to discuss the issue with interested municipal officials and schedule a public hearing on the subject before the council. The entire issue stemmed from the legacy of the Sojourner Truth Homes controversy, after which Jeffries and the Common Council had imposed a policy of preserving neighborhood characteristics, in effect limiting locations for the construction of segregated units. See *News,* 3 March 1944, 10; 8 March 1944, 21.

4. The National Conference on Palestine convened on March 9 to press for passage of the Wagner-Taft-Wright-Compton resolution, which recommended that the United States favor opening Palestine to Jewish immigration for the purpose of establishing "a democratic Jewish Commonwealth." However, for reasons of international political developments, Roosevelt delayed a congressional vote on the resolution for over a year; finally, despite President Harry S. Truman's continued opposition, the Senate and the House passed it in December of 1945. Clearly Jeffries's role at the conference was one of spectator, presumably for moral support. See *New York Times,* 10 Mar. 1944, 1, 3; J. Joseph Huthmacher, *Senator Robert F. Wagner and the Rise of Urban Liberalism* (New York: Atheneum, 1968), 306-07, 332.

Detroit. March 10, 1944
Edward J. Jeffries Jr. to Jack M.
Dear Jack and Peggy: *and Peggy Carlisle*

I am combining my note to the two of you on account of I don't know where you live, except that I remember Silver Spring [Maryland] used to be the name of a mixer. Consequently I remember the town but not the address.

I don't know whether I properly thanked Peggy for meeting us at the airport.[1] If I did I want to do it again. It's the very thing that is going to get me out of bed in time to meet a train bringing a Russian General to the Pere Marquette station, Monday morning. I know the certain satisfaction which comes from being met at a railroad station or airport. . . .

Jack, you've a great opportunity to be a great writer. You are at the crossroads of the earth. Where you are practically everybody is somebody. You might not like . . .[or] have much of an opinion of some of them, but, somewhere somebody thinks they are potential number one men. You can't discount them completely. The fact of the matter is you have a great opportunity to fathom human nature as the individual represents a type. No newspaperman can be really good until he thoroughly understands life in all its phases. You couldn't run a metropolitan paper well until you knew what it is that makes life run. There is no other place where you can see as much of it so concentrated as in Washington.

I don't wonder at your being homesick, but there is no easy way to be good. It takes work and lots of it, and postponing what you want to do in order to do what you should do. You have a lot of ability. You can only make the maximum use of it with a well rounded background. You have more energy than most newspapermen . . . and I don't think there is a substitute for that attribute. You should be in a newspaperman's paradise and, with the information you can gather, and with the stories you can write, you could be outstanding. It doesn't make any difference what game you are in, the champ is always recognized.

I am going to try to go down to Washington in a couple of weeks and just talk to some of you folks as to what's going on. I will find out exactly when the hearing is to be had on the road bill, and I would like to combine it.[2]

In the meantime, give her both barrels and just remember that they don't call you names unless they are either respectful or scared of you. Hayden would never have made that crack unless you had unusually impressed him. I will guarantee that if you can impress enough people you are on the high road to success.

You folks were awfully nice to me and you made a very pleasant trip out of what could have been a little boring.

Luck to you!

Sincerely,   J E F F

NOTES

1. When Jeffries visited Washington for the National Conference on Palestine.
2. Jeffries appeared before the House Committee on Roads on 27 March 1944, representing the views of both the city of Detroit and the American Municipal Association on the $3 billion federal highway appropriation bill. Nineteen months later the bill became law, providing significant monies for urban areas. See *News*, 20 March 1944, 4; *New York Times*, 3 Oct. 1945.

                                    Camp Van Dorn, Mississippi. 11 March 1944
Dear George: *Walton S. White to George C. Edwards*

If that mimeographed masterpiece of yours doesn't produce mail for you I don't know what will. I hasten to add my bit; I got the thing yesterday. For your information, the above is my address. I noted that you apparently didn't have your address book in the hospital, and that you addressed me . . . in care of my father. The thing reached me in good order. . . . In the future, if you forget the address, but if you can remember the number of the division, that will do: Hq 63rd Inf[antry] Div[ison]. If you can remember the "APO 410" so much the better. . . . The "PRO" [Public Relations Office] is not necessary at all because the mail sorters at Div Hq know me well enough.

Your letter not only amused and delighted me and Peg (who is currently visiting me for a few days . . .); it created a sensation in Detroit. Probably you know that [W.K.] Kelsey reproduced part of it. You doubtless see the *News* more often than I do, but you must know that you made a profound impression on Kelsey a long time ago and that he frequently mentions you. . . . (Apropos of nothing, in the same column ["The Commentator"] in which he used your stuff, Kelsey did a masterful piece on the traffic ordinance. . . . He is having another fight with the constituted authorities, this time because he got a pedestrian ticket. It's driving Slutz crazy . . . because Kelsey is giving a lot of unfortunate publicity to the pedestrian ordinance.)

Anyway, I must berate you for dragging me through the public prints, but there is nothing I can do about that now.

I gain the impression from your masterpiece (obviously a typical Edwards job of soft-talking the southern gals in the hospital into lending you the mimeograph) that you really are getting training. At the risk of exposing myself to your merciless comments, I must tell you that I've had practically no training compared with yours. I get the same impression that you do, that at the end of your training, or soon thereafter, you'll be shipping out. . . . I imagine that's the lot of most guys being called now; they probably will go either to IRTC or . . . [as] replacements in divisions about to move. It's entirely probable that a lot of guys called after I was will get overseas long before I do, if ever. Today is my six-month anniversary in the Army. I have no particular expectation of getting overseas until and unless the 63rd does. I'm not saying much about it, and I'd appreciate it if you wouldn't either, but I have feelers out with both YANK [service newspaper] and OWI [Office of War Information]. YANK needs more field men; that would be great professional experience and would make me feel I was doing a hell of a lot more than I'm doing here. OWI has a new set-up for which Fred Gaertner[1] and others have recommended me; they need men and are trying to get them released or transferred from the Army to publish papers, do radio work and general public relations jobs in occupied territory, following the invasion. Probably nothing will come of either application, but they are worth the try.

To reply categorically to your letter: Apparently the cries of "Needle bait" and "You'll be sorry!" are universal. They were standard at [Fort] Custer, and everyone tells me he got the same stuff at Meade, Upton, Devens and other reception centers.[2]

We heard a rumor before we left Custer that we were going to [Camp] Van Dorn. No one ever had heard of it; of course it's less well known than [Camp] Wheeler. The rumor had a sound basis, because two previous shipments had come the same week from Custer. Naturally we didn't know, even when we got south of Memphis, where we were going for sure.

On our troop train the GIs didn't work KP. A permanent detail of cooks and KPs worked the chow car all the way, as apparently it had been doing on other troop movements, some of them as far away as California.

The officer and GI versions about both Van Dorn and nearby Centreville [Mississippi] are identical. The cadre for this division came from [Camp] Blanding, which was not far from Jacksonville [Florida], and they found Van Dorn and Centreville suffered by comparison. This is a combat camp, we are on field (not garrison) rations, and conditions approximate those of a theater of operations. Consequently there are no softening or alleviating influences, and officers and men alike do not like either camp or town.

I was tremendously interested in your G.I. rumor that [Walter] Winchell, etc., was reported to have belittled Wheeler in a broadcast. This was the first time I knew it had been said about another camp. We were told last fall that a year ago, when the 99th Div was here, Winchell made a broadcast in which he said Van Dorn was the worst camp in the country and not even fit for prisoners of war. Now, if never before, I doubt that Winchell or anyone else ever made such a statement about any camp.

There is a tendency in nearby towns, excepting Natchez [Mississippi] . . . to gyp soldiers, but not in small things. That is, there is no apparent robbery in stores and such places, but the OPA is worthless when it comes to rent control, the quality of housing, etc.

I am one of the few gents who was aptly classified. As nearly as is humanly possible in the Army, I am doing exactly the same work I was doing last summer. I had the advantage of being classified by two friends of mine, one a newspaperman. They recommended me for public relations work and that's what I'm doing. Of five men who were sent here as fillers with the reception center recommendation that they be classified for PRO, I was the only one actually so classified. My favorite current story is from YANK or somewhere . . . about the postal clerk who told the classifiers that he sorted letters and put them in pigeon holes. He was classified as a pigeon fancier.

Having been assigned to Div Hq–incidentally, anyone who asks "What did you do to get such a soft job?" is uttering strictly shit for the birds, as the saying goes; I was assigned here with not even the choice of being a rifleman (God forbid!) . . . –I had relatively little basic training. Actually, we had slightly better than 30 days of elapsed time. The training period in a division, as opposed to that in an IRTC is 13 weeks. We trained on alternate days, thus getting 6½ weeks. On a number of occasions I had to work in the office . . . so the total probably was not much over a month. However, we apparently learned our stuff convincingly, because . . . we passed the regular corps test–this comes at the conclusion of Basic in divisions–without much trouble. . . . As a matter of fact, we were commended later for having done an especially difficult job . . . we learned soldiering and our office jobs at the same time, whereas, although the line outfits probably know a hell of a lot more about soldiering, they have only one job to do and can spend six days a week at it.

I expected to wind up in a line outfit and when I didn't the physical training proved much less arduous than anticipated. However, I was in pretty good physical condition—I never was in bad condition, even in civilian life, but I was a lot harder at the end of Basic—until Basic was over, when I went back to an ordinary desk job. We now have relatively little exercise, but living more or less out of doors all the time (you might as well be out of doors as in our more-than-adequately ventilated barracks) keeps me in pretty good shape.

I join you in condemning [Jack] Pickering[3] for having alleged that he volunteered for KP. If he really volunteered, which I doubt, he is either stupid or the same prick he always was, both in college and in Detroit.

KP for us is substantially the same as with you, except that it looks as though your kitchen was larger. . . . At least we don't seem to have as many containers and pots as you described scrubbing. This is, as far as I can learn, the only division in which Div Hq pulls KP and guard. I get KP about once every three weeks, frequently in the staff officers' mess, which has more pleasant surroundings but which has the disadvantage of using about 300 dishes. We, the buck-ass privates, eat out of mess kits.

I know relatively little about the M1, although I have disassembled, assembled and cleaned plenty of them. I have never fired one. My weapon is the carbine, a dandy little device.[4] Nearly all Div Hq is armed with the carbine and many other outfits are, too. As a matter of fact, there are nearly as many carbines in an infantry division now as there are rifles.

There is no manual of arms[5] for the carbine, so I was spared that, though back in October I had 20 minutes of manual of arms with the M1.

We had plenty of both close and extended order drill.[6]

Our longest march in Basic was about three miles (the infantry outfits do 10 or more . . .); subsequently we have had a couple of slightly longer (about five-mile) marches with full equipment. When we go on bivouac or . . . into the field, we . . . go by truck. That may sound soft to an infantryman, but don't forget that we pack the entire field equipment of an office (desks, tables, chairs, typewriters, safes and office supplies) and that loading and unloading them one or more times daily is at least the equivalent to carrying a pack on your back. We do plenty of rolling and unrolling packs, but we are at least spared carrying them for great distances.

We had about the same first aid instruction you did. . . . The reaction of everyone here to bayonet drill is about the same as yours. It is hard and distasteful work. No one likes to growl. No one likes the weapon. Fortunately there has been no bayonet for the carbine until one was developed a few days ago, and it should be light—if we ever get them.

We had no grenade throwing at all, but will get some this spring.

We have had a tremendous amount of gas training, none with the unfortunate effect you described. My OCD training was surprisingly valuable in the gas course, and I had none of the trepidation about the gas chamber or field tests that most others had. We have been subjected twice to gas chambers with lethal concentrations of chlorine, and have made field tests with all the other war gases.

We have had relatively little on interior guard. . . . We had a lecture on the theory, but the station complement does all the guarding in camp except for the ordinary regimental and company area guards, who are little more than fire guards.

We ran the obstacle course twice during Basic.

We had no cross-country runs, though they are common in the line companies.

We've had all the lecture and movies you have had. . . . The so called training aids, including the films, are . . . excellent. In addition, I took a six-week intelligence course with the G-2 [military intelligence] staff, which repeated a lot of stuff we had had in Basic, with . . . a lot on security, censorship, mapping, operations, enemy uniforms, etc.

I am tired of the sex hygiene film and of the film and lecture on the Articles of War. The latter I've caught only twice, but that was enough. You get it every six months in the Army.

Our food, though plain (field rations, as I said at 67 cents a day), is pretty well cooked and we have a marvelous baker in our mess. All cooking, serving and eating is done outdoors, as part of field training. The mess halls are used only for storage since December or January.

I have played no poker and done no other gambling. . . . I'm afraid to. I think I learned my lesson the hard way around the green cloth at City Hall. I love the game, but I avoid its temptations and I'm not good enough to insure myself an income. Instead, two nights a week for about a half-hour a night, I pick up beer bottles on the grounds around a PX and get a dollar or two a night, which adds $10 or $12 a month to my $54 (net of about $20; that $54 sounds like a lot of dough, but you know as well as I do that it never amounts to much real cash-in-hand).

It has taken me all morning to do this letter, what with sandwiching other jobs in between paragraphs, and it's getting near lunch time. I have a pass starting at noon and ending Sunday (tomorrow) night, which I'll spend with Peg, so I'm about to take off.

Your letter was a swell idea and tremendously interesting. I'm glad the hand is healing all right, and I'll look forward to a more personal letter from you eventually and to seeing you on the battlefield.

STOD

NOTES

1. Managing editor of the *News* and White's former boss.
2. Fort Custer, Michigan; Fort Meade, Maryland; Camp Upton, New York; Fort Devens, Massachusetts.

3. The *Times* reporter mentioned in SOL 1, 21 Feb. 1944.

4. The M1 or Garand rifle is the semiautomatic, rapid-firing .30 caliber weapon of the infantry: approximately nine and one-half pounds, eight-cartridge clip, 300-yard range. The carbine is a semiautomatic, rapid-firing .30 caliber weapon of the officer corps: less than four pounds, fifteen-cartridge magazine, 150-yard range. Division headquarters personnel received the smaller carbine for close-in fighting should the infantry units be overrun.

5. Manual of arms is the set of drill movements one goes through when handling the rifle: right-shoulder arms, present arms, and so forth.

6. Close order drill is shoulder-to-shoulder; extended drill permits more spacing between soldiers.

Detroit. March 20, 1944
Edward J. Jeffries Jr. to John M. Carlisle

Dear Jack:

I received your two letters. I enjoyed both.

Incidentally, how did you get those excerpts on municipal problems? Is that a service or are those just handouts that you get around Washington. It seems to me that if we got all those things here and somebody read them, it would give us a pretty fair idea of what is going on around the country in relation to municipalities. . . .

Slutz, [Glenn] Richards, [Lloyd B.] Reid and Jeffries are all planning to descend upon Washington next Sunday.[1] I am to testify before the House Committee on roads in relation to Federal help for urban roads. These plans are as yet tentative and might be cancelled, but I don't think so. We would be glad to discuss with you "the state of the nation."

You will remember my talking to you about the Wyoming–Eight Mile Road problem. We went to the Council last week and Bill Rogell suggested that there be temporary Negro housing. Edgecomb and Jeffries almost fell off their chairs, but because of our sophistication and our practice in dealing with shocks, we maintained a semblance of equilibrium, and this morning . . . Edgecomb recommended to the Council that this project be built according to a model and plan drawn by the City Plan Commission. Charlie in his own inimitable way put in the plan submitted to the Council that it was at the recommendation of Councilman [William G.] Rogell.[2]

I swallowed hard a couple of times and finally shrugged my shoulders and let Charlie do it. I still hate myself for it a little, but he asked for it. I presume that if you ask long enough and often enough, you no doubt get what you are asking for.

Mr. Cobo is mad at me for good this time, he says, because I, in an unguarded moment, suggested that it was hokum that his [city treasurer's] office had to close on a legal holiday when all the rest of the city was open. He has taken the position that that was the last straw, and he is telling everybody who will listen how much better he could . . . [run the city] if he were given the opportunity.

I am bowling in what I like to think is a mid-season slump. . . .
That's all the news that is new which presently occurs to me, at least.
I will no doubt see you next week.
Good Luck, and say hello to Peg.

Sincerely,   JEFF

NOTES

1. Richards, DPW; Reid, successor to Grant Mickel as city traffic engineer.
2. Rogell, former Detroit Tiger infielder and conservative Catholic who had opposed assigning the Sojourner Truth Homes to black defense workers, now took the lead in having Common Council request that the State Land Office Board withhold from private sale 842 lots in northwest Detroit. In short, he advanced plans for a federal housing project for black defense workers as requested by the City Plan Commission (CPC) and its supporters. He did so doubtless in part because the area was "long recognized as a Negro community" (whereas the Sojourner Truth Homes had been located in a mixed neighborhood of middle-class blacks and Polish Catholics) and in part because the commission feared that uncontrolled building of low-cost individual homes might create a "new slum." Although perhaps duped by Edgecomb of the Detroit Housing Commission, Jeffries played a greater role than this letter implies. Earlier, in response to the CPC's original appeal, he had met with Edgecomb, CPC secretary George F. Emery, and chairman William J. Norton of the Mayor's Interracial Committee, and then called the public hearing. Indeed, two days after writing to Carlisle, he approved the council's action. See Jeffries to Edwards, 8 March 1944; *News*, 8 March 1944, 21; 11 March 1944, 13; and 24 March 1944, 12.

Camp Wheeler, Georgia. 21 March 1944
George C. Edwards to Assorted Friends

Standard Operational Letter II

Subject: From 1A to GI (with a delay enroute in G1).

1. You may be interested to know that Private Edwards has already been through the "graduation exercises" which wind up the 17 weeks training cycle. What? Precocious or Premature? Well. . . .
I have now been through the 1st, 2nd, 3rd, 8th, 9th, and 17th weeks of the training cycle, and am about to start back to fill in the gaps. You can imagine that my delight is unbounded.
You remember the story about for want of a nail the shoe was lost, etc. Well it seems that I like to play football. . . .
2. The origin of the strict requirement that all trainees must participate in all training sessions is said to be something as follows:
Scene: advance post under heavy machine gun fire. Officer: "Private Doakes, you and Private Blow take this Bazooka and go out there and get that damn machine gun." Private Doakes: "But sir, I don't know how to

fire a Bazooka." Officer: ". . . didn't they give you work on blankety blank Bazooka at that blankety blank training camp?" Pvt. D: "Oh yes sir but I was on K.P. that day. . . ?"

3. High point of the graduation exercises: Colonel: "And I know at times you men have hated the guts of every non-com and officer in this outfit." (Cheers) "But that's what we're fighting this war for—so that you won't have Corporals & Captains & Colonels telling you what to do all the rest of your lives." (Cheers, wild applause . . . and an "Amen Brother" from me.)

4. S.O.L. I left off with Pvt. E[dwards] . . . hospitalized with a broken hand (oh yes—the football game). I had all but become reconciled to the idea of spending the war with my right arm in a plaster cast. All of a sudden at inspection . . . (where all of us fracture cases stand at attention and a Colonel strides past saying to each man . . . "How do you feel?" . . .) said Colonel . . . called back to the Ward Corporal, "Take that thing off his hand—He goes to G1." Shortly thereafter I was gingerly picking my fingers apart and discovering my wrist still worked.

5. G1 (Not G.I.) is the exercise ward where surgical and fracture cases are "rehabilitated." I have been rehabilitated. I spent the week in G1 on work details shovelling dirt, swinging a pick axe (work reasonably related to . . . building an athletic field) and gold-bricking (work reasonably related to my enjoyment of fresh air and warm spring sunshine).

6. One afternoon . . . [e]ight of us were sent out on a truck to dig some sod for the athletic field. . . . it was a beautiful afternoon—*we got completely out of the camp* (my second time since arriving here)—we worked very little. . . .

Digging sod at the same place were a group of Italian prisoners of war. They were all young—like the German prisoners we see but unlike them they were smiling, friendly and as garrulous as the circumstances permitted. There were at least 15 of them guarded by one very casual M.P. whose carbine was unloaded.

In spite of orders . . . we and the Italians promptly [endeavored] . . . to establish some contact. One of the Italians spoke a little English. The M.P. and our truck driver spoke a very little Italian. The rest of us got along by some words and violent use of the hands. We learned. . . .

They had been captured in Tunisia. They liked the United States. They "needed for nothing" at the prison camp—except girls (we explained: us too). They were happy. They considered Italy as out of the war. Some wanted to stay here after the war.

The most interesting of the lot was a Sergeant who had learned a little English. He . . . was apparently pretty wealthy as the owner of vineyards and a winery at Brindisi (on the heel of the Italian boot—now occupied by the 8th Army). He showed us pictures of his girl (quite lovely), his family and his home which fronted [the Adriatic Sea] on Brindisi harbor. He was a Sergeant in the Italian tank corps—captured at Gafsa [Tunisia] by [Gen. George S.] Patton's Army.[1] His comments included "the Germans are very stubborn. They will not quit for a long time." "The fighting was very bad. I was very lucky." "I am ashamed for my country. We are a defeated nation." All in all I figured that he had not done too badly under fascism and might have more regrets for [Benito] Mussolini than he cared to tell us. . . . But he was a personable and likeable fellow.

These men who were engaged in such friendly palaver had shortly before been killing and being killed by Americans like us. Such is life—my first experience of fraternizing with the enemy. . . .

Early in the afternoon I tried whistling a few bars of *Bandiera Rosa* which was the song of the Italian labor movement before Mussolini.

It brought an immediate, voluble and, to me, totally incomprehensible response.

But all afternoon one of the prisoners kept coming around and saying to me knowingly, "Padre Italiano [Italian father]?" I would say, "Non." Undisturbed he would say "Madre Italiano [Italian mother]?" My denials failed to register on him.

7. Post Hospital Letter with qualified apologies to Macon for S.O.L. I.

This is really the first undisturbed moment I have had since Sunday. I am seated peacefully in the PX [Post Exchange] garden with a glass of G.I. (i.e., 3.2) beer in front of me. It is a beautiful evening. . . . So I herewith give an account of myself.

Saturday I walked into Co. D orderly room and the Supply Sgt. said, "just back from the hospital—fine, come clean rifles"—so I did until noon. In the afternoon I went out with the company but I ducked inspection. Saturday night I . . . [hastened] to Macon for my second visit to that lovely city—met another G.I. at the Dempsey [hotel]; we had a bottle of real beer—my first since January 1. Then we ate at the Dempsey Coffee Shop. Then away for a big evening of drinking & helling around. First we learn *there is no whiskey of any variety in Macon at any price.*

We end up the evening at the Dempsey tavern with a bottle of Sparkling Burgundy. But all things considered, it was a good evening. Free air—not a single order—stripes and bars looked insignificant, and you could go where you pleased or go nowhere when you pleased. We pleased.

Sunday I went back to Macon. . . . Breakfast at the Dempsey, a show, dinner and back to camp early. I had just decided . . . that I couldn't afford Macon on my salary when a new character in the first Platoon invites me to join a poker game and then since I look like a lamb suggests raising the limit. I argued a little about this but not too much and then the boys donated me my week end expenses and those for next weekend. Tell me a college education doesn't pay.

Comes Monday and back to work with a vengeance. A.M. brings 2 hours of class work and 2 hours of bayonet drill. . . . P.M. brings four hours of light machine gun instruction and then a march back to camp about a mile and a half with packs and a light (31 lbs) machine gun.

Monday was a picnic. Comes Tuesday. We turn out early with full field packs, rifles, belts & bayonets for a march to a bivouac area 6 miles away.

The trip out I actually enjoyed. We marched . . . past a small lake and through very lovely Georgia pine woods and hills with the sun just coming up. We marched into the bivouac at about 10:30, pitched tents, posted guards, had a practice air raid alert, struck tents and assembled for chow in the field. The cooks brought a meal from our mess kitchen. . . . Anything would have tasted good Tuesday, but this would have tasted good any day. We ate most heartily, sat down for ten minutes and Holy smoke here we go again.

The march back was something close to agony. It was hot. It was dusty. We were tired. Our feet were sore. And the C.O. made us hit a pace up hill and down that was pretty close to murder. A few fell out—the rest just sweated and muttered and suffered.

Eventually we arrived in camp. Good Lord it was only 3 P.M. and we had two more hours of work. We were given 25 minutes to rest and then turned out for an hour of physical training and an hour of practice parade.

The day finally ended with the announcement that the company would have a beer party . . . at 8 P.M. "What, tonight?" wept everybody—"When we can't even stand up?". . . .

Anti climax dept. The party was held—everyone was there, everyone had a good time and they had to chase 'em out to bed. I'll hate to leave this outfit which I will have to do as soon as the red tape department gets my transfer made out.

8. Some of my friends comment on the fact that Army letters rarely refer to other G.I.s and . . . suggest that maybe they all look alike under Army regimentation. In my experience t'aint so. There are more character studies here than I ever saw . . . and you get to know each man quicker. Something about adversity bringing out the traits in a man.

But letters don't speak of the other men because no one at home knows 'em and it would take some time to describe them enough to make 'em real.

One of the men in our platoon was a pretty successful Chicago real estate man, 35 years old and already plump. His Corporal was a rosy-cheeked stripling of 19—fresh out of high school. The constantly re-arriving drama was . . . Corporal Berry . . . [indignantly] demanding, "Beeman, didn't I tell you to scrub this floor? Well, what sort of a job do you call that? Get down there and really G.I. it." Beeman meekly lowers his bulk to his knees and complies.

But the loveliest situation in the company was provided by the adventures of (let's say) Pvt. Gorman and Platoon Sergeant "Spindleshafts." Sergeant Spindleshafts came to the Army from . . . Rutgers [University]. Here his experience lecturing, instructing, wheedling and coaxing the youth . . . had given him a definite view on the desirability of discipline. Unfortunately this view ran into difficulties with irate parents and the Dean's office.

But this was the Army. . . . Pvt. Gorman was the very prototype of those Rutgers freshmen—at least we came to imagine so from the attention

Sergeant S lavished on him. Not that Pvt. G wasn't a character in his own right. He was 19, a sophomore in college, the beloved son of a fairly wealthy parents, smart as hell but accustomed to his own way. . . . Sergeant Spindleshafts must have spotted Gorman as he walked in the barracks. At any rate Pvt. G was the first man in the company to get K.P. for extra duty and he stayed on it almost without interruption.

The typical scene was: Pvt. G returns to barracks from a shower preparing for an evening of freedom and whistling to advertise the fact. Sgt. S: "Gorman you're out of uniform; where's your belt?" Pvt. G: "Must have left the darn thing in the latrine–oh well, my pants stay up without it."

Sqt S: "But in the Army Gorman we wear belts whether our pants stay up or not."

Pvt. G: "Oh you and your Goddamn Army."

The last thing I recall of Co. D of the 15th was Pvt. Gorman staggering out of the kitchen with a load of ashes–black with soot from cleaning the stoves.

9. My new outfit is Co. D of the 12th Battalion. I am in the First Platoon–better known here as *the SNAFU Platoon*. (I follow *Life's* translation for want of a more printable one: "Situation Normal–All Fouled Up.")

My old Platoon was filled with the entirely laudable ambition to be "the best damned platoon in the infantry" and . . . [platoon members] would tell you about it to *Hinky Dinky Parley Vous* on the slightest provocation.

My new platoon is at least equally proud of being the worst. (They assure you privately that they are really darn fine combat troops and if practice makes perfect they may have something there.)

They hold (or claim) the all time Camp Wheeler record for AWOLs.

They have been consistently last in drills and competitions.

They are the despair of their non-coms whom they rib unmercifully and obey only occasionally.

I walked into the barracks on a night when the 1st Platoon was on Guard duty. Three steps behind me storms in the Officer of the Guard and abruptly assembles the guard. As I slid inconspicuously out the back door I could hear his voice booming, "That was the worst . . . job of guard mount I have ever seen. After 16 weeks you men don't drill any better than a bunch of rookies."

The following night the Company was restricted to the Battalion area due to shipping orders and . . . the 1st Platoon was on alert. There was much grousing. . . . Later I couldn't understand the complaints. 50% of the Platoon missed bed check that night anyhow. It seems they had a date to conquer the Air Corps in Macon–and kept it.

Every nite that week there were men out of bounds and much horse-play after bed check from those who looked too long at the grapes of the vine. The horse play, the short sheeting (making up a G.I. bed so that the top sheet is tucked in at the top and folded back to make a collar—resulting in the sleepy G.I. being unable to get in further than halfway), the bed dumping, all seemed amusing enough to me until . . . second floor beer drinkers decided the latrine was too far away. When the flood started leaking through the ceiling, I thought that was really going a bit far. But the first floor victims of the rain of reprocessed beer took the situation with surprising good humor.

The officers and non-coms alike greeted the departure for P.O.E. (Port of Embarkation) of the Snafu Platoon with undisguised relief, and many oaths that the next cycle would be different. Oh me, the future doesn't seem bright.

10. There were fewer predictions of the doom of the Snafu Platoon after Sgt. Kelley (really Pvt.—the rating was an afterthought) got the Congressional Medal.[2] We gather that at Wheeler he was a bit of a Snafu too. Wheeler now of course is vigorously claiming him as their own and playing down the couple of AWOLs that got our hero kicked out of the paratroopers. The faint suspicion persists nonetheless that maybe spit & polish aren't absolutely essential to a combat soldier.

11. From an A.P.O. San Francisco island J.P. Simpson A.A.A. [Anti-Aircraft Artillery] 1st Lt. (God save the mark) and a former SMU [Southern Methodist University] colleague, contributes these three paragraphs:

"Welcome to this damned old boondoggling army. I'm glad you got in the infantry, since you seemed to want in the infantry; but I still feel the same way I always did about exercise, and wouldn't care for any myself.

"Get ready for a shock which will follow your emotional realization of what you already know intellectually . . . war ain't exciting—it's boring. During my little sojourn here I have done an average of three hours useful work per consisting mainly of insisting that people do petty administrative things right, when they would probably have done them right anyhow. . . . The rest of my time has been spent in diligently rationing out the things I can think of to do in an effort to spread them throughout the time to be occupied. I have walked miles to perform leisurely ablutions in mountain streams, helped dig a well with shovels, joined the Battalion Surgeon in building us a fine one-room house out of lumber tediously obtained from packing cases.

"I have formally invited my wife [Anna Beth] to prepare herself to be a missionary's wife and look me up a job with some non-Prohibitionist Church as a missionary to the south seas for after the war. It looks to me like a swell job. The missions outdo Hollywood in beauty and comfort. The natives are simple, childlike, friendly, willing workers. There is no more fertile land in the world than around here, and cultivation is easier than falling off a log. . . .

"It's fairy tale stuff to wander down a cool path and casually chop out a dozen ripe pineapples. It's more fun than for a kid to find an easter egg. They taste better than a malted milk. This is the promised land. I hope we clomp on to some of it and get the hell out of Europe. . . ."

Sounds like heaven to a Wheeler trainee. But then Homer [R.] Marson[3] claims S.O.L. I made Wheeler life sound like *the distillation of the essence of Pleasure.* Yes, he's the Tax Assessor.

12. Pvt. Edwards is spending all his idle moments . . . pacing the floor. The second Edwards offspring is due to arrive April 7th. The Army proves surprisingly uncooperative to us anxious fathers. They quote us the Navy saw about "the Father is essential to the laying of the Keel but not at all necessary to the launching of the ship." Then they assure us that an emergency furlough is granted immediately if mother or child are in "a critical condition"–what a comforting thought.

Fortunately at home all goes well, and I am in the ridiculous position of having to hope that I don't see wife or child until weeks after the event. Needless to say Peg is the real soldier in this family.

Best regards,   GEORGE

NOTES

1. On 7 April 1943 the U.S. First Army and the British Eighth Army joined at Gafsa to encircle German and Italian units in Tunisia, initiating the Axis surrender and the conclusion of the North African campaign in early May.

2. Cpl. Charles E. Kelly, a replacement infantryman with the Thirty-sixth Division of the Fifth Army, fought seventy days and killed forty Germans in Italy. On 13 and 14 September 1943 he engaged in repeated acts of heroism near Altavilla, for which he became the first from the Italian campaign to receive the nation's highest military honor. At twenty-three years of age, the 5'7" and 145-pound Pittsburgh native, who bore only scrapes and tiny cuts for his all his bravery, quickly became an unofficial "legend." See *New York Times,* 10 March 1944, 9; 12 March 1944, 20; and 14 March 1944, 5.

3. Member of the Detroit Board of Assessors.

                                     Camp Wheeler, Georgia. [early April 1944]
Dear Jeff: *George C. Edwards to Edward J. Jeffries Jr.*[1]

Thanks for your letter. I agree on the race track business–someone there must really be on the inside.

I was glad you won on the Grosse Pointe business[2] and the OCD. I wrote in [to City Council] to add my two cents worth–I gather too late on both counts.

You know, of course, of James McConnell Edwards' arrival on April 7. The Army up-to-date has failed to comprehend my desire to see the finished product.

Thanks for the Washington business. I've been up before the OCS Board here–no answers down yet.

Regards to the wife and to Miss Ford.

Sincerely,   GEORGE

NOTES

1. Handwritten on the back of the last page of Jeffries's copy of SOL II.
2. Following an initial setback, which drew Jeffries's ire, the Board of Supervisors permitted the reapportionment of Grosse Pointe communities into the legislative district of Wayne County. In essence, this redistricting gave Detroit another seat in the state legislature, but it required vote-changing by several Dearborn and Detroit officials (including some councilmen who also served as supervisors). See *News*, 22 March 1944, 22; 5 April 1944, 23.

Detroit. April 24, 1944

Dear Martin: *Edward J. Jeffries Jr. to Martin S. Hayden*

I am the last one to complain as a correspondent. However, I just mention in passing that you owe us a letter.

Life is humdrum—just more of the same old thing, only . . . the bickering that is always with us seems to be of a more bitter nature than usual. So far as I am able to dope out, only Carlisle, from his vantage point in Washington, seems to be charged with enthusiasm, primarily, I think, because he wants to get home. People are becoming so worried about their near and dear ones scattered all over hell's half acre, and they are working so hard that they don't have much time for other people's troubles except as they interfere with themselves. . . .

My work has lightened considerably. The only things that matter are the great, broad, human problems that I can't think of the answers to anyway. Therefore, all I am able to do is worry about them a little but not do much about them. Hand to hand contact with folks has lessened a lot.

The Great Slutz is circulating about as busy as ever, trying his hand at all kinds of new games of chance, all of which seem to work out badly whenever I see them in action. But he insists that is the exception rather than the rule. I am inclined to believe it because I can't understand how he could engage in these activities as frequently as he suggests with as poor results as I am able to witness. He came out to the house the other night and took Florence on, and even she pinned his ears unmercifully at gin rummy.

The political situation in Detroit is in the doldrums. The Democrats cannot find a candidate for governor. The Republicans, as you probably recall, dealt from off the bottom of the deck and gave a blow to the Democrats by providing in the last session of the Legislature that the presidential ballot would be separate from the State ballot. Therefore, the State ballot will not carry the name of Mr. Roosevelt, and it will be very difficult to find a Democrat who is willing to run without the great draw which the President's name has on the ballot.

The CIO took over en masse the Democratic Party at the State Democratic Convention. Judging from newspaper accounts the Democratic Party and the CIO, insofar as they relate to Michigan, are synonymous terms.

The Republicans appear locally to be riding the crest. I don't think Mr. Roosevelt or the Democrats will do well in Michigan.

The late [U.S.] Senator Prentiss M. Brown has a new job as Chairman of the Board of The Detroit Edison Company. He is the personal representative of Mr. [William G.] Woolfolk.[1] The Gas Company now owns and controls the Detroit Edison Company.

I talked to your Dad in Washington a couple of weeks ago. He was well and seemed to be in good spirits. Miss Ford talked to Betty the other day and she also was apparently all right.

Florence and Gary are well. Gary is having all the troubles that a healthy, vigorous youngster can enjoy. On the way home from Sunday School yesterday he was apparently enamored of the idea of climbing a fence. He did, and he tore his best and only trousers. He said nothing about it when he got home. To quote him, "I forgot to tell you, Mother, about the little tear in my trousers." I literally am not exaggerating when I say that it was a three-corner tear, six inches long in all directions. He was practically naked. In fact, if it hadn't been for his top coat the police probably would have picked him up as a wayward waif.

We read in the papers about the invasion about to come off. If you are in it, good luck. If you aren't, good luck to everybody who is.

Drop us a note and let us know how the world has been treating you.

Sincerely yours,   J E F F

NOTE

1. Prentiss, Democratic senator from Michigan, 1937-42; Woolfolk, president of Michigan Consolidated Gas Company.

Llanover Park, Monmouthshire, England. 18 May 1944
Martin S. Hayden to Edward J. Jeffries Jr.

My Dear Jeff:

I received a letter from you about ten days ago in which you file charges in re my delinquency as a correspondent. As Tommy McIntyre[1] would say but not advise, "I hereby cop a plea." I will try and do better next time and perhaps at that time will be able to let go with a little more information than a most rigid censorship now permits.

I today received a letter from Betty in which she enclosed the clipping on Bill Walker's[2] resignation. She also had some terse . . . remarks as to Bill's quotation on his prospective deferment which she compared with a previous statement as to his disinterest in such matters. I think Betty is probably getting a little touchy on the subject of deferments but it still does not seem . . . Bill was doing . . . a [good] job of public relations for himself. . . . I rather expect that you did not feel too badly about the resignation.

Betty also forwarded Blair Moody's piece on me.[3] While it somewhat over-emphasized my importance for the war effort it did set forth my future plans in more complete detail than the censor would let me do it. There will be considerable satisfaction in getting to put into use the things we have learned during the past couple of years but I would be just as satisfied if it were all over and I was on the way back to Detroit.

. . . This business of being in the army typifies a reversal of the old chestnut of from rags to riches. Our living standard declines as time goes on and we are now at the point of doing our own laundry. You should see the Great Hayden out in the latrine with a bar of G.I. soap, a de-capped lard can and a pile of "unmentionables." I know now what the copy writers meant when they spoke of "tattle tale grey." As far as I can see the sole result of my laundering effort is to diffuse the specific dirt spots into a sort of overall smudge.

At the time your letter arrived I was ensconced in the hospital recovering from medicine's most undignified and–from my experience–unpleasant operation.[4] After several days of acute discomfort I finally began to enjoy the hospital life but my colonel cut it short by conniving with the hospital commander for my early release. I am now completely recovered and can sit down without planning the maneuver in detail and in advance.

I find that sitting down to write a letter these days calls for real mental work. We can't describe what we are doing and what interests us the most, and the passing of each day results in our immediate job taking up more and more of our consciousness. The BBC news and the *Stars and Stripes* gives us sketchy accounts of what goes on back home but it is getting to the point where it all seems very distant and other-worldly. I was tickled the other day when the American Forces news broadcast carried a one sentence Detroit bulletin stating that 22 . . . persons were injured in a collision of a DSR bus and street car. Without really meaning that I enjoyed your discomfort I could not help grinning to myself at the picture of the *Free Press* descending in righteous indignation to ask his honor why his buses and street cars could not get along better.

Despite the lack of meat in this I hope you and Nancy will keep the mail coming. It is quite likely that our mail deliveries in the future will be spasmodic and I am going to be looking forward to a good haul each time they do come.

My best to Florence, Nancy, Gwynn [Davis] and Elsie [Mills], to Paul Krause and any of the journalistic profession which is left.

Regards,   MARTIN

NOTES

1. *News* reporter.
2. Detroit DPW commissioner.

Llanover Park, Monmouthshire, England. 23 May 1944
Dear George: *Martin S. Hayden to George C. Edwards*

Today I received your long and interesting report on Edwards The Dog Face. Realizing that it may already be too late, I am shoving this on the way in the hope that it will catch you before you start the torturous trail of APO numbers which only God and an Army postal clerk can unwind.

I unfortunately am at present in a situation where I can say virtually nothing about myself. Your address was right, "Captain" Hayden but I am hoping it will be wrong in about ten days as my promotion recommendation is in and I am spending most of my spare time trying to figure out how to look sufficiently dignified for field grade.

Peg may have forwarded to you a piece which Blair Moody wrote about the Great Hayden during his recent whirlwind tour of the ETO [European Theater of Operations]. It tells far more about our prospects than the censor would ever let me pass on and is on the whole very accurate outside of the implication that I am the God and brains of the outfit while the colonel just works here. I assure you that . . . he is much in evidence. And, incidentally, Brother Edwards let me disillusion you if you think advancement . . . will in any way relieve you from the troubles you presently have with corporals, sergeants and second lieutenants. In the army it always goes on. Let me point out the routine as it works up from the misdemeanors of say a Pvt Edwards who goes out with the brushes and mops but *does not* clean the latrine. The camp commander makes an inspection and finds the floor dirty.

The camp commander calls my colonel and because they are both colonels he, just kind of pally like suggests that the latrine is not what it should be. Then the colonel calls me. I can tell what is coming by his tone. It is "Martin" when he wants to play cribbage in the evenings; it is "Captain Hayden" when the latrines . . . smell.

"Now Captain Hayden," says he, "you are aware that it is my policy that this organization shall in every camp which it visits win itself a reputation for soldierliness and cleanliness. You are also . . . aware that as Executive Officer of this Battalion it is your duty to see that my policies are carried out. When Colonel Smell goes smelling around our latrines and finds that they smell that means that your manner of performance stinks. Pray get the latrines de-stunk."

Having already heard his lecture A-1 which begins, "In my 32 years in the Army I have learned one thing and that is that no subordinate gives excuses," I meekly say, "Yes, colonel" and act 2 of the drama begins when I call the Company Commander whose men are on detail.

. . . My speech is then the same as the speech of the colonel which was the piece de resistance of Act I. It gets a little rougher, however, as I usually end with a succulent reminder that there are "lots of other officers in this battalion who would like to be company commanders and who wouldn't let the latrines stink."

Act three finds the company commander talking to a Second Lieutenant and saying "Jesus, Lieutenant you have me jammed up again. If you can't get that platoon of yours to do its details for Christ sake start busting some non coms." It will be noted that in this scene there is no threat of reduction. Second lieutenants like privates, have little to lose.

Act IV finds the lieutenant and his platoon sergeant having a heart to heart talk. . . . Act five finds the Platoon Sergeant telling the corporal who was in charge of the Latrine Detail that chevrons can be taken off as quickly as they are put on.

Act V finds the corporal threatening to put Pvt Edwards down the G– d—d latrine if he doesn't get the G– D—d thing cleaned up. . . . That Act is climaxed when Pvt Edwards wearily returns to the latrine muttering, "Nuts to the whole damned war." . . .

But there are serious sides to this business too. I don't mean the prospects which Moody describes for our outfit—we think of those in terms of supply, equipment and training . . . and in other, more lonely terms after "lights out." . . . As you know we have colored troops and they present problems all of their own which make hair turn grey but keep life interesting.

While it is true that a certain percentage of our boys are turned inside out by their over-consciousness of the racial problem, most of them are good soldiers and I see red when I bump into some half baked headquarters officers with ideas on "shipping those niggers back home." If I may do a little boasting, this outfit at its last station consistently maintained a record for the lowest number of arrests by MP's of any outfit in the district and ours was the only Negro one. In eight months we have had only 13 men in the Battalion up before Special or General courts and that is amazing over here where they court martial at the drop of a hat and cast five year sentences about like rain on the roof. You mentioned AWOL's. If your outfit is headed this way advise the boys to lay low. In this theatre two days is good for six months and a second offense will probably bring a General [court martial].

On the whole the Negro soldier is well treated in this Theatre. Eisenhower is a bug on the no-discrimination question and has cracked down sufficiently so that all but a few of the most recalcitrant boys from the deep South know he means it. The bad problem, however, comes up when the colored and white soldier bump when they are at play. There being no girls of their own race, the colored soldiers of course go out with the local product. . . . Trouble starts when a Hill Billy . . . arrives on the scene. . . . The Negro soldier almost never starts trouble although he often contributes to keep it going by regarding any gesture [as] . . . a racial affront. As shown by our low record of arrests we have gotten our men pretty well educated and have had no racial "incidents" at all.

Betty wrote me of the safe arrival of the new and small [James McConnell] Edwards. It was too bad that you could not make the unveiling but I can only say . . . "Wait until you have been as far from your family for as long as I have." I think probably nothing contributes so much to home-sickness as the feeling that kids are growing up and you are not there to be in on it. Our one hope these days is that "first in" will also be followed by "first out and home." Whether such a formula exists is a constant subject for speculation.

We have . . . a captain and our only Negro officer, who is planning to seek a church in Detroit. . . . He has a very close friend, George Crockett, a Negro attorney who was just hired by the UAW in Detroit.[1] Chaplain [Edward G.] Carroll would be a distinct addition to our somewhat depleted Detroit Negro leadership. He is a Yale graduate, has studied in India and figuratively is as white as they make them. Fully aware of the Negro problem, he is intelligent enough not to let his belligerency be stirred by every slight. He seeks Negro rights but at the same time preaches to our men that all Negroes must develop what he calls "the capacity for self criticism." If we can get a little of that doctrine spread in Detroit and then harness down some of our industrialists and their "fellow liberals" in some labor organizations, we may get somewhere. I have told him all about you and our continuing good relations despite your distress at my being on the "wrong side" of the Guild fight.[2] He is prepared to like you and I have assured him that the army will not change you unless they make you a first sergeant. God, just imagine Edwards in a place where the boys of the movement would be organizing against him.

If this letter has at times become disconnected it is because it was interrupted by numerous phone calls and a brief transition into my roll [sic] as Summary Court. I trust it reaches you and that I will get an answer—not a mimeographed one.

Regards,   MARTIN

NOTES

1. Former attorney with the U.S. Department of Labor (1939-43) and the Fair Employment Practices Committee (1943-44); hired by the union to head its FEPC.

2. Hayden had opposed the effort by Detroit journalists to establish a guild, the equivalent of a union.

England. 29 May 1944
John J. McElhone to George C. and Peggy Edwards

In the spirit of some of my compatriots here, this could be called S.O.B. Story No. 1, but I won't infringe on George's copyright, and anyway, I don't feel that way at this particular moment. I wend my winsome way from war, around war, but never quite to it. They must be saving me for the big dance, after the game.

This is a sweltering English holiday. In most places I'm a nice tomato color, the result of that old English sport, "punting on the Thames," only it was the Avon, and a skiff. In addition, we cycled to the Avon and back, which was much too long in the sun, but it was well worth this "misery." The bike makes me a mechanized unit in this war. [William F.] Dufty[1] and I bought second-hand bicycles near Manchester . . . which definitely puts us in a privileged class. The last bus from town leaves at 9:30, you "queue up" an hour earlier in order to get on it. . . .

In this country one queues up for everything. (That's a carefully considered statement.) Most necessities are scarce, and these people are pathetically funny in the apologetic manner they use in explaining a shortage. Most of them are a little shabby, by some standards—theirs, at least—and they're both sensitive and apologetic about that. You've probably heard about English rationing. . . . People get 60 coupons a year for clothing. A dress or suit is from 15 to 30; shoes are 9; handkerchiefs 1 . . . and other items accordingly. I'm TOLD that many English girls no longer wear underclothes or nightclothes, because they prefer to use the coupons on more visible items. That, of course, depends on their occupations or hobbies, and the subtlety with which they pursue them. Food is quite a shock to the newcomer, but if these people have stood it for nearly five years I'll be damned if I get very excited about it for the time I'll be here. Besides, I had two glasses of milk yesterday, which makes this a week apart.

You won't be surprised to learn that I had seven days "disembarkation" leave, a nice orientation period. I spent two days in London seeing a couple of plays and Jennie Lee,[2] and the rest near Manchester with Liberator Dufty. He has some wonderful stories about the awful fate awaiting the peoples of the occupied countries when AMG [Allied Military Government] arrives, but I'll let him tell them. Suffice to say that the people who ran Liverpool during the blitz made most plain to Bill's visiting party that their principal function was not to get in the way of the civilian authorities. Bill's down near me now, and we're trying to get together again before he moves closer to the war and I, as usual, move farther away from it. He had been very ill, with pneumonia, but he's all right now.

In London, I had lunch with Jennie [Lee], including "gin 'n orange." About that time Aneurin [Bevan][3] was in the middle of a Labor Party crisis. He had jumped the coalition to vote against the strike-penalty law, which provides some drastic infringements of civil liberties. The real issue was "collaboration" of Labor Party leaders with the Tories [Conservatives], which Aneurin feels will extend . . . into the post-war period. It ended in an Irish draw, in favor of Aneurin, in terms of prestige. Another case of the rank and file being ahead of the leadership. As Jennie puts it, it's the old question of the lesser lights in comfortable jobs and the leaders in jobs that feed their egos without straining them. J. and A. think [Ernest] Bevin & Co. are afraid of the responsibility attached to leading a government. . . .

Jennie . . . [said] British popular feeling isn't what it was in 1940, that the people are tired, and that a tremendous groundswell of popular pressure will be necessary to avert the limited fascist state of collaborationists. That was quite a shock to me: I . . . had been hoping for great things of England after the war. Talks with English soldiers haven't entirely dissuaded me. She seems to feel that the real things will come from Europe, if a reactionary Russian policy is not too influential.[4] (America is the growing corporate state.) She speaks of the English common wealth party of [Sir] Richard Acland[5] in terms of Trotsky's definition of "social dust," crediting them with serving a useful purpose in 1940 and '41 when progressives of that type had no place else to go, lamenting that the labor party isn't progressive enough to absorb them, but minimizing their effectiveness, even their sincerity.

. . . You'll probably be in Georgia . . . when this reaches . . . [you, Peg], but send it on to George later. I'd like to get his S.O.L. experiences. The best to all.

JACK

(And what about your S.O.L. experiences?)

NOTES:

1. Dufty had been first publicity director, national CIO War Relief Committee, New York City, before his induction in May 1942; he had worked under and befriended Edwards in the UAW Welfare Department, Detroit, during the late 1930s.

2. Longtime socialist and Labour Party member from Scotland who served in Parliament in 1929. During the war she defied the "coupon" election arrangement made by Winston Churchill's coalition government to protect seats that became vacant for the party—Conservative, Labour, or Liberal—that previously held them. She ran for Parliament in the Conservative-held Bristol Central by-election of February 1943 but lost and was expelled from the Labour Party. See Paul Addison, "By-Elections of the Second World War," in *By-Elections in British Politics*, ed. Chris Cook and John Ramsden (London: Macmillan, 1973), 165, 183, 188, 373.

3. Welsh husband of Jennie Lee, known as Nye or Ni by those who knew him, entered Parliament in 1929. He became the major parliamentary spokesman for the left wing of the Labour Party during the war, constantly challenging Churchill's ministry. Beginning in April 1944 he openly criticized Minister of Labour Bevin, who sought to curb unauthorized mining strikes by penalizing their instigators with five years in prison, a £500 fine, or both. He broke ranks with Labour Party leaders and trade

union officials over what he considered a violation of both civil liberties and the best interest of working men. Unwilling to lose his socialist voice within the party or Parliament, however, he ultimately agreed to the demand of Bevin supporters and pledged, in the future, to "abide by Standing Orders of the Parliamentary Labour Party." See Jennie Lee, *My Life with Nye* (London: Jonathan Cape, 1980), 102, 116; Michael Foot, *Aneurin Bevan: A Biography*, vol. 1, *1897-1945* (New York: Atheneum, 1963), 15-19, 96, 185, 250-56, 309-10, 440-63.

4. Like many, Lee misread the mood of British voters, whose wartime sacrifice and experience with central planning gave impetus for reform in the postwar era. Both her by-election effort and Bevan's opposition to the strike-penalty law indicated a leftward swing within the Labour Party and electorate generally, which culminated in the defeat of Churchill and his Conservative Party in the election of 5 July 1945. McElhone proved more accurate in his assessment, though it was a welfare state—as compared to a socialist society—that emerged after 1945. See Stephen Brooke, *Labour's War: The Labour Party during the Second World War* (Oxford: Clarendon Press, 1992), 1-11, 57-103.

5. Liberal Party MP from Barnstaple, founded the Common Wealth Party on June 26, 1942, combining Christianity and socialism to convert the war into a moral crusade whose victory would require the abandonment of private property. Acland attracted members from the suburban middle class, particularly professionals and idealists, with the view of transforming an antiquated, corrupt, machine-oriented Labour Party. He provided significant financing for the Common Wealth Party, which boasted 12,049 members in the fall of 1944, when his bid to affiliate it with the Labour Party was rejected. Only one [of twenty-three] Common Wealth candidates won election to Parliament in 1945, and Acland ultimately joined the Labour Party. See Addison, "By-Elections," 179-82.

New Guinea, South Pacific. 31 May 1944
James P. Simpson to George C. Edwards

Dear George:

I've been to Milne Bay and all over and around the peninsula to the North and East of it, and I've been to and up and down the coast a bit along there. I'm now somewhere else in New Guinea, in one of the loveliest places I've seen, encamped in a coconut grove beside a fine beach of sand whose grains are mostly black. It's cool and beautiful. That is by day. It's hell at night though. Japs are out at night. We've found a use for our AA [Army Artillery] shoulder patches. In the mornings the boys go out and stick them on the dead Japs around the gun position, thus staking out their claims. . . . While our AA patches hold out, we'll keep it up. Which is not to say that we do not love the infantry, for we do. We're getting our infantry training the hard way.

George, it's true about these damned Japs. They really don't seem to care whether they die . . . as long as they die trying to achieve their objective. They are cunning like wild beasts—dead they look like wax figures of fierce beasts killed in an attack and not like humans at all—and they are the personification of the offensive spirit. They're reasonably easy pickings for well trained infantry but they sure as hell keep on coming. And they don't pick on infantry much.

This is my night on duty in the CP [Command Post] behind a battery of telephones, and not much is doing. The last two have been tough. I just figured out that I've had my shoes off 4 hours out of the last 65. Our baths consist of swims in the surf, and it's been 2 days since I had one of those.

Before you come or go overseas, get some kind of case—preferably fine-weave canvas—for your rifle, to keep the grit out of it. It will come in handy. I'm using silk from a Jap parachute. And start collecting cigarette lighters. Matches are always wet, and so is the abrasive surface.

There is very little that I can say about my experiences. For more information, consult your local newspaper. I'd like to keep hearing from you, however, and I want you to know that, as an infantryman, you'll be mighty damned popular in a combat zone. Everybody here loves them and respects them. The airmen are not the fair haired boys they once were.

I'd better start unsticking an envelope and get thru with this before [Gen. Hideki] Tojo makes me jump into a hole.[1]

Write by V-mail. That's the only mail we've received so far at this place.

JPS

NOTE

1. Prime minister of Japan, 18 Oct. 1941 to 18 July 1944.

Botwood, Newfoundland. 6 June 1944
Dear Jeff: John M. Carlisle to Edward J. Jeffries Jr.

Left New York by Pan American Clipper Saturday afternoon and have been stuck here for two days—first engine trouble; then, bad weather. It is very monotonous. This is the dullest, most desolate place in the world. If some of those CIO agitators in Detroit could spend two days here, they would be better satisfied with conditions in Detroit. I am wearing among other things woolen socks, woolen underwear, a woolen shirt, a heavy trench coat—and freezing to death. But this is some war. A lookout on a high bluff overlooking the [camp] sits beside a Bofor gun[1]—in a swivel chair. I am hearing about the invasion from the radio.[2] I played poker last night with some R.A.F. and American flyers, till 3 A.M. You know what happened, being an old card player yourself—they got me. Good luck.

Your best World War Correspondent,   JACK

NOTES

1. A 40mm automatic, rapid-firing antiaircraft fieldpiece.
2. Assigned by the *News* to cover the war in Europe, Carlisle found himself enroute just as the Allied Expeditionary Force was landing in Normandy.

Like our erstwhile confrere, Pvt. George Edwards, I have no time to write letters to the handful of Detroiters who might be interested in what happened to Schachern, so I have resorted to the mimeograph machine.

One advantage to this procedure is that you will be able to read it. My penmanship is usually quite illegible.

My wife [Florence], in her most recent letter, asked me if I really like it here. Like all but a handful of the members of the Armed Services, I would a damned sight rather be home, but as long as I am in, this would be my first choice in all the Armed Services.

The set-up is this: Things got a little fouled up in the opening offensives in the South Pacific. The fliers were too busy to run the Marine Air Force. All they had time . . . for was flying planes and fighting the enemy. Secondly, the Air Ground Force officers . . . [in] the ranks hadn't the proper background for administrative and technical work. So the Marine Corps, for the first time in its history, decided to open up its commissioned ranks to civilians. The order went out . . . for 550 trained specialists in certain designated fields. These were to be trained in eight classes of from 60 to 70 men. For example: 2,400 men passed the physical exam for the class I am in, the sixth. Of those 2,400, 450 were approved by the local procurement districts, passed the mental qualifications and were recommended to Washington. Washington cut the 450 down to 70, the actual size of this class, and if you don't think this is a fast league, you're crazy.

Five men got off the train at Quantico with me. After we got acquainted, I asked each one what he had done in civilian life. One was an Aircraft Engineer from Lockheed, one a Mathematics Professor, and one an instructor in Meteorology and Celestial Navigation, one the Production Manager for Stromberg-Carlson, and the fifth, an F.B.I. agent.

Some of my other classmates are Winston Guest, the International socialite polo player, and nephew of Winston Churchill; George Putnam of "Putnam Edits the News," NBC and Paramount News; Marty Glickman, All-American from Syracuse and more recently a N.Y. Sportscaster; Alex Raymond, creator of Flash Gordon and Jungle Jim; Ray Heatherton, singer and orchestra leader, and many others not so famous, but all topnotchers.

We have construction engineers who will build hangars and barracks; mechanical engineers and aviation engineers who will oversee the maintenance of planes and motors and guns; radio announcers who will be fighter directors; newspapermen who will become combat intelligence, or liaison officers; eight FBI men who will go into Intelligence; caterers and restaurant managers who will be mess officers, and radio engineers who will be in communications.

That only covers half the field. We even have an engineer whose specialty has been draining and grading swamp land. It's easy to see what he'll be doing for the Marine Corps: just two jumps behind the assault troops with those steam shovels and bulldozers.

The thing that is the toughest to take is the terrific physical beating along with the mental cramming.

They will drill you on the dusty parade ground for hours. You will be covered with grime and sweat. Naturally, you would think they would give you 15 minutes to clean up for class, but no, they march you, hot . . . dirty . . . wet and tired into a classroom and throw hours of map reading or tactical orientation at you.

By then it is 17:45 (5:45 to you civilians), and time for chow. You have to dress for that. After chow and a few minutes at the radio, back to class we go. But do we go back in our nice clean uniforms? Not by a damned sight! You crawl back into those dirty . . . wet . . . smelly field uniforms and, brother, 70 of those in a packed classroom is something out of this world!!!

That is typical of the procedure which makes it hard for the civilian to adapt himself to Military Life, especially Marine Corps life.

. . . Marine Corps training is a calculated attempt to break every ounce of individuality and morale you ever had. If they succeed, you fail, and they want no part of you. On top of it, they throw that "Marine esprit de corps" at you all the time, . . . that you are a member of the greatest fighting machine in the history of the world, and that no enemy or task can possibly be too tough for you.

That is why [when] a Marine officer points to a Jap position and says, "Go," everybody goes. The Marine is so used to being told to do the damnedest things, so puffed with pride in the Corps and so convinced he's a . . . cinch to fix the enemy's kite, that it never occurs to him to hesitate.

Richard Tregaskis recently wrote that after watching the Afrika Korps and [Gen. Bernard L.] Montgomery's Eighth Army, he was still convinced the American Marine is the best fighting man in the world because his morale is higher.[1] I think his morale is higher because he has stood the acid test of morale wrecking and come out so damned proud of himself and the officers who command him, that he'd start for Tokyo in a rowboat.

One of the basic elements of Marine Corps training, as in the Army, is close order drill, but the Marines start where the Army leaves off. The average Army G.I. gets a maximum of 13 weeks basic training which includes a few hours of . . . drill.

The Marine recruit does it 7½ hours a day for 16 weeks. Marine "bigwigs" claim this not only gets them into better physical condition, but also gives them better coordination and quicker response. Of course, the marine Boot has to master all his technical training in addition to this 7½ hours a day of close order drill. He's usually a pretty tough and tired cookie by the time he gets out of Boot Camp.

This Marine is still not quite convinced he is a capable member of the toughest fighting unit in the world. He is at the stage of wondering when his blisters will start turning to callouses, and when the stiffness is going to start leaving his legs. "Esprit de corps" still seems a fair distance away.

Our daily schedule . . . : Up at 5:30, 20 minutes of exercise with a rifle, back up to the third deck (by ladder, not stairway) to make our sacks (Marine for bunks), police the barracks, swab the deck, dust the window sills, and lockers, stow everything in sight and be ready for breakfast at 6:30.

After breakfast we have a short blow and then alternate periods of drill and classes until . . . noon chow. The afternoon is the same until 6 o'clock chow, and then more classes until 9:00 P.M. Lights go out at 10, so you see we have a whole hour to study notes . . . from about six to ten classes, clean our M1 rifles, write letters and get our gear in shape for the following day. Inevitably, you just get your rifle dismantled (field stripped) when the O.D. [Officer of the Day] . . . turn[s] the lights out a few minutes early, so you tote all the pieces up to the "Head" (Marine for Latrine), and re-assemble them there. Not being much of a mechanic, I'm not yet sufficiently adept to do it in the dark. Everybody has to be in his sack by 11, and brother, you need no coaxing. . . .

But your day isn't quite done yet. At least two or three nights a week you have to stand a watch. Last night I had the 2 to 4 watch here in the barracks. Tonight I have the 2 to 4 at an abandoned building up on the hill. Do they still shoot you for going to sleep at your post in wartime? Tomorrow . . . I get my first chance to drill the platoon. That is one of the most important things in the course, your command presence. All day . . . I have been giving silent commands to myself to guard against giving "to the rear on the left foot, or, by the left flank on the right." To the by now well-know "SNAFU," the Marines have added another, "FUBAR," meaning "fouled up beyond all recognition." I fear the second platoon will be "FUBAR" tomorrow. . . .

Here is another example of how the Marine regards himself. Our C.O. gave us a talk almost the first day . . . : "If you get up to Washington and are doubtful about whom to salute, here is what I would do. Start with Army Colonels and Navy Commanders. Not Lieutenant Colonels or Lieutenant Commanders, but chicken Colonels and three stripers. You may salute them for, after all, they are about equal to you Marine Lieutenants in rank, and in deference to their age, you may initiate the salute. But make damned sure they are fighting officers. Don't let me catch you saluting any of those swivel chair task force commanders from that Goddamn Navy Department!"

One thing that has seemed a little unreal to me the past week is . . . that the biggest news story in history got under way with the Invasion, and I don't even have time to read about it. When we do get five minutes to listen to the radio in the recreation room, the soap operas or baseball scores have taken over.

I did manage to get hold of the *New York Times* today, and read the lead story and a couple of commentators which brought me fairly up to date, but it was a long time coming. The home folks got a damned sight better and quicker coverage on the Battle of Gettysburg than I'm getting. Hell, I haven't seen "Terry and the Pirates"[2] since I've been here, and that was one of the bright spots of my civilian day.

There are two other newspapermen in my class. One is a swell boy named Bob Meeker, who was a reporter for the *N.Y. Times.* . . . The other is Captain L.W. Roberts, a reservist, whose family owns a string of papers in Kansas.

How Schachern ever got into the company he is in will always remain a mystery. Everybody here had a lot bigger job and made a lot more money in civilian life. I blushed when I wrote my qualifications and background for the Procurement Officer, but it seems to have worked. On top of that, the people who wrote my letters of recommendation, and those who were interviewed about me, must have told some whoppers.

With the exception of Leo LaJoie,[3] who has been through the Marine Corps mill, many of you, especially Private Edwards, will disagree with some of the things I have told you. . . .

As for you, Private Edwards, is that proposition about the Camp Wheeler Infantryman being able to lick any two Marines, still open? If so, I have a couple of pretty good boys line[d] up. One is a Solomons killer, with 37 notches in his carbine stock. When he shakes hands with you, he sizes you up in a very deliberate manner and you just know he's figuring out . . . just how many seconds it would take him to kill you with his bare hands. He took but a quick glance at me.

I, apparently, came under the classification "Job too small, refer to 1st Sergeant."

I'd just as soon spend the whole night telling you about the Marine Corps, but there just isn't time, as our instructors keep yelling, "We haven't time to talk about the Invasion. We have a hundred invasions of our own to make, before we get to Tokyo." . . . If you're a minute late for muster, you hold up 70 men for one minute, or 70 man minutes, and the Marine Corps can't afford 70 minutes. There isn't time, get going, on the double. . . ."

. . . one of the things we have learned . . . isn't restricted. The Marines . . . have discontinued their "Raider" battalions, and "Para-marines." "Why the hell should we maintain a Raider outfit when we can make every Marine a Raider, and why in hell should we train Air Borne Troops . . . when we can put any marine in a transport and land them or put parachutes on them and kick them out?" our C.O. said.

With that final bit of Marine lore, I will close, hoping to see you before I'm off to the wars in the fall.

Apprehensively yours,   HAROLD

P.S. I forgot. . . . One regulation forbids us to wear ties to chow. I don't know why. It's just a regulation and nobody ever knows the "why" about regulations.

Anyway, needing a beer between drill and chow the other evening and having about three minutes in which to get it, I dashed out the door, intending to catch one on the fly at the officer's bowling alley across the street, but I ran smack into a full Colonel, stern as rock and at least a veteran of the Spanish American War and Vera Cruz. "Lieutenant," he barked, "what do you mean appearing outdoors without a field scarf? Haven't you read Order No. 87306, USMCR [United States Marine Corps Reserve], MCS [Military Communications System], AGOS [Air Ground Operations System], dated 12 May, 44, States, covering this regulation? Do you not realize that the Landing Force Manual, Chapter 38, Section 12, paragraph 14 strictly forbids this? Are you aware . . . are you cognizant . . . etc., etc.?"

After fumbling my way out, I began to see the light. That wasn't a Marine veteran, it couldn't have been! But, how the devil did John Christian Lodge get in the Marines and get to be a Colonel so fast?

NOTES

1. Tregaskis, author of widely acclaimed *Guadalcanal Diary* (New York: Random House, 1955). Montgomery's Eighth Army victory at El Alamein, November 1-4, 1942, forced Gen. Erwin Rommel to retreat from Egypt.

2. A popular comic strip.

3. Detroit assistant corporation counsel.

Detroit. June 22, 1944

Edward J. Jeffries Jr. to John M. Carlisle

Dear Jack:

As you know, your articles are appearing in the paper daily. They have been good—in fact, excellent. However there has been a certain sameness to them. A little admixture would contribute to their interest.

Your friends have talked about you a lot. I must confess, good.

The timeliness or the untimeliness of your departure added zest to your adventure from our point of view. Here's hoping that you are getting into the places that you want to, and absorbing the news and information that will later be very interesting history.

. . . [I opposed FDR's reelection bid before the Executives' Club in Chicago] the Friday [June 9] after D-Day. It is astounding how much publicity it got in competition with D-Day. Most of the newspaper writers criticized me for participating in what they termed partisan politics. Your paper [*News*] became literally childish in an editorial. Brother [W.K.] Kelsey became so acrimonious that he overdid it. Even I could tell that the speech was more deserving than he insisted. To make a long story short, we stirred up a hornet's nest. The results and repercussions are still in the realm of the unknown.[1]

I have seen Peggy a couple of times. Florence and Peggy went to lunch yesterday. From all surface appearances Peggy is holding up all right. According to Florence's reports, Peggy has been sleeping with the horses, understands their every mood, finds the game [horse racing] very simple and profitable. If true, she has my profound respect.

Carl Muller wrote a piece about my speech and said that I was running Republican, that I sounded like a Republican, and that Dowling would now have to pay for the support he gave me last fall. It was a very good piece in Dowling's behalf. It certainly should rally his supporters. Karl Seiffert wrote a piece about a party which Steve Maher had arranged for tomorrow night. The theme of the piece was, who was host? Seiffert suggested that I was doing it as a peace offering. The sum and substance of it was that all newspapers printed a public endorsement of Brother Dowling by me. They don't know that there is anything sure about his nomination. He should be elected, but I don't know how much influence the CIO will have behind O'Brien and the Democratic Party.[2]

Take care of yourself and keep out of the path of robots.

Sincerely yours,   JEFF

NOTES

1. Never mentioning Roosevelt by name, Jeffries's speech lambasted him for having "broken the spirit of the American people" by usurping local and state rights through New Deal programs and war-related policies, and by denying the middle class its part in the governmental process. He also portrayed the president as posing a threat to free enterprise, raising the specter of federal competition with private industry in the production of consumer goods after the war. Yet though assertively opposing a fourth term for FDR and seeing the best hope for his defeat in a strong Republican Party candidate, Jeffries concluded by identifying with rank-and-file workers even as he criticized union leadership and its left-wing allies. Kelsey, for one, considered Jeffries's logic "pitiful," contending that the city's problems stemmed from its own inability either to borrow funds or to raise taxes rather than from federal programs or revenues (commercial and industrial), which certainly were raised to fund depression and war programs benefiting a society in crisis. The people "fighting and winning the greatest struggle ever fought upon this planet" did not seem broken-spirited or the middle class—however defined—liquidated. And it seemed to Kelsey a "leap" to imply that organized labor could "seize the Government" and a "boogie" to suggest that the president could replace democratic rule with divine kingship. Indeed, "under heavy strain" of late, Jeffries appeared more like "a Board of Commerce reactionary" than the mayor of a city with ample home rule powers. See *News*, 9 June 1944, 1; and Kelsey, "The Commentator," *News*, 13 June 1944, 14.

2. Dowling and O'Brien were campaigning for the Wayne County prosecutor candidacy in the Democratic primary election scheduled for July 11. Muller, a *News* reporter, wrote that before Jeffries's Chicago speech Dowling opponents thought that he "had a better than even chance" to beat O'Brien; none felt it was improved by the mayoral address. Seiffert noted that the party at the home of Maher, the deputy com-

missioner of buildings and safety engineering, was organized by mayoral secretary Robert M. Dalton, who, like Jeffries, denied any connection between it and the Chicago statement. In fact, the mayor claimed that the party had been planned long before he delivered the speech. See *News*, 14 June 1944, 7; 20 June 1944, 4.

Dear Martin:

Detroit. June 22, 1944
Edward J. Jeffries Jr. to Martin S. Hayden

It was good to hear from you, Martin. I have thought an awful lot about you in the last couple of weeks and worried some.

As I probably told you, I talked to Blair [Moody][1] after he talked to you, and he told me some of the things that you told him that he wasn't able to print.

I am convinced that it is impossible for us to appreciate here what the boys who were really in this invasion have gone through. In order, however, to do that, I have thought of the worst thing that I could imagine and hoped that it was something better than that. The best of luck to you.

Harold Schachern is in the Marine Aviation Corps as a Cadet Lieutenant. I have a letter on my desk pointing out how hard they are working. I think he has understated it, and I suspect that when we see him he will only be a shadow of his former self.

I gave a speech. . . . It was directed at the President's candidacy for the fourth term, and it barbed labor as it relates to its powerful organization and lack of any forces for checking or regulating the use of the tremendous power of organized labor. I was immediately branded a Republican. The fact of the matter is I have been branded everything since. It has gotten a very wide publication, and about the only result that I am sure of is that there is a tremendous bitterness on the part of those who are opposed to Mr. Roosevelt, and those who hope he will be re-elected. I suspect that the presidential campaign, when it really gets underway, will be the liveliest and possibly the nastiest certainly this generation has ever seen in this country.

As you know, of course, the State and County primary will be on July 11 this year so that you boys will have ample opportunity of voting wherever you are. Bill Dowling is running for reelection. He is actively opposed by Negroes and the CIO, and his opposition is Jerry O'Brien. He may have some difficulty in the primary. He doesn't seem to be worried, but I am a little. Perhaps he knows more about it.

Things have been a little quieter than usual here. All sorts of threats, of course, but nothing really materializes. The wage controls are working a little better, but I fear it is only temporary. I make no guesses for the future. I report only on the present and the late past.

D-Day quieted the city down considerably. How long this will continue—your guess is just as good as anybody else's.

The family is all well. The office is doing business as usual with everyone in attendance and . . . "in the pink." Mr. Lodge just walked in the office. He, even, looks good—aging a little but good. I will have to stop now and talk to him.

Keep your eyes open so you can duck. Best of luck!

Sincerely,   JEFF

NOTE

1. Moody while assigned to cover the European theater, had met with Hayden in London during the week of April 16-22 ("Diary of Martin S. Hayden," 80).

Detroit. June 29, 1944

Dear Harold: *Edward J. Jeffries Jr. to Harold J. Schachern*

We got your operational letter and certainly enjoyed it. . . .

I suspect that you are but a mere shadow of your former self, properly described as in the slim pink. Incidentally, I don't think any of us are taking on weight here these days as the thermometer has been well above 90.

With Carlisle in England and dog days upon us, the tempo of the beat here has slowed to almost a walk. Even the prevailing rate wage of the controller's office failed to start an incipient revolution. D-Day quieted . . . the area, and it is pleasant no matter how long it lasts.

Karl Seiffert who is sitting here . . . suggested that I tell you that things are so quiet . . . that the pigeons are no longer eating our vegetables in the victory garden on the City Hall lawn. His explanation is that the pigeons can't tell the difference between the weeds and the vegetables.

The campaign tempo is picking up. Apparently a merry race for prosecuting attorney on the Democratic ticket is in prospect. . . . At best it looks like a horse race. Many people seem to think that O'Brien has a better chance than Dowling. In my opinion Dowling is only doing fairly well, but I am not discouraged. July 11, as primary election day, will without doubt spring with surprise on thousands of Detroit voters. The past record would indicate that we always have a very large primary vote in [a] presidential election year. How the changed date will affect it, I don't think anyone, even an expert, can tell.[1]

Aside from this one contest, however, there is hardly a ripple on the surface. I have been doing what I could to get Dowling back in. Many of Mr. Dowling's enemies and mine have been using my obvious and ostensible help as a reason why Mr. Dowling should not be returned to office.

Keep us informed as to your progress. We all are very much interested in you. . . .

Good luck, and I suppose by now the callouses have turned into corns.

Sincerely yours,   JEFF

NOTE

1. The primary date was changed from September to July in order to print and distribute ballots to servicemen in time for the November general election. See *News*, 10 July 1944, 2.

[Solomon Islands, South Pacific.] 29 June 1944
Joseph P. Lash to George C. Edwards[1]

Dear George:

Your operational letter #2 was awaiting me on my return from New Zealand. I had ten days down there by virtue of having logged 100 flying hours. It was nice but no substitute for home and every appurtenance of civilization accentuated the pangs. However, I shan't burden you with my private woes. I stayed at a rest camp for enlisted men in the air corps. It was organized with surprisingly good taste—private rooms, crisp sheets, beds made up for you, steaks and fresh milk in abundance, a liberal liquor ration which you placed in the custodianship of the barman who produced it on request, and Red Cross hostesses, gals quite skillful at making one feel their concern for you personally and at the same time firmly warding off all aggressions!

I was quite fortunate running into several young New Zealanders active in politics and spent most of my time with them. The political situation in N.Z. is not as rosy as it looks from the outside. If elections were held now I don't think labour would come out with a majority again. Partly this is a result of the grievances that inevitably accumulate against a wartime administration. But it is more than that. Labour and conservatives are in a stage of attrition warfare and the majority of people feel that the outcome of the fights in Parliament won't affect them in any case. There is a general "agin" feeling. The younger people feel that the Labour Party has no interest in utilizing them and the party has no post-war program to enlist their enthusiasm. As a result there are a number of independent movements modelled on Acland's Commonwealth Party in England,[2] but I don't think they will amount to much. A couple of years ago Americans were very popular in N.Z. They aren't today and that is quite understandable if you think of the same change in attitude in American towns located near army camps. What is surprising is the resurgence of empire sentiment. I think this is a result of a feeling that small nations will have little influence in the post-war world unless they are part of a larger power combination such as the commonwealth.

I found it quite cold in New Zealand after 14 months in the islands and immediately came down with a cold. Then when I returned to the heat here the cold came back, but this time accompanied by a heat rash! But in all I am disgustingly healthy.

The war news is swell. I bet some fellow (he gave me 5 to 1) that both wars would be over by March 1945. My reasoning is that by Fall 1944 it will be clear to both Berlin and Tokyo that the alternatives are either surrender or national suicide. The Japanese may not be able to salvage any part of their conquests, but by surrendering before defeat they may stave off revolution at home. Such a development of course would in part depend on the conservatives reasserting their control over the fanatical military and they may not be able to do so. But it is with such speculations that I keep my spirits up.

You ask me how my impressions of APO San Francisco square with Simpson's. They don't. His description may be accurate so far as rear echelons are concerned but not the forward areas. Of course we have a great deal of time on our hands. Even if you pull an 8-hour shift there is still little to do in this theatre in the 8 hours one is not asleep. A great many factors affect the amount of work that is to be done. When we first arrived here and there was only jungle, we worked like dogs setting up our tents, getting our station operating, flying on weather reconnaissance trips. Now the forward area has moved again, and so there is less to do. This must be even more the case with line troops. As for finding these islands beautiful—well—the jungle does have a fierce, brilliant and lush kind of beauty, but it's hell to live in or near. The heat is more endurable than I would have anticipated because the ocean climate predominates, but the monotony of unchanging seasons, the torrid mid-day sun, the torrential rainfall make life pretty hard. I am not complaining just expressing my differences with Simpson. Some outfits, of course, are mainly paperwork outfits and Simpson's remarks may apply to them, although my personal experience is that the men who have to do the paper work are the most overworked in the service.

Congratulations on the arrival of your second son. I hope you get to see him before you are shipped. My best to Peg.

Cordially,   J O E

NOTES

1. At this time Lash was a technical sergeant with the U.S. Army, serving an eighteen-month tour as a weather forecaster in the South Pacific; his entire military tenure lasted from April 1942 to October 1945. In September 1933, when Edwards visited his sister Nicky in New York City before proceeding to Harvard University for graduate work, Lash was newspaper editor of the Student League for Industrial Democracy. They were introduced by socialist leader Norman Thomas, who knew Edwards's father. Edwards became college secretary of the student league after graduation, and the two "shared an apartment for some years" during the mid-1930s. See Joseph P. Lash, *Eleanor Roosevelt: A Friend's Memoir* (Garden City, N.Y.: Doubleday, 1964), 290; George Edwards, *Pioneer-at-Law: A Legacy in Pursuit of Justice* (New York: Norton, 1974), 138, 156; interview with GCE, Cincinnati, 8 April 1983.

2. See above, John J. McElhone to George and Peggy Edwards, 29 May 1944, n. 5.

Detroit. June 30, 1944
Edward J. Jeffries Jr. to George C. Edwards

Dear George:

It seems as though it were a long time between drinks. I don't have any very good excuse except that inevitable inertia which seems to overcome us all from time to time. But anyway, whether I have been writing or not, I have been thinking about you. I presume that you have felt no news was in the nature of good news.

Things are much quieter here both area-wise and government-wise. The Council passed the prevailing rate wages with much less bickering and name calling than usual.

The primary campaign is warming up a little, and a lively race between Jerry O'Brien and Dowling for Democratic nomination of Prosecutor is taking place. Dowling, in my opinion, is only doing fairly well. Many of his supporters are worrying intensely. I personally don't think it looks rosy by any means, but I am not discouraged.

I saw [Rollin M.] McConnell[1] the other day. I get periodic reports from him as to your health.

There is never a dull moment in the Housing Commission. The latest episode revolves about a soldier who came back AWOL and called unexpectedly on his wife [and her lover] and, in the orthodox manner, he up and shot them both. His aim apparently was only good at the man. I doubt if he has the marksmanship medal, but at least he is batting 500%. This incident followed shortly on the heels of the eviction of a war widow by accident as poor Charlie [Edgecomb] in his own inimitable way described the problems of the Housing Commission.

For the last seven or eight months the Police Department and our Inter-racial Committee[2] have been keeping graphs on racial tension in the community. Race incidents as they relate to 1. words, 2. blows, 3. missiles, 4. weapons, have been going down for the last 40 or 50 days. The graph as it relates to rumors has gone up so high that it has gone right off the paper. Actually these graphs are amazing. The weird stories that are circulating about the planned and programmed riots are more absurd than the term ridiculous defines, except that they are very serious. For the life of me I cannot understand how people can be so naive as to tell seriously some of the stories that I have had told to me.

[John] Ballenger, incidentally, is working out very well as a Police Commissioner. I think he has been especially good as his activities have related to the race question.

We are about to embark upon an overall survey of our transportation needs in the future. We are going to hire an outside consultant, engineers and experts. I have in mind three different types—highway engineers, sewer and subway experts, and transportation city planner. We hope that from this conglomeration we can get a first class plan for handling private and public mass transportation. We will see that you get a copy of the report. One is forthcoming.

Good luck to you. The heat of the day reminds me of Southern Georgia this year. We can possibly match thermometers with you.

With kind regards, I am

Sincerely,   J E F F

NOTES

1. Edwards's father-in-law.

2. Following the race riot of 1943, Jeffries appointed a peace committee of citizens that evolved–through councilmanic action–into the Mayor's Interracial Committee, which had eleven members, a director, an assistant director, a small staff, and a $15,000 budget. The first public agency of its kind nationally, the committee came into existence in January 1944 and launched a program to defuse racial conflict and promote harmonious race relations through combining research, action, and education. Hence the Community Barometer, a part of the research division (the graphs described by Jeffries), sought to record the pulse of racial hot spots and pass along rumors and complaints to the action division for reconciliation, while the education division advanced programs–conferences, lectures, workshops–to change racial attitudes. In 1953 the committee was replaced by the Commission on Community Relations, and Detroit entered another chapter in its racial history. See Tyrone Tillery, *The Conscience of a City: A Commemorative History of the Detroit Human Rights Commission and Department, 1943-1983* (Detroit: Wayne State Univ. Center for Urban Studies, 1983), 3-10.

Detroit. June 30, 1944

Dear George: *Gloster B. Current to George C. Edwards*

Pardon my delay in answering your letter. Detroit is still the hot spot of reaction, the home of the Fascist and the center of liberal activity.

Gerald L.K. Smith[1] was barred from use of the schools by the Board of Education on petition of the Jewish Community Council, the Left Wingers and a number of community groups. We were not a party to the mess because it was our opinion that barring . . . Smith from the use of the public schools, established a danger precedent which the school board might attempt to use on minority groups.

An announcement has been made relative to the opening of some of the units in Willow Run for Negro occupancy and the shifting of others to other sites. The Federal Housing Authority promised 2,398 units of housing for Negroes by the end of the year. This is about 17,000 short of the required number of units needed at the present time.

We have just completed a successful membership campaign and have attained 22,000 members. Contrary to some downtown opinion, Negro and white Republicans did not withdraw their support from the Association this year because of its militant stand in the election of last year.[2]

We sincerely miss you in the Common Council and now that . . . Jeffries has torn his pants on Republicanism, I am sure the people will see
the light and elect a new, young and liberal Mayor.[3]

P.S. I suppose by now you have recaptured your southern accent.

NOTES

1. Fundamentalist preacher, America First Committee founder, anti-Communist,
and anti-Semite, Smith had arrived in Detroit a year earlier and challenged the black-
liberal-labor coalition on every issue.

2. In the 1943 mayoral election the Detroit NAACP had mounted a full-blown (unsuccessful) effort to defeat Jeffries because of his handling of the housing situation,
police-community relations, and especially the riot. Still, it emerged as the largest
branch nationally.

3. Reference to local criticism of Jeffries's speech before the Executive Club of
Chicago on June 9, and to Edwards–"new, young, and liberal"–as potentially the next
mayor.

Normandy, France. 1 July 1944
My Dear Jeff: *Martin S. Hayden to Edward J. Jeffries Jr.*

It has been a long time between letters but for once I have a good
excuse. Put mildly, we have been a little busy since we hit the shore on
D plus not-very-much.[1] For a bit it was, as the British put it, "a good
show." When it was all over I was in command of a somewhat depleted
but otherwise calm Battalion. If I ever needed it, I got complete proof of
the fallacy of the theory that Negroes scare easier than other people. Our
men were scared a couple of times–me with them–but no more of them
evidenced it than did the white troops working beside us and when it
was over they bounced back to normal in the same amazing way as the
chosen race. Even after it happens to you, you cannot believe that, after
being so completely distorted for a while, your emotions and thoughts
could so quickly drop back into the groove where clean clothes, food and
letters from home are the chief thoughts.

To me the whole three and a half weeks has been a little satisfying. I
suppose like most other people I have often wondered what I would do if
someone was shooting at me. When it happened I discovered that you
couldn't do a hell of a lot about it. My suspicion that I might cut out and
start running for home didn't pan out but that isn't much of a testimony
as there wasn't any place to run to if you stopped to think. The few that
did not stop to think were the only ones who evidenced any cowardice.
They did so in more or less ostrich fashion by taking defensive tactics
which served no purpose but to make them ridiculous and strangely
enough nobody kidded them about it.

I became head man when my colonel [James Pierce] stepped on an anti-personnel mine while digging a fox hole. He lost a leg and the same explosion made casualties of our Bn [Battalion] Adjutant and our Sergeant Major. Besides the inconvenience of taking over a Hqts short two important key men it was a little rough on the emotions as the adjutant, the colonel and I had worked, eaten and slept together for the past nine months. I was lucky, however, in having a company commander who has 24 years of service, the latter part of it as a First Sergeant in the 2d Cavalry. He became executive officer and, despite his having served in this business exactly 12 times as long as I and our being the same rank at the time, he cracked the whip to demonstrate to the others that the new CO was boss. He has my eternal gratitude for I will admit I felt a little shaky the first morning. Since then you will note I have acquired a pair of gold leaves [lieutenant colonel insignia] and would be very swanky if I were not so dirty.

There have been a number of interesting anecdotes some of which you may have already gotten if you have seen Betty. I will repeat them, however, on the assumption that you have not talked much to her.

The field hospital that we took the colonel to the morning he got it was a fantastic place. The invasion was not yet 40 hours old but it was running full blast. There were of course no nurses, no electric lights and no such fineries as sheets or pillows. In the operating room three teams of surgeons were working on two tables while orderlies were either removing or preparing a patient on the third. The doctors had on rubber gloves and masks but that was their only concession to the usual surgical sanitation. They simply dropped sponges and dressings on the grass floor of the tent and, while orderlies bustled in and out picking them up, setting up apparatus, removing completed patients and carrying dead ones to a shockingly long line outside, the doctors were doing things to heads and stomachs which back at Harper [Hospital] would have called for a full house of spectators.

In the wards it seemed as though everyone was getting Plasma. That and sulpha drugs certainly rate with the jeep and the Bulldozer as the prime new instruments in this war. Again the wards were more or less of a constant bedlam and thereby I get at last to the point of this story. In one corner of the colonel's ward tent was a French woman and her ten month old baby girl. They had been hurrying away during the bombardment and picked up some shrapnel. The mother was pretty well banged up, the baby only slightly but no one knew where they belonged and this was the only place to take them. The doctors gave orders that the baby should not be allowed to add its cries to the general confusion and the orderlies met the situation by keeping a bottle of milk constantly on the fire. Every time the kid woke up they stuck a bottle in her mouth and she ate herself back to sleep. When I arrived, however, the ward men were in complete confusion. It had been discovered that the young lady had soiled her pants and something had to be done about it. They had her out of her basket on a cot and were trying to figure out how to fold some sort of a square surgical dressing into the prescribed diaper design.

A passing doctor, too busy to stop himself, spotted me and asked if I was married and a handy man with diapers. I said I was in the six-second league back in Detroit so I was assigned to do the job and teach the orderlies for the future. The mother who had watched the previous procedure with considerable exasperation at her inability to give instructions in English heartily approved the handiwork of "Monsieur le capitain" and the soldiers were overcome with admiration for my skill. When I stopped by the next day however they woke their charge up especially to turn her upside down and show me how well they were doing on their own hook.

Some days ago I met a very nice elderly French couple. They had their own story of "D" Day from the receiving end. The old man is a former Paris architect who retired some years ago to live with his wife on their country estate in Normandy. He said that the night the bombardment started they awoke but he told his wife, "We are very old; if we are to die tonight we will do it in bed, not in a hole in the fields." So they stayed where they were until morning when they heard voices outside speaking English.

"I put my head through the window where the glass had been and looked right into a very big gun," the old man said. "The man behind it said, 'Come the hell out of there!' I said, 'By Jove, yes I will come the hell right out.'"

They are of course enthusiastic about the liberation and show it by trying to hand as much as possible of their limited stock of food to every American soldier who stops by their door. In that respect they are however profiting by a little reciprocation in the form of American coffee, chocolate, sugar, jam, soap and canned meat the likes of which they had forgotten existed in the last four years. There were of course the usual stories of unbelievable heroism and luck here. One engineer private at a few minutes after "H" hour jumped into a tank which had been abandoned by a panicked crew and sailed on into a German pill box although he had never been in a tank before. Another engineer similarly commandeered a half track anti-aircraft vehicle with the purpose in mind of getting it out of a line of traffic. While he was driving it a heavy calibre German machine gun literally hem-stitched the cowling at the base of the windshield. The bullet holes were from side to side and not more than an inch apart but somehow not one hit the soldier. No one knows where they went any more than they know what happened to a bullet that went through one man's helmet, pierced the liner but did not touch his head and was not in the helmet when he took it off. Bearing out my previous comments on Negroes being about the same as everyone else, four of my men and their white platoon commander have been recommended for the Soldiers Medal for going back into the channel waters to rescue sixteen other members of their Platoon who were dumped into deep water when a landing rope broke while they were working their way ashore. Unfortunately three others they brought in were already dead.

One Seabee over here, and even Ripley won't believe this, drove a tent peg straight through the cover of a German Shu mine.[2] It broke the cover and bent the trigger wires but did not go off. But to show that the opposite kind of luck also pops up, a sergeant in our companion Port Battalion was killed, when a tree fell down on him while he was asleep. He had been successfully under fire and there was no wind or other reason for the tree which had stood for a good many years to fall down. It just decided to fall when he was under it.

With things now pretty well stabilized our life is getting routine. The men still live in fox holes under their pitched tents. Every time we have a casualty there is a lot of flying dirt the next morning as they dig a little deeper. A couple are going to need elevators before they are through. The Great Hayden, however, has acquired himself a canvas cot by the simple process of going down and picking one up from the litter on the Beach and moved into the headquarters tent. I might mention that it has a row of sand bags around it. That solved the bed problem but I lie awake nights dreaming of a bath tub—a great invention that.

Several days ago I ordered our band instruments broken out and every evening there is, first, a formal band concert which the men greet with restrained enthusiasm and then a jam session which would go on into the wee hours if I didn't go out and break it up. A Signal Corps outfit down the road has provided a loud speaker and a QM [Quartermaster] company turned up with a quintette of harmonizers that would turn Broadway on its ear. When it starts soldiers come out of holes for what seems like miles around and the MP's have a hell of a time with truck drivers who insist on stopping for a while to listen.

I will write again but meanwhile get out your own pen and hand. As I look at the length of this I should be able to coast for the rest of the summer. My best to Nancy and the boys and to Florence.

Regards,   MARTIN

NOTES

1. On D-Day, June 6, Hayden and his stevedore unit had watched from off shore; he reconnoitered Omaha beach on June 7 and set up battalion headquarters on June 8.

2. A small anti-personnel explosive.

Detroit. July 7, 1944
Dear Jack: *Edward J. Jeffries Jr. to John M. Carlisle*

We have been reading with interest your epistles from England. In a roundabout way, however, I heard that you are now in Normandy, and we are waiting with bated breath for what you can tell us about that.

Louis Colombo[1] and I have been giving much thought to your articles so that we can cable you as to whether we think they are extraordinarily good, fair, or not too good. I imagine that before you get this letter you will have had our cable. We are running a survey among our friends for their reaction, but for the purposes of this letter I have no report to make.

Bill Dowling is having a hectic struggle for renomination. I am sure that by now you know the majority of the CIO and the Negroes are all out to take his scalp. The weakness of his position, of course, is that the opposition has great strength in the Democratic Party. His chances look better day by day, but he is, by no stretch of the imagination, not a sure thing yet. The *Free Press* endorsed him with an editorial this morning. Whether it will do him any good or not remains to be seen. But won't do him any harm.

I am ashamed to admit that I haven't seen Peggy lately, but . . . Louis . . . reports that she is in good shape. I will look into the situation at home, however, and if there is anything that I feel needs reporting I will let you know.

We have set up a Transportation Board in the City for the purpose of hiring outside experts to make an overall transportation survey so that we can have the proper kind of equipment, highways, etc. . . .

Things have been relatively quiet here, especially since the weather has turned hot, and people are taking their vacations. My golf has been getting more attention, but unfortunately it has not been reacting very favorably to it. I am still on the wagon. My health is, relatively speaking, good.

The best of luck to you, and keep pitching.

Sincerely yours, JEFF

NOTE

1. Detroit lawyer and member of the Public Lighting Commission.

Detroit. July 7, 1944
Dear Martin: *Edward J. Jeffries Jr. to Martin S. Hayden*

I have done a lot of worrying and wondering about the part that you are playing in the invasion. I sure would like to hear what is happening.

Miriam Hewlett[1] has been in Detroit for the last week, staying with Grace [Cogan]. She is taking her examination again for overseas duty and hopes that this time she may be able to make the grade.... she has been stationed in Montana for almost a year now, and her stories are as broad as is space out there. She is the same old Miriam, very much liking her work, very much interested to get to more exciting places, and, in fact, as usual, impatient.

George Edwards was in the other day on furlough. In fact, he is still in this part of the country—in Lansing—taking the bar exam. He has had no preliminary training, unless boot training in Camp Wheeler got him in such good physical shape that he just plain mentally clicks. He looks swell.

The Democratic contest is getting even hotter than the weather. The primary is next Tuesday, and I think (discount it for wishful thinking) that Bill [Dowling] has a fair chance to succeed. It still is not a pushover, however.

I was interrupted while writing this letter by a Negro, by the name of [Louis] Taylor, who is running for the State Senate in the Fourth District. That is Arthur Wood's district. He is a Democrat.[2] Whether he is just mad at the party, or whether he knows what he is talking about, I do not know, but he would not be a bit surprised to see some Republicans elected in Detroit and Wayne County this year. I don't know whether that is true or not. I haven't made up my mind as to how strong the two parties are in this area. For sure the Republican Party margin here is much stronger than it ever has been. Whether it will get enough votes or not is still in the equation.

With the best of everything to you, my boy, I am

Sincerely yours,   JEFF

NOTES

1. A social worker and close friend of Jeffries and his sisters, Grace Cogan and Lola Hanavan.
2. Taylor drew third in the Democratic primary, in a field of seven led by realtor Daniel J. Ryan. Wood, a veteran of state government, having served one house and nine senate terms (including that of 1943-44), won the Republican primary against one other candidate, but he lost to Ryan in the countywide landslide for Roosevelt that November. See *News*, 13 July 1944, 1; 9 Nov. 1944, 10.

Quantico, Virginia. 16 July 1944
Dear Friends: *Harold J. Schachern to Dear Friends*

The sixth basic class of the Aviation Ground Officers' School is heading into its 8th and final week with colors flying, bugles blowing and pants dragging.

Much of the correspondence I have received has been in the form of round robin letters, so . . . I will reply in kind.

Mr. William Lampe[1]
Dear Bill . . . The time I spent visiting around the picture desk was wasted. Leg art and human interest don't count in Marine Aerial photography. While studying a picture taken at 10,000 feet, I marked one object "haystack." It turned out to be a Chic Sales masterpiece, Japanese variety.
Searchingly yours, H.S.

Mr. John MacLellan[2]
Dear Mac . . . I just want to assure you I am keeping up my loyalty to the Hearst Organization. Each evening at sunset, I shift my pack, face toward San Simeon[3] and salaam three times. Perhaps, between our Great White Father of the West and the Marine Corps, Democracy can yet be saved.
Hopefully yours, H.S.

Private George Edwards
Dear George . . . I still have the best interests of the Army Infantry at heart. I hadn't intended to discuss the Marines, but have you read Marion Hargrove's recent piece on the Corps?[4] In one place he says: "A Marine describes himself as a soldier who can read and write."
Affectionately yours, H.S.

Honorable Edward J. Jeffries Jr.
Dear Jeff . . . The Marine Corps travels fast but seldom light. My field transport pack has become like a Siamese twin. The transport pack, as Private Edwards undoubtedly can verify, consists of everything an infantryman owns in life. If it were two pounds heavier, he would no longer be in the infantry, for they would then have to put him in the Cavalry to get him a horse to help him carry it.
Your round-shouldered friend, H.S.

Honorable John C. Lodge
Dear Mr. Lodge . . . In our study of tactics, we have learned the mechanics of such things as frontal attacks, enveloping movements, pincers movements, flank attacks, enfilade fire, and numerous other maneuvers for reducing the opposition.
Scarcely practical in a body so small as the Common Council, I should think they could be applied admirably in the Board of Supervisors. The author of the text probably hails from Ecorse.[5]
Affectionately, H.S.

Mr. Leo Donovan
Dear Leo . . . Your note saying Jeff's Chicago speech has made the heat dead of late surprises me. I should have thought the opposite would be the case.
It seems to me that Higyoneo [Donovan], from his newly-claimed seat in the howdah [City Hall],[6] could observe a better field of fire and better

maneuver his native beaters and gun bearers than from Aft of the donkey [Democratic Party].

Miss Mabel N. Ford

Dear Nancy . . . I received and enjoyed your letter. I was beginning to wonder how long you were going to waste your charm on the civilians, and how long it would be before you started blowing some my way.

Passionately yours, H. S.

Mr. John M. Carlisle

Dear Jack . . . Perhaps this will never reach you short of Berlin, but if you get tired watching the army operate, come over to the islands and see the Varsity in action.

Mr. John F. Ballenger

Dear John . . . As a former Army Man, Welfare Director and present law enforcer, I thought you might enjoy a few lines about the best disciplined, best maintained and best policed and policing organization in the world. To borrow again from Marion Hargrove: "When a Marine hears that one third of the nation is poorly clothed, poorly housed, poorly fed and poorly educated, he automatically knows which third it is. It is the army, the navy and the coast guard."

Mr. Charles Weber[7]

Dear Charlie . . . Take heart, chum, there are tougher beats than city hall, and all of them are in the Marine Corps. What's more, the city editors here are harder to con.

Mr. Karl Seiffert

Dear Karl . . . Your description of vacationing on the shores of Lake Huron gave us something in common, for I also have been spending a lot of time in the water, but under full pack and vainly trying to keep my rifle dry.

Mr. Richard A. Sullivan[8]

Dear Dick . . . A veteran boatman like yourself would probably have enjoyed the past week here. We took part in three amphibious landing operations from an LST [Landing Ship Tank] . . . once in a "Duck" [DUKW], twice in an LCV [Landing Craft Vehicle]. This week we go over the side in pitch blackness to establish a beachhead somewhere along the Potomac [River], which differs somewhat from bringing a "snipe" into the Detroit Yacht Club.

Mr. Leo Lajoie

Dear Leo . . . Architecturally, Quantico has undoubtedly changed greatly since you were here in 1917, but the spirit lingers on. There aren't as many marching feet to kick the dust up in your face because they train only officers here now, but the wind still whips in from the Potomac and blows it in your eyes.

I, also, have sweated it out on the rifle range, taken my turn "in the butts,"[9] and the range officer still yells . . . "Ready on the right . . . ready on the left . . . all ready on the firing line . . . lock and load . . . aim in . . . fire at will." To this he always adds: "All right, you first relay, pick up all that brass and put it in the brass can. Pick up all the paper and cigarette butts and put them in the G.I. can. Get going, you gismos.

Mr. Ernest Jones[10]

Dear Ernie . . . If you meet any Marine Purchasing agents, please, please tell them to buy some rifles that don't rust!

Mr. William Comstock[11]

Dear Bill . . . You have the reputation of being a great man to take long hikes in the woods around your native Alpena [Michigan]. I think a few months in the Marine Corps would cure you of this. You would never again be interested in walking . . . especially in woods.

I have a list of at least 50 I wanted to include, but there isn't time. To you who have written, many thanks. I enjoyed every word. To you who have not, I just want to remind you that you are doing nothing to improve the morale of the world's greatest fighting organization.

All my best,   H A R O L D

NOTES

1. *Times* picture editor.
2. *Times* staff member.
3. The California estate of William Randolph Hearst.
4. *See Here, Private Hargrove.*
5. A municipality located on the Detroit River, just south of the city of Detroit.
6. A reference to the title of Donovan's column, "The Tenth Councilman."
7. *Times* reporter assigned to cover city hall upon Schachern's enlistment in the U.S. Marine Corps.
8. Detroit corporation counsel.
9. The area beneath the target.
10. Detroit Department of Purchases and Supplies commissioner.
11. Detroit Common Councilman.

Detroit. July 18, 1944
Dear Martin: *Edward J. Jeffries Jr. to Martin S. Hayden*

Your letter was far and away the best thing I have seen or heard as it relates to a fellow's experience when the chips are down. We all have thoroughly enjoyed it, and I wouldn't be a bit surprised if it would be in the afternoon Bugle [*News*].

Your experiences fill us with envy and awe and thankfulness that we are not there.

The local primaries are over. Jerry O'Brien beat Bill Dowling by 14,000 votes.[1] It was a relatively light primary because of its unusual date. As a result the verdict was quite conclusive. [Governor] Harry Kelly, according to Dr. Eugene C. Keyes, Lieutenant-Governor, tried to purge Keyes and did. Vernon J. Brown was selected as Lieutenant Governor on the Republican ticket.[2] Ed[ward J.] Fry, brother of Phil Fry who used to be State Treasurer, is now the nominee for Governor on the Democratic ticket.[3] Mr. Cobo has been offered, by at least part of the Republicans, nomination for Auditor-General. All the Congressmen were renominated with substantially the same opponents. The real surprise at the primaries was a chap named George O. Cornell. I never heard of him before. I don't think I have ever seen him. He defeated [Ray] Hafeli for the nomination of County Auditor.[4] I imagine that Hafeli is the most astounded man in this part of the country. I don't imagine he knows yet what happened. Bill Friedman, who was appointed to the vacancy caused by the death of Harry Keidan, was nominated along with Frank B. Ferguson, brother of [former U.S. Senator] Homer. Friedman ran pretty well in front of Ferguson in the primary.

Bill Dowling is talking about running as a sticker [independent] candidate. He asked me this morning what my reaction was. I told him I would make some inquiry. I think I am going to tell him that I don't think he can be elected.

The CIO is red-hot after me—at least a segment is. At their State convention the other day they passed resolutions telling the public what a no good fellow I was. I was out of town over the week-end and didn't see them, but from reports they resolved that they didn't think much of me.

It is hard to tell what the attitude of the general public will be on anything. They are confused, diverted, worried and plenty hard to get along with.

I don't think anyone can tell you for sure how the national election is going. I think, however, that Mr. Roosevelt still has the inside track. But the people are dissatisfied. They don't like what they have and I don't think they know what they want—but they don't want what they've got.

It certainly is good to hear that you are a Major. I am getting proud of knowing young men who in such a short space of time have had so many promotions. I suppose there are a lot of good stories that go with that, too. We are waiting impatiently until we hear them all.

The best of everything to you, my boy, and may the Good Lord look after you.

Sincerely,   J E F F

P.S. Did you know that John Carlisle is over there somewhere as a correspondent?

NOTES

1. *News,* 13 July 1944, 13.

2. Brown overwhelmingly defeated Keyes, "a nonconformist in the Kelly administration," thus handing the governor "a tight rein" on the Republican Party in Michigan. Indeed, Kelly was renominated without opposition (*News,* 12 July 1944, 1).

3. Edward J. Fry defeated William J. Cody, Wayne County Circuit Court commissioner, and Earnest C. Brooks; John J. Kozaren, Wayne County treasurer, was nominated by the Democrats for lieutenant governor over political novice Lester G. Stoll. Theodore I. ("Phil") Fry had been four times state treasurer. See *News,* 13 July 1944, 13.

4. Cornell, Michigan Department of Labor and Industry deputy, defeated Hafeli, the incumbent, by 1,500 votes to become the Democratic Party nominee.

Detroit. July 19, 1944

Dear Jack: *Edward J. Jeffries Jr. to John M. Carlisle*

Your articles are good. They are getting a good reception, but they are not as good, Jack, as you could write them. Your letter to me is better than your articles, and I've finally caught on to why. You are putting too much of the other fellow in and not enough of yourself. What you wrote to me about your experiences is what we want to hear concerning the experiences of the other boys. If you will pardon me for saying it, one of your best articles is your letter to me. We are beginning to get the stuff you are writing from France. I like it.

Incidentally, the primary has come and gone. Our good friend, Bill Dowling, took a shellacking. . . . They [blacks, liberals, labor leaders] did the same thing to him that they did to me only it was confined to the Democratic Party and, needless to say, he was at a terrific disadvantage. . . . I tried to help in every way I could, and I am sure that physically I did more for him than he did for me, but I won and he lost. One of the arguments they used against him was that he had helped me, and that I had turned out to be a rotten Republican. . . .

As a parting shot, my boy, you are a Columnist now. Put in a few "think" phrases. Tell a little of your own experience. You are doing the same thing as other boys are doing. Don't make it a plain reporter style. If you are going to determine editorial policy or write editorials in your later years, you never had a better opportunity to practice than right now. The folks back home are just as interested in what Carlisle is doing, experiencing and seeing as they are in Joe Doakes. You all are from Detroit—remember? Your stories are written to too narrow an audience. If any criticism can be made of them it is that they are like a letter home to the family of the affected person. Give us the background. Give it a general reader appeal. I repeat you are a Columnist now—not a reporter. Whether you like it or not, my boy, you are going to have to write some of those think stories. Why don't you write some of these stories as you did your Sunday features? Good Luck to you, my boy. We all are envious of you, thinking about you, and missing you plenty.

Sincerely,   J E F F

P.S. I had to smile when I read that you think it is a little noisy there. Paradoxically it is quiet here with you there.

3

The Crucible

(July–December 1944)

More than during any other period of the war, the second half of 1944 proved to be a time of testing for Jeffries, his friends, and their families. Correspondence amid problems of delivery and censorship revealed deep love, yet occasionally touched raw nerves and threatened longtime relationships, such as that of Jeffries and John M. Carlisle. Other friends expressed interest in the national scene, particularly the presidential election, and the local home front, where Jeffries juggled what seemed irreconcilable issues of race and labor with more hopeful plans for municipal revenue and postwar Detroit. Still, he kept in contact with George C. Edwards, Martin S. Hayden, and Walton S. White, doubtless wondering about the silence of Harold J. Schachern. That he found time as the chief executive of the most important industrial center of the war to write often revealed his deep concern for their welfare. Indeed, the harsh reality of training, combat, and military life in general continued to occupy the letters of the boys in the movement, who increasingly thought "aloud" about the people and world being liberated by their blood sacrifice: a price driven home–from battlefield to Detroit– by word of a fallen warrior among them.

Sustaining connections during a war proved frustrating for everyone. Jeffries and Hayden went back and forth over who had written last, the mayor claiming that "the notches on the wall" indicated that Hayden owed him a letter or two; the major claiming otherwise.[1] Their friendly debate revealed what Jeffries deduced, that some of his letters had never been delivered.[2] For Hayden and others, letters and newspaper subscriptions sometimes arrived belatedly and in bunches.[3] Sometimes, however, the press of municipal and military business dashed the best intentions, or the desire to write became lost in another assignment."[4] For whatever reason, the lack of mail–and cigarettes–proved to be, in

Figure 4. John M. Carlisle, courtesy of William O. Carlisle.

Hayden's phrase, "bad morale factors" for front line soldiers and, doubt-less, everyone stateside.[5] Perhaps this reality motivated Jeffries to tell uniformed confidants of one another's safety and to lend their letters to mutual friends in Detroit.[6] Recycled or late-coming, bits of news kept loves afire and hopes eternal from one mail delivery to the next.

For servicemen, word from the family proved most uplifting. Hayden, for instance, recorded like a historic event that the "deadlock broke" in mid-December when nine letters arrived together, seven from wife Betty.[7] Even more profoundly, time spent with one's wife, took "much of the curse off military life." So said White, whose visit from Margaret turned into her permanent move to Mississippi, complete with joint living quarters, a government job, and recreational excursions into New Orleans.[8] Most of his friends enjoyed no such luck, though a stateside serviceman such as Edwards "fully lived" with Peggy an occasional furlough, which he described as "lyrical."[9] Those in combat zones, of course, could only wish for the ecstasy of Carlisle, who, upon completing coverage of the European front and reuniting with his Peggy, exclaimed: "Second honeymoons are best!"[10]

Between close friends, morale was affected greatly by what they said to each other. Carlisle was devastated by Jeffries' criticism of his front line reports for the *News*.[11] Qualifying his anger with assurances of having done his best and the admission that Jeffries was "undoubtedly right,"[12] he revealed that his ego had been bruised at its core, very possibly because Jeffries served as a big brother or father whose much-needed approval seemed to have been withdrawn.

Jeffries himself soon realized that their relationship was special indeed—and that he had crossed a line. His conscience bothered him, he told Carlisle in a second letter, and he visited Peggy that evening as a family member seeking forgiveness.[13] His third communication, endeavoring to reduce his previous criticism to much ado about nothing, soothed the columnist's hurt feelings: Jeffries telegraphed that he was a "louse" and Carlisle's writing was "excellent."[14] Thereafter, the two quickly picked up their friendship without ceremony and, upon the reporter's return to the city, enjoyed themselves at a Miami conference that winter.[15]

To Edwards, in contrast, Jeffries seemed a political confidant, even a tutor—a figure of significance rather than one of authority. He urged Edwards to seek reelection to the Common Council despite his absence as a full-time soldier: "You owe it to yourself and you owe it to the city." Edwards should declare his candidacy and line up friends to run his campaign—which he did, in part because of this advice from a comrade and special politician.[16]

Neither friend let ideological differences affect the relationship, despite the councilman's having joined those who chided the mayor for opposing a fourth term for President Roosevelt. Jeffries believed the criticism for his speech before the Executives' Club of Chicago was quite overdrawn, in some cases "acrimonious,"[17] yet he dared not dismiss Edwards's contention that it lacked his "usual standard of thinking or political acumen."[18] Possibly because of the depth of the lambasting, the truth of his friend's remarks, the demands of his own office, and the damage to his requests of federal monies, Jeffries thereafter stayed out of the presidential campaign.

Privately, however, he confided his views to Hayden. Having placed his hope for FDR's defeat on the Republican Party's choice of a strong presidential candidate, he gave Roosevelt the "inside track" over Thomas E. Dewey.[19] Later, noting that Dewey was stronger than his predecessor, Wendell L. Willkie, and Roosevelt weaker than before, he wondered whether those factors would be enough for a Republican victory. More certain of triumph for municipal Democrats and state Republicans, he remarked that politicos in both parties were concentrating on the "national picture" and, thankfully, behaving themselves locally.[20] In the wake of the election, he credited the president's win to Political Action Committee efforts and public fear of changing executives at a "critical stage of the war."[21]

Ironically, given the Chicago speech and his genuine concern over increasing big government, Jeffries considered himself "unprejudiced" and "non-partisan" and, as late as election day, in doubt of the campaign's outcome.[22] Perhaps he voted Democrat, as may have fellow progressive Republican Hayden, who viewed the war from a military perspective, as did many soldiers.[23] More likely, to protect democracy from what he called the threat of divine kingship and remain true to his philosophy of government, the mayor pulled the lever for Dewey.[24] Perhaps, too, he was knowingly opening his way to state office as a Republican gubernatorial candidate.[25]

Long before that failed effort in 1946, Jeffries struggled to govern his city according to Jeffersonian tenets in a war demanding Hamiltonian centralization. Endeavoring to assuage race tension, he sought firsthand information from Philadelphia when that city experienced a near-riot over its transportation policies, and prepared for the quick removal of an ineffectual Harold Thompson as director of the Mayor's Interracial Committee.[26] He began to reconsider his policy of limiting public housing sites to restricted areas, thereby preserving neighborhood racial characteristics—and preventing much needed construction. To liberal and black critics, Jeffries's motivations seemed suspect, combining practical and political concerns: balancing the desire for some control over the housing crisis (which was extending beyond city limits and involving a myriad of government officials and citizen organizations) with the need for political fence-mending with blacks, liberals, and laborites (supposedly for having appointed their nemesis as Corporation Counsel).[27]

In reality, Jeffries probably understood that the housing situation required attention in itself and that it was much more complicated than suggested by either the left-leaning coalition or their racist opponents. He always listened to Edwards, for example, who observed that blacks and whites in Officer Candidate School lived together "seemingly for years" without incident.[28] Though predisposed to uphold white middle-class concerns in socioeconomic issues, including those involving race relations, the mayor's appointment of William E. Dowling as corporation counselor appeared more an act of political gratitude for the former Wayne County prosecutor's support during the race riot than an attempt to score points with right-wing voters. Jeffries probably believed that his Chicago speech had contributed to Dowling's lost bid for renomination as prosecutor because left-wing Democrats associated him as a friend and ideological cousin. Equally important, he chose Dowling in order to advance his own friend and counselor Paul E. Krause to the Recorder's Court.[29] But to have selected Dowling simply for the benefit of conservative voters, only to alienate those same supporters by moving toward a more liberal housing policy, seemed incongruous if not impolitic for a politician of Jeffries's ability.[30] In short, as in the case of encouraging Edwards's councilmanic candidacy, he fused politics with friendship and public service.

Although mayoral action on the housing front lay in the future, Jeffries continued to spar with the Common Council over several issues, including wages for municipal workers. He also looked to the future, appointing a high-powered committee to recommend an airport site, and developing a ten-year plan for capital improvements. In the process, he sought greater sources of revenue from the state, realizing that the level of postwar planning lay in the balance. He also revealed additional dimensions of his view of public service and government philosophy, criticizing powerful citizens who "duck civic responsibility" unless it could advance friends or hobbies, and state fiscal policies that favored sparsely populated areas over municipalities.[31]

Meanwhile, firsthand military information emanating from training camps reminded Jeffries of a crisis far greater than those confronting him. Edwards graphically described his vigorous training, from the intricate workings of his M1 Garand rifle to the dangers of infiltration courses featuring live fire. "Neophytes" like himself understood well the difference between preparing for combat and "doing it for keeps"; few called themselves soldiers, a title reserved for veterans of the front to whom they paid "profound respect." Yet Edwards and his comrades hoped for any fate save that of remaining in a training camp.[32] Promoted to corporal, then set back in his training because of an injured hand, he later entered Officer Candidate School, already convinced of the need for discipline—"pretty rough justice"—and astounded by the quality of instruction.[33] Similarly, White reemphasized the rigors of training with live ammunition and the belief that it best prepared one for combat, while also recounting the lot of a public relations sergeant at a stateside division headquarters.[34]

More than anything, news from combat zones brought home the grim reality of war. Like Hayden's letters from Normandy, those from Carlisle relived the exciting highs and the boring lows of war: liberating a chateau's wine cellar with Ernest Hemingway; writing about every imaginable subject with a pencil ("my hand grenade adjective thrower").[35] Most poignantly, he described the horrors of seeing war up close, "scared to death," and—as a reporter—unarmed: Germans cut to pieces in pitched battle at Le Mans, Americans killed by cannon fire, aircraft strafing and nighttime sniper fire; little or no sleep, "lousy food," and always the fear of being hit. Shaken by action and noise that drove him to drink, Carlisle nevertheless carried on, knowing the significance of his work for those who fought and for their families and friends back home in Detroit.

Most letter writers at the front commented on the course of war and prospects for future developments in Europe and the Pacific. In fact, by year's end, Hayden opined that France was "going to Hell," a county wracked by "political confusion," class hatred, and economic dislocation.[36] Similar uncertainty characterized England, though Jack McElhone expressed hope should that country follow Aneurin Bevan, minister of labour and Labour Party leader, in the postwar era.[37] Indeed, Edwards's unionist friend considered a greater problem for Britain other leaders in the Labour Party than the failure of Winston S. Churchill to tilt his coalition government leftward.[38]

Contrariwise, James P. Simpson shifted from initial pessimism to greater hope for the Pacific. He expressed concern that American presidential candidates seemed ignorant of "this side of the world," which he thought worthy of protection only if the United States owned territory west of Hawaii.[39] He came to respect the Filipinos especially: underprivileged but courageous, intelligent, moral, "not inferior people," whose admiration for the United States would become a "valuable international asset" in the postwar era.[40]

These glimpses into the future resulted from great sacrifice in the present, none more troubling than the death of an acquaintance or friend. The killing of Associated Press photographer Bede Irvin, half a mile away near St. Lo, slowed Carlisle down "a couple of days"; he realized, as did everyone on the front, how "very easily" he could have been slain instead.[41] Edwards, in turn, was rocked by news of the death of close friend Bill Lamson, wounded as his armored unit pressed into Germany. He knew the machine gunner from earlier days in the UAW, as did Jeffries, who became "depressed no end" upon learning of the tragedy.[42]

Under these circumstances, Detroiters entered the new year more knowledgeable about themselves and more appreciative of one another. Hayden's self-discovery in Normandy preceded that experienced by his friends in the latter part of 1944. Jeffries realizing the true meaning of his friendship with Carlisle and Edwards, White finding greater significance in his marriage, McElhone awaiting a combat assignment in England, and Simpson already fighting in the South Pacific—all survived in crucibles wrought by war. Only Harold J. Schachern had not been heard from recently; he would reconnect in the final year of uncertainty, hope, and triumph.

NOTES

1. Edward J. Jeffries Jr. (hereafter EJJ) to Martin S. Hayden (MSH), 11 Oct. 1944, Box 5, Mayor's Papers, BHC (hereafter all Mayor's Papers citations refer to Box 5, 1944, unless stated otherwise); MSH to EJJ, 24 Oct. 1944.

2. EJJ to MSH, 7 Nov. 1944, Mayor's Papers.

3. "Diary of Martin S. Hayden: October 1943-August 1945" (author's possession, courtesy of MSH), 175, 181; John J. McElhone (hereafter JJM) to George and Peggy Edwards, 4 Aug. 1944, Box 5, pt. 2, Edwards Collection, ALUA (hereafter all citations to the Edwards Collection refer to Box 5, pt. 2, unless cited otherwise).

4. Walton S. White (hereafter WSW) to Select Little Band, 8 Dec. 1944, Edwards Collection; EJJ to Geroge C. Edwards (GCE), 12 Dec. 1944, Box 3, Mayor's Papers.

5. "Diary of Martin S. Hayden," 178.

6. EJJ to GCE, 4 Aug. 1944, Box 3, Mayor's Papers; EJJ to MSH, 13 Nov. 1944, Mayor's Papers.

7. "Diary of Martin S. Hayden," 181.

8. WSW to Select Little Band, 8 Dec. 1944, Edwards Collection.

9. GCE, SOL VII, 4 Dec. 1944, Box 14, pt. 1, Edwards Collection (hereafter the location of all SOLs unless cited otherwise).

10. "Diary of Martin S. Hayden," 129; JMC to GCE, 27 Dec. 1944, Edwards Collection.

11. EJJ to JMC, 7 July 1944 and 30 July 1944, Mayor's Papers.

12. JMC to EJJ, 11 Aug. 1944, Mayor's Papers.

13. EJJ to JMC, 3 Aug. 1944, Mayor's Papers.

14. EJJ telegram to JMC, 25 Aug. 1944, Mayor's Papers.

15. EJJ to GCE, 27 Dec. 1944, Box 3, Mayor's Papers.

16. EJJ to GCE, 12 Dec. 1944, Mayor's Papers; GCE to EJJ, 17 Dec. 1944, Box 2, 1945, Mayor's Papers.

17. EJJ to JMC, 22 June 1944, Mayor's Papers. See Chapter 2 for the letter.

18. GCE to EJJ, 24 July 1944, longhand note on back of SOL III-VI, Box 3, Mayor's Papers.

19. EJJ to MSH, 11 Oct. 1944, Mayor's Papers.

20. EJJ to MSH, 7 Nov. 1944, Mayor's Papers.

21. EJJ to MSH, 13 Nov. 1944; "Diary of Martin S. Hayden," 181, for Sidney Hillman's PAC and Jay Hayden's view that the votes of soldiers carried Michigan for FDR.

22. EJJ to MHS, 7 Nov. 1944, Mayor's Papers.

23. "Diary of Martin S. Hayden," 173, for Hayden's elation over the defeat of isolationist Republicans: Congressman Hamilton Fish of New York and U.S. Senator Gerald P. Nye of North Dakota.

24. W.K. Kelsey, "The Commentator," *News*, 13 June 1944, 14.

25. In 1946, Jeffries finished third in the Republican primary.

26. EJJ to GCE, 4 Aug and 12 Dec. 1944, Box 3, Mayor's Papers.

27. George Schermer to GCE, 21 Dec. 1944, and Gloster B. Current to GCE, 21 Dec. 1944, Edwards Collection.

28. GCE to EJJ, 17 Dec. 1944, Box 2, 1945, Mayor's Papers.

29. The political deal involved Governor Harry F. Kelly, Republican, who controlled the court appointment, though his motives for wanting Dowling, a fallen Democrat, are unclear.

30. EJJ to MSH, 13 Nov. 1944, Mayor's Papers; EJJ to GCE, 27 Dec. 1944, Box 3, Mayor's Papers; *News*, 14 June 1944, 7, and 20 June 1944, 4; "Diary of Martin S. Hayden," 181.

31. EJJ to MSH, 11 Oct. 1944, Mayor's Papers; EJJ to GCE, 12 Dec. 1944, Box 3, Mayor's Papers.

32. GCE, SOL III-VI, late July 1944.

33. GCE, SOL VII, 4 Dec. 1944.

34. WSW to Select Little Band, 8 Dec. 1944, Edwards Collection.

35. JMC to EJJ, 30 July 1944, Mayor's Papers.

36. MSH to EJJ, 24 Oct. 1944, Mayor's Papers.

37. JJM to George and Peggy Edwards, 4 Aug. 1944, Edwards Collection.

38. JJM to Peggy Edwards, 24 Dec. 1944, Edwards Collection.

39. JPS to GCE, 23 Aug. 1944, Edwards Collection.

40. JPS to GCE, 18 Nov. 1944, Edwards Collection.

41. JMC to EJJ, 30 July 1944, Mayor's Papers; *New York Times*, 26 July 1944, 3.

42. GCE, SOL VII, 4 Dec. 1944; EJJ to GCE, 27 Dec. 1944, Box 3, Mayor's Papers.

LETTERS: JULY–DECEMBER 1944

Camp Wheeler, Georgia. [late July 1944]
George C. Edwards to Beloved Correspondents

STANDARD OPERATIONAL LETTERS III, IV, V, and VI

1) Private Edwards is now by Army regulations, a trained infantry replacement, Dogface, Model M1 1944. By the same definition I can field-strip, reassemble, place in action and fire for effect:

1) The Garand M1 Rifle.

2) The Browning Automatic Rifle.

3) The Carbine.

4) The Light Machine Gun.

5) The 60 Millimeter Mortar.

By the same definition I am qualified to assault an enemy with the Bazooka, the Rifle-Grenade, and the Hand Grenade, which, with the Mortar comprise the dogface artillery. If all else fails, I also have had much training with a peculiarly wicked instrument known as the bayonet and have also been given a little incidental instruction in knifing, kneeing, gouging and garroting. By the same definition I can read a military map, lead a squad through the woods at night on a compass bearing, give and carry out hand and arm signals for a rifle squad in combat formations and . . . most important . . . assume a prone position behind a four inch rise in Mother Earth in something less than two seconds.

By the same definition I can march a minimum distance of twenty miles in 8 hours, carrying a rifle, cartridge belt, bayonet, gas mask, steel helmet and full field pack (about 60 lbs. weight).

OK I hear you saying, "By definition you can—but can you?" Oh yes I can . . . and doubtless will. Same is true of 90% of the other Joes in my company. And the same would . . . be true of anyone between 18 and 38 who was warm to start with . . . had been here 17 weeks and was still alive.

You might be interested in . . . Pvt. Edwards' first promotion. Since the second week of this cycle I have been . . . "a safety pin Sergeant." I hasten to add that you won't find the title in the military manuals, that it doesn't carry any increase in pay, and that it doesn't vote a salute even from a second lieutenant. Nonetheless it does have its privileges and its responsibilities. For example I escape the onerous duties of table waiting, but in turn have the heavy responsibility of seeing to it that the 2nd Platoon Latrine is properly cleaned up every morning.

In plainer language I am platoon guide—a post held in a regular platoon by a sergeant but which brings us Wheeler trainees the rather temporary decoration of an arm-band with three stripes. . . . The four squad leaders and I decided we'd get along somehow without wearing the detachable stripes.

The result, however, with me, has been that I've had to be a better soldier than I probably had any particular desire to be.

The guide marches at the head of the platoon, sets the pace, maintains the interval with the platoon ahead and with the squad leaders sets the pivot on column movements.

Almost every other trainee gets a second guess at a command. Not the guides. . . . I learned the hard way. I shall not soon forget leading four of my trusting confreres in a forlorn "platoons column right" when the Captain's command of "column right" to the company meant . . . "Forward march" to me. That parade ground was awfully big and we felt awfully lonely for a long 60 seconds.

So by moral coercion I had to learn the manual of arms and close order drill . . . in spite of a considerable distaste for it. I had to learn the class work because the instructors . . . [picked] on the guides to recite.

In marching I had to learn to set a quicker shorter pace so as not to wear out the little guys at the tail of the platoon and how to speed up that pace and slow it down by degrees so as not to wear the platoon out changing step.

And because the guide led off I had to do the obstacle and bayonet assault courses with more simulated enthusiasm than I really felt; and on marches or runs I couldn't or wouldn't drop out though the man doesn't live who has been through basic without wanting to.

When the non-coms were on committee work or leave I had to learn to take the platoon at reveille, retreat and occasionally . . . during duty hours. Which leads up to the neatest trick . . . getting guys who are on . . . equal footing with you to do thoroughly unpleasant work at your orders and not end up hating you in the process. Oh well some of the work didn't really have to be done anyway.

2) By the time you receive this my two weeks bivouac which winds up Wheeler training will be over and my file card . . . will be moving to wherever at the moment the Army needs a 30 year physically Class A Wheeler trainee with a variegated civilian background and an unsullied (in fact practically virgin) military record.

Trainees leave here every week on routes that lead to Cherbourg, Bouganville, New Delhi, Chungking, and . . . to Alaska, Iceland, Shelby, Tenn. and Van Dorn, Miss. I may be sent overseas. I may be sent to a division in this country. I may be sent for advanced training. Worst of all I may be sentenced to stay a training camp soldier. Neither I nor any other G.I. has the slightest need to worry about the above, however. Fate, the Classification Office and a few machines have the situation well in hand.

3) Several people have inquired how the hell I got these letters mimeographed. That . . . is a military secret. But an even greater one is how the hell I got time to write even these. This opus has been more than a little delayed. The following . . . should reveal how Pvt. Edwards progressed . . . and why you didn't hear about it sooner.

4) S.O.L. III is being started . . . at Toombs Range with live fire snapping overhead. I have given up trying to write in the evenings and on these pit details we sometimes get a little waiting time. At the moment I am comfortably seated with my back to a concrete and earth embankment above which we raise some 180 10 foot targets which stretch out over a half mile. 500 yards to the rear is the firing line where C Company is firing slow fire with the Garand M1 rifle.

They tell us that the 30 caliber bullet fired from the M1 will go clean through a ten inch tree and kill a man on the other side.

I believe it—immediately in front of me is a dense forest with every tree at 10 foot level. Up to a 10 foot height there is a thick woods—then suddenly your gaze is projected half a mile away where about a 20 foot strip of beaten dust runs in a half mile belt along the hillside, that's the "beaten zone" for . . . the largest rifle range in the world.

We fired this morning for record. I scored 170 out of a possible 210, which is good enough for a sharpshooters medal but not high enough for me to worry about finding myself tied in a tree as a sniper. High man for our company is a stringy 18 year old Italian kid . . . who fired 187.

(5) This is now weeks later on Baming Range and for this afternoon I have the best goldbricking job I've run across since I've been in the Army. I am ensconced in the control tower as phone orderly, with exceptionally little to do and a fine view. This is a field firing range where we practice technique of fire by squads. We fired it this morning and so far our platoon has the record for the battalion.

On this course our squad started to advance up a hill. About the middle of the hill we were fired on and hit the dirt. (Those words . . . are most expressive. If you do it right you pick up quite a bit of terra firma and leave some of your own skin behind.) We advanced in short rushes through two firing positions to a skirmish line on the military crest on the other side of the hill. There we could see the whole valley below, and the hillside opposite and silhouette targets began to pop up at ranges from 375 to 700 yards. We fired three clips of ammunition and it is amazing to see how much fire power twelve men have. We scored hits on all but two targets in about 2 minutes. . . . In actual combat we would doubtless have won this skirmish. . . .

6) Late at night at Wheeler a visitor catching the last bus is likely to be greatly puzzled by the sight of a lonely trainee walking solemnly around the quadrangle halting at each corner to let out a wail "I love my Rifle."

Such a character has doubtless committed one of the most heinous of infantry crimes—by accidentally dropping his rifle or having a bit of dirt at inspection. On the walls of each barracks is a printed tribute to the M1, starting off: "I love my rifle. It is my best friend. If I take care of it, it will save my life," etc. .

In this regard . . . I am a model infantry man. While the M1 has hardly displaced my family or friends in my affections I like it quite well enough to give it the care it requires and I get the most kick out of the days we spend in the field firing it.

The M1 fires 8 shots one right after the other as quick as you can aim and pull the trigger. It is not hard to hit a 24 inch silhouette target at 500 yards distance. It operates on a very simple but ingenious principle. When the rifle is fired the expanding gas from the cartridge builds up 50,000 lbs. pressure in the barrel, pushing the bullet out. Just before the bullet clears the muzzle, there is a little hole in the barrel called a gas port which diverts some of the gas into another barrel called the gas chamber which runs back toward the stock of the rifle. In this chamber the gas pressure strikes a piston called the operating rod throwing it sharply to the rear. This rod is attached to the bolt and cams it open, ejecting the used shell and cocking the rifle. As the rod slams to its rearmost position, it also compresses a spring which promptly forces it back forward, carrying the bolt . . . with a fresh cartridge and the M1 is ready to fire again.

7) If I seem excessively interested in some of the technicalities of infantry training, forgive it. You must remember that this is now my sole occupation and that I always talk shop.

8) But what of Pvt. Edwards? SOL II ended abruptly with me pacing the barracks floor awaiting the birth of Andy's brother or sister. Promptly on April 6th Peg [hastened] herself to Harper Hospital and exactly on schedule James McConnell Edwards, weight 6 lbs 15 oz, arrived. His first words are said to have been: "Where in hell is Daddy?" He is reported . . . to be machined to specifications within a ten thousandth. The inspection may have been prejudiced, but I believe every word of it. Andy on being told that his baby brother had arrived said with just a touch of scorn—"Well its about time!"

9) Currently I am looking forward to a visit by my beloved wife. As a result I have been attempting to pull every sort of detail that I could think of in order to have at least a few free evenings. I should have cleared off K.P., table waiting and guard duty, which leaves only weapon cleaning, alerts and night problems. There better not be too many of them or my hopes for unblemished AWOL record may suffer. 5 months is quite a while! (Yeh I know, you overseas G.I.s, three years is quite a bit longer.)

In front of me the last squad is hitting the dirt on the firing line and tracers are beginning to kick up the dirt around the targets. It is now 4:30 on the easiest Saturday afternoon I've spent in the Army. . . . All we have to do now is march the three hot dusty miles back to camp with full field equipment and rifles (a total weight of about 60 lbs.). We should be policed up here and in camp by 6 o'clock with all Saturday evening free (except of course for cleaning our beloved MI's which must be inspected before we sign out)—I love my rifle.

10) They are now trying to glamorize the infantry. What a helluva job that must be. The sad facts are that the infantry just doesn't "off we go into the wide blue yonder"—or "anchors aweigh, my boys." It doesn't even think it is the "greatest fighting machine in the history of the world" (quote 2nd Lt. Harold Schachern on the Marine Corps). The infantry doesn't even have the most dangerous job in the armed forces. Sure more dog faces get killed than in any other branch but percentage-wise the Air forces . . . and Marines can claim that dubious honor. . . . When the War Dept. P.R.O. boys are looking for superlatives, most infantry G.I.s would suggest for consideration these—the dirtiest, sweatiest, hottest, coldest, toughest, least romantic—most miserable (and I reckon—most essential).

11) One of the standing and overworked infantry jokes is to say to a sweating G.I. elbow deep in dishes, "That's all right Joe—Someday you'll make someone a good wife." In my case t'aint so. I may come home with more knowledge than I ever wanted to gain on mopping, sweeping, washing dishes, etc. But I also will come back with less disposition to do any of the above than ever before (which . . . previously was zero). Many a marriage may be marred by hubby standing by demanding hospital corners on his bed or silver washed at 190 [degrees] but refusing point blank to do same himself.

12) I'm the only infantryman around here whom I've ever heard say that he wanted to be in the infantry, and I've stopped admitting it. It just

isn't popular. The average G.I. loves the Air Corps, its planes, the Artillery, its guns, the armored force its tanks, the Navy its ships, and the Marine Corps its P.R.O. (Kindly note Schachern.) The only people he admits respecting are combat infantrymen and paratroopers (who were infantrymen first).

13) . . . let me put myself in proper perspective. To date I am a training camp Joe. Few men call themselves soldiers unless they have been in combat and damn few who have will talk much about it. We get combat training here of a pretty vigorous and realistic nature enough to convince us all that doing it for keeps must be a thousand times worse. We have many men back as cadre at Wheeler who swear they'd rather be back overseas than here. But when they say that they are not thinking of combat, they are thinking of those base camps where there is said to be less spit and polish and in some instances less rigorous training and fewer regulations. Apparently overseas duty and combat duty overseas are two horses of different colors. We neophytes with little seniority pay profound respect to the G.I.'s who have been there and done the job that we are just being trained for.

14) In the sixth week of the cycle we were introduced to live fire. . . . We crawled the infiltration course . . . a hundred yards square of rough ground, filled with simulated shell holes, real logs and three very real barbed wire entanglements. Our platoon was marched down a connecting ditch to a trench along the rear of the area. On command fixed machine guns opened up with live 30 caliber bullets and tracer ammunition. Our job was to crawl the 100 yards from the trench we were in to the one from which the machine guns were firing at us, negotiating the logs, holes and barbed wire enroute—and, oh yes, keeping all of our anatomy within 30 inches of the ground in the process, since that was the height of the machine gun fire. We were to start on signal. If there ever was a whistle I never heard it over the cracking of the bullets, but half of the platoon . . . started moving forward. We did too. I thought the worst job was going to be getting up the slope of the trench and on to the field. As a matter of fact once the outfit started moving you moved almost automatically, and in your place. Then the work started. Creeping on your belly propelling yourself with your elbows and knees flat out to your sides is miserably hard work. After a couple of minutes we were choking with dust, sweat was pouring off of us, we were grime from hair to toes and the machine guns were the least of our worries. Here was a log. We go over it carefully each man having a healthy respect for his anatomy and trying to keep all of it low. I am crawling left to get away from a simulated shell hole where the dynamite charge in it goes off. More dirt. Now the first barbed wire, wait for the next burst from the gun firing just above you. Now turn over quick on your back, stick your bayonet under the wire and ahead of you and shove yourself along on the back of your helmet. Now you are looking up and the tracers are going right over you— close but not too close and anyway you are too damn uncomfortable and

busy to pay much attention. There are a dozen or so strands of wire and each one seems to have a special barb to catch on your rifle, your fatigues or you. All of a sudden the guns cease firing, there is a whistle and much shouting. According to instructions we lie still and wonder what the hell. Then there is another whistle and the guns fire again. It seems that . . . [someone] from the 1st Platoon thought he was past the firing line and stood up. He wasn't. Fortunately an alert gunner saw him and ceased fire in time. . . . [The lucky soldier] is reported to have been unmoved by all the fuss—but they had to relieve the gun crew. The rest of the course was the same . . . more [obstacles] . . . dirt and sweat and the guns firing steadily. Finally I got under the last strand of wire, guided left to crawl around a hole—looked up right into the muzzle of the nearest machine gun. It looked as if it were pointed right at me—but since . . . it was firing and I was still there, I guessed not. At any rate I did some fancy crab-wise creeping, found the entrance to the trench, rolled down into it, scrambled to my feet, charged up the bank, bayonetted the dummy at the top and went on another 25 yards, hit the dirt and took up a firing position to wait for my rifle to be inspected.

We ran this course three times that day—twice during the day and once at night. We got off duty at 10 o'clock. I pitched my tent at the command post only 100 yards from the firing line and with the machine guns still firing away over the heads of C company I went sound to sleep in a second.

15) . . . From the 12th week on all we get is simulated combat. By then we have completed training as an individual soldier and are taught squad and platoon tactics on the offense and defense with each of the weapons that we use.

Since a couple of friends asked, let me describe a fairly typical 48 hour period in the 13th week.

Friday morning first call comes at 5:30. Since we have a 3 and ½ mile march . . . before we start work at 8 A.M. we do not stand reveille. By the time we have dressed, shaved and made our beds it's 5:50 A.M. and the chow whistle blows. We get some kind of fruit, a cold cereal and either eggs or pancakes or some other pretty substantial breakfast and coffee (incidentally the best of the army meals . . .).

By 6:15 we should be back ln the barracks, sweeping and mopping the floors, getting our equipment ready and in my case performing my onerous responsibilities as guide by seeing to it that the proper squad cleans up the latrine.

By 6:45 we fall out in the company street with full field packs—rifles, belts and bayonets. We spend 5 minutes policing the area around the barracks (picking up scraps of paper, cigarettes, etc.) and at 6:50 we are in formation ready . . . to move out.

Between 6:50 and 8:00 the whole battalion marches about 3 and ½ miles. . . . The morning march is not half bad. As yet it isn't too hot—some of the trails over the Georgia hills are very pretty and we all feel pretty good.

At 8 we march into area M, get a 10 minute break and are ready to start the day's work.

Today we are working on the light machine gun section in a rifle platoon. . . .

We spend the morning attacking a ridge from which we are supposed to drive an enemy force. Our platoon is formed into 3 tactical rifle squads and 3 light machine gun squads. As guide I have the . . . easy assignment of bringing up the rear. Our platoon forms in a thin woods in a valley. At a whistle we move out each squad taking a different route of attack and spreading out its men in a dispersed group called the diamond formation. We seek such cover . . . as we can find behind bushes, trees, rocks or little gullies.

A little way up the ridge the "enemy" spots us and opens fire. Our advance halts momentarily; the squad leaders bring up their men to form a skirmish line; and I bring the machine gun section up to the flank chosen by the Platoon Leader from which . . . [to] fire on the enemy. Each machine gun is served by 5 men and when the position for mounting them has been carefully chosen in advance, they can be put into action in almost no time. . . .

As soon as the machine guns have simulated fire and "pinned down the enemy," . . . the rifle squads move forward in the assault, the machine guns lift their fire and one platoon moves triumphantly to the top of the hill to be told, "That was lousy, I don't know what's the matter with you men. You act like you were dead." And down we go to run the problem over and over. The temperature by now is 95 degrees. . . .

At 12 o'clock we assemble and march to a bivouac area for chow. The chow trucks come out with the food prepared in the mess kitchen and carried out to the field in 50 gallon G.I. cans which in other days I would have called garbage cans.

Chow is the best hour of the day. We spend a quarter of it eating and washing our mess kits, a quarter of it griping about the quality and or quantity of the food, and a half hour sleeping.

Suddenly there's the whistle [to] fall in—here goes the afternoon's work.

Back we go to the top of the same damn ridge. It seems we took it after all this morning but the enemy is preparing to counter attack. . . . Soooo— we have to dig in.

The thermometer is now at 100 in the cool shade of the weather bureau office.

The machine gun crews have to dig emplacements for their guns. All the rest have to dig fox holes for themselves. And "dig in right, damn it— this may mean your life," so we dig. We just about get dug in, when all of a sudden comes the whistle—"hurry up and fill em in. We're moving back to an alternate position—the enemy has mortar fire on our guns."

We fill 'em in, move back 100 yards and do it all over again.

The temperature has now broken the top off the thermometer. We are all Georgia red clay from head to foot and sweat is pouring off of us.

Strangely enough the dimensions of the fox holes tend to shrink until by late afternoon very few of us would like to have this fox hole be the one that we had crouched in a few weeks earlier while a tank ran over us. . . .

By now the enemy counter attack has driven us back down the hill which we so laboriously won in the morning and we are digging in the woods where we originally started from when we get the command: "all right fill 'em in, you should have had 'em filled in already. Do you want to be late for chow?"

. . . As darkness falls we are assembled [again] and marched to another section of the area. Each squad is given a compass, an azimuth reading, and told to attack a hill roughly a mile to our front. . . . Each squad takes off at 10 minute intervals, so we all promptly fall fast asleep while waiting our turn.

Tonight we are doing the same thing as this morning, except that we have to stop every 50 feet for a new compass bearing and . . . moving through the woods in the dark is a pretty eerie experience. You never set your foot down with positive knowledge that the ground is there—and sometimes it isn't. I am acting as scout for the 4th squad. . . . We move through the woods on our [compass] bearing and suddenly . . . a machine gun opens up on us. . . . Aha! we've hit it on the head. Now to form our skirmish line, get set and charge and this day is finally over. . . . the squad leader gives the signal for the skirmish line, then . . . the charge and bolts for the machine gun position. . . . As he passed me I had a fleeting thought that maybe I ought to be moving faster . . . when all of a sudden . . . [his] feet are jerked out from under him and his whole six foot length flies through the air to crash and bounce and then hang suspended in six or eight strands of a barbed wire entanglement that hadn't been mentioned to us in the briefing. . . .

For the following week . . . [the squad leader] had no taste for realism in simulated combat. . . . I was just glad he was a faster man. Half a dozen guys went to the hospital that night, but as was pointed out to us none of them died and we'd be pretty careful about barbed wire at night from here on.

When the last squad came in we collected a few stragglers who had got lost. The battalion was formed and we took off for the 3 and ½ mile march to the barracks. This was vastly different than coming out. It was midnight when we started the march in—we had been up since 5:30. . . . [It seemed] like a bad dream. Night marches are made "at ease" with no talking, and the columns swing along the dusty roads in a seemingly endless silent procession. You suffer and you sleep. I have marched for half an hour, kept step, kept my eyes open and maintained the 25-pace interval to the next platoon and been sound asleep all the while. It is not the most refreshing sleep I've ever known, however.

At the barracks we are greeted with coffee and cake . . . and very welcome they are.

I won't go through the rest of the next day except to say (1) we got to sleep about 2 A.M.; (2) we stood reveille at 7:40 A.M.; (3) we worked all day. (4) At 3:30 in a broiling sun we took off with combat packs and rifles for the four mile forced march which we were supposed to make in 50 minutes. Our company was paced by a 1st Lt. who took us through in 39 minutes to set a camp record. I hope he was happy about that record. I . . . didn't enjoy it a damn bit.

That night our platoon was on the alert and hence restricted to the barracks. It didn't matter much. We hadn't planned to go any place anyhow.

Op. [Operational Letters] III, IV, V, VI are being completed on the Southern R.R. enroute from Detroit to Macon. Miracle of miracles Pvt. Edwards has been home. By some devious method Dick Sullivan[1] connived a certificate of completion of my law school work out of the Detroit College of Law. It seems there's a statute about soldiers and law schools. Under it I was entitled to take the Michigan Bar Exam (if I could get there). With no hope of getting it I applied for an emergency furlough which would give me a day in Detroit to appear for an oral hearing and 3 days in Lansing to write the quiz. To my delight it developed that my first Sergeant had studied some law and regarded the Bar Exam as a matter of considerable importance.

So Tuesday A.M. of this week I boarded a train with one law book under my arm and came in on a book and a prayer.

I conceivably may even have passed the darn thing though I don't see how in all logic that could be.

At any rate I did get to see my by now not-so-brand-new son Jimmy, whom I can report to be all that a fond father could desire. He can smile by now, and Peg claims he can talk. I guess I haven't learned that language yet.

Andy filled his pappy's heart with joy by recognizing me with enthusiasm at the station.

After hearing the long discussions of the problem of readjustment to civilian life, this G.I. can report that he thinks it will take for him a bath, a change of clothes and 15 minutes.

This is now Sunday afternoon in the Chattanooga R.R. yards. I join my company tonight and tomorrow we start the 2 week bivouac which ends basic training. Do I need to say that I shall be delighted to see it over?

Best regards

NOTE

1. Law school friend of GCE and attorney in corporation counsel office.

Camp Wheeler, Georgia. 24 July 1944
Dear Jeff: *George C. Edwards to Edward J. Jeffries Jr.*[1]

Thanks for your recent letter and I'm sorry I couldn't answer sooner—but enclosed the adventure of Pvt. Edwards up to recent date.

I am now thru training and just waiting shipping orders for God knows where.

The transportation program looks good to me. I just can't fathom the DSR officials' attitude toward transportation planning.

Each of three OCS Boards that I have been before has examined me on the subject of Detroit's race problems. How that relates to infantry combat officer training I leave you to judge. But I was glad to have your comments to pass on to the last board.

My regards for all. I may be seeing you soon—or I may not be home for some months. Thus it is with the Army.

Yours,   G E O R G E

I was disappointed in [Henry A.] Wallace's defeat[2] but think R [Franklin D. Roosevelt] will win handily. Most service men will vote for him I think for the good of their own hides if for no other reason. For the above and other reasons I am, of course, with the dissenters on your Chicago speech. If you aren't too plagued by discussion of it I would greatly like to know that background of it. I hope you'll pardon my thinking that it didn't . . . live up to your usual standard of thinking or political acumen. But that's one incident and life's full of 'em.

NOTES

1. Handwritten on the back of the last two pages of the copy of SOL III-VI sent to Jeffries.
2. In order to avoid conflict within the party from the right during his bid for a fourth presidential term, Roosevelt permitted conservative Democrats to force Vice-President Wallace, an avowed liberal, from the ticket; he accepted U.S. Senator Harry S Truman, a moderate yet proven New Deal supporter, as his running mate in 1944.

Normandy, France. 30 July 1944
Dear Jeff: *John M. Carlisle to Edward J. Jeffries Jr.*

Finally got your letter of July 7th. My mail has had a hard time finding me. I was six wks without mail; rough, over here, not to hear from home. I was interested in the survey you & Louie [Colombo] are taking on reactions to my stuff. Like to hear what it is. I hope I am not being judged on what I did in England. That was done merely to start writing, under terrific pressure, because I was alerted for 14 days to go to France before I got cleared to go, and every day I had that pressure sitting on me, afraid I might get too far away in southern England; afraid I might miss the chance. They finally gave me 10 minutes notice. I barely made it, and without half my gear.

It has been a lot of fun writing about the war. However, Bede Irwin's[1] death (he was killed down the front lines about a half mile from me; it could have been Carlisle instead) slowed me down a couple days. But have had fun in the Army. Took an outdoor shower today; almost froze when I got out from under the hot water. Ernest Hemingway and I captured a Chateau with a guy named Stevie [Lieutenant Marcus O. Stevenson of San Antonio, Texas]. I wrote a story about it and left myself out of it.[2] The 1861 French sherry was great. Got half stiff on it. Had a hangover the next day. Got shelled. Shelling no good with hangover.

I finally got my laundry done for a package of cigarettes, a bar of soap and two candy bars. I got my cigarette lighter fixed by giving a G.I. a German officer's cap I had.

By now you should have read my story on John Ballenger's boy Johnny.[3] I hope Ballenger liked it. He has a great kid and I ran into him by chance. His lieutenant was telling me about a boy who blew up a tank, and I asked him to send for him, not knowing who he was or where he came from, and . . . when I asked him what his name was he said, "John Ballenger, Jr."

Good God, when I got back to . . . camp . . . there was my first mail in 6 weeks—and a letter from Ballenger . . . with a paragraph about the boy I had met. What a coincidence. John Ballenger can be proud of that kid. He is a hard going youngster. He looked terribly young. He had a nice way about him. He had a swell smile. He had so little to say about himself. But the other guys in his company told me all about him. Jesus, imagine having a kid who has guts enuff to crawl out and knock out a tank. . . . I talked to him for an hour. I hated to leave him. He is one swell kid. . . . I hoped I did the story justice. It was a swell yarn, but I got feeling a little fatherly over this son of our friend and maybe I spoilt it. I hope not. It should have been one of the best I have ever done, but maybe that isn't good enuff over here.

A captain from headquarters came over . . . last nite and brought the second clipping of mine that I have seen. Nice play. . . . The captain was very pleased at being mentioned . . . in the story. I made a friend. If that Sweet Lady, Miss Mabel Nancy Ford, is not too busy, you might ask her to send me a few clippings of my stuff. Hell, I'll ask her myself. She reads your mail before [Leo] Donovan and Karl [Seiffert] do. Send me a clipping a day, will you, Nancy, wonderful?

Glad I didn't bring any cigarettes. There are millions of them over here. No pipes, tho Jesus, I should have brought a pipe. I have a suitcase full of French francs (worth two cents a franc), so I bought some paratrooper's boots yesterday to get out of those damned leggings. Some bastard with the mind of a moron kicking small babies in the stomach invented those leggings to irritate guys like me.

I have been playing bridge nights with the colonel and lieut-col[onel] of our outfit (200 of us in this camp including 55 prima donna newspaper wizards), and a radio gent. A tough bridge game. But there is very little to do at night. Some excitement now. Three irrepressible photo[grapher]s brought in five German versions of the Jeep. . . . They also brought enuff German equipment to fight another war. I had three Jerry [German] machine guns but I gave them away. I think my hand grenade adjective thrower (my pencil) is good enuff. Have Mabel send me a couple of notebooks, will you? I offered 1,000 francs (20 bucks) for one today and got no takers. There isn't a notebook in France.

Well, Jeff, you are a tough reader-critic and I know I never will satisfy you over here, but write anyway, will you?

Best of luck to you.

Faithfully,   JACK

NOTES

1. Associated Press photographer who had lived in Detroit before the war.
2. "Hemingway Goes to War," *News*, 4 Aug. 1944 [dateline], in Carlisle, "World War II: June 1944–October 1945," (author's possession, courtesy of Anita E. Carlisle), 31. This compilation of Carlisle's stories as war correspondent for the *News* was presented to him at his retirement.
3. "Detroit's Bazooka Kid Bags Nazi Tank Alone," *News*, 3 Aug. 1944 [dateline], in Carlisle, "World War II," 32.

Detroit. August 3, 1944
Dear Jack: *Edward J. Jeffries Jr. to John M. Carlisle*

My conscience has bothered me ever since I wrote that last letter. Your stuff is favorably received and it is good, Jack. But your letters are better. . . .

Those boys you interview must have experiences like that. Write your own experiences occasionally, too.

We think about you a lot, we talk of you often and, of course, everywhere we go around town your mug is on the billboards.

Florence and I stopped in and saw Peggy last night. She is hale and hearty, plenty lonesome and certainly wishes you were back. She claims she is working like a beaver and I presume it is to pass away so many of those idle hours.

The Police Department is in a dither. The *Free Press* and the *Times* are screaming bloody murder because Ballenger is going to let Louis Berg[1] go. Louis has been on furlough at New Baltimore and apparently calling all his friends in Detroit to get in touch with either Ballenger or Jeffries and say it isn't so. I have said nothing, and Ballenger will neither affirm nor deny. Because local news is at a low ebb the editorial writers and news writers have had a picnic over it.

I couldn't wait for your return to fall off the wagon. Anyway I can have a cup of grog with you when you get back and probably, judging from the present outlook, you had better bring a jug of that cider with you because sometimes liquor is so scarce here that even cider would serve as a good substitute.

We are keeping the home fires burning. Don't let yours go out.

Sincerely,   JEFF

NOTE

1. First deputy police commissioner and superintendent.

Detroit. August 4, 1944
Edward J. Jeffries Jr. to George C. Edwards

Dear George:

I was tickled to death to hear that you had passed the bar examination. At least you can carry another scalp at your belt now. Cap McConnell called me at home the night he heard. He was certainly pleased.

City news of real value is at a lower ebb than usual. Currently the *Free Press* and the *Times* are very much alarmed over the possibility of re-tiring Louis Berg and some other top police officials. Mr. Ballenger is getting a few bumps by the local press. . . . [He] seems to be bearing up well under it, and Berg is acting . . . a little hysterically. Perhaps I am doing Louis an injustice. Perhaps it is only his friends who persist in bringing the matter to a head. Those things work usually only to the detriment of the victim.

Gene [Eugene I.] Van Antwerp's[1] boy is coming home this weekend. He has had seventy-five missions over France and Germany. I should say he had earned a rest.

I sent Charlie Edgecomb to Philadelphia last night to gather the low-down on their transit-racial troubles.[2] In addition to that the Police Department sent a couple of policemen down there. I am exceedingly interested to know what their reports will be. I will let you know. . . . Horace [A.] White[3] . . . left word that he also had gone so I will probably hear from him, too, on what caused the situation and what will be done about it.

The Council and the D.S.R. have appropriated $48,000 jointly for W. Earle Andrews, an engineer from New York, working with De Leuw, Cather & Company of Chicago, and Ladislas Segoe, the City Planner, for the purpose of surveying transportation in Detroit. They estimate it will take about three months. . . .

Incidentally Detroit is in its eighteenth day without a traffic fatality of any kind—a new record since we have been keeping statistics.

I have heard from both Carlisle and Hayden since the invasion. Hayden is now a major . . . and, so far, has been unscathed. Carlisle is . . . plenty homesick and, as he tells his wife, . . . streamlined and in that early college condition.

Good luck, my boy. Will write later.

Sincerely,   JEFF

NOTES

1. Councilman who defeated Jeffries in his 1948 bid for a fourth mayoral term.

2. The director-secretary of the Detroit Housing Commission visited Philadelphia to investigate a wildcat strike against the training of blacks as streetcar operators. Several months earlier the Fair Employment Practices Committee had directed the Philadelphia Transit Company to upgrade blacks, and the Transport Workers Union had wrested control of employees from the Philadelphia Rapid Transit Employees Union and negotiated a nondiscriminatory contract, whereby the company—pressured by a War Manpower Commission ruling that the hiring of male workers nationwide would be done through the United States Employment Service—moved to train black platform operators. That action sparked the strike on 1 August, led by a longtime subway motorman. Quickly 5,000 army regulars rode the municipal vehicles, federal agents arrested four ringleaders (for violating the Smith-Connally War Labor Disputes Act of 1943), and selective service officials threatened to draft or dismiss strikers without the benefit of government certificates for employment elsewhere; this firm external force, assisted by the tension-reducing efforts of local black organizations, white journalists, and city policemen, avoided violence and ended the shutdown within a week. See Allan M. Winkler, "The Philadelphia Transit Strike of 1944," *Journal of American History* 59 (June 1972): 73-89.

3. Jeffries appointee and sole black member of the Detroit Housing Commission, minister of the Plymouth Congregational Church, and newspaper columnist. See "The Facts in Our News," *Chronicle*, 12 Aug. 1944, 6, for his report.

[Censored], England. 4 August 1944
John J. McElhone to George C. and Peggy Edwards

Hello, matron, and the cadre, too, since I hope you'll pass this trivia on to be what use it can in moments out of the Georgia sun. I'm recovering from my first feeling of exasperation when I read about the circumstances under which George took the bar exam. He has absolutely no right to pass that test. It separates him from the common herd and provides fuel for the private enterprise boys. But when I think of that last year of school he'll miss by passing I can only extend my best wishes, too.

I enjoyed hearing from you. I hadn't known that my letters were so vital to the success of the invasion, and it was getting a little wearisome reading letters from people complaining about not hearing from me. But letters arriving with yours cleared up the problem for awhile, and . . . [113] newspapers flooding in the next day solved my reading problems. . . . I have a daily subscription to *PM* and the *FP*[1] and until Monday I had received one each, both of which I had read before embarking some moons ago. The local mail facilities nearly collapsed under the onslaught–as I did–but they were welcome. I'll ration myself to one or two a day pending the next deluge.

The Edgecomb story is priceless. Is Charlie still Housing Secretary? Something in one of Donovan's columns makes me wonder. . . . What happened to Martin Dies?[2] What's Jeff going to run for, that he's so Republican in his public remarks? Just what is a cadre? And are you two–and the juniors–as well as you sound?

Things with me are uneventful. "There's less here than meets the eye." For possibly the fifth time since I hit England the sun is bothering me, shining through the windows into my eyes as I type. I'd like to bottle some of it for tomorrow morning. It's precious stuff here. . . . It's 8:15 P.M. and I've been lying out in it for an hour talking with a Denver pilot who's billeted near me. We agree on the Philadelphia business,[3] but he's a little more vicious against the whites. . . . An Ohio boy turned out to be incorrigible when the matter first came up . . . so I'm proceeding to isolate him on his own little island of prejudice. It'll work, until one of the boys . . . sees his own girl–it's different with other fellows' girls–dancing with a colored soldier. The boys aren't too bad, tho, I wish there were more like them.

For every North American serviceman in England the classic cartoon of the war appeared in Beaverbrook's *[Daily] Express*[4] the day after the invasion. It showed an American tank roving through France with a sign loudly proclaiming "NO GUM, CHUM." Kids don't let us walk a block without asking. One little girl, when told by a Yank that he hadn't drawn his week's ration yet, asked to see his ration card to make sure. . . .

I may as well keep writing, I'm tired of reading *Free Presses* and I'm hoarding the *PM*s. I've read John [S.] Knight's[5] impressions of England, some of which were very cogent, indeed. And Sprague Holden's[6] entry in *The Editor's Notebook*, telling very beautiful[ly] and in the best history-book tradition why fascism cannot come to the United States gives me this feeling of unreality about that fabulous land. The same sort of feeling reading Jurgen[7] provides, but without the humor, and you can skip the Freudian implications, too. So nostalgic a tone did it strike that the mechanized era seemed to fade away and all the sharp modern colors become lavenders and mauves. . . . All I could think of while reading it was Jennie [Lee][8] telling me just a week ago about all the notes she brought back from America, intending to make them into a book, and about her inability to make them add up to anything but the corporate state, and of her unwillingness to put those conclusions on paper, partly because of the needs of the times, more because she never gives up, quite. And, of course, in terms of the day after tomorrow, it's just possible that all these violently clashing ingredients in the US may indeed prove to be its salvation.

Ni Bevan[9] impresses me as no one I've ever met. If he isn't Prime Minister of England someday then there's little immediate hope for England. His combination of the emotional and intellectual revolutionary isn't completely sublimated in the practical politician, and I think never will be, but he's sound, and his information and use of it makes me fight to keep my head above water. That was a week ago and that stuff in my lungs is still [Red]. He impressed Bill [Lamson] the same way, only Bill's a better swimmer than I. It was a wonderful evening, though, and I hope to get back next week. I have a couple of Ni's books and there are some people I want to meet and a trip to the Commons in session he wants me to make. I had dinner with them the night after I carried coals to Newcastle and heard . . . [a] lecture to the London Fabians on the Labor Movement in the U.S. . . . Jennie and Ni are a little impatient with the Fabians[10], looking upon them much as they do upon their American counterparts.

A friend of Jennie's brought Camembert [cheese] sent her by her soldier-husband in Normandy. Ni hadn't seen any for four years so I only ate enough to curry him. And to prove to myself that the second front is not without its fruits. (Today's headlines make me eat those words.)[11]

Nearly a month now since any of us here have heard from Bill, as he must be there by now. The liberators may yet be liberators, if nothing else but the law of averages gives us hope.

I hope Flo is well. Greet the new member [James McConnell Edwards] for me. And I eagerly await SOL III, for the G.I. rapport.

JACK

NOTES

1. *PM* (New York) and *Free Press*.

2. Texas Democrat and chairman of the House Committee to Investigate Un-American Activities (later HUAC), created in 1938 to investigate Communist, Fascist, Nazi, and similar organizations.

3. Philadelphia transit strike, August 1-7; see above, EJJ to JMC, 3 Aug. 1944, n. 2.

4. Owned by Canadian-born self-made millionaire and English politician Max Aitken, the *Daily Express* became under his control "a paper for everybody." He began financing the newspaper founded by Sir Arthur Pearson in 1911 and bought it outright five years later, employing it for personal and political advantage. He received peerage in 1917 as Lord Beaverbrook, served as minister of information in David Lloyd George's government during World War I (1917-18) and as minister of aircraft production, minister of state, and minister of war production in Winston Churchill's

government in World War II (1940-42). He resigned his last position for reasons of health, political differences with deputy prime minister Clement Attlee, and limited power over production; he publicly supported the need to open a second front and soon returned as lord privy seal, an adviser outside the war cabinet. A conservative close to Churchill, he invested in other newspapers, but his *Express* was probably the most widely read yet least influential national journal in wartime Britain. See A.J.P. Taylor, *Beaverbrook* (New York: Simon & Schuster, 1972), xiii, 99-100, 413-26, 446, 467-69, 508-16, 524-29, 545-46, 565-68; Angus Calder, *The People's War: Britain, 1939-1945* (New York: Pantheon, 1969), 100-101.

5. Owner of the *Free Press*.

6. *Free Press* editorial writer and columnist.

7. In *Jurgen: A Comedy of Justice* (New York: Edward M. McBride, 1919), James Branch Cabell's mythical protagonist searches for truth and beauty in a cosmic setting. See Desmond Tarrant, *James Branch Cabell: The Dream and the Reality* (Norman: Univ. of Oklahoma Press, 1967).

8. In 1932 and again in 1941, Lee visited the United States—as, respectively, lecturer and unofficial government representative—where she befriended numerous union leaders, including Victor and Walter Reuther, who introduced her to McElhone. Whenever they came to England, she put them up as house guests, indicating an American-British labor link. She also knew George and Peggy Edwards. Jennie Lee, *My Life with Nye* (London: Jonathan Cape, 1980), 86-87, and 140-41; Michael Foot, *Aneurin Bevan: A Biography,* vol. 1, *1897-1945* (New York: Atheneum, 1963), 465-66; phone conversation with Peggy Edwards (Cincinnati), 18 May 1995.

9. Representing the left wing of the Labour Party, Bevan opposed the nonpartisan coupon elections and Bevin's postwar "employment policy" as an insufficient program of public works; he supported equal pay for women teachers and national ownership of the property necessary to replace housing destroyed by German bombs. He sought to reestablish party competition and pressed for socialistic postwar plans, challenging Prime Minister Churchill, who considered every parliamentary vote one of confidence in his government. Bevan and intellectual Harold Laski stressed the need for party independence, lest wartime coalition politics overwhelm the Labour Party, its ideology and goals. See Foot, *Aneurin Bevan,* 454-98; Stephen Brooke, *Labour's War: The Labour Party during the Second World War* (Oxford: Clarendon Press, 1992), esp. 9.

10. Named after Roman general Fabius Cunctator, who stressed delaying tactics and infiltration (in this case of the government), the Fabian Society was founded in 1883 and advocated these—rather than more drastic—measures as the means to bring a socialist state into existence in England. Among its early members were George Bernard Shaw and H.G. Wells, and it joined with unionists to form the Labour Party. See A.H. McBriar, *Fabian Socialism and English Politics, 1884-1918* (Cambridge: Cambridge Univ. Press, 1962).

11. The announcement of Hitler's purge of the German Army officers who had attempted to assassinate him on 20 July. See "Hitler Denounces Nine Generals," *Times* (London), 5 Aug. 1944, 4.

	[Censored], France. 11 August 1944
Dear Jeff:	*John M. Carlisle to Edward J. Jeffries Jr.*

The GI Joes have a phrase for it, a harsh, typical man-to-man phrase. They call it being "all pissed off." That's what your July 19th letter did to me. I came back to our camp after being away five days. I hadn't shaved. I had washed out of my helmet. I had slept on the ground. I never had my shoes off. I had never had my field uniform off. Three nights I wore my helmet as I slept. Hell, a helmet never was meant to sleep in. I was dead tired. I went to the mail box. Three letters. None from Peggy. But a letter from you. You are supposed to be my best friend. I ate that letter open. I read it through three times. Christ, it put me in the dumps. I was in the dumps anyway.

I went with a spearhead driving into Le Mans; not with just the Yank force, but with the spearhead up front. And I went alone. None of our great war correspondents, who write about their own private heroism (spending their time at division headquarters miles from the front, and making the folks back home believe they are at the front) would go with me. I went because I wanted to see a little more of this goddamn war. I went with the spearhead for three days. We cut through the Jerries for 45 miles. I saw more of the war than I ever wanted to see. Christ, I was scared to death. On a Monday afternoon, a column of Yanks drove 800 Jerries down a railroad right smack into the company I was with. We fought them on three sides, front, back and rear. I sat in a ditch, with brambles all around. They gave me two riflemen for protection. We are not allowed to carry arms. Christ, they came up within 50 yards before we cut them into pieces. I hid all my German souvenirs in case I got captured. They shoot you if they catch you with them. I kept looking out, watching the action, making notes. A captain roared at me through the hedgerow to "Keep your goddamn head down."

Well, that's the way the goddam fight for Le Mans went. We hit them all the way for 45 miles. I named our jeep Peggy O'Neil after my gal, God bless her; and painted the goddam sign on while we were being shelled. I walked along a hedgerow to talk to a general. A shell came screaming over. I hit the ditch with the general. The shell hit 20 feet back of us; never exploded. The general said, very calmly, "Have you got a cigarette?" I was so shaky it took me minutes to find one. For three nights the snipers popped at us. The Jerries flew overhead trying to bomb us. They strafed the rear of the column. They killed a kid I had come to know. I wrote two stories in the field. Sent them back by courier. The goddam courier got killed. I had to do the stories over.

That night, after reading your letter, I wrote three stories without having eaten for 10 hours. Our lights went out. Took 30 minutes to get them fixed. They wanted to send the courier on to the radio sending outfit. I kept hollering, "Hold that goddam courier." The censor trimmed some of my stuff. It didn't even make sense. I thought, "To hell with it," it's the best I can do. I went to bed with my clothes on. We had moved our camp. While I was gone the Jerries came over, dropped flares, bombed the fields all around, missed the camp. So the new camp was strange to me. I fell over tent guy ropes. I finally got to bed. All the time I was thinking, so I can do better. I can write like a columnist. I can put more of a punch in it. I wrote better on my Sunday pieces! Jesus, I was disgusted. Jeff, I have done the best I can do. There is no better. If my stories stink, well, they stink. This motorized war is tough to cover. It took me four hours, fighting convoys to get back to camp, driving that jeep down to the floor board. We almost tipped over five times. I have lost 32 pounds. I have written my stuff the way [Fred] Gaertner wants it. I have never lost with him yet. Not in 17 years. Using Detroit names, we keep 400,000 Detroit families watching, waiting for the paper. I refuse to be a military smart aleck.

Perhaps you are right. Undoubtedly you are right. But I meet guys at the front with clippings of my stuff. Their mothers and wives sent those clippings to them. Well, it makes them happy anyway.

All I can say to you, pal, is that I have done the best I can. I have worked seven days a week. I have got about four hours sleep at night. I have lived in a tea cup. We move around so much you can't get any laundry done. Half the time I stink. Half the time I feel lousy. The office never sends me any clippings. They never tell me anything. Now and then Gaertner cables me, "Everything fine. Good work." What the hell does that mean? He is too laconic. My money got lost he sent me. I have been living without any money for three weeks. What's the use wiring for more money? The Army will only lose it in red tape anyway. By the end of the war I will get it.

What the hell, I'm no soldier. I never heard a gun go off until the Race riot, and that was peanuts compared to this. But I am a reporter at heart. I am going up there where the news is as long as I can get up there. I am proud of one thing. The outfit I was with—I wish I could tell you what outfit it is and whose it is—made me a member.[1] I had just got in an argument with a goddam snotty captain because I told him his food was lousy, he was lousy, and he had the guts of a chipmunk. So when the colonel called me in front of his staff, out there in a field in front of Le Mans, I thought I was going to be dressed down. Instead he made me a swell speech, gave me a shoulder patch of his outfit, and patted me on the back. He did say that "You're the only goddam war correspondent who had guts enuff to go with our outfit and you're one of us." He said a lot of other nice things. I felt very good. We got drunk together that night, and I told him I was scared to death and he said, "Hell, at times I didn't feel so good myself." The colonel and I got drunk because the snipers almost got us in Le Mans. They came close, Jeff; very close. I noticed this morning that my beard is getting a little gray. So don't be too critical, pal. I am doing the best I can. I am no goddamn hero. I am the worst goddamn coward in the army, but I am a reporter first, last, and always. My best to you.

Yours,   JACK

NOTE

1. Carlisle accompanied units of the U.S. Third Army under the command of Gen. George S. Patton.

New Guinea, South Pacific. 23 August 1944
Dear George: *James P. Simpson to George C. Edwards*

I pass for the moment the fact that you—as ever—owe me a letter.

Here's a little item I whipped up for the boys last nite. Our latrine has no walls, so I have nothing better to do with it than this.

SONG FOR A CIVILIAN
WHO BELIEVES WHAT HE READS

It gladdens my heart when I think of the part
That we're playing and who it is for,
And I freely admit we're all doing our bit
For the soldiers who're fighting the war.

I believe ev'ry word that I've read or I've heard;
For the Office of War Information
Would censor or curb any story or blurb
That they thought was a falsification.

And I think that it's nice that we all sacrifice
All the things we can give up with ease,
And I'm glad that I know all the comforts that go
To our soldiers who've gone overseas.

No song ever sung with a press-agent's tongue
In General Somervell's[1] cheek
Could tell deeds that are vaster than our Quartermaster
Can match any day in the week.

Each hundred men get a good radio set
For whiling away their spare time,
And a phonograph, too, with records—brand new—
Of music both hot and sublime.

All jungle fighters get cigarette lighters;
If they smoke, they get two or three more;
And each of our men gets a good fountain pen,
Guaranteed for a lifetime or more.

And, if you should fail to find watches for sale,
Be patient; don't be too outspoken.
Our boys over there all get one watch to wear
And a spare one in case it gets broken.

You don't hear us mutter at having no butter;
We're glad to be just a bit skinny,
When ev'ryone knows that our butter all goes
On the bread of our boys in New Guinea.

Yes, ev'rything good made of metal or wood,
And the best things to drink and to eat,
For convenience or pleasure, in bountiful measure,
We pile in huge heaps at their feet.

And the magazine ads show the mothers and dads
An oil painting of how it's all planned
So the finest food reaches our boys on the beaches
Just two hours after they land.

Without any compunction—with some little unction—
We pat our own backs for this stunt.
Let it be understood that *nothing's* too good
For our heroes who fight at the front.
Positively the final edition; Destroy all others[2]

We sing it to such tunes as "Home on the Range," "Believe me if all those endearing young charms," "The Man on the Flying Trapeze," and "It's a Grand Old Flag."

The war is very tedious again at this place. I hope you're finding it so these days.

Willard Baker[3] made Major, as S-3 [operations officer] of a combat engineer battalion that was up in front on D-Day in Normandy.

I can't vote because my wife forgot to pay my poll tax. However, I'm not sure who I'd vote for [in the presidential election], if I could. Neither candidate [Roosevelt or Dewey] has ever made any remark indicating that he has any conception of the International Situation—Past, Present or Future—on this side of the world. It seems clear to me that if we hang around out here without owning anything, we'll provoke somebody else into attacking us again, and make nothing out of it for our pains. So I see only two rational courses. (1) Call it off, move back to Hawaii, and let whoever wants to use these islands do so if he's man enough. (2) Assume control of them if we're going to defend them against everyone who wants to use them. It was the failure to adopt either course that got me out here this time, and I don't ever want to come back on a similar mission unless I've got something at stake.

As for Europe, I'm not interested, and I never was.

If we don't develop some statesmen with savvy, we'd better become isolationist as all hell. Let's have a letter.

Love and kisses,   JP SIMPSON

NOTES:

1. Brig. Gen. Brehon B. Somervell, Army Supply Program.
2. Simpson closed an earlier version of the poem with these stanzas:

> When the war has been won, will your husband and son
> Go back to their old ways of life?
> —Pay with trouble and sweat for whatever they get
> For themselves and the girl-friend or wife?

> How will they react to the cold, cruel fact
> That luxuries, such as they've had,
> Can only be gotten by chopping some cotton,
> Or doing something else equally bad?

> I'm afraid that these millions of former civilians
> Now love these new luxuries so,
> That after we win they'll all fight to stay in,
> And our army'll continue to grow.

> Though some have the gall, while enjoying it all,
> To contend that they're having it tough,
> Yet each wants to keep his own personal jeep.
> And keep living—as now—on the cuff.

> And I very much fear that they won't volunteer
> To become poor civilians again.
> But, when peace has occurred, let *none* be deferred!
> Draft all of them out when we win.
> > Box 5, pt. 2, Edwards Collection.

3. A friend and Kappa Sigma fraternity brother of Simpson and Edwards.

Detroit. August 25, 1944
Edward J. Jeffries Jr. to John M. Carlisle [telegram]

You win. I am a louse. Your stuff now excellent.

New Caledonia. 16 September 1944
Joseph Lash to George C. Edwards

Dear George:

I wonder whether this letter will find you in Europe, the Pacific or OCS. I have run into so many old friends since coming down to New Caledonia from Gacon Is[land], that it wouldn't surprise me at all to see you suddenly swing down the road—no surprise but darn real pleasure. I was brought down here in August to set up an orientation program for the squadron's detachments which are scattered throughout the S. Pacific. After 15 months in the Solomons, this place's coolness, cosmopolitanism, etc. is a real treat and the work has been enjoyable, altho having set up the program I am currently busy with administrative work at Hdqtrs.

A group of us–a Harvard philosophy instructor, a Texas chaplain, a former U.P. [United Press] man and the youthful Dutch consul–meet regularly for dinner and discussion. These evenings are like a breath of life, and reconcile me to this place for all its recently acquired spit and polish.

And the news is excellent–so much so that one can reasonably hope to be demobilized by the end of 1945. I had a letter from Anna. She and Paul are having great difficulty and the Vansittart views on the treatment of Germany seem to have gained wide acceptance among liberals. Paul has always been a stormy figure in the emigration and now the whispering campaign against him is reaching a climax.[1] One could write an eloquent piece on "learning the wrong lessons from history."

My best to Peg when you write her and much good luck to yourself.

JOE

NOTE

1. In the early autumn of 1940, Sir Robert Vansittart, chief diplomatic adviser to the British government, aired several broadcasts that portrayed Germans as innately brutal and bellicose, responsible for all the wars of Europe over the previous seventy years. His racist tenet became even clearer in his December 1943 plan for the unconditional surrender and treatment of Germany: Allied occupation, government, and approval of all economic assistance; war crime trials, military demobilization, and "closing down" of any potential to wage war; reparation payments and reeducation programs. Though he was no longer associated with the government at that time, Vansittartism attracted many revenge-minded English citizens, including trade unionist leaders (but not Aneurin Bevan, who denounced such anti-Hun demagogy).

Anna's full identity is unknown, but Paul refers to Paul Hagen–in actuality Karl Frank–who led a small group of German resisters identifying themselves as *Neu Beginnen* (New Beginning) and living in London. Earlier in the war he had received assistance from the British government to smuggle individuals out of Nazi-held France. He had also sought aid from the Roosevelt administration before the United States officially entered the war, through a meeting with Eleanor Roosevelt arranged by Lash. Having drawn criticism from various quarters, including the American Friends of German Freedom, who viewed him "now as a German, now as a British agent," Hagen experienced the full force of such rumors after Vansittart tapped anti-German feelings. See Calder, *The People's War*, 489-91; Foot, *Aneurin Bevan*, 197 n. 1, 422-23; *New York Times*, 5 Dec. 1943, 5; Joseph P. Lash, *Eleanor Roosevelt: A Friend's Memoir* (Garden City, N.Y.: Doubleday, 1964), 30, 32, 36, 84, 111, 113 n. 1.

Detroit. October 11, 1944
Edward J. Jeffries Jr. to Martin S. Hayden

Dear Martin:

I read your letter to Hermie [Krause] and I am very much disgusted with the mail service. The notches on the wall would indicate that I have written you two letters since I last heard from you. However, it was very good to hear from you even through Hermie.

I noticed therein that the novelty of invasion and being in France has completely worn off. You have my sympathy. Aside from the danger in warfare, I think that the worst feature of it is the diversion of men from their home life and their normal walks of life. It is a terrible thing that this country has suffered; that you boys in particular are suffering from. If hoping and praying will finish it quickly, you may be sure that the folks back home are doing their bit in that respect.

Municipal affairs are relatively quiet. The Council has been indicating its independence of late by overriding my vetoes—singling out the nurses for increased pay to the exclusion of everybody else—and last night they amended the salary ordinance providing for straight time instead of overtime for salaried employees by resolving that out of the 8,000 or 9,000 salaried employees, 33 Election Commission employees should be paid time and a half while the rest should be paid straight time for their overtime. But that keeps life exciting.

Most of our activity is one of planning and talking about what we are going to do when the opportunity presents itself for so doing. Almost all of this revolves about the acquisition of physical improvements like parks, highways, rehabilitation programs, schools, libraries, police stations, etc.

Peggy Carlisle got a cable from Jack that he is on his way home. I couldn't help thinking that he was very lucky to be able to come home when he got tired and sick of it. I presume that there are several million others who would like to come home by now.

I appointed a committee this summer to study a suggested airport on made land in Lake St. Clair. It has Walter S. McLucas as chairman. The members are K.T. Keller, C.E. Wilson, William E. Anderman, William Scripps, John S. Knight, George M. Slocum and Oscar Webber. Allen Dean called it the Taj Mahal committee which isn't a bad name for it.[1] We have had two meetings. It's amazing to me how we gentlemen like to duck civic responsibility unless we desire to use our influence for a favorite individual or personal hobby. Anyway they have decided that they will allow an overall survey to be made by the State in competition with Oakland, Macomb, Wayne Counties and Detroit, and that they will await, if necessary, this report. So after two free luncheons we are adjourning, awaiting further call. I didn't even accomplish one of my cute purposes— I didn't even get the newspaper representatives to agree on anything, much less any crystallized idea on air needs. Each of the three newspapers, it seems to me, is fighting for a different location. Come hell or high water, surveys not to the contrary. Incidentally, none of them agreed on the location to be studied.

I haven't seen those Hayden youngsters since you have been away. At the rate the war has gone, they will probably be in the finishing up process.

I was interested in your comments on Mr. Roosevelt and Mr. Dewey. I don't think that anybody knows which will be elected. The polls are confusing. I don't mean the Polish. I still think Mr. Roosevelt has the inside track plus the fact that it is a good axiom to string along with the old one until the new one comes along.

Detroit, of course, is overwhelmingly Democratic. The wise-acres apparently think the out-State is overwhelmingly Republican. Most of the prognosticators feel that Michigan is safely in the Dewey column. Something that Dewey or the Republicans said or did has piqued Mr. Roosevelt. He is much more bitter in his harpooning of the Republicans and Dewey than he has been in other campaigns. He picked up a relatively hum drum campaign and gave Mr. Dewey the first opportunity he has had to look relatively good. The home front boys are a little confused, and, I repeat, I think anything can happen but that probably history will repeat and that Mr. Roosevelt will be our President for better or for worse.

Incidentally, we came within an ace, in fact just one pitched ball of winning the American League pennant. Without any doubt in the closing six weeks of the campaign we had the best team in the league, but the Brownies'[2] luck, plus a late start on our part, nosed us out. It is astounding how enthusiastic we can get in this town of ours. My God, I was going to the baseball game every day in the week when I had been to only one during the summer. I am sure that Mr. [Walter O.] Briggs[3] had a field day, but it wasn't to be. The Browns won the last day and we lost the last day, and we lost the flag by a single game.

Miriam Hewlett[4] is in Italy with the Red Cross. I think her headquarters are in Rome. Grace received word that she arrived, but I don't think she has heard since from Miriam as to what she is actually doing. In my next letter if I have any news about her, I will tell you.

It is good to hear from you. Your letters are very interesting and I will make you a bargain—if you will write more often I will try.

Sincerely,

JEFF

NOTES

1. Dean (Detroit Board of Commerce) was alluding to the eminence of its members: McLucas, chair, National Bank of Detroit; Keller, president, Chrysler Corporation; Wilson, chair, General Motors Corporation; Anderman, publisher, *Times*; Scripps, president, *News*; Knight, publisher, *Free Press*; Slocum, president, Slocum Publishing Company; Webber, chief executive officer, J.L. Hudson Company.

2. St. Louis Browns baseball team.

3. Owner of the Briggs Manufacturing Company, Briggs Stadium, and the Detroit Tigers baseball team.

4. Social worker and friend of Jeffries and his sisters.

Normandy, France. 24 October 1944
My Dear Jeff: *Martin S. Hayden to Edward J. Jeffries Jr.*

I several days ago received a letter from Nancy in which she indignantly denied a Hayden allegation to Hermie [Krause] that you owed me a letter. Of course, since Nancy is carrying your cross, I cannot besmirch it too much but I still have the feeling that I am right and Nancy prejudiced.

Here in this part of the world things still go on although the excitement which the newspapers convey as accompanying life in the ETO [European Theater of Operations] is considerably dulled by rain and mud. I have been in a lot of rain and seen a lot of mud in my day but, Brother, it is nothing as compared with the Normandy variety. On the rare occasions when it stops coming down we know that it is just so that the celestial water makers can refill their pumps—so we keep our umbrellas continually up and waiting for more.

The mud is everywhere. Despite the fact that half the German army of a few months ago is currently employed in slopping mud around with shovels, the roads are a horror and our bivouac areas are beyond description. They tell me that the cows of Normandy are noted for their strong legs which resulted from the fact that, in winter, they had to wallow through pasture mud which was belly deep. We are now living in those same fields except that the cows would not recognize them as all of the grass disappeared when we dug fox holes last June. Now the holes are filled up but the resulting disturbed surface would no longer make even a respectable mud wallow. All in all it is weather worth talking about.

The war is of course "off the record" in our correspondence and anyhow, with access to the newspapers and radio, your information as to what in Hell we are doing is undoubtedly more up to date than mine. However, almost as interesting to me is the opportunity of watching a country going to Hell which France is doing in a sure and terrible way.

I think probably some people at home have the idea of the political confusion. The hatred between classes which I think had a lot to do with France's decay prior to 1940 has been accentuated rather than calmed by the German occupation. According to the well-to-do people the FFI is largely communistic and bent solely on the objective of seizing the government. On the other hand an FFI Lieutenant, formerly an actor, whom I talked to in Paris, denied this. As expressed by him the FFI is primarily opposed to the old Regular Army officer class whom they claim deserted their men in 1940. The rich (who really aren't rich anymore) intimate that the working classes really didn't mind the occupation too much and the poor make it clear that they are bitter because the rich were able to buy in the black market and eat better than did they.

Momentarily everyone seems to recognize [Gen. Charles] De Gaulle[1] as the top man but they do so in a sort of temporary manner. No one seems to have anything against him but everyone seems to feel that he will not last.

Economically things are worse. As a first example, take this district of Normandy. In peace time . . . it was the meat and dairy center of France and exceedingly prosperous. The fighting across the country destroyed many of the cattle. . . . Worse still, however, was the destruction of their land. For centuries these Norman farmers had built [a] series of small pastures, each fenced in by a thick hedgerow of woven vines and under-brush growing out of mounds of earth. When we landed we found the hedges bristling with Germans and the ensuing fighting tore many of them open and ruined others completely. Then, after the fighting, came the American transformation of this peninsula into a giant supply base. For awhile every field housed troops, rations, ammunition, fuel, vehicles, guns and all the rest which goes to make up and supply an army of a million or so. As we occupied each new field . . . bull dozers bobbed in to tear out the hedgerows completely. Now there are virtually no fields which are still enclosed and Normandy does not have . . . the wherewithal to artificially fence fields. As a result they have no way to keep their cattle in.

Adding to their difficulty is the fact that many of the men are being mobilized by the French government so it is impossible to hire anyone to work as farm hands. Finally, there is no transportation to bring in the winter feed necessary to augment the pasturage and no transportation to take the beef to the Paris market where it is needed so badly. If a farmer can find a truck and some gasoline, he cannot, under French law, carry the cattle to the Paris market himself.

I heard the net result summed up last night by an old couple who live near our camp and are in the middle of it. Everyone is trying to sell [their] cattle before they starve but there are practically no buyers. At an auction in the village last week a prize cow went for 2000 francs which, according to our 50-to-one standard (and no one but the Americans values the franc so high) is $40.

Everywhere it is the same. For lack of a single machine part whole factories are closed. Everyone needs coal but the mines can't run because they need timbers for reconstruction. The wood is in another part of the country and there is no transportation. Around Paris the perfume factories are closed for lack of blossoms and in the south of France the flowers died in the fields for lack of transportation. The last is a matter of importance only to the people who eat from growing the flowers and making the perfume but it is typical of every business and every industry.

Paris itself is a daffy place but still wonderful for Americans if their money holds out and they don't look under the surface. In one respect it is the least warlike looking capital in the world. There are a lot of American soldiers about and you see the FFI running up and down the streets with nowhere apparently to go but the civilian population seems to be thinking on a different line than the rest of the world. As has been the case since 1940, eating enough is still their prime object in life and everyone concentrates on it with his full energy.[2]

The Germans, as part of their system of milking the country, deliberately issued food coupons in insufficient quantities to keep a human alive. That made black marketing a necessity and during the occupation there were two which the French referred to respectively as the "good" black market and the "German" black market. The former sold things at "reasonable" rates of only five or six hundred percent more than the legal price. The latter was much steeper. The Germans profited by paying high rates in their printed currency for anything from candle sticks to used shoes and the people peddled their possessions to buy food.

Out of it has grown a whole class of French profiteers. Many of them are youngsters in their teens who made fabulous sums by taking sometimes a bicycle and sometimes an automobile and going forth into the hinterlands to buy for re-sale in Paris. They are still at it with the result that the wife of the FFI Lieutenant whom I have already mentioned showed me a pound of imitation Swiss cheese for which she had paid eight dollars according to our valuation of the franc.

All during the war, wages and salaries were frozen in Paris. With the necessity of eating from the black market, people could not live on the frozen wages and they became a joke. Any employer who kept his help did so by paying them so much for the record and then slipping them an illegal addition "under the table." Last month the freeze order was lifted to the extent that the new government "ordered" that all wages go up what apparently amounted to forty percent. Naturally the prices at once went up too so everything stayed the same including the number of francs American soldiers get.

As I mentioned we are paid on a basis of fifty francs for the dollar. Steps are taken to see that no soldiers get their hands on dollars and trafficking in them is a serious court martial offense. The reason for the precaution is easy to see. The last report I got was that the merchants of Paris were willing to offer 300 francs in cash or merchandise for an American dollar. That makes it a little rough on the pocket books of the American stationed in or lucky enough to get to Paris. For instance, on the night before I returned to these mud flats I paid off on some hospitality by taking three people to the Ritz for dinner. It is about the only restaurant running normally and is open only to allied officers and their guests. The service was excellent but the food virtually non-existent and the bill took what our finance officer claims is $44 worth of francs. A bottle of champagne (of which plenty was hidden from the Germans) cost 500 francs when I was in Paris. Later returnees report the price is now 800. I saw a wrist watch in a jewelry store window. It was apparently comparable with a good Hamilton and I inquired as to the price, more out of curiosity than with any idea of buying. The list price was 12,000 francs but that was only on the condition that you had some old gold or enough cash to buy some in the black market. I pointed out that American soldiers didn't usually carry old gold around with them and he said that in that case the price would be 24,000 francs which is $480 in terms of our pay. Need I say that I still wear the watch that runs only if shaken every two hours.

But now I have writ my piece and, if I did owe you a letter, you now owe me two on the basis of this wordage. Give my best to Nancy, Florence, Hermie and the boys in the lavatory and of the executive suite and write me all the gossip. Incidentally, where did [John S.] Knight get the wherewithal to buy the *Chicago Daily News* as recently reported in our journals?

Your friend,

                                                                MARTIN

NOTES

1. De Gaulle formed the French National Committee (June 1940) and in May 1943 teamed with Gen. Henri Giraud to create the French Committee of National Liberation, which became the French Provisional Government-in-Exile in London in June 1944. On 23 October the organization was recognized by Great Britain, Russia, and the United States as France's provisional regime.
2. France was under Nazi occupation from early June 1940 until late August 1944.

Detroit. November 7, 1944
Dear Martin: *Edward J. Jeffries Jr. to Martin S. Hayden*

Very apparently some of my letters have not been delivered. For your edification, I have written you four times, not including this letter, since I received your letter describing D-Day. This is only for the record because I so thoroughly enjoyed your recent letter that, as you said, it made up for all the answers I might have had.

Today is Election Day and, for the first time, I was unable to vote this morning because of the long queue outside of the booth. I will try again later. They have extended voting time until ten o'clock and, in spite of the huge vote we expect, and the green help secured for the purpose, I expect that the votes will be taken care of substantially. I don't feel, however, that election parties tonight will be very successful as it is anticipated that the vote will be close practically all over the country and, therefore, the results will hinge upon the finals, and it looks to me as though the election parties should be Wednesday or Thursday night.

The campaign locally has been a desultory affair. The CIO and the PAC have completely taken over the Democratic Party. Their chief concern was national and, therefore, the local allegedly Democratic ticket centered all its activity on the national picture. The local Democrats will all be elected, and apparently the State Republicans will all be easily elected, and both sides have been concentrating on the national picture. It has been a long time since there was as much doubt on the part of one of the unprejudiced, non-partisan as to the result. [Thomas E.] Dewey, however, or at least the Republicans, must be stronger than [Wendell L.]

Willkie, or else Roosevelt is weaker than he was in '40. Whether either factor is sufficient to defeat Mr. Roosevelt you will know, I am sure, before you get my letter.

Jack Carlisle is back and, incidentally, glad to be back. He says that he has seen enough of France and the war to last him for some time. Somebody invited him to go hunting, and we suggested that he might jump out of his skin if he heard a gun shot. He says he never wants to hear that again. He lost a lot of weight but otherwise is hearty and sound. He is a big-shot war correspondent and it apparently irks him.

I have been enjoying . . . two months of relative quiet on the behavior front. All the wild-eyed boys have been with Brother Roosevelt, and they apparently have sincerely tried not to rock the boat, at least during the campaign. The [Common] Council, however, has set the scene for trouble if I am any judge of the future. Right out of the blue they dipped into the bag and raised the nurses' pay which already was higher than any other nurses in the whole world, and neglected to include anybody else. The County [Wayne] in their budget raised all their help above the schedule of the City of Detroit, and we have still got eight months to go before a new budget goes into effect. I suspect that about four or five days after the election the merry-go-round starts again.

There have been many rumors flying to the effect that the little steel formula[1] will be raised, and if that happens it will take more strength of character than I am sure exists in the City Hall to prevent re-budgeting as of about January 1, February 1, or March 1, or some other more indeterminate date. But then a lull such as we have had the last six weeks might get a gent intolerant and smug if it continued too long.

Karl Seiffert has left the paper [News] and gone with McManus, John & Adams Inc., 2400 Fisher Building. We gave the usual going away party the other night at the Public Lighting Commission and Jeffries got out with his hide and a little fresh money. I had to stay to hang the last dog and use my skill to the utmost in that dirty poker game called baseball. . . .

My kid nephew Jeff [Benjamin Jeffries] is on the high seas somewhere in the Pacific.

I will drop you a line when the returns are in, and give you an analysis maybe of what did happen.

Sincerely,   J E F F

NOTES

1. Established by the War Labor Board in July of 1942, the "little steel formula" tied wages in all industries to the cost of living, permitting no more than a 15 percent increase above the scale of January 1, 1941.

The election is over and, of course, you know the results. Michigan, we think, went to Mr. Roosevelt. The election machinery here broke down, and the tabulation for President may or may not be accurate, but the best guess is that Mr. Roosevelt carried Michigan by about 20,000. So far as I am able to determine, the only large amounts of money that were lost on the election were lost as a result of Dewey's failure to carry Michigan. I think it safe to conclude that the combination of PAC and the fear of the general public to change Presidents at this critical stage of the war were the controlling factors. The latter, I feel, is much more important than the activity of the PAC. Bear in mind, however, that the PAC was tremendously active and did help.

[Georges] Clemenceau's[1] grandson was in Detroit Friday as the speaker in the Town Hall series. I met him at noon at the Book-Cadillac [Hotel]. I had your last letter in my pocket and I told him that I thought it would be very interesting for him to read it. He read it and was quite insistent that I give him a copy. I did. I hope you don't mind. In fact, this is the second letter that you have written me and it was so good that people have taken copies. So I am warning you that other people read my mail and you will be careful what you put in it. But for emphasis, I do repeat that your last letter was the best I have seen on conditions. You are right, our papers are filled with war activities, but we get very little of the information that you supplied. When we do—speaking for myself at least—I always take it with a grain of salt. But knowing you or, for that matter, whoever does the writing, makes it considerably more interesting and accurate.

Now that the presidential election is over, conversation and thinking have turned to the next municipal election. Mr. Cobo . . . is again publicly trying to make up his mind whether or not he is a candidate for Mayor.

[Recorder's Court Judge] Tom Cotter passed away a couple or three weeks ago and Mr. Dowling and a few other customers are trying to get the job. Your paper, or at least some segments of it, is interested in a proposition whereby Mr. Krause might be appointed, especially if I would appoint Mr. Dowling Corporation Counsel in his place. By the way, that is very confidential. Don't write it back to anybody that you have heard it. I don't know what the result will be. Incidentally, I am in quite a predicament myself because my good friend, John D. Watts, thinks he is going to get it. . . . We have been friends for 35 years. That's a long time out of my life—his, too, for that matter. But I presume Mr. [Governor Harry F.] Kelly will do as he wishes and the Lord only knows what he wishes.[2]

Good Luck and take care of yourself.

Sincerely,   J E F F

NOTES

1. French premier (1841-1920) who represented France at the Versailles Peace Treaty negotiations ending World War I.

2. Cotter died at the age of sixty-seven on 15 October, having served in the Recorder's Court for a quarter-century. He was replaced by Krause rather than Traffic Court Judge Watts.

Philippine Islands. 18 November 1944
James P. Simpson to George C. Edwards

Dear George:

Your letters . . . eventually reach me. They would come in ⅙th of the time however if you would (a) send them by 6¢ air mail, or (b) send them by V-mail. I got yours of 11 September about 5 November, along with several of late October from others. I didn't answer it, pending our move to the Philippines, which has now been peacefully and safely accomplished. The censor likes to have me say that I am somewhere in the Philippines. I guess he thinks that in case you show this letter to any of your Jap friends, they'll perhaps suspect that I'm in Manila, or Davao or some such place, and thus be misled into some sort [of] error. Confidentially, the Japs know where we are. They send planes over quite frequently to keep in touch with us. The only one that has come within range of our guns got in direct contact with us and fell in flames.

You got into the army at the right time. You'll probably get to return to the states after a normal tour of duty overseas. It appears that a good sergeant in the infantry has an excellent chance at getting commissioned in the field. I wouldn't be surprised to hear that you were commissioned. If the war lasts 50 years, I'll still be a 1st Lt. in my job. There are no promotions in AA [Anti-Aircraft Artillery] to speak of. My job is administrative, and the next higher echelon of command, the Group, has no administrative offices.

We are very glad to be out of New Guinea, where we stayed almost a year without ever seeing a civilized civilian or any sign of civilization. The Japs who lived within artillery range of us there are still there, and can have the place for all I care. Maybe the Dutch want them to leave. If they do, they can run them out themselves.[1]

I hope you get to see the Philippines. This section is much like the damp tropical parts of Mexico and Central America. The people are poor. They are farmers and fishermen. The interesting thing about them to me is that they are higher in morals, culture, intelligence and physical beauty than I had thought.

They take pride in wearing clean clothes, though they are in rags. They neither beg nor steal, but seek work or exchange for what they want. All of them over about 10 and under about 30 speak and understand at least a little English. Their admiration and gratitude to the Americans is evident and touching. I would not have believed it. They have completely won the hearts of the Americans, who are causing no end of trouble to the Quartermaster, by giving away clothing in exchange for services, and to the authorities responsible for procurement of labor, by giving them rations and clothing of value in excess of the prescribed wage rate.

These people never knuckled under to the Japs. Many houses near here were burned down because the people were not obedient. A seventeen year old girl, mother of one with another in the oven, who does my washing, tells me that her father was captain of the guerrillas in the nearby village. The Japs killed her mother and she thinks they killed her father. One of the guerrillas was around here a day or so ago, bare-footed, as every Filipino I've seen but one has been, dressed in shorts and a polo shirt. He looked about like Douglas Fairbanks would have looked in his heyday if he had tried to portray a Filipino guerilla.

This is the same sort of people we are. I did not think so before. They are, as the saying goes, underprivileged, but they're not inferior people in any other sense.

As for their spirit, many of our patriots could take lessons from them. When we arrived they saw our men carrying ammunition out of the LST's [Landing Ship Tank]. Men, women and children, without being asked and without being paid, fell into line and helped carry it out. Similarly, when we were setting up a bivouac, the neighbors fell to and helped.

Theirs is a rich country in resources, and they are a clever and industrious people, civilized in their tastes and morals. I suspect that their admiration for us will be our most valuable international asset during the next few decades.

JP SIMPSON

NOTE

1. West New Guinea had been under Dutch influence and control before the war.

Fort Benning, Georgia. 4 December 1944
George C. Edwards to Friends

STANDARD OPERATIONAL LETTER VII

1) . . . Just in case you get no farther here's wishing you all—in Detroit, Dallas, New York, Washington, The Philippines—as merry a *Christmas* as operations, supplies and space allow, and for all of us a much happier *New Year,* and I hope that next Christmas at any rate can truly be dedicated to *Peace on Earth—Good will to men.*

We will now flash back to the beginning of SOL VII some months ago at "Old" Camp Wheeler—(darn if I can't already work up some nostalgia for the place).

The chief news with me is that I am now Corporal Edwards. Corporal is an army rank somewhat below that of General. But it is important none-the-less. For one thing it means $16 more on pay day. For another the stripes help in giving the orders which are part of my current job here. And then of course there are real possibilities of advancement–just look at [onetime "corporals"] Napoleon and Hitler. I reckon that's not a good parallel, however.

S.O.L. VI ended just before bivouac with me wondering what next. Much has happened since then. Bivouac, to me, was tough but interesting and enjoyable. . . . Then came shipping orders and . . . all my friends shipped out to all corners of the country and the world. I and 6 others out of the battalion were assigned to cadre and the dismal prospect of staying at Wheeler as instructors.

For two beautiful weeks we were at NCO [Noncommissioned Officer] school. I began to think Camp Wheeler could after all be tolerable. We rode to the instruction areas in *trucks*. (For 7 months I hadn't even been near one of "these luxurious vehicles.") We had almost all of the evenings free. We didn't work very hard during the day, and most wonderful of all, the food was good. For the first time since I've been in the army I ran into food which was not merely edible (which it almost always is) but in addition was appetizing (which it almost never is).

But all good things finally end and so did NCO school. Back I went to the 12th Bn. and the most dismal month that I have spent in the Army. The first thing that happened was a proposal that I take over the company clerk's job. This, of course, covers a rating but it is just the sort of office assignment which I've had nightmares about ever since receiving my "greetings from my friends and neighbors." My very earnest and rigorous protestations persuaded a friendly 1st Sgt. not to make that assignment. I was assigned as a field instructor and attached as an acting corporal to the 2nd Platoon of D Co.–the same Platoon in which I had taken my training.

And what was so dismal about that? Well the neophyte non-com (as is true with all neophytes) gets all the worst assignments. . . . One fascinating job is standing 8 hours under the burning sun turning pages on a chart while an officer lectures a class. I had that one. One wonderful task is guarding prisoners . . . who are serving sentences for AWOL, MP reports etc., but who must . . . be taken out to training every day . . . (or else every trainee would want to get a short rest in the stockade). Yes, I had this one too, and . . . hated it.

But this wasn't all that was dismal, about the last of August and the first part of September Paris fell, there's a rumor that Cpl. Wm. Dufty, now with AMG [Allied Military Government] was there to watch our first troops march in. . . . *Major* Martin Hayden was somewhere in France and PFC Wm. Lamson was a machine gunner in the Brittany push[1] and in the line for 30 days before going back to a rest camp. And certain it is that Jack Carlisle was in Paris to write of the welcome that seemed to bring alive the idea that this war after all was a crusade against tyranny and oppression and that the people of the world who wanted to be free looked on our armies as something more than conquerors. Oh yes and I was a trained infantry soldier and all dressed up and no place to go.

Added to these minor miseries, I was expecting a furlough and desperately homesick for it. And each week it was put off just a little longer.

Came Sept. 20—and with it my first furlough. You can't conceive of just what that phrase means to a guy in uniform. No ten days of my life have ever been as fully lived or as thoroughly enjoyed. Furloughs for soldiers lucky enough to get 'em in the states mean coming back home and back to life as they want to live it. I could write poetry about that word. "Furlough." Beautiful sound, eh?! . . . sounds positively lyrical to me.

Well all good things end, but this furlough didn't . . . the memory lingers on.

I came back to a regular assignment and the life and troubles of an IRTC Corporal. Here's a sample.

Sick call . . . is at 6:15 P.M. If you happen to get sick or get hurt at any other time of day, that comes under the heading of T.S. (an army abbreviation . . . translated as Tough Stuff). And the unfortunate soldier is advised to report to the Chaplain to have his T.S. card punched. Some weeks ago . . . I got a hand smashed up. Although I didn't know it . . . , one of the bones was broken into three pieces. But that was in the first hour of the day. . . . T.S.! I made it through the day without too much trouble until the second hour of bayonet drill in the late afternoon. . . . All of a sudden I heard Cpl. Martin yelling: "Whassa matter with you Edwards. You wouldn't punch your way out of a paper bag that way."

That seemed to me to be too much, so with some heat I pointed out the rather obviously damaged mitt and asked, "How the hell am I supposed to do any good with this?" Cpl. Martin reminded me with equal heat and more authority that I wasn't off duty, that this was bayonet drill and he was damn well going to see that I did it. So back I went to punching the dummy with the prescribed fury and with many mental promises of dire vengeance on Cpl. Martin. . . .

Time has passed. I am now a *Corporal* and to save my self-respect my opinion of Corporals in general and Martin in particular has changed. Martin was then and is now a competent non-com and a nice guy. But he and I and thousands of other "two stripers" have the thankless job of enforcing at the point of execution all the countless rules, regulations, policies and orders of the Army. At least the discipline of the Army is pretty rough justice (though doubtless essential to the grim purpose for which armies are designed). At its worst army discipline can look to the new trainee like unthinking brutality. In either case it is a corporal who finally enforces the order on the long-suffering G.I. I can hear myself now for the weeks past, "All right Hunt, if that hangover was so bad that you were late for reveille they'll cure it for you in the kitchen. Sunday K.P. for you." "Hertz, Kenner—what's the matter with you? This isn't but a

2 mile course and we aren't but half way around. I'll be damned if you'll walk in. You 18-year-old kids ought to be ashamed. Look at Hazel up there. He's twice your age and he isn't kicking." "Hale, you'll ride the range (i.e., clean the kitchen stoves) for all that racket. How many times do I have to tell you to keep quiet in this barracks after light's out?"

And what's worse . . . I would defend each of the above decisions as essential to the maintenance of the health, morale and efficiency of the United States Army. Can a Corporal Be Human? Probably the easiest answer is "No."

2) Sometime ago I filled out an innocent appearing document entitled "Application for Officer Candidate School." The reasons for doing so have by now grown dim in my memory. The one I recall best was given in a *Yank* cartoon wherein a G.I. [is] asked by an imposing OCS board, "Just why do you want to be an officer?" He replies, "Well frankly gentlemen I just can't get along on what you're paying me." (Note, in case the above comes to official attention, I hereby label the above comment JOKE–the more so since I subscribed to the more conventional and heroic sounding reasons when they asked me the same thing.)

At any rate after a seemly delay (plus two or three odd months and a barrel of red tape) I was suddenly notified to report to Ft. Benning . . . Infantry Officer Candidate School on Nov. 8.

I did.

I am now attending what our Wheeler 2nd Lieutenants referred to as "The Benning School for Boys." I don't think *The Infantry School* would like that appellation. Still less would T.I.S. (yep . . . they capitalize . . . "The" and use "T" as part of the initials) appreciate their graduates conversion of the T.I.S. slogan *Follow Me* into the more popular *Quit Pushing*.

T.I.S. is very proud of itself and . . . with considerable justification. Our instruction is excellent–our instructors are almost all fresh from battle zones and speak of their subjects with [authority]. . . . The program is geared to the very maximum capacity of the classes and no college course that I've ever taken traveled over complicated material with the speed and effective teaching technique of many of these. The academic standards here are pretty high; the physical standards are terrific. The first three (of about a dozen) requirements of the physical test are 9 pull-ups (palms out), 40 push ups and 71 sit-ups. Try these . . . and you'll know why your correspondent is frequently very tired. This is now the fourth week of a 17-week course. If I survive . . . I will be here another 3 months and then my number will be dropped back in that greatest of all lotteries–the Classification and Assignment pool. (There will be plenty of time . . . for return mail.)

3) Since it is sometimes well to remember what we're fighting about, I quote again from a letter from my college Texas friend 1st Lt. James P. Simpson. . . . [See above, Simpson to Edwards, 18 November 1944, regarding liberation in the Philippine Islands].

4) I can't end this letter without referring to the sad news of Bill Lamson's death. He was wounded in Germany on October 10 and died in France 5 days later. He was a machine gunner in a heavy weapons company that had earlier seen hard fighting in France. I think his outfit was in the assault on Brest.[2] He must have been in action somewhere in the Aachen area[3] when he was wounded.

The news shocked me more than I care to talk about. Bill was my good and loyal friend and I can't comprehend coming back to Detroit and not finding him there. He was one of those who believed in a better world for the common man and was willing to fight for it. Bill wouldn't want to be mourned but he would want to be remembered by those who get to carry on the [union] work he's had to leave.

Sincerely,   GEORGE EDWARDS

NOTES

1. The Brittany Peninsula–200 miles long and 100 miles wide–jutting into the Atlantic Ocean southwest of the Normandy beachhead.

2. Located in northwest Brittany, Brest served as a major submarine base for the Germans. It fell to the Allies on 18 September, though it never served as a strategic military port for the second front. See Geoffrey Perret, *There's a War to Be Won: The United States Army in World War II* (New York: Random House, 1991), 340-45.

3. Aachen, on Germany's western border and a direct path to the industrial Ruhr Valley, fell on 21 October (following nineteen days of assault), the first city in Germany overrun by AEF forces. See Perret, *There's a War to Be Won*, 354-55, 359-60, 381, 387-88.

Camp Van Dorn, Mississippi. 8 December 1944
Walton S. White to Select Little Band

No one can say that I personally constitute any threat to the nation's forests in my consumption of writing paper. There are people . . . who wrote me as long ago as Jan. 29, 1944, and never received an answer. It isn't that I don't, or didn't, want to write. . . . Something just seemed to come up every time, as it will in the Army.

Before I entered the Army I had a horror of duplicated letters. Subsequently I altered my opinion, chiefly because duplicating seems to be the only way to burrow through the pile of unanswered correspondence.

This shall be . . . the first annual review of the military life of White. I have been in the Army not quite 16 months. I have been on active duty 15 months. (You enter the Army when you are inducted at home; you go on active duty when you report to the reception center.) I have been stationed at Camp Van Dorn–a so-called "temporary" camp of tar paper buildings located near Centreville, Wilkinson County, southwest Mississippi, between Baton Rouge, La., and Natchez, Miss.–since a week after I reported for duty at Ft. Custer [Michigan] in September, 1943. For this I have been awarded the Good Conduct Ribbon. This is not a Boy Scout badge. It is a red-and-white ribbon which is awarded automatically to most men who have managed to stay out of the guardhouse for a year. The best that can be said for it is that it signifies the wearer is no rookie.

I have spent my time at Van Dorn in the public relations office of the 63d Infantry Division, known as the Blood and Fire Division. Recently this office has been incorporated into what is known throughout the Army as the Information-Education Office, which handles public relations, a weekly newspaper, orientation of the soldier in world affairs, current events, the reasons for fighting, etc. It is pleasant work. For a year it took me nearly every week to Baton Rouge, where we printed our Division newspaper. It took me to New Orleans for 10 days last June, doing publicity for a huge Infantry Day show. Those things break the routine of camp life. Public relations, whatever its liabilities, is work familiar to me and which I do easily, so I have a little more pleasant life than many men; and, for me at least, the Army classification system worked well.

I finished Basic Training last New Year's Eve. I became a Private First Class (Pfc.) two weeks later. On April 15 I was made a Technician Fifth Grade (T/5); this takes the holder off KP and entitles him to be addressed as "corporal." On Oct. 17, while home on furlough, I was made a Technician Fourth Grade (T/4); this, my present rank, takes the holder off guard and entitles him to be addressed as "sergeant." (Ruder persons know the holders of technician ratings as "Model T corporal" and "Model T sergeant" because the stripes bear the letter T. This signifies that the bearer holds a rating as a specialist rather than as a noncommissioned officer of the line. But . . . the technician is a soldier as well as a specialist.)

The Public Relations Office is part of Division Headquarters. In Headquarters we all had full infantry basic training, the difference between us and the men in the rifle companies being that we spent our 13 weeks doing Basic *plus* . . . technical training; that is, we studied the soldier's profession and our . . . specialty as well.

I learned to fire . . . the carbine, a sweet little .30-caliber semi-automatic weapon which now is used by about one-third of the men in an infantry division. I was sent through a lethal concentration of chlorine gas in a gas chamber. I have been over the infiltration course (where you crawl 50 yards through mud, on your belly and back, under barbed wire and live machine gun fire) both by day and by night. I have been through . . . the Close Combat Course, advancing through a woods, firing at dummies which pop up out of the ground and from behind trees, and the Nazi Village course, where troops "take" a group of abandoned schoolhouses and wooden sheds. I have fired the .45 caliber automatic pistol, thrown a dozen or so hand grenades, fired grenades from an adapter attached to a rifle (. . . [which hurls] a grenade about 10 times as far as . . . by hand), fired the "bazooka," or rocket launcher, the wonderful portable weapon which makes two men into an Antitank weapon, and I have familiarized myself with the M1 (Garand) rifle, basic weapon of the infantry. I have had brief study of the machine gun and anti-tank guns and have done considerable other training. . . . Most of it has been extremely practical and realistic; this Division prides itself on its constant and extensive use of live ammunition, and I like to think that if I see combat I will have some idea of how to behave. . . . In addition . . . I took a three-month course in intelligence work (secrecy, interrogation of prisoners, map reading, handling of information, etc.).

Until recently we made a 10 mile hike monthly, with full field equipment. We have had occasional field problems and bivouacs, which sound easy to the rifleman because we ride to them in trucks; but the rifleman forgets that we pack the heavy desks, typewriters, safes and other office equipment and do our work in the field—and the work must continue as though we were in garrison or the business affairs of the Division would bog down. We have eaten exclusively from mess kits for a year, except on Christmas and Thanksgiving; I never see a plate except when I am out of camp. Most of us in Headquarters are qualified jeep drivers, and I am licensed as well to drive ³⁄₄-ton command cars and medium-sized trucks; we also learn the maintenance of four- and six-wheeled vehicles.

(Purely for the benefit of relatives . . . a bit of bragging:

I scored a modest victory with the carbine and earned a Sharpshooter's medal—not the best, but pretty good. . . . I scored 54 out of 100 the only time I ever held a .45 pistol . . . , received a commendation from the public relations officer . . . [and] been recommended for Officer Candidate School by a brigadier general and a lieutenant colonel, although I am not applying.)

The best part of my 16 months in the Army is that which has taken much of the curse off military life. My wife has been with me for nearly 10 months. Peg came down in March for a three-day visit and just never went home. She started out in a branch tailor shop on the post and wound up in the Camp Special Service office. There she hired on as a clerk-typist, having passed a Civil Service exam for that job; such is the Army way of doing things that she now is a bookkeeper and payroll clerk. She lives in a trailer, part of a Federal housing project, about a mile from camp. The trailer is the best living accommodation we have found in the Centreville area; it is not unlike living in the boat we want after the war, and we enjoy it thoroughly. Generally I am allowed to leave the post each evening and I may spend a weekend and one other night overnight. So, with occasional lunches together, we see a lot of each other. We spent a magnificent four days in New Orleans in November, eating and drinking our way through the French Quarter in belated celebration of our seventh wedding anniversary. . . .

For all your indulgence, in writing, in not getting answers, in reading this, many thanks. Best . . . wishes that Christmas will be merry, the New

Year happy and successful and that the next holidays . . . will find us all restored to peace.

STODDARD WHITE

This was done personally, NOT at the expense of the City of Detroit. But keep up your own reports.

Detroit. December 12, 1944
Edward J. Jeffries Jr. to George C. Edwards

Dear George:

I am sorry that I haven't written before. The fact . . . is I told Peggy that I would write to you immediately and express my attitude on your potential candidacy for re-election. That immediately is quite awhile in the past. . . . It apparently slipped my mind.

Peggy said that you were thinking it might not be appropriate for you to run for re-election inasmuch as you were not here and didn't know exactly when you would be here. If my opinion is worth consideration, it is just exactly opposed to your thinking on this matter. I know of no reason why you should not run and, for your future and for the good of the city I most surely think that you should. The council is so constituted that it can work on an eight-man basis, and fame is fleeting, my boy. If you are gone so long that it might make for difficulty in the operation of the Council, it might be so long that it would be necessary for you to start all over again. If you are not gone that long it doesn't make any difference to the Council. Consequently, do as some of our local judges have done. If I were in your place I would enter my name in the lists, get my friends to conduct my campaign, and do my best to be re-elected. You owe it to yourself and you owe it to the city.

Brother Krause has just been appointed to fill the vacancy of the lately deceased Thomas Cotter, Judge of the Recorder's Court. It was a good appointment for both [Governor] Kelly and Krause. Knowing Krause's disposition as well as I do I think he has the proper temperament for a judge. He certainly knows as much, if not more law, than his associates. His education has been good and his training and practice have been such that he has developed more than many men who occupy similar positions. He, of course, stands for re-election or rather election almost immediately–primary in February and election in April. He may have a little name trouble at this time, but then again, as you well know, elections are always uncertain. But I think that he has better than an even chance, and if he can make it he can, no doubt, stay there for life. That is social security.

A chap was in here the other day who is stationed at Ft. Benning. I have forgotten his name. He is a captain and he said that he would look you up. . . .

We have about developed a plan of how we would spend money for capital improvements over the next ten years if we get the money. That if is about as big as it was when you were here. The Governor's survey committee that was set up last year as the answer to the municipality's request for return of the sales tax . . . [is] about to recommend: First, that the [state] sales tax be reduced to 2 ½ percent and that permission be given to municipalities to adopt a ½ percent local sales tax, and the State will collect . . . and return . . . [it] to the municipality without . . . charging the collection cost. Second . . . , a change in the rates on the income tax upward so that [the state] will collect approximately three times as much as presently. In addition the State will refund to the local levels of government on a population basis without collection charge, the total amount collected. Third . . . , that the State weight and gas tax be revised and amended so that it will no longer be necessary to spend a certain portion in the Upper Peninsula . . . [and] in the upper portion of the Lower Peninsula, but that the money be divided 40 percent to the State, 35 percent to the Counties, and 25 percent to the municipalities.

The question . . . of the local sales tax is already being debated. There seems to be no discussion . . . of the intangible tax, and there is no doubt that the amendment to the gas and weight tax would tremendously improve the position of Detroit, but I suspect the Upper Peninsula and the upper portion of the Lower Peninsula will start to ride like Paul Revere through the State. The County Road Commissions . . . may not go along. . . . they have been getting about 35 percent, and it would not change their position materially. They might, however, want more, and . . . their reactions, if crystallized, have not been brought to my attention. If these things actually materialize at the next session of legislature it will mean some additional revenues to the City . . . estimated at between $10,000,000 and $12,000,000. As you can appreciate, it will give us sufficient monies to have a relatively decent post war capital improvement program.

The race situation from an incident reporting point of view both on the streets and in our transportation system is fairly good. The housing situation becomes increasingly acute. In fact it has gotten to such a state that I personally am sure something more has to be done about it. I am in the throes of making up my mind as to what.

Harold Thompson, Director of the Inter-racial Committee was the butt of a resolution by the N. A. A. C. P., requesting his removal.[1] Off the record, the resolution was probably timely. As usual, however, they could probably have accomplished more if they had operated more quietly and with a little more finesse. But if a good man could be found, Mr. Thompson would be quickly replaced. . . . More important, some of the members of the committee are on the lookout for a successor to him.

How have you been doing? I would enjoy very much hearing from you. If I don't see you between now and Christmas, have as much pleasure as being in the army many miles from home at Christmas time will allow.

The best of everything to you, my boy.

Sincerely,   JEFF

NOTE

1. On 13 January 1944, when Common Council replaced Jeffries's temporary peace committee with the permanent Mayor's Interracial Committee, it was headed by William J. Norton, executive secretary of the Children's Fund of Michigan, who agreed to serve only until a full-time director could be named. Thompson, public relations expert of the Detroit Trust Company and executive council member of the Episcopal Diocese of Michigan, was appointed six weeks later. Originally greeted with hope by NAACP officials, Thompson drew increasing criticism for inaction and ignorance of race-related issues, which culminated in the December resolution that he be replaced by "an individual with a background of wide experience and training in social problems." See *Chronicle,* 22 Jan. 1944, 4, and 4 March 1944, 4; *Detroit Tribune,* 15 April 1944, 8; 17 June 1944, 8; 25 Nov. 1944, 6; and 9 Dec. 1944, 8.

Dear Jeff:

Fort Benning, Georgia. 17 December 1944
George C. Edwards to Edward J. Jeffries Jr.

Thanks for your very kind and thoughtful letter. The [reelection] matter had been bothering me and I appreciate your advice more than I can say. This time I'll try not to be so darn late acting on it.

I am more than a little curious about the housing matter you mentioned. Peg last Thurs. told me something on Negro housing was in the wind but I haven't got either papers or [the] *Council Journal* as yet which referred to it.

I never knew [Harold] Thompson . . . but I am impressed with what John Ballenger is trying to do in the Police Dept. and am praying for his success. I think that the community . . . [needs to be placed] on some plane of reasonable mutual respect before we can feel very secure about another June 21st [race riot].

Incidentally you will be amused to know that the Army has finally given me the conclusive answer to Joe [Joseph P.] Buffa's[1] question—How would you like to live with one? Hell I am living with 'em. Negroes, seemingly for years, have been going through Infantry O.C.S. with white candidates and with absolutely no segregation. Just to put the clincher on the matter, however, last week we had a six day bivouac and one of the Negro candidates was assigned to the same four man pup tent (two pup tents pitched together in cold weather . . .) that I was in. I reckon you can't live in much more restricted quarters than that.

How did I like it? I can hear Buffa asking. The *bivouac* not a damn bit—sleeping on the ground in 18-degree weather is not my idea of soft living—but as for Jesse I reckon most of the time I was too busy and too uncomfortable to spend much energy thinking about the color of his skin.

By the way before I sign off this station and retire for the night is there anything that can be done to build a fire under George [F.] Emery[2] and the City Plan Dept.? I am not a City Planner but I am morally certain that a pretty fair job of completing a logical and defensible master plan should have been done by now. The infinite detail of such a plan probably won't be worked out for sixty years anyhow. What we need now is a broad general outline within which the Depts. could work and plan. Oh well the mills of the Gods grind finely but they grind wonderously slow.

Merry Christmas to you and Florence and Gary.

Yours,
                                                          GEORGE

NOTES

1. Buffa, a builder organized the Seven Mile–Fenelon Improvement Association in opposition to black occupancy of the Sojourner Truth Homes, which led to the disorder of 1942 and, many believed, set the stage for the massive riot a year later.

2. City planner for Detroit, a municipal position, and secretary of the private City Plan Commission.

Detroit. December 21, 1944
Dear George: *George Schermer to George C. Edwards*

At Peg's suggestion I am writing to give you some first hand facts about Edgecomb's recent housing proposal. I assume that you get the papers or clippings. . . . The stories in this case were quite complete. Edgecomb wrote a letter to Jeffries asking that Jeffries request the Common Council to approve a change in the racial public housing policy in Detroit. That is, to abolish the current policy of not changing the pattern of any neighborhood.

Considerable publicity accompanied the submission of the letter and all of the Councilmen were asked to comment. The proposal was a shock to those who had assumed that Edgecomb was safe on the racial question, and a surprise to those who had been pressing for a more liberal approach. As far as I know, Edgecomb consulted no one on this move. Certainly, he did not raise the question with any of the groups which have been pressing for some such move as this. I don't think, either, that he ever cleared with the various anti-negro groups. He did tell Ed[ward D.] Connor[1] and myself that he was going to do it with the implication that he was going to give us a way out of the Dearborn proposal. However, we don't want a way out of that and we told him so.

I know that Charley has a specific area in mind. He wants to open up Southwest Detroit (the little thumb section west of River Rouge next to

Ecorse). I don't know why he did not specify that area in his letter–the Common Council would be more inclined to vote favorably on it. Also, if he were to wait six months or so he would not need to ask for a change in policy because that area is changing anyway. The private builders are going to build in there for Negro occupancy.

There are two possible reasons why Edgecomb made this move now:

a. (The most likely) Jeffries just announced Dowling's appointment as Corporation Counsel. The appointment is cheering news for Jeffries right wing support but will be unpopular with labor, liberals and Negroes. Jeffries needed some other appointment or proposal to counteract or neutralize the opposition to Dowling. Ergo–Charley's proposal.

b. There is a growing movement on foot toward a broad area approach to the Negro housing problem in Detroit. The general plan is to push simultaneously for (1) Expansion of Negro or unrestricted areas in the City of Detroit, (2) Post war slum clearance in Detroit, (3) Breaking down the barrier in the industrial suburbs, particularly Dearborn, (4) Development on a large scale of one or two satellite communities, unrestricted, in currently unincorporated areas. This last to be sponsored and underwritten by the County rather than Detroit.

The movement is well underway and FPHA's [Federal Public Housing Authority's] proposal to go into Dearborn is part of it. The idea is headed up by Ed Connor and myself with much support from Bill [William G.] Nicholas, several in [Ford] Local #600, Wm. [William P.] Lovett, Pat[rick V.] McNamara, NAACP, Ray[mond H.] Foley, many others.[2] Much support is coming from Mayors of River Rouge, Ecorse, Inkster, Wayne. The idea of Wayne County financing the land improvements and probably setting up a County Housing Authority is very popular.

Now, Charley has been pooh-poohing these ideas for a long time but he is beginning to show signs of being impressed. It is just possible that he believes it might work. Charley loves the spot light. Why not get on the bandwagon and into the driver's seat? Why not become the guy who takes over the reins and says "you boys know where you are going, but let a man drive you over the rough part of the road."

So much for analysis of why Charley did what he did at this time.[3] Regardless of why, he has stolen the show. If he knows where he is going he certainly can make progress for a while. There is nothing to do at the moment but to let him go because he is going in the right direction. I don't think he can steer us up a blind trail or slow us down because there are too many people now who know where we should go.

I am not trying to put words into your mouth. I warn you in advance that I am very strongly biased on this matter. Feeling as I do, if I were Councilman, my position would be, "I am in favor of Mr. Edgecomb's proposal that the policy of the City of Detroit be changed. However, I believe that in considering specific sites, the Housing Commission should take into consideration possible plans for a broad area approach to this matter. I believe further that the Detroit Housing Commission should participate with public and civic agencies in evolving an overall plan for housing which would place a fair share of responsibility upon all communities in the Metropolitan area."

Incidentally, we have adopted a term which seems to be very suitable to both white and Negro groups. We don't talk about "Negro housing" or "Negro projects." We say "unrestricted." The understanding is that in "unrestricted" areas anyone may live.

GEORGE SCHERMER

NOTES

1. Executive director of the Citizens Housing and Planning Council.
2. Nicholas, chair, UAW Housing Committee; Lovett, executive secretary, Detroit Citizens League; McNamara, vice-president, Detroit and Wayne County AFL; Foley, state director, Federal Housing Administration.
3. For the accuracy of Schermer's analysis, see Charles F. Edgecomb to GCE, February 22, 1945, in chapter 4.

Detroit. December 21, 1944
Dear George: *Gloster B. Current to George C. Edwards*

On January 4, 1945 the Common Council will hear representatives from the Detroit Housing Commission and the Mayor's Committee on "Housing in Detroit."

A few days ago Charles Edgecomb and the Detroit Housing Commission wrote the Mayor that no more housing can be built for Negro occupancy under the present policy of not changing the racial characteristics of any neighborhood in Detroit through occupancy standards of housing projects under their jurisdiction. Various councilmen who have been polled on the matter have indicated opposition to change the policy which would allow the erection of either mixed projects or Negro projects in so-called white neighborhoods. You will remember that in April, 1943, the Mayor presented this policy to the Common Council . . . and it was informally approved eight to one (8-1) with you dissenting. This action took place after the N.A.A.C.P. had importuned for a mixed policy for housing war workers in Detroit.

We hope that your statement on this matter will be more intelligent, and we know that it will be, than the prejudiced statements of [Councilmen Eugene I.] Van Antwerp, [William G.] Rogell, [Fred C.] Castator, and others who, seemingly, are totally unaware of the difficulty of selecting sites. I promised Mrs. Edwards that I would write you re: this matter.

There is speculation, however, that the Mayor is insincere in dumping this into the laps of the Common Council because it comes at a time when he made the appointment of former Prosecutor Dowling to the Corporation Counsel's office. Moreover, the policy alluded to was not a formal decision of the Common Council, but an administrative decision of the Detroit Housing Commission which was merely concurred in, as an opinion by the Common Clerk. We await your views on the matter.

GLOSTER B. CURRENT

London, England. 24 December 1944
Jack McElhone to Peggy Edwards

The date and my presence in London form no coincidence nor, as usual, do they have any legal affinity. I'm AWOL again. Camp just didn't seem an inviting place to spend Christmas, with no serious duties to justify my presence there. I dropped in for two days last week, after the Labor Party Convention here, to be greeted by my envious compatriots as a more reserved and less guilty father might have greeted the prodigal son. I'm starting to fly again Thursday, so this is my last escapade for awhile.

The Labor Party Convention was brass hat heavy, depressingly so. Ni Bevan rode rank and file resurgence of spirit into new strength, which is some consolation. Britain's tragedy of the period is not so much Churchill's forsaking of the barricades bugle as it is the leaden quality of the LP leadership.

I spent some time with [Norman] Thomas and [Sidney V.] Hillman a week ago. Hillman took me away from the depressing spectacle of Thomas and [Emil] Rieve playing Gin Rummy in Claridge's to find out about me but mostly to extol PAC.[1] I tried hard to find some mental reservation he may have about the final efficacy of the PAC method, but he was too flushed with the November successes to see rationally, I suppose. I gave up—but diplomatically—when he gave PAC the credit for the reshuffling of the State Department.[2] Nauseating, eh?

If I come home in disgrace one of these months you will thereby know that they have tried to give me a Greek or similar assignment. They haven't yet, and I hope they don't. I'm not particularly anxious to be a sackcloth martyr.

Labor Baron[3] will be welcome. . . . [William] Dufty will get it posthaste and thanks a lot. People over here are interested in the book. Bill is in an unhappy period, comparatively speaking, but his are depressing surroundings from a military point of view. Uncivil affairs, etc.

I sympathize with George's present grind. I did it for months and I haven't yet regained interest in what I am supposed to be doing.

For your future reference, Shakespeare has been successfully filmed. The near-fantasy of *Henry V* has been given *a good* production by Laurence Olivier and is worth your attention when it comes your way. I saw it with Jennie [Lee] and Ni [Bevan] last night. A new stage of technicolor development. A Merry Xmas or something to you, George and all.

JACK

NOTES

1. Thomas, Socialist Party leader in the United States; Hillman, official, Amalgamated United Clothing Workers of America, and the CIO's PAC chairman; Rieve, official, American Federation of Full-Fashioned Hosiery Workers.

2. Cordell Hull, Roosevelt's secretary of state since 1933, was forced out of office by ill health in early October, but—at the president's request—withheld his resignation until after the November election; he was succeeded by Under-Secretary of State Edward R. Stettinius Jr. in early December. Immediately Stettinius announced a reorganization of the State Department, combining a "forward-looking policy with level-headed and business-like efficiency" through the appointment of several entrepreneurs (for example, William L. Clayton and Nelson A. Rockefeller) as assistant secretaries. In fact, his plans had begun earlier in the year as the war enlarged diplomatic responsibilities during Hall's tenure: long before Roosevelt's re-election or PAC's influence. See *New York Times,* 27 Nov. 1944, 1,10, and 2 Dec. 1944, 1, 8; Robert H. Ferrell, ed., *The American Secretaries of State and Their Diplomacy,* 18 vols., vol. 13: *Cordell Hull,* by Julius W. Pratt II, 765-68 (New York: Cooper Square, 1964), and vol. 14 (1965): *E. R. Stettinius, Jr.,* by Richard L. Walker, 17-26.

3. James A. Wechsler, *Labor Baron: A Portrait of John L. Lewis* (N.Y.: Morrow, 1944).

Detroit. December 27, 1944
Edward J. Jeffries Jr. to George C. Edwards

Dear George:

I read with a great deal of pleasure your SOL. It was very newsy and, incidentally, well written. Your letter was interesting, too. I am certainly glad you have made up your mind [to run for reelection], and I know you are right.

I suppose you know that Paul Krause was appointed to fill the vacancy caused by the death of [Recorder's Court Judge] Tom Cotter. He stands for election almost immediately—primary, February 19, and election, April 2. In fact, it seems to me that we just go from one election to another for some reason or other. I appointed Bill Dowling to take Paul's place, and it stimulated a lot of conversation and discussion. As you can imagine, there were excited debaters on both sides. I am sure, however, that Bill can do the work, and even in public life gratitude is not the most unattractive reaction, I hope. . . .

The council is not happy over the question of Negro housing. They are going to have one hearing for discussion and probably several more. Your guess is as good as mine as to the outcome. But in any event it should give ample opportunity for a thorough public discussion.

I received a lucky break. Pan American is bypassing Miami. Miami is very much disturbed, and is trying to get the midwestern mayors to attend Miami from December 31 to January 4 to talk about what should be done. I am going as the guest of Miami. It is not often that a fellow gets to do business at a winter resort at such a timely season. John Carlisle bamboozled the *News* into sending him. He claims the story was that the *News* couldn't afford to let Jeffries get into the hands of the [John S.] Knight industries as it relates to the *Miami Herald* without someone down there to take care of its interests. Anyway it worked and he is going there with me.

The news of Bill Lamson has depressed me no end. He was a good boy and I liked him.

Here's hoping that '45 has better things in store for you. May you have the best of everything.

With kind regards, I am

Sincerely yours,   J E F F

Detroit. December 27, 1944
John M. Carlisle to George C. Edwards

Dear George:

You are right, I owe you several letters. I am afraid I was a lousy correspondent in France, tho I was eager to get mail from you. The trouble was that just getting a story a day at the front, getting back to our censors and our radio station, and staying alive kept me so damned busy I never felt like writing. My wife complained, too. Since I never married Corp. Edwards, but was only going steady with him, you can see I had a good alibi.

We had a party for Judge Krause the other night. I was toastmaster; about 90 there. So I called on Your Little Woman to amaze the gathering with the Activities of Corp. Edwards. She made a cute little speech and called on Ernie Jones'[1] wife, who made some cute remaks and then called on my wife. My gosh, the gals really crossed me. But they made the party a howling success.

We wished you could have been with us. A lot of folks were talking about you, and only in lyrical terms, as a result of your wife's reminder that you were not in a mausoleum, only buried in the officer's school.

I am glad you are going to be an officer. I know you will make a good one. While I was with the 3rd army I lived with a lot of officers of varied ranks, and, believe me, son, they had stuff on the ball! They fight well, they lead well—and they die well! Best of all, the front line infantry officers are close to their men! I know one company that just kicked the living Jesus out of a battalion of Heinies [Germans] after the company's captain had been killed. So it is good to know that you will be an officer, too, and with your inherent liberalism you should make a good one.

Ed Jeffries, known as Junior or Our Little Mayor, is still telling everyone who will listen that someday you will be our first labor mayor of

Detroit. I have heard it so often that I have surrendered and even I agree.

Incidentally, Jeff and I are going to Florida by airplane Saturday for a week in an aviation conference in Miami. Now isn't that just tough, Georgie! . . .

Like a lot of gents who come back, I had one helluva time acclimatizing myself. I had dropped 37 lbs. and was down to 130 and was a bit whacky, I guess. But now I have picked up 20 lbs. and I am back in shape so I can even launch a laugh with the Great Yale Stuart.[2]

Let me know when you are coming to Detroit on furlough and we will kick over a couple of tubs of beer.

Good luck, George.

Faithfully,   J A C K

NOTES

1. Commissioner, Department of Purchases and Supplies.
2. Union organizer of the Department of Public Works, known for his outgoing personality and leftist political beliefs.

Dear Martin:

Detroit. December 28, 1944
Edward J. Jeffries Jr. to Martin S. Hayden

We have all been wondering how close this German surge[1] is to you. Here's hoping not too close. Incidentally there has been a mass change of mind in this country about how the war is going. I think it has sobered everybody, and the people are settling down now to a good, long, steady grind.

I presume you heard that the Great Krause is now Judge Krause. . . . I appointed Bill Dowling to take his place [as Corporation Counsel]. . . .

The best thing that has happened, as relates to personnel, has revolved about one of those parties at the Public Lighting Commission recreation rooms. [Councilman] Bill Rogell shot a deer this fall and decided that he would give a venison dinner for the newspaper boys and some select friends. I qualified under one head or the other. The date was set and arrangements made. Shortly thereafter Brother Krause received his appointment. Jack Carlisle, who had been appointed as the master of ceremonies, suggested to Bill Rogell that they make it a combination venison dinner on behalf of Mr. Rogell and a going away party for Mr. Krause. He said all right. In a couple of days he apparently changed his mind and said that he would not supply venison for that purpose. The newspaper boys angered quickly and decided that they would call the whole thing off. Then they decided they wouldn't give him that satisfaction. So, we had roast beef and a very representative group. Of course I prefer beef to venison anyway, so I enjoyed it.

Why don't you write, you stiff? In spite of what you think I have been fairly regular and your letters are more interesting than mine anyway.

My wishes for a great and successful '45 to you, incidentally as pleasant as possible under the circumstances. Good Luck!

Sincerely yours,　　　　　　　　　　　　　　　　　　　　　　JEFF

NOTE

1. In the Belgian Ardennes, the German army launched and lost its last great offensive in the Battle of the Bulge, December 16-26. See Perrett, *There's a War to Be Won,* 397-415.

4

Meliora Resurget Cineribus

(February 1945–January 1946)

Entering the final year of war, Detroiters at home and abroad managed to maintain regular contact with one another, despite the ongoing wartime inconveniences of censorship and mail delivery. Jeffries continued as the center of correspondence, dispensing updates on contemporary problems and future plans, which culminated that fall with his election to a fourth term as the mayor of Detroit. Meanwhile, he reinforced his friendships with those who moved in and out of the fronts. John M. Carlisle reported on the war in the Pacific, his second battlefield assignment in two years and one from which he returned in October, as did Martin S. Hayden from Europe. Walton S. White, who had followed his division into Germany early in 1945, remained safe yet unheard from for a long time. Harold J. Schachern and George C. Edwards found themselves headed into the Pacific that summer, fully expecting to invade Japan. Tragically, Jack McElhone's combat death punctuated the meaning of war and saddened those who knew him, genuinely diminishing their lives. Everyone pressed on, however, expressing increasing optimism for victory and exchanging views on war, its impact worldwide, and the long-awaited peace. Edwards, clearly representative of the boys in the movement, began the new year hopeful that the motto of the City of Detroit–*Meliora Resurget Cineribus*– would prove prophetic: "Better things will rise from the ashes."[1]

Censorship and postal delays or losses were increasingly tolerated, if unappreciated, as factors of war. Hence Edwards, on one hand, jested that he was "rigidly barred" from disclosing instructional techniques of officer training while "invaluable field manuals" like *Time* discussed them regularly and, on the other hand, apologized for the very late delivery of Standard Operational Letter X because of unreliable mail service.[2]

Letter writers from Detroit, including Jeffries, informed those in military camps and war theaters of municipal developments. Thus Edwards learned that personnel changes in the Mayor's Interracial Committee and efforts by federal and private agencies signaled hope for peace on the racial front.[3] Surprisingly, he heard from Jeffries's housing director that a black project on the most recent proposed site, in southwest Detroit, might actually be forthcoming in order to ease the city's "present overcrowded conditions." Nothing was assured, however, wrote Charles F. Edgecomb, for "the 'Love Thy Neighbor' crack" of most whites existed only as propaganda.[4] Perhaps that prejudice was why others discounted the mayor's and the housing director's supposed change of their own de facto segregation policy, leading federal official George Schermer to look beyond local boundaries for a solution to what had become the flash-point of racial conflict.[5] Various individuals and organizations, including the restructured interracial committee, succeeded in reducing the tension of February, if not in solving the housing crisis, so that Jeffries could report to Hayden five months later that the race issue was "not so burning" and quieter than in most other metropolises.[6]

Other issues continued to confront the mayor. Revenues from the Detroit Street Railway flagged as gasoline rationing eased, while "an acute meat shortage" led to steakless dinners and skimpy picnic baskets.[7] More significantly for Detroit's future, Jeffries struggled with plans for the location of a modern air terminal. He succeeded in adopting a site at Eight Mile Road and Wyoming (pending the Board of Commerce's ability to raise the necessary purchase price of $1,000,000), outmaneuvering opposition in council by having Edwards furloughed from military service to cast the tie-breaking vote in a contest as intense as that over biracial housing.[8]

That move indicated both Jeffries's political sagacity and his relationship with Edwards, which converged again in their reelections that fall. Earlier he had encouraged the councilman-soldier to run for reelection, as did many individuals among both supporters and opponents of the mayor. Edgecomb assured Edwards that he had everything to win and prospects of becoming the city's first mayor from labor, and Louis E. Martin, editor of the *Chronicle*, affirmed that he was popular "on this side of town"; both mayoral appointee and black journalist pledged support for an Edwards campaign.[9] Once he decided to seek reelection, Edwards drew on their offers, and his dramatic presence in council for the airport vote combined conscientious public service, mayoral friendship, and smart politics. He also found himself backed by the CIO's Political Action Committee, along with Wayne County union leader Tracy Doll and popular black activist Rev. Charles A. Hill.[10]

Jeffries faced a more divided electorate. Very few if any *Chronicle* readers, white liberals, or labor leaders would endorse the mayor. Ironically, much of his opposition came from voters (as opposed to campaign workers) who did support Edwards. Jeffries understood, as did everyone else, that the mayoral campaign would be a replay of 1943, his major threat coming from Richard Frankensteen, former vice-president of the United Automobile Workers, who entered the race in May. He also considered James D. Friel, former Wayne County auditor, a possible spoiler in what shaped up to be a "three-cornered race." Not opening his own headquarters until early July, the mayor soon worried over the lack of interest in the campaign, fearful that without an "upsurge to remove Jeffries," it would be difficult to rally friends.[11]

Jeffries's prescience became fact in the small primary, for Frankensteen ran hard and finished first.[12] Determined to win the November election, the mayor returned to the race-baiting and red-baiting tactics that had brought him victory in the previous campaign. Frankensteen, in turn, equivocated on the issue of biracial housing, and the CIO ranks split over his candidacy. In Jeffries's own words, the campaign quickly turned "nasty" and "bitter," as his supporters claimed that Frankensteen's election would result in a black invasion of white neighborhoods and a government of Communist-leaning unionists. Thus he concentrated on turning out the very heavy vote necessary for a fourth mayoral term, his criticism of Roosevelt seemingly forgotten. He carried white ethnic and middle-class districts, separating rank-and-file union members from their leaders while consciously ceding 90 percent of the black vote.[13]

Edwards won big, too, though the other PAC-supported candidates, Hill and Doll, fell under the avalanche of antiblack, antilabor votes triggered by Jeffries's campaign. He drew the most votes of all councilmen, thereby becoming council president and demonstrating popularity across ideological, race, and class lines. Edwards benefited from being a serviceman overseas and absent from the volatile campaign; he escaped having to advance personally his unqualified support of biracial housing or to criticize his close friend and political benefactor's mayoral campaign. He benefited even more from the well-organized, smooth-running campaign mounted by his friends and administered expertly by Peggy. Surprised by his overwhelming victory and doubtlessly aware of the political pitfalls he had sidestepped, however unavoidably, Edwards sincerely thanked those friends who addressed Detroit voters on his behalf while he was investigating Japanese prisoners of war halfway around the world.[14]

Friendship proved as lasting between Jeffries and Carlisle, particularly during the journalist's return to the war zone from late April to early October. Throughout his coverage of the Japanese defeat, which carried him throughout the South Pacific and into Japan to witness its formal surrender, Carlisle shared his adventures—combat and otherwise—with the mayor.[15] Jeffries, in turn, was careful not to repeat the mistake of the previous year, when his candor had bruised Carlisle's feelings and tested their friendship. Instead, he complimented his writing frequently, boasted of it to their mutual friends, and buoyed Carlisle's spirits, sensing when they needed propping up.[16]

Responding to one inspirational letter as "just what the Great Doctor ordered," Carlisle revealed why the boys of the movement were drawn to the mayor. Jeffries projected himself into their own "dark moods" (in this case brought on by the rain and mud of jungle living) and dashed their depression in a handful of lines carrying "the zip of a radio pin-up boy exulting over Wheaties," offering uncommon strength and unconditional support.[17] He accepted individuals for who they were, assisting Carlisle to overcome his professional insecurities and Edwards to fulfill his political ambitions, never expecting payback of any kind for himself.

Of course, there were some limits to Jeffries's friendship. He and Carlisle kept in regular contact until the primary loss to Frankensteen; then, despite a promise, he failed to inform the chagrined war correspondent of his second-place showing. Unknown to Carlisle, however, who carped about being "quickly forgotten," the mayor had shelved all his letter writing to concentrate on winning the November election.[18] Finally, learning of Carlisle's return to the States in mid-October, he welcomed him back and asked about his "third honeymoon" (the second having occurred during his return from the European assignment the previous year). "The shooting may be stopped in [the] far Pacific," Jeffries telegraphed in unmistakable reference to the mayoral campaign, "but it's still going on here."[19]

Before and after that local political skirmish, global war continued to rage and allied peace hung in the balance. Consequently, Edwards and James P. Simpson carried on serious discussion of officer candidates and their training and worth, one preparing for such a responsibility and the other passing on the truth of those who failed to cut it in combat. Simpson also considered life more pleasant in combat zones—which were less "salute-crazy" than training centers—so long as one stayed out of the line of fire.[20] Others too—Carlisle, for one—relished the thrill of action despite its very real danger and their own very real fear.

The correspondent who covered the war in both theaters, including the liberation of Paris, found "the absolute epitome of excitement" flying fifty feet up in a B-24 bomber.[21] So did McElhone, who died on his last bombing assignment over Germany; that "hurts like Hell," exclaimed an angry Edgecomb, who, like Edwards, had known the pilot from earlier union days. Clearly, the death of friends and acquaintances continued to haunt servicemen and civilians alike, though they realized that blood sacrifice this late in the conflagration would prove redemptive rather than futile, signaling the end for both Germany and Japan.[22]

In fact, the second front opened by thousands of American and British troops the previous year came to fruition when Germany formally surrendered to end the war in Europe on May 8, 1945: V-E Day. Thereafter, invading and victorious GIs, such as Hayden, reported their experiences and pondered the future. Although the Germans "were more thoroughly licked" than any other people in history, every man, woman, and child picked away at bombed-out rubble to rebuild their homes and towns. This admirable "self-reliance" notwithstanding, contended Hayden, they could not become a powerful nation; mourning the loss of an entire generation of young adult men (approximately 3.5 million servicemen) and facing widespread starvation, they also appeared to be in danger of dividing themselves into patriots and collaborators—a dangerous political cul-de-sac. French residents, by contrast, sat "scratching their fleas" rather than restoring their cottages and villages, and they too confronted problems of food and politics. The black market and political turmoil loomed large and intersected when those who ate well often found themselves labeled, rightly or wrongly, as collaborators. Whether the popular and militarily influential Gen. Charles De Gaulle, the man of the moment, could succeed remained to be seen, opined Hayden, but both liberated France and vanquished Germany revealed a postwar Europe in dire need of economic reconstruction and political stability.[23]

War in the Pacific dragged on for another three months, marked by the steady, costly retreat of Japan and, suddenly, ending with the atomic bombing of Hiroshima and Nagasaki on 6 and 9 August. Carlisle accompanied U.S. forces as they "smashed Japs" in the Caraballo Mountains of northern Luzon, bombed enemy-held territory in the area, and hunted "for trouble" on surrounding seas.[24] Convincing military authorities to name him one of "the first war correspondents into Japan," he was among the 238 journalists who covered "the biggest story in the world" from the fantail of the U.S.S. *Missouri.* There on 2 September he witnessed the formal surrender of Japanese dignitaries to Gen. Douglas MacArthur and reported the world "aglow in the bright sunlight of complete peace."[25]

Within six weeks Carlisle returned to the States triumphant, while Schachern continued to serve in the Pacific. Mobilized in midsummer, expecting to participate in the invasion of Japan, he found himself thankful for the atomic bomb, which eyewitnesses near Hiroshima said had unleashed "a terrifying, burning wind which flattened everything in its path." He provided incomparably frank accounts of the initial occupation, covering subjects from romance and souvenir hunting to evaluations of the Japanese culture and people, whom he judged generally friendly yet helpless and idle.[26] He compared life in Yokohama, which lay in "absolute ruins," with that in Detroit, among other things commenting on the smell and docility of its people. He marveled at Kamakura, which stood "completely untouched by bombs" and came as close to a prewar existence as any city, intrigued by its rickshas, exquisite wood carvings, and famed Buddha shrine.[27]

Southwest of Japan, Schachern shipped into the Mariana Islands where Japanese guerrillas remained at bay, refusing to believe the war over. He recounted the saga of the commander of fewer than 100 members of the Imperial Army on Saipan demanding proof that Japan had surrendered. There Schachern also observed "grim reminders of the war": beaches littered with helmets, canteens, weapons; caves lined with "bleached skulls and bones of Jap defenders."[28]

Schachern toured other ports, including Hong Kong and Manila, before heading home via Guam and Hawaii. He described the commercial riches, night life, and intriguing characters of the Crown Colony, which contrasted sharply with the bombed-out spectacle of the once beautiful Manila. There he attended the war crime trials, necessary morality plays connecting victory to peace, but arrived too late to enjoy the company of Edwards, who had departed the Philippines only weeks earlier.

Edwards, too, had been mobilized to participate in the invasion of Japan, noting that preparations had been made for every possible contingency save the Japanese surrender without a fight (which produced "indescribable" confusion). In Manila he found "the Pearl of the Orient" a "pile of rubble," its people surviving on "black market trade," and himself assigned to the war crime trials. Significantly, Edwards prepared the legal evidence against those responsible for atrocities committed at the Los Banos Internment Camp, and he located its most offensive culprit, chief warrant officer Lieutenant Sadaaki Konishi of the Imperial Army. Unlike Schachern, who noticed an obvious disregard for courtroom rulings on behalf of the accused yet cared little whether they "got a break," he struggled with the concept of a "victor's justice." He probed the issue of guilt and moral responsibility thought-

Figure 5. Harold J. Schachern, 1944 or 1945, courtesy of Kathlyn Nies.

fully and concluded that the trials at Nuremberg and Manila provided hopeful efforts to create "a standard of world ethic" and "a world organization to enforce them." Indeed, he said, the future would produce "either *One World* or None."[29]

Thus playing on the title of Wendell L. Willkie's well-known book, Edwards revealed the concern of many servicemen for the postwar world. In fact, early in the year he had contended that the United States needed to remain internationally active after the war and engage in collective security, largely through commitment to "some sort of World Government and a police force to guarantee its decisions." He recognized the need to include Russia in such an endeavor and to press

England to recognize "skeletons in her closet" by freeing colonies such as India. Impressively in advance of the Yalta Conference agreements, he advocated self-determination for Greece and Poland; restoration of prewar governments for Norway, Czechoslovakia, and other Nazi-occupied nations; removal of Francisco Franco and his fascist dictatorship from Spain; and the return of Hong Kong to China. He expressed great admiration for the French and Filipinos, declaring that France, like China, should play a major role in the ongoing struggle for democracy and that the Philippine Islands receive their promised freedom.[30]

Simpson and Schachern also admired the Filipinos' spirited resistance to Japanese aggression but viewed their future differently. Simpson implied that their loyalty and rich resources should benefit the United States; Schachern believed that most Filipinos preferred freedom from Japan rather than complete independence and that hanging "onto Uncle Sam" would guarantee the rebuilding and future economic security of the islands. And where Edwards depicted the dangers of strong dictators and disciplined armies when considering the world beyond the South Pacific, Simpson and Schachern tended to focus on economics. Simpson questioned whether major powers such as the United States and Great Britain would set aside their self-interest. He hoped for international cooperation, perhaps under a federal union that would open markets and encourage democratic participation, declaring himself "a free trade, equal voice and vote man." Schachern envisioned China as the best possibility for America's trading future, one requiring heavy investment in that country's industrialization to ensure the prosperity of both partners. No other economic opening existed in an Orient "bottled up" by British and Dutch merchants.[31]

As the war and the year came to a close, what everyone most desired was a quick return to loved ones. Hayden, who witnessed V-E Day in Europe, for instance, wanted "out of this blasted Continent" and, despite fears that he might be reassigned to the Pacific, was mustered out in early October 1945.[32] He was followed within days by Carlisle, who in his six-month coverage of the Pacific war had witnessed as much combat as any soldier. Edwards departed the Philippines in December; Schachern left the Pacific and White left Germany during the new year. Simpson, who had come stateside earlier, also left the service in 1946. Perhaps, like Carlisle, those who had experienced combat remembered their tours of duty as "a nightmare," and each one who had worn a uniform grew "quieter, more mature, more introspective, more appreciative of the Little Things of Life."[33]

In truth, what began as national travail sometimes ended as personal triumph. Military promotions and decorations—such as Hayden's reaching the rank of lieutenant colonel and Carlisle's becoming the only correspondent in the Pacific to be awarded the Bronze Star—recognized the ability and valor of many.[34] In Detroit, meanwhile, Jeffries and Edwards scored major political victories that would influence peacetime reconversion throughout the metropolitan area.

Having served their country and survived their ordeals, in no small way because of concern for one another, the boys in the movement were satisfied with having been true to their country and themselves. They had survived the "good war" and, in Schachern's words, figured "on being too old for the next one."[35] They had changed, as had the city that awaited their collective help to resolve those "social and economic problems" accelerated by war and—most notably in race relations—left begging for answers.[36] Peace meant the return to family, friends, and civic duty.

NOTES

1. George C. Edwards (hereafter GCE) to Assorted Friends, 20 Feb. 1945, Box 14, pt. 1, Edwards Collection, ALUA (hereafter all citations to the Edwards Collection refer to Box 14, pt. 1, unless stated otherwise). The motto comes from the city seal, adopted in 1827 to commemorate the fire of 11 June 1805, which consumed Detroit. The seal was sketched by J.O. Lewis and bore the wording *Speramus Meliora* above and *Resurget Cineribus* below two female figures, "one weeping over a city in flames, and the other pointing to another city in a growing state"; the motto was translated as, "It has risen from the ashes" and "We hope for better things." See Silas Farmer, *The History of Detroit and Michigan* (Detroit: Silas Farmer, 1884), 138-39.

2. GCE to Dear Friends, 7 March 1946, Box 2, Mayor's Papers, BHC.

3. Gloster B. Current (hereafter GBC) to GCE, 9 May 1945, Box 5, pt. 2, Edwards Collection.

4. Charles F. Edgecomb (hereafter CFE) to GCE, 22 Feb. 1945, Box 5, pt. 2, Edwards Collection.

5. George Schermer (hereafter GS) to GCE, 28 Feb. 1945, Box 5, pt. 2, Edwards Collection.

6. Edward J. Jeffries Jr. (hereafter EJJ) to Martin S. Hayden (MSH), 30 July 1945, Box 3, Mayor's Papers (hereafter all citations to the Mayor's Papers refer to Box 3 unless cited otherwise).

7. EJJ to John M. Carlisle (hereafter JMC), 25 May and 30 July 1945, Mayor's Papers.

8. EJJ to JMC, 2 and 30 July 1945, Mayor's Papers.

9. CFE to GCE, 22 Feb. 1945; Louis E. Martin to GCE, 9 Feb. 1945, both in Box 5, pt. 2, Edwards Collection.

10. Alan Clive, *State of War: Michigan in World War II* (Ann Arbor: Univ. of Michigan Press, 1979), 166-67.

11. EJJ to JMC, 25 May 1945; EJJ to JMC, 11 July 1945, both in Mayor's Papers.

12. EJJ to JMC, 30 July 1945, Mayor's Papers.

13. EJJ to Harold J. Schachern (hereafter HJS), 12 Nov. 1945, Mayor's Papers; Clive, *State of War*, 168; Robert Conot, *American Odyssey* (New York: William Morrow, 1974), 395.

14. GCE, SOL X, 12 Dec. 1945, Box 2 (1946), Mayor's Papers. In August, Edwards was ordered into the Pacific expecting to participate in an invasion of Japan; however, given the Japanese surrender, his rank (second lieutenant as of March), and his legal education, he instead became a member of the War Crimes Division in the Philippines from September through mid-December.

15. Carlisle, "World War II: June 1944-October 1945" (author's possession, courtesy of Anita E. Carlisle), 97-217 for his stories from the Pacific.

16. EJJ to JMC, 8 June 1945; EJJ to HJS, 11 June 1945; EJJ to MSH, 30 July 1945, all in Mayor's Papers.

17. JMC to EJJ, 17 June 1945, Mayor's Papers.

18. EJ to JMC, 30 July 1945, Mayor's Papers; JMC to EJJ, 25 Aug. 1945, *ibid.*

19. EJJ telegram to JMC, 16 Oct. 1945, Box 5, Mayor's Papers.

20. GCE, SOL VIII, 20 Feb. 1945, Box 14, pt. 1, Edwards Collection (hereafter the location of all SOLs unless cited otherwise); James P. Simpson (JPS) to GCE, 5 May 1945, Box 4, pt. 3, Edwards Collection.

21. JMC to EJJ, 17 July 1945, Mayor's Papers; Carlisle, "World War II," 177-78, for the story of Carlisle's first bombing mission; Geoffrey Perret, *Winged Victory: The Army Air Forces in World War II* (New York: Random House, 1993), 99-101, 250, for development of the heavy, long-range B-24 Liberators.

22. Jennie Lee, *My Life with Nye* (London: Jonathan Cape, 1980), 151-52; CFE to GCE, 22 Feb. 1945, Box 5, pt. 2, Edwards Collection.

23. MSH to EJJ, 30 June 1945, Mayor's Papers; Norman Polmar, ed., *World War II: America at War, 1941-1945* (New York: Random House, 1991), 193.

24. JMC to EJJ, 3 June and 17 July 1945, Mayor's Papers.

25. JMC to EJJ, 25 Aug. 1945, Mayor's Papers; Carlisle, "World War II," 197.

26. HJS to Dear Friends, 31 Oct. 1945, Mayor's Papers.

27. HJS to Dear Friends, 16 Nov. 1945, Box 3 (1946), Mayor's Papers.

28. HJS to Dear Friends, 27 Nov. 1945, Box 3 (1946), Mayor's Papers.

29. GCE, SOL X, 12 Dec. 1945, Box 2 (1946), Mayor's Papers; HJS to Dear Friends, 11 Jan. 1946, Box 3 (1946), Mayor's Papers.

30. GCE, SOL VIII, 20 Feb. 1945.

31. JPS to GCE, 5 May 1945, Box 4, pt. 3, Edwards Collection; HJS to Dear Friends, 11 Jan. 1946, Box 3, Mayor's Papers.

32. MSH to EJJ, 30 June 1945, Mayor's Papers; "Diary of Martin S. Hayden: October 1943-August 1945" (author's possession, courtesy of Hayden), 256.

33. JMC to W.S. Gilmore, 12 Oct. 1945 (author's possession, courtesy of Anita E. Carlisle).

34. "Diary of Martin S. Hayden," 256; *News*, 25 Sept. 1945, 2.

35. HJS to Dear Friends, 11 Jan. 1946, Box 3, Mayor's Papers.

36. EJJ to MSH, 25 May 1945 (in author's possession, courtesy of Martin S. Hayden, Jr.).

LETTERS: FEBRUARY 1945–JANUARY 1946

Detroit. February 9, 1945
Dear Corporal: *Louis E. Martin to George C. Edwards*

Thanks for the interesting letter. I hope the OCS appreciates what fine material they have in you. I do hope also that this damn war ends

quickly. Detroit is still the same old jig-saw puzzle and on the race relations front here there is never a dull moment.

Now that the mayoralty race is around the corner the political monkey
business is picking up. Your esteemed colleague [Councilman] Billy
Rogell is carrying on in his wonderful reactionary way. Your friend,
the Lord Mayor, (my verbal punching bag) is going in for the fine arts.
He went to New York to hear the Detroit Symphony at Carnegie Hall in
the company of Butch LaGuardia.[1] The Lord Mayor is greying around the
temples and he is looking more like Hamlet everyday.

Charlie Edgecomb called to have me get petitions out for Vic Reuther[2]
for the Board of Education which I did. You know Charlie has decided
that the lily-white neighborhood policy is impractical. I am still waiting
for the Lord Mayor and the Council to decide where people like me may
be able to live in this lovely town. Billy Rogell and company believe
that the Lord made us to lie down in green pastures, but this weather is
against them and us.

I suppose you heard that the *Detroit News* editor told Governor [Harry
F.] Kelly to put Paul Krause in that Recorder's Court vacancy and told the
Lord Mayor to take care of Bill Dowling. Perhaps you know also that
[Harold] Thompson of the Interracial Committee is on the skids. The guy
meant well but was too naive. He wanted to make all these heathens act
like Jesus. Saw your madam at the Executive Board meeting of the Michigan Citizens Committee which is headed by Pat Nerty. Pat's brother-
in-law, Brien,[3] appointed two brown brothers as assistant prosecutors,
[attorneys] LeBron Simmons and Elvin Davenport.

John Ballenger's doing a nice job with the brass buttons and Negroes
have a little more confidence in the police department. He is quite proud
of his efforts too. He hinted to Negro kingpins out at Beulah Whitby's
house not long ago that Negroes ought to go along with the Lord Mayor
for a fourth term. [Reverend] Horace "Lips" White gave him an assist at
the meeting but most of the boys balked.[4] I talked with [UAW president]
R.J. Thomas about the mayoralty race and he said he was looking for a
candidate. He mentioned you and I told him that you had to run again
and that we were going down the line for you.

George Schermer is being pressured to go to Cleveland. He is a straight
guy and we need him here. Edward Conner, a Chicago Wonder Boy, is
sparking the Citizens Housing and Planning Council. [Joseph P.] Buffa
and his pals are active again and eager as ever to gum up the works in
[public housing] site selections. Lt. Com. Harold Stoll is trying to get
Jimmy Friel's job at the County Building.[5]

A state FEPC [Fair Employment Practice Committee] bill has been
introduced in Lansing and we are laying plans to get the GOP boys
behind the measure. Charlie A. Roxborough got a nice letter from your
dad replying to a note of congratulations on the Dallas speech. We ran
your dad's speech in the green sheet.[6] Your stock is up on this side of
town. If you can get a few 100 per cent Americans [white conservatives]
on your side you can get any office you want in this burg.

I have been busy as a cat on a tin roof during the past year. During the campaign I was assistant publicity director of the Democratic National Committee under Paul Porter. I had a nice office at the Hotel Biltmore headquarters in New York for three months. My job was to get the Negro Press behind FDR and to lay groundwork for rallies, radio programs etc. It was a great experience. During this time I was running the *Chronicle* by long-distance telephone and with the help of my wife.

Two months before Washington called me to handle the Negro publicity in the campaign I started a national monthly magazine called *Headlines.* You can imagine my dilemma. It is going over slowly and the paper is doing fine. We are getting an ABC [Audit Bureau of Circulation] audit which should put us in the 25,000 circulation class. We have some new staff members on the *Chronicle* and for the first time I think I have a fair newspaper organization although only fifteen are full time workers.

Besides this work I am trying to get a book finished for John Woodburn of Harcourt and Brace. Both of my kids are in school and I am the only member of the family in need of rest in a good hospital. If you wish me to do anything on the local front, don't be reluctant to ask me. When you get to be President I want a soft job in the Library of Congress dusting off the Atlantic Charter, that is if FDR has found it by then.

Sincerely,   LOUIS MARTIN

NOTES

1. Fiorello H. LaGuardia, mayor of New York City, 1933-45.

2. Assistant director of the UAW War Policy Division, brother of UAW board member Walter P. Reuther.

3. Gerald O'Brien who defeated Dowling for the Wayne County prosecutor nomination of the Democratic Party, won the office in November by defeating the Republican candidate Elmer G. Rice, 224,693 to 125,914. See *News,* 7 Nov. 1944, 1.

4. Whitby, a Jeffries's appointee, supervised the Alfred Welfare District (1941-42) and served the OCD (1943) before becoming assistant director of the Mayor's Interracial Committee; White, also a mayoral appointee, was a member of the Detroit Housing Commission.

5. Buffa, the builder instrumental in mobilizing white opposition to black occupancy of the Sojourner Truth Homes in 1942; Friel, Wayne County politician and auditor; Stoll, Wayne County Register of Deeds (1933-42), long-time leader in the Wayne County Democratic party, and a naval reserve officer who entered active service in March 1942.

6. George C. Edwards, Sr., delivered "Negro Progress and White Justice" before the Dallas Bar Association in the fall of 1944. See George C. Edwards, *Pioneer-at-Law: A Legacy in the Pursuit of Justice* (New York: Norton, 1974), 208-22. Roxborough was a longtime black attorney and occasional office seeker active in the Republican Party; Martin's newspaper was printed on green paper.

Fort Benning, Georgia. 20 February 1945
George C. Edwards to Assorted Friends

STANDARD OPERATIONAL LETTER VIII

I. *Ft. Benning Trivia.*

1) SOL VIII is being finished as the Fifth Company is sweating out the 14th week Board. These are military tribunals which periodically review the records of would-be Second Lieutenants and summon the doubtful ones . . . for interview, admonition or elimination. Those of us not listed this time have a pretty good chance on March 19 of having a pair of gold bars and the accolade of "gentleman" bestowed upon us by Act of Congress. We are all trained as combat platoon leaders and why gentle birth is essential to that assignment has not yet been made clear to me.

But in any event T.I.S. [The Infantry School] does its part to see that its brand new officers get no exaggerated idea of their importance. The favorite instructor "joke" runs . . . like this—"Men don't let anyone tell you that Second Lieutenants and tent pegs are expendable. You'll find you have to account for every one of those pegs."

2) . . . There's just a hint of dire prophesy in the appellation my comrades . . . have hung on me. When they remember to, they gleefully greet me with "There comes the China Clipper." Actually the title is derived from no past or future expedition farther away than the mess hall. I won it, one morning by taking a cereal bowl which proved to be the keystone of a two foot high stack. The resulting crash made me famous. I still don't know how I escaped a statement of charges.

3) Which reminds me of a question which has been worrying me—"Is Edwards really a chow-hound?" This cruel appellation was hung on me by a former Southern California football player by the name of [George R.] Gist [Jr.] (known here of course as "Gist in time") who was an obvious candidate for the title himself. I have tried hard to explain that it is not that I eat so much—its just that I eat more slowly that causes me to be the last at the table. My compatriots however pooh pooh this theory by pointing to the dessert bowls from three tables which some one discovered on our's, when only Gist and I were left. Can I help it if Gist likes dessert? Anyway the official Army definition of a chow hound is a G I who takes more food than he can eat. That's *never* happened to me.

4) This is just prior to our last bivouac. I reckon I'll survive it but . . . winter bivouacs are really sump'n—yep even in Georgia. . . . Our first one here was a week's duration and in weather 18° above zero. A pup tent . . . is no palace, but the real rigors set in when you have to get out of it. In ten seconds all of your carefully hoarded body and candle heat is gone with the wind. I reckon that sometime in each man's life he ought to "break the ice in the bucket" (in this case a G.I. helmet) to wash his face. . . . I've now done that enough to satisfy me for the rest of my life. I really greatly prefer indoor plumbing in the winter. Most of that week,

chasing around the Georgia hills or sitting in open stands . . . with a freezing wind whipping around from all sides, I felt more like one of [George] Washington's colonials at Valley Forge than a G I in *Sunny Georgia.* I guess I am strictly one of Tom Paine's summer patriots. "Whatcha bitching about candidate? Ain't nobody shootin' at you is there?"

5) Bivouac reminds me of one of my mates in the 4 man pup tent. . . . He was a college football player named Eggleton[1]—one of the three Negroes in our platoon. It is interesting to note that O.C.S. accept[s] Negro officer candidates and allows no discrimination against them in any phase of life on the Post. This doesn't mean that they don't have a hard row to hoe to get through here. They do. But those in our Platoon were genuinely popular with the men and I never heard a word of complaint about the policy which certainly must have been new to many of our Southern candidates.

6) The most interesting phase of life at Ft. Benning is the actual instruction at which we spend at least 8 hours a day out in the field. (Don't let me give you any false impression of the O.C.S. work day. Our duty hours start at 6 A.M. and end, unless we have a night problem, at 9 P.M.) But about this instruction, I can tell almost nothing since discussion of military topics at Ft. Benning is rigidly barred. (You of course, can find much of it discussed at length in those invaluable field manuals *Life* and *Time.*) Yet I would like to pass on some comments on the techniques used in the instruction.

I have been continually impressed by Army training methods and the really surprising results they achieve. It is standard practice for every subject to be taught by the use of every means of communication [conceivable]. . . . The standard educational devices of books and lectures are supplemented by continual use of charts, pictures, maps, photographs, motion pictures, skits, demonstrations and the final inevitable practical work. And woe be it unto the instructor who tries to teach a class without a set of training aids. . . .

The most publicized Army training aid is the *map chart* of Betty Grable[2] used to teach the location of terrain features by the map coordinate method. This map has in fine print at the bottom the customary legend "any changes in the area and terrain noted will be promptly reported to the Chief of Staff Army Eng. Corps, Washington, D.C."

None of the above (except maybe, Grable) is at all news in educational theory but . . . in reviewing some personal experience . . . the Army has done a really superior job of putting many of these educational theories into practice.

Nowhere in my education was any such use made of the motion picture as the Army has made of it in the fine series of Orientation films called *Why We Fight.* I think reprints of these are now available for civilian showing. . . . *The Battle of France–The Battle of China* and . . . the *Negro Soldier* seemed especially good to me. In re: *The Battle of France,* I have always wondered how that film got by with picturing DeGaulle as the only figure capable of leading in the rebirth of France at a time when our State Department still was making faces at him.

While I know well that the problem of military training and civilian education are entirely different I still suspect that educators in both public schools and colleges could get some interesting data from observing the work done and results achieved at I.R.T.C.s and O.C.S.s.

7) Having noted some things that I approve of about O.C.S., here are two other matters:

a) I do not care for Spit and Polish. (The G.I. has another name for it.)

b) I do not care for Ft. Benning's insistence on *The school solution* (i.e. one stereotyped way of working out every problem). Discretion leads me to say no more.

II. *Letter to the Governor [Ellis Arnall] of Georgia:*

Dear Sir: *11 Feb. 1945*

For the past year I have been a temporary resident of the State of Georgia and one of your war-time constituents. Since I am shortly scheduled to leave your state I am giving myself the pleasure of writing this note of appreciation for the contributions which the Governor and the State of Georgia have made to the morale of this particular soldier.

This appreciation is not derived from the undisputed hospitality of Georgians, nor from the mildness of the Georgia climate or the beauty of the Georgia pine woods. Most people in most Army towns try to do the best they can by soldiers; and I regret to say that no infantryman *ever* likes *any* weather or *any* terrain.

My constantly recurring joy has been in the columns of the *Atlanta Constitution* and *Journal* and their daily record of the brave, unflagging and highly skillful battle for a living Southern democracy which you have been conducting.

Though by inclination, legal residence and pre-war occupation, I am a citizen and public official of Detroit . . . (currently on military leave from its City Council), I am a descendant of a Southern family and born and educated in the State of Texas (which currently seems to recall the Civil War more vividly than other Southern States . . . actually more closely connected with it).

As a consequence some knowledge of the battlefield on which your operations have been conducted gave me even greater pride in watching a progressive Southern governor lead his state in wiping out some dark spots on the South's escutcheon.

Your dramatic appearance before the Georgia legislature when the bill to abolish the poll tax appeared defeated must have taken much political courage. But your success in persuading the legislature to pass the bill took an even rarer statesmanship.

To know that the Georgia of the chain gang and the poll tax has been replaced by the Georgia of a reformed prison system and a free ballot must give you a great amount of satisfaction. And I think that liberals all over the country should be wishing you equal success in your fight for fair freight rates, for constitutional reform and for an improved educational system for Georgia's people.

One other episode which helped speed a week of combat training on the Georgia hills was great. The reception which you and the people of Atlanta gave Vice President [Henry A.] Wallace the week after his defeat at the Chicago convention. I read the story not only as a tribute to the dignity and courage which the candidate had exhibited, but also as an evidence of a determination that a man who had come to symbolize full production and a concern for the common man in post-war America should not pass from the national scene.

I don't imagine that the millennium has arrived in Georgia; but I do think that the citizens of your state have earned a right to the pride they express in the accomplishments of their Governor and their State. And I think the whole country should feel more secure in the knowledge that Georgia's eyes are on the future and not on a dead if often stirring past.

Respectfully yours . . .

III. What One G.I. *Thinks* He Thinks About the Peace.

1) The title is occasioned by my strong suspicion that my information is inadequate, my conclusions very fallible and that I am quite likely to have changed my mind by the time anyone quotes one of these ideas back to me. But the British challenge for us . . . to make up our minds [about] what we want if we don't like what they are proposing seems fair enough. And since . . . I am currently being urged to think about world affairs by the Army Orientation Service and since I dunno whether . . . a 2nd Lt. is allowed such privileges—here goes.

2) This time I think we're in it for sure and up to our necks. We can't fight two world wars to save democracy and then for the second time pull out to our side of the Atlantic and say the heck with the rest of the world.[5] . . . we have to have some sort of World Government and a police force to guarantee its decisions. I fancy if the U.S., Britain, the Soviet Union, China [and] France were definitely committed to such an organization that voluntary association would bring most other nations into the fold and that the infinite repercussions of economic sanctions could be used to prevent trouble with recalcitrants who stayed outside.

There is much that is implied in the above that goes deep against my own mid-western grain.[4] But if we couldn't have peace in our time, I certainly pray my two sons can have it in theirs. Some of my friends will doubtless say "how can such a world league work with Stalin in it? Or with Churchill in it?" The answer is I don't know. But it sure can't work without 'em; and without some effort more hell-on-earth like the current war seems inevitable.

3) So . . . let's get down to cases. . . . To me the bright spots of American foreign policy as far as the conquered countries are concerned are France (and a grudging policy it was), and the Philippines. In both our military progress has [been] unmeasurably speeded by the cooperation of people who wanted to be free. I think France has endured her hour of travail and should be aided in every way possible to regain her authority as a democratic nation and be given all help possible to train her army and re-enlist in the battle.

As to the Philippines we should never forget that it was because of our promise of freedom that the Filipinos trusted us and fought on our side; and with such measures as would be necessary for our mutual protection that promise of freedom must be kept. I think it a source of tremendous pride to Americans that the Japs found no such embittered natives in Luzon as they found and used in Malaya and Burma and the East Indies.

4) As for Norway, Holland, Belgium and Czechoslovakia it would seem logical . . . to restore their pre-war governments and allow them to work out their [own] destiny . . . [with] the belief that they would pull their weight in whatever Federation of Nations was formed.

5) . . . I would like to see Greece and Poland (about whose former governments there is at least a reasonable doubt) by joint U.S.-British-Soviet pacts guaranteed a chance at free elections of their governments.[5] I believe that Poland, whose people have fought hard for freedom on every battlefront, is entitled to much more than a puppet regime. And I am equally sure that the Soviets are entitled to (and will make darn sure they get) a friendly neighbor. As for Greece I fail to see why Britain is entitled to restore a bedraggled monarch to the original home of democracy—particularly when his devoted people seem more ready to welcome him with hand grenades than with flowers. Apparently Churchill has . . . about given up this idea but I doubt that he allayed American suspicions of British Imperialism by making the attempt.

6) . . . After Hitler and Mussolini, we still have left a fascist dictator whose contributions to this war were as great and as evil as he was capable of making them. [Gen. Francisco] Franco [of Spain] gave the Nazis a proving ground for both the blitzkrieg, and for the type of psychological warfare that . . . overwhelm[ed] Europe. He seems to have furnished during the war every type of military aid to the Nazis which he thought he could get by with. And had military circumstance been just a shade different he would certainly have been ready to provide the Nazis with their soundest road of attack on the American continent thru Franco-inspired fascist groups in Latin America. And I . . . say out with him—by peaceful means if possible and if not by giving the Spanish people the aid we denied them in [the civil war of] 1937. . . .

7) And finally another word or so for our British cousins. . . . our Govt. ought to make some comments on a few phases of the British Empire which have in the past endangered world peace and will no doubt do the same in the future.

. . . it was Britain's plight in 1940 that conquered my own deep-seated isolationism and . . . nothing exceeds my admiration and gratitude for her steadfast and lowly courage when France fell and Hitler stood across the channel. But . . . I see no reason to overlook the skeletons in her closet. If Britain gave the world and us a chance to save its freedom we've certainly had a major hand in giving Churchill a chance to say he didn't "become the King's first minister to preside over the dismemberment of the British Empire." And there are certainly some parts of it which I think would be better dismembered.

Specifically . . . India should be free and the argument about how doesn't particularly appeal to me as too germane. . . . If Britain wanted to do it I suspect . . . [it] could find a way. We've had a lot less time with the Philippines than Britain has had with India and allowing for the greater difficulty of the Indian problem . . . we still have done a better job. Nothing in recent months has reminded me (in a repulsive sort of fashion) of the gap between the Atlantic Charter and its application to the world than a picture (datelined from India) of a half dozen American W.A.C.s[6] with *their lady bearers* apparently published as an indication to prospective W.A.C.s of the joys of Empire which we shared by our military alliance with the British lion.

Finally I think Hong Kong should go back to China and have yet to see any reasonable excuse to the contrary except the not too enlightened "what we have we hold."

8) All this before the Yalta results were announced and . . . I'll let it stand. So far as this G.I. can read . . . Yalta accomplished an unusual amount of good. Certainly the first and major objective of united military action until victory was achieved. And apparently with this comes an agreement to seek a common ground and support common decisions in the making of the peace. Maybe with such an understanding there is at least hope that "Meliora Resurget Cineribus." (Yeh! that means something like "Better things will rise from the ashes" and the reason I knew how to spell it was because I still have my badge with its City of Detroit motto.)

9) And re-reading the above reminds me vividly of the quote from some famous politico—"a politician is a man who never writes a letter and never destroys one." Oh well I never wanted to be called that anyhow.

10) It will be "Goodby Ft. Benning" three weeks from date, and (I trust) hello Detroit for 10 days. Where away thereafter no one can predict but wherever it is you may be sure I'll be wanting to hear from and about you.

Sincerely,   GEORGE EDWARDS

NOTES

1. Years later, Edwards had forgotten Eggleton's first name.
2. Actress, most adored GI pinup of World War II.
3. A reference to the U.S. failure, despite the efforts of President Woodrow Wilson, to ratify the Treaty of Versailles (1919) or join the League of Nations, established after World War I.
4. For ethnic and geographic reasons, the Midwest was well known for its isolationist attitude. See Selig Adler, *The Isolationist Impulse: Its Twentieth-Century Reaction* (London: Abelard-Schuman, 1957).
5. Though some of this was addressed at the Yalta Conference, February 4-11, Edwards did not learn of that until after he had written this section. Thus his views demonstrated insightful analysis and perception.
6. Pushed by Eleanor Roosevelt and Congresswoman Edith Nourse Rogers, against governmental and military opposition, the Women's Auxiliary Army Corps (WAAC) was created as a separate entity to serve with the army in March 1942; despite further opposition, much of it from soldiers, it became the Women's Army Corps (WAC) part of the army itself, in June 1943. See Geoffrey Perret, *There's a War to Be Won: The United States Army in World War II* (New York: Random House, 1991), 458-61.

Detroit. February 22, 1945

Dear George: Charles F. Edgecomb to George C. Edwards

I received your letter and your fan mail . . . [which] must have given you a thrill.[1] I will answer these letters and say in effect; "your letter to Councilman Edwards has been referred to this office for consideration." And we, in the Housing Commission, are intent on giving them just that, period.

As to your future status of statesmanship in Detroit, George, I can honestly say that even if you went to Europe or the South Pacific, or the CBI [Complete Background Investigation] area, you would still be more constructive as a councilman than your eight colleagues who meet futilely every morning in Detroit. I am sure that you should run for re-election because: Number 1, I think you will be re-elected without any difficulty. Number two, even if you were defeated, your name would be kept before the public and that is important insofar as your post war program is concerned.

In other words, George, you have all to win, and nothing to lose. . . . Your fan mail to the contrary, you still have a few comrades here who will do a certain amount of campaigning in your behalf. I have listened to so many citizens go through a flag-waving program that I can hardly wait to get even with them in a campaign for a councilman who is fighting for democracy. . . . I have questioned many people . . . and I have heard no one disagree with the idea of you running again.

The present site we have selected for Negro Housing is in Southwest Detroit, vulgarly called the "dog's leg," down in the area around Fisher

Homes.[2] The Council and the Housing Commission tossed the housing grenade back and forth several times so finally we recommended a thousand units on this site and tossed it back to the Council. We, in effect, pulled the pin on the grenade. The Council in their usual straightforward, aggressive manner, decided that they would hold an open hearing on this issue March 9th. The only constructive thing said at that Council meeting was by the elder statesman who said, "this meeting should be held in the Olympia [Stadium]." It will take more than statesmanship to kick this issue around until after the next election, which I think is their ultimate aim. I personally believe that the area will be Negro in five years without our help, but I also believe that some Marines may be necessary to complete our project down there at this time. One of the things you discover sitting on this Housing throne is that the Whites apparently have no sense of humor, and the "Love Thy Neighbor" crack is just propaganda.

Seriously though, this type of move must be made if we are going to alleviate the present overcrowded conditions in Detroit and I feel that three years in this job is gradually pushing me into a corner with the social workers. This latest move on our part will alienate the last Klu Klux [Ku Klux Klan] friends I have in Detroit.

I have just interrupted this letter to go to lunch with Victor Reuther and Jack Carlyle [Carlisle] in the interests of Vic's campaign for the School Board. I introduced Vic to our friend, [columnist W.K.] Kelsey, and I believe Kelsey is favorably impressed, which might help, and Carlyle is working on Doc [W.S.] Gilmore[3] with the intention of getting the *News* to eliminate any anti-Reuther statements. This latter program is still in the bargaining stage, because Gilmore is definitely not a push over for a CIO Candidate, particularly a Reuther who has been to Moscow. I don't think Vic can make it but we are having a lot of fun trying.

I hear Jack McElhone is reported missing and that hurts like Hell, too. It seems as if only our good guys are getting clipped. All of those jerks who were screaming for a second front apparently are no where near the front.

Getting back to your campaign for Councilman, I honestly believe that you can be the first Labor mayor of Detroit and that makes it important that you stay in the political picture. In discussing this around town I have come to the conclusion that you could even get the newspaper support. . . . That would not be this term of course but the next term rolls around pretty fast. Jeff hasn't [decided] . . . whether or not he will run and if the Gods should become nasty and put Cobo in the Mayor's office, I believe he is strictly a one termer and would be ripe for the plucking two years hence. If you come to Detroit before [the] filing date I hope we can get together for a while and I'll try and bring you up to date on the most important conniving . . . since you left.

To close with a familiar theme, we believe that the racial tension in Detroit today is more serious than at any time since I have been in this job. The disturbance has filtered down through the rank and file in some of the factories and anything can happen.

It is considered good policy in writing to a Serviceman to give him the brightest side of our Home Front picture and I guess I have hit the Jack Pot, negatively speaking.

Best Wishes.

Fraternally yours,   CHAS.

P.S. I think it is smart to add, please do not photostat a-la-Dufti [William Dufty]!

NOTES

1. Letters from irate white residents opposing Edward's January request to fellow councilmen that they rescind the ban on black public housing in predominantly white neighborhoods. See p. 241 below, n. 1 at top of page.

2. Built by the National Housing Administration and operated by Detroit Housing Commission as a temporary project for whites, the John R. Fisher Homes—bounded by Schaefer Highway, Marian Park, Visger Road, and the City of River Rouge—opened for occupancy in July 1943. See Freda Siefert Yenney, "Areas of Tension in the John R. Fisher Homes as Revealed by 100 Wives Living on the Project" (M.A. thesis, Wayne State University, 1944), 8-11, 21-22.

3. Editor of the *News*.

Detroit. February 28, 1945
Dear George: *George Schermer to George C. Edwards*

In response to your note of the 18th written on the back of S.O.L. #7, you're right, you did send me one before with a note. . . . your previous note asked if you had done alright in your letter [on the housing situation] to the Council.[1] The answer is, you did damned good. The vote still runs 8 to 1. The Council still bats the question around and postpones action by intervals of three or four weeks at a time. I realize us civilians ain't got the slightest idea of the ruggedness of army training or the horrors of war, but brother its mighty disgusting to be a civilian these days.

In answer to your most recent note, I do not think it will be northeast Detroit again. I doubt that it will be Detroit at all. As far as I am concerned, I wrote Detroit off as a lost cause sometime ago, and hope that some solutions can be found through new planned community developments beyond the present boundaries of the city. Remember you submitted a suggestion along that line to the City Council once a long time ago. The idea may develop faster than you ever thought it would and then again, of course, maybe we will just muddle along like we always have—postponing our problems with the hope that we will be in heaven before too much hell busts loose down here.

To give you a brief resume—Charley [Edgecomb] submitted his proposal last December, the Council postponed action until January 18. In the meantime, the Interracial Committee requested that the CHPC [Citizens Housing and Planning Council] and the Victory Council[2] submit recommendations to the [Detroit] Housing Commission as to sites which they would support. Edgecomb and Horace White tried to get both organizations to officially adopt a specific recommendation which they had; namely, southwest Detroit. The CHPC refused to be a mouthpiece for any individual and prepared a comprehensive study of three areas; namely, southwest Detroit, northeast Detroit, and far northwest Detroit. In their statement to the Housing Commission they pointed out that it really was the responsibility of the Housing Commission to select sites, but that the CHPC would support the Housing Commission in locating developments in any of those three areas. The Victory Council conformed to Edgecomb's and White's request recommending only the southwest Detroit site.

In the January meeting before the Common Council, Edgecomb did a strange thing. He submitted no recommendation himself but read the CHPC's letter to the Council and then said that the Victory Council had recommended the same thing. The result was that people in all three sections of the city became quite worked up. The Council then postponed action until February 13. Later the meeting was set for the 14th. On the 14th, Edgecomb appeared before the Council and asked them for a decision at which time John Lodge stated that he would vote on nothing until the Housing Commission came in with a specific recommendation for southwest Detroit. Billy Rogell was Chairman for the day and without any discussion set March 9 for a public hearing. In the meantime, Rogell is working with an athletic club from southwest Detroit which will surely mob the Council chambers.

As far as I am concerned, I expect absolutely nothing from the City of Detroit. While in Washington this week, I will try to get the Commissioner[3] to approve our locating a site outside Detroit, preferably in Dearborn. I am in favor of locating all future public war housing outside the city, unless the city specifically requests an allocation.

Bernice and I spent an evening with Peg about a week ago and had an extremely pleasant visit. The kids were in bed when we got there so that we didn't get to see them, but Peg and we had fun beguiling each other with the exploits of our youngsters. We were much impressed with the girl Peg has staying with her [Phyllis Dickinson] and are glad that she has such good company. Peg told us that you have been on bivouac much of the time lately, which I understand is the next thing to being in the front lines. How you get time to keep up with Council affairs and write the only intelligent thing which ever comes out of that Body is beyond me.

Best regards from both Bernice and myself.   GEORGE

NOTES

1. In a letter dated 3 January, Edwards urged his fellow councilmen to abandon the eighteen-month-old municipal policy that prohibited the alteration of neighborhood racial patterns in the construction of defense housing. Since black residential areas already were "narrowly restricted" and "almost no vacant land" existed "in the popular mind" for black projects, he contended that the policy codified race prejudice and denied black citizens their "right of equality before the law." In effect, he said, the City of Detroit had established racial boundaries similar to "the walled boundaries of certain areas in European cities." See *News*, 3 Jan. 1945, clipping in Box 2, pt. 1, Edwards Collection.

2. The Detroit Victory Council was formed in October 1943 by several management, labor, and other interested organizations to promote solutions for manpower problems, which ultimately included adequate housing for defense workers. In 1945, Ned A. Gorrell served as executive secretary and Detroit's superintendent of schools, Warren E. Bow, as chairman of the council. See Gorrell, "Resume and Presentation to the Detroit Victory Council," 9 October 1944, 1-2, Box 25, UAW War Policy Collection, AULA.

3. Most likely, NHA administrator John D. Blandford Jr.

Camp Maxey, Texas. 1 April 1945
Dear Jeff: *George C. Edwards to Edward J. Jeffries Jr.*

Enclosed a Dallas brochure in which I think you would be interested. They really have done a very impressive job of city planning in my home town in the past 20 years which has paid dividends in flood control, reclamation of much waste land, traffic artery improvement, railroad unification and removal of R.R. tracks from the downtown area etc. They are now making a very determined start at getting district planning through a drive to unify the area by assimilating the Three Park Cities (Dallas' Grosse Pointes) and seem to have a reasonable chance of winning 2 out of 3 elections this coming Tuesday if not all.

I thought you would be interested in the politics of this as well as the pictures they are using for their sales campaign.

Meanwhile I am assigned to Co. B 83rd Bn 21st Regt at Camp Maxey . . . and would like to hear the news when there is time.

Best regards,   GEORGE

P.S. Would you pass the enclosed and this note on to Geo[rge F.] Emery?[1]

NOTE

1. Detroit city planner, and secretary of City Plan Commission.

Zamboanga, Philippine Islands. 5 May 1945
James P. Simpson to George C. Edwards

Your letter of 19 April got here by air mail . . . . They get here much faster by air.

I'm glad you're still in the states. It looks as if you're too late for the show in Europe. I know you're disappointed. But cheer up. There's plenty to be done here.

Incidentally, now that you're an officer and a gentleman, I'll let you in on the big open secret of the army's officer system. When an officer becomes intolerable to his immediate commander, said commander gets rid of him, which process, in literally 99 out of each 100 cases, means that the GFU [General Fuck Up][1] gets to go to a better job, and usually gets promoted. This sounds cynical, but look around you. And stop and think how you would be if you commanded a company or battalion. Would you send away your best, and keep the ones that always had you in trouble and were personally offensive? Of course not, for it would actually endanger you. All the lieutenants we sloughed off back in the states as being the worst in the battalion got better jobs and promotions. Most of them are captains, while this battalion is full of good officers who've been 2 1/2 to 3 years in grade. There is very little to be gained by not being a GFU. One officer who almost got court martialled when we were loading for an operation last winter got banished from the task force, and fined, because court martials are too much trouble. The battalion he's in now has a very fine assignment, and his battery commander and exec are on the next rotation quota, which will leave him the ranking officer in the battery, and 5 will get you 10 he's wearing railroad tracks [captain's bars] come Christmas. There are at least 15 officers here who'd have been so promoted before he would have. . . . Now you know the awful secret about the army. I've been adjutant of this battalion for 2 1/2 years and a 1st lt. with a superior efficiency rating for 2 years. The army's full of administrative officers in grade of Captain or Major who got both the job and the rank following reclassification proceedings [for dealing with unsatisfactory officers].

We're having spit-and-polish trouble with the 8th Army these days. They like . . . guns to shine, and things like that. I liked the 6th [Army] much better. It's not so salute-crazy. Life, oddly enough, is actually more pleasant in combat areas with combat going on, provided you're more or less out of range of the mortar fire.

I got into an army hospital for the first time recently. Headaches resulted in an X-ray that looked like sinus surgery might be indicated, so I took a plane ride. Back at a general hospital, they called it neuritis of the spheno-palatine ganglion and wanted to destroy the ganglion. I wouldn't let them, so I came back to duty. Vitamin B1 has helped a lot. I saw at first hand something of what I had heard so much about—casual camps. The man said I'd have to wait for a ship to get back here, air transport not being available. So I caught a cargo plane next morning at 5:00, flew a couple of hundred miles beyond here, and then came back. I could have gotten here the same day, but I stopped over with one of our platoons in a quiet nook[2] with no one around to interfere with the idyllic existence except a few japs, who were not inclined to fight as long as they weren't fought.

If you come over as a replacement, you'll get good and sick of casual camps unless you're lucky. Our men usually go AWOL from them after a month or two and catch a plane ride and come back to duty. It's all right. Nobody minds. ATC [Air Transport Command] is priority stuff, but cargo planes will put passengers on the manifest and carry them, and bombers will usually do so, either officially or sub rosa. Don't hesitate to catch a ride beyond where you're going. It's a cinch to get away from the front. It's transportation forward that's difficult. And, also, if you keep track of your friends, you'll find you'll have bed, board, and transportation available at nearly any base.

Reports here about the San Francisco conference are scanty and hard to follow, but from what I've heard, [U.S. Senator] Tom Connally [of Texas] seems to have had the distinction of casting the first monkey wrench into the machinery. He doesn't want the proposed union to have any authority over the size or activity of the US Navy. In other words, the whole is not to be greater than any of its parts. The *New Yorker,* oddly enough, has for nearly a year been beating a drum and proclaiming what seems to me to be the only sensible course.[3] I wonder if you've kept up with their comments on world security unions and world governments. I think they're more sensible than any others I've seen. Almost no public figure seems to be able to make any kind of lucid statement about what he thinks ought to be done, and I've about given up hope. Britain and the US seem bound to perpetuate the systems that caused the last two [wars], while every body else seems to want to alleviate the situation. [The average] Joe apparently thinks, with good reason, that we don't have sense enough to see that we're doing it; and he is carefully preparing to stay out of the next one.

I had some hope that Roosevelt might be able to swing something. Personally, I'm a free trade, equal voice and vote man. But I don't think Britain or the US can be sold either notion. I don't see how we'd lose money, after a little period of shifting of industries, by complete free trade, and don't see how any war could get started if we had it under a federal union similar to the one originally intended by our constitution. It seems to me that if we don't have that we're certain to have more trouble.

I'm wondering how you view the matter. Does it look as discouraging to you as it does to me?

As for me, personally, I did once disobey an order to report to a Medical Disposition board for discharge, so I guess you have some justification for saying I wouldn't take a discharge if it were offered. But I think I would. I had a bit of asthma once at Camp Cooke,[4] and had to take some adrenalin one night. I took a one day leave–3 days if you take it on Monday–and went to Hoff General Hospital for tests. It was western ragweed, and they told me to appear before their board on Thursday. I told them I was an out-patient on leave and doubted their authority to compel me to. They doubted it, too, so I went back. But, hell, I'd been with the outfit a year, liked them, had a job I knew I could do, and would have felt pretty ashamed to leave while they were alerted to go overseas. But I've been over here 18 months, and I'm not doing anything worthwhile. I'm beginning to think I was silly. It's nice to see the show, but I'm not enjoying much of it, and the people like me who didn't go are going to be a hell of a lot better off the rest of their life than I am.

Which brings up another point. I'm probably no longer competent to practice law, and now that I know I can, I'm not so eager as I once was to do so. Do you think chances of employment are likely to be any good, for one of my dubious talents, in Detroit after the war? Personally, I wouldn't hire an ex army officer, because they're too accustomed to not doing anything, but I guess civilians don't know that. I've thought of trying to learn a little tax law by a year's "refresher course" under the so-called GI Bill of Rights,[5] but it sounds like a lot of work and I'm getting awful lazy.

Gosh, it looks as if I'm writing a diary. I have to stay in the CP all night, because it says somewhere that we must keep an officer here at all times, so I'm taking it out on you tonight.

Anna Beth is working in Corpus Christi–C.C. Hardware Co.–and dwelling chez nous at 314 S. Morningside Dr.

Every other person on the battalion has a monkey these days. They have tails, notwithstanding a widespread notion to the contrary. They have every bad trait of a 4 year old boy, and are fascinatingly human in moods, emotions, and conduct. An example of a remarkably accurate picturesque terminology, buried and unrecognized in every day speech, is the so-called "monkey-bite" in amorous dalliance. You'd never realize how picturesque it is until you watch monkeys.

My regards to all your family. And keep the letters coming. They're highly stimulating, and few things around here are.

JP SIMPSON

NOTES

1. "General Foul Up" in polite company.

2. Bongao, a small island in the Tawitawi Group between Mindanao in the Philippines and Borneo.

3. The San Francisco conference, beginning in April 1945, established the United Nations and wrote its charter. Several "Talk of the Town" commentaries (see *New Yorker*, 24 Feb. 1945, 11; 3 March 1945, 13) advocated a constitutionally structured

and popularly backed United Nations with greater "overall authority" than that of "any one member or any combination of members"; they opposed a League of Nations like that which emerged from the First World War, whose insistence on sovereignty would mean that "a nation shall be its own law."

4. Now Vandenberg Air Force Base, California.

5. In force from mid-1944 to 25 July 1956, authorizing educational and other benefits to veterans of World War II.

Detroit. May 9, 1945

Dear George: *Gloster B. Current to George C. Edwards*

On Tuesday, May 8th, Reverend [Charles A.] Hill, Frank Winn,[1] Louis E. Martin and I conferred re: your campaign in the Negro neighborhood and what type of cooperation could be worked out mutually helpful to both candidates. It was felt that no real discussion of this matter could take place except in conference directly with you and Reverend Hill. Since this is impossible we have decided to confer by telephone and Mr. Winn states that he can put through a call to you on Monday, May 14th at 5:30 P.M.

Reverend Hill, we feel, has an excellent chance for victory in the councilmanic race. The question uppermost in the minds of his sponsoring committee is: What coalition needs to be formed in order to best advance his candidacy in white communities? Accordingly, in our telephone conversation we would like to discuss whether or not you are in agreement with a cooperative campaign, and if so, the extent of that cooperation such as; speaking at each others meeting or in the absence of the other candidate, say a word in his behalf; distribution of each others literature depending on agreement between the people who are cooperating in the campaign; and seeking endorsements for both candidates from organizations.

You might be interested to know that PAC, today, endorsed the following in its first meeting on endorsements: George Edwards, Tracy Doll,[2] and Rev. Charles A. Hill.

Give my regards to Mrs. Edwards and we shall endeavor to discuss this matter more in detail by telephone.

Sincerely yours,   GLOSTER B. CURRENT

NOTES

1. Hill, minister at Hartford Baptist Church, led the Citizens Committee for Jobs in War Industries, which grew out of the Sojourner Truth Citizens Committee; Winn, a white unionist, an official in UAW Ford Local 600, was a close friend and political operative of Edwards.

2. Head of the CIO Council.

Dear Jack:

I am ashamed that I haven't written to you before, but I stayed in Florida longer than I anticipated, and I didn't have your address. Of course I could have been energetic enough to get it, but the weather was much better than when we were there, and I didn't seem to have time and energy enough for anything except play.

I enjoyed your letter immensely. Your articles appearing in the paper are excellent, and if you will pardon me for saying it, they are *better* than those from France. You know nobody but Jeffries would tell you that. All you have written, and I have read most of it, is good.

The campaign is about to commence. Jimmy [James D.] Friel and [Richard T.] Frankensteen seem like the logical contenders.[1] Apparently enough of the Jeffries haters will settle on Friel to make a potential three-cornered race, and there have been rumors to the effect that [Robert E.] Hannegan, who remembers well that Frankensteen would never allow his part of the Michigan delegation to switch to Truman, is anxious to see the non-CIO portion of the Democratic party go to Friel, and the Democrats are scared about the congressmen in this area in the next election, as a result of Archie Leadbetter beating Jimmy Friel for County Auditor.[2] It is difficult to tell, of course, yet how this will materialize, but at least that is the present propaganda. . . .

The local airport question is really a tangle. The experts hired by the [Detroit] Metropolitan [Aviation Planning] Authority have said that the Dequindre site is useless. We just got the verdict to the tune of two million three [hundred thousand dollars] on it Tuesday. They recommend that we use the Romulus or old Wayne County airport. The town is so befuddled that hardly anybody knows what to do next, including me, and I am going to have to find out within the next week or two weeks, and I don't envy my position very much because it looks very much as though I would be damned if I do or damned if I don't. However, there seems to be no alternative.[3]

The DSR is in trouble. Their revenues are beginning to go down and the announced increase of gasoline rations will probably contribute further to it and, without doubt, unless some reorganization of some sort is set up, they will start to run in the red. Poor Sam [Gilbert] is rubbing the few hairs he has on his head, off. Naturally I am not too happy about it myself. Frank Picard got Sam . . . a gold badge from the State Police, exactly like Ace Wilson's.[4] Sam is beginning to look like a returned war veteran only he has badges instead of medals.

We stopped in to see Peggy the other night and she apparently likes her job, and is glad she is working. Your Mother's Day flowers knocked her for a loop. I am sure you would have enjoyed her reaction.

We had a lot of fun in Florida. We played golf every day but three. Jeffries went native and finally ended up by playing golf in shorts. We had a quiet and, for me, restful time. Played golf so much that we practically wore Florence out. That is about all we did so I got along all right.

I got Wilson out fishing one day, and apparently my bad fishing luck continues. All of the other boats that were out got quite a few fish. We only caught two. Wilson got a six foot sail fish. He was so tickled he almost jumped out of the boat. I got a 24 1/2 pound king fish which is the largest one I ever saw or heard of, but it is not the largest one ever caught by quite a bit, but it was really big and it disappointed Wilson a little because it weighed more than his sail fish by a couple of pounds. But Joan[5] and Gary went with us and got a kick out of it. It was a beautiful day and even Carlisle would not have been sick. The fact of the matter is, we went in the afternoon because I had to wait until the ocean was like a mill pond before I could get Wilson out.

I have been very busy since I have been home. I have neglected practically all my intramural sports and kept my nose to the grindstone.

Your letter[6] made me wish that I had some of your experiences not all–but some. I would have loved to see you at the party. Having seen you at others I am not sure that your description of it does you justice.

I will do better in the correspondence department in the future.

Best of luck to you and *be careful.*

Sincerely yours,   J E F F

NOTES

1. Friel, former Wayne County chief deputy and clerk; Frankensteen, UAW vice-president.

2. Hannegan, Democratic National Committee chairman; Leadbetter, brother of city clerk Thomas Leadbetter.

3. A modern airport to serve the entire metropolitan area had been talked about for some time, but wartime exigencies accelerated plans for its construction. The authority endeavored to serve the interests of several affected municipalities, with Councilman Charles E. Dorias representing Detroit. Shortly before writing this letter Jeffries learned that a condemnation jury of the Macomb County Circuit Court had granted the city one square mile of land on Eight Mile Road–between Dequindre and Ryan roads–for the airport, appraising it at $2,326,226. That location proved unsatisfactory, but he thought the Eight Mile Road–Wyoming Avenue site might have possibilities, whereas the Wayne County Airport, located too far from Detroit, would provide only a temporary answer. See *News,* 22 May 1945, 1.

4. Gilbert, DSR Commission chairman; Pickard, U.S. District Court judge; Asa E. Wilson, executive, Ira Wilson and Sons Dairy Company.

5. Daughter of Ace and Doris Wilson.

6. This letter of Carlisle's has not been found.

Detroit. May 25, 1945
Edward J. Jeffries Jr. to Martin S. Hayden

Dear Martin:

You are half right–I am a very bad correspondent–almost as bad as you think I am, but not quite. Miss Ford relented and let me see your last letter to her, in spite of your instructions to the contrary, and I enjoyed it.

Our early campaign is about to start. . . . Friel was beaten in April for County Auditor . . . so I don't know how strong a candidate he will be. Frankensteen . . . will have the CIO support. . . . He has a lot of enemies in that organization, . . . but I suppose that he will be able to beat the guns to a sufficient extent to make him a substantial formidable candidate. I will know a great deal more about it later. . . .

I have been very busy since I have been back, and Detroit is jittery. The cut backs in war orders that are inevitable have not materialized enough to call for or make possible large sized conversion to civilian economy. The uncertainty as to what may happen employment-wise, has accentuated the shrinkage in employment here. Consequently people are not sure of what's around the corner.

Casualty lists from the Pacific are growing higher daily. The shortages of civilian goods, especially food and meat, have aggravated people's dispositions more than they have created any hardship. The problem of returning people to a normal week without the large bonus of over time premium pay is no small matter. It is not real yet, but is obvious for the near future, and the unions are beginning to scream their heads off about it. I suppose it is always wiser to yell before you're hurt on the theory that if you yell loud enough you might not get hurt. Anyway it is always harder to yell after you get hurt. My own guess is that we inevitably must raise the base wage scale because if we materially reduce the national income our economy could collapse. Many social and economic problems have been abated for the war's duration, but they will have to be met at the termination, and V-E Day has stimulated the conflicting forces to put their best foot forward.

It would seem to me that you might have the 85 points necessary to get out of the service and, judging from your reaction to [Samuel Lyman Atwood] Marshall's[1] suggestions to go to China, you would no doubt like it. Can we be looking for you home one of these days? Sure would love to see you.

Our jurist friend, Brother Krause, is becoming as smug as a veteran. He apparently really likes it and, from all reports, he is well liked by his colleagues and by the legal profession.

Charlie Oakman is a candidate for the Council. I think he has a good chance to make it. Henry Sweeny is not running for reelection and, therefore, there is one vacancy. There is a long list, as usual, with a chance for some other folks, but if Charlie can't make this he can't be elected to anything, but I still think his chances are pretty good.

With kindest regards, I am

Sincerely yours, JEFF

NOTE

1. Marshall, a veteran of World War I and journalist with the *News*, was instrumental in establishing historical sections of the U.S. Army, which collected data and ultimately produced a multivolume study: Office of the Chief of Military History, *United States Army in World War II* (Washington, D.C.: Government Printing Office, 1947–), the so-called "Green Books." See "Diary of Martin S. Hayden," 237; Perret, *There's a War to Be Won,* 538-40.

Northern Luzon, Philippine Islands. 3 June 1945
John M. Carlisle to Edward J. Jeffries Jr.

Dear Jeff:

Well, Jefferson, how the hell are you and how many folks have you insulted the last few days? Please don't change your style. It would be a pity. I sort of miss your raucous comment myself.

Well, I have gotten out of the mountain campaign. Our outfit smashed the Japs and came into a rest area and it gives me a chance to find some Detroit lads.

Some of the boys are going home. I am glad for them. But I made some new friends in this [U.S. Army] division and I hate to lose them.[1] I told my pal Bill Agy, a warrant officer of the 32nd [division], 128th regiment, to walk right into your office and talk to you when he gets back home. Bill is a Detroiter who has been 38 months overseas. Done a great job. He is the boy who got the supplies—the ammo, the water, the food, one hot meal a day, too—up the 25 miles of the Villa Verde trail to his regiment. He had 900 to 1,000 Filipino carriers taking supplies over the trail, down the slopes, through the draws, and up the mountains to battalions and companies.

Now Bill is going home. Before he went into the Army he took a Civil Service Examination for the City of Detroit. He will probably get mustered out of the Army in short order. So, Jeff, take care of this pal of mine. Find him something good. Because he is good. He is the kind of a guy who gets things done. I know you like those kind of gents.

My best to you & Florence, and thank you for dropping over to see Peggy. Let me know the date of the election. Give my best to Ace [Wilson]—and write, Jeff. Best regards,

Faithfully, JACK CARLISLE

NOTE

1. See John M. Carlisle, *Red Arrow Men: Stories about the 32nd Division on the Villa Verde* (Detroit: Arnold-Powers, 1945).

Dear Jeff:
Tacoma, Washington. 4 June 1945 (postmark)
Harold J. Schachern to Edward J. Jeffries Jr.[1]

This is the New Marine Corps carrier aboard which I am to serve as a fighter director officer. She'll be a fighting ship, I warrant, if the B-29's don't end the war before we get there [Japan]. My best to everyone in your official family.

HAROLD

NOTE

1. This note appears on the back of an invitation to Commissioning Ceremonies of the U.S.S. *Puget Sound*, 19 June 1945, in Tacoma.

Dear Jack:
Detroit. June 8, 1945
Edward J. Jeffries Jr. to John M. Carlisle

The stories and the pictures are very colorful.[1] They are winning a wide acceptance. Everybody is enjoying them immensely.

It was good to hear from you. I suspect that the day you wrote the letter you were a little low, however, but that happens to everybody.

We have dropped in on Peggy several times lately. She is plenty lonesome, but both she and the youngsters apparently are sound physically and mentally—just wishing the old man were home.

I have never been so busy at this time of the year. It has raised hell with my golf, and the combination of bad weather and too much work has limited my golf to once a week—either Saturday or Sunday.

We went out the other night to see Joe Norris and Buddy Bomar bowl Andy Varipapa and George Young[2] at the Palace Recreation. They bowled 56 games—28 in New York and 28 in Detroit. Incidentally, Bomar, who is the national individual match game champion and Norris got a good shellacking. Andy Varipapa bowled ten strikes in a row and then, to show his nonchalance, while waiting for the ball to come back, he turned around to shake hands with Florence. Then he threw the eleventh and didn't touch the pins. Florence threw up her hands and said, "Do I jinx him or do I jinx him." Our timing was bad, however, Andy rolled a 300 game. As a practical fact, he rolled 16 strikes in a row the night we were there, but it was six to finish one game and ten to start the next game. I played "hearts" with Allen[3] that same night and we knocked his ears off. We left him in a very tearful mood.

The political pot has not yet really started to boil. I suppose it is the calm before the storm. Charlie Oakman, on the surface at least, is generating a lot of steam as a candidate for the Council. . . . Good Luck to you, my boy, and be careful. You only think you are made of steel. You wear out, too.

Sincerely yours,   JEFF

NOTES

1. Carlisle's stories of the Pacific front appeared regularly in the *News* and were collected in Carlisle, "World War II."
2. Professional bowlers on tour.
3. Perhaps Allen C. Dean, secretary of the Board of Commerce Aviation Committee.

Detroit. June 11, 1945

Dear Lieutenant: *Edward J. Jeffries Jr. to Harold J. Schachern*

Certainly wish we were there to help you commission . . . [the U.S.S. *Puget Sound*]. We hope that the B-29's are able to take care of the job and that you will soon be back to take your place here.

Wally Hushen[1] wants you to know that the most arduous activity around here is a lot of words. The matters of major importance are as you left them. The partition between the reception room and the press room has been raised to the ceiling to shut out or keep in the sounds emanating from the Fifteen Minute Club poker table which flourishes early and late.

Your successor—Charlie Webber [Weber][2]—returned this morning from a week's honeymoon. This morning there were three calls for him— "Please call your wife."

As you probably know, John Carlisle is with MacArthur's boys and doing a fine job of putting it in words for the home folk. We have not heard from Stod [Walton S. White] since he went across months ago. Jim Inglis[3] sent a copy of a German newspaper to adorn the bulletin board in the press room. He did not give us any information about himself, though.

What with improved transportation prospects and new airport plans we are kept busy. The food industry has us guessing, too. The August 7th primary is not far off, and it means a lot of excitement.

Write to us when you can and tell us all about it. Good Luck and take care of yourself.

Sincerely,   JEFF

NOTES

1. *News* reporter covering city hall.
2. Weber, *Free Press* reporter covering city hall.
3. *Times* reporter serving in the U.S. Army.

Bad Neuenahr, Germany. 30 June 1945
Martin S. Hayden to Edward J. Jeffries Jr.

Dear Jeff:

At this writing I am in the final stages of another Army assignment[1] and suffering from the usual uncertainties of such a situation. With this Headquarters breaking up I have arranged to be transferred in the relatively near future to Paris where Sam Marshall has offered me a spot which is about ideal under present conditions.[2] In other words he says to come to work for him and he will release me whenever I can figure a way to get out of this blasted Continent.

There is still a chance that a shuffling of cards will send me off to the Orient or to some longtime occupational job but I don't think so. I am well-stocked with points for discharge and hopeful. The main trouble is that if you are declared excess in this Theatre you are then up against the problem of no transport for home and the prospect of sitting for months in a redeployment camp. That is the chief reason I appreciate Sam's offer. I would much rather sit it out in Paris.

I have arranged for my particular pal of this war, Bill Knowland, to be transferred with me. Bill is the former Republican National Committeeman from California, a job which he acquired when he was about 32. He is an ardent supporter of Gov. [Earl] Warren and a type of Republican who would give the Party some hope if there were only more like him. We have had a lot of fun together and are playing our cards to stick together on the theory that any fate is made less unpleasant if you have good company.

This life in Germany has been strictly a pain in the neck. Our Army has had its headquarters in a small resort town called Bad Neuenahr. It is just west of the Rhine and about halfway between Coblenz and Cologne. Physically the surroundings are good. We took over the center of the town including several very modern hotels and put up a barbed wire fence through which no Germans are allowed to pass. It is very boring, however, as we live a completely contained life. Being an army headquarters discipline is strict, the saluting non-ending and the spit-and-polish considerable. Our General [Leonard T.] (Gerow) is an exceedingly capable gent but strong on the military end and he has us all jumping through hoops. Having three of those twinklers on your shoulder would, incidentally, be not too hard to take. When one of our generals moves about the screaming sirens and flashing Cadillacs is enough to put Mr. LaGuardia's dignitary parades to shame. The more stars there are the more sirens go along and when Eisenhower arrives it sounds like the opening day at a Detroit race riot. The processions usually travel at about sixty miles an hour which is, I believe, a matter of self protection for the enclosed dignitary. At that speed it is impossible for all the GI's to tell whether or not he returns their very proper salutes and he is thereby saved from the necessity of more or less having to propel himself along with his right arm.

Last week I jeeped down to Paris and back, a process exceedingly hard on the tail feathers but more interesting than flying as it gave a better chance to see what is going on.

There is a marked difference between the French and German people. Germany is more thoroughly licked than any other nation in history. Their suffering in the coming months is going to be beyond imagination. But still they have a basic self-reliance which you cannot help admiring and which is definitely not present among the French.

In France, where towns were smashed in the fighting, the wreckage is essentially untouched and the French are sitting around scratching their fleas and waiting for someone to come and fix it. In comparable German towns every man, woman and child is out picking away at the unbelievable heap of rubble. There aren't many results yet evident but they are at least trying.

I was particularly interested in the town of Prum which is about 80 miles from here and on the route to Paris. When I went through it four months ago it was as depressing a piece of war evidence as you could find. It had changed hands several times in the fighting and not a house was left. At that time the town site was utterly devoid of life, not a dog, car or human.

The other night about 9 PM I drove through again. Some percentage of the townspeople are back. Most of them are living in basements which they have reached by tunneling through the rubble of collapsed homes. And they were all out. Little children were stacking bricks and usable pieces of stone. Women were scraping the bark off of newly-cut trees and men were up fitting the trimmed logs into place as rafters over stone walls which had been left standing.

Despite the energy, however, Germany cannot in my opinion come back. First, of course, they will be affected by a loss of a whole generation of manpower. I saw a recent report which stated that in the town of Freiberg, of 60,000 people who had registered for ration cards, only 318 were men in the age group between 18 and 30. This situation has been somewhat relieved by American and British releases of thousands of prisoners, primarily farmers, miners and transport workers. But neither the Russians or French are releasing prisoners and I don't believe they will until the prisoners are too old to come home and breed more Germans. All of the powers have agreed that SS Troops will remain prisoners.[3] There are thousands of them and they were, of course, the pick of German manhood. Adding these permanent prisoners to the thousands which Germany lost in dead and permanently crippled, you will see literally the loss of a generation.

Others will be lost this winter through starvation. The British general commanding military government recently made a statement that 1,000,000 people would starve this winter in the Ruhr and that nothing could be done about it. Starvation which is going to be existent in France, Holland and Belgium makes it out of the question for the allied powers to give Germany any food even if they wanted to.

The British general's estimate was based upon a taking into account of results of the British and American policy of making every effort to plant every field and produce every possible pound of food within Germany. Now, however, we are turning over the Southern Rhineland to the French. There are indications that they are going to work there as they did in the areas they already occupy and ship everything out to France. This is, of course, what Germany did to its victims but it is going to mean that that farm area will do little more than feed itself and that the predicted starvation in the Ruhr will go up for lack of expected imports from the agricultural regions.

I don't mean to imply that I have any particular sympathy for the Germans but I cannot see a healthy world coming as long as so big an area is starving.

France is little better. My friends In Paris reported that the legitimate food market is virtually non-existent and that everything they eat comes from the black market. They only shrug when asked as to what will happen next winter when the season brings an end to the flow of fresh stuffs which are now keeping things going for the poorer people. Politically also France is in a turmoil. De Gaulle is unquestionably the boss primarily because there is no one else and his position will be strengthened as he continues to re-build the army. But France is being flooded with returned German prisoners and slave laborers for whom their economic system has no place. These people feel a vested right in a living is their due and they are raising Hell when it is not forthcoming. There is considerable confusion on the question of who is a collaborationist and the answer of the less fortunate is that everyone who can eat well is prima facie guilty. It is a peculiar situation with discontent rising but De Gaulle's power to control it is increasing proportionally as he adds more and more battalions of trained and equipped troops. He seems to have pretty well licked the FFI question by incorporating the ex guerrillas into the army, reducing the rank of their officers and interspersing them with trained and professional soldiers.[4]

In Germany politics is, of course, completely confused. In the British and American zones our military government, in addition to turning aside all former Nazis in the search for civilian administrators, is also avoiding the communists. The result is that almost all of the civilian administrators functioning are former members of the very-conservative Catholic Centrist Party. Political organization as such is forbidden and although we have made a couple of gestures towards labor, unions also are being kept generally down. The result is that the Catholic Church is the one organization being given freedom and it is presently the most powerful civilian organization in Germany. What the results of this will be is hard to assess. We are giving them a running start over their opposition but this may boomerang if the Germans prove to be like all other peoples of the world and get around to dividing all men into two classes: those who collaborated with the occupation authorities and those who do not. We may find that all our efforts to find non-Nazis to act as government officials has simply served to eliminate them from any consideration in the Germany of the future.

Yesterday morning I arose at 3 AM to attend the execution of the first three convicted war criminals. My job was as guardian of the press and to keep the photographers present from completely upsetting the dignity of the affair. The victims were three very ordinary gents found guilty of having killed an American flier who had parachuted down during the bombings last August. During the trial my attitude drew a strong reprimand from my good wife. I had written Betty that I could not help, during the trial, recalling our enthusiastic receipt of news of a bunch of British farmers who had applied a pitchfork treatment to a German pilot who landed during the air blitz of England. Also I remarked that there would probably be some violators of the "Laws and Usages of War," the crime for which the three died, if a Jap pilot had the misfortune to bail out over San Francisco. I was answered by a letter admitting our right to kill their pilots because the Japs and Germans are the aggressors while we are just defenders. Perhaps Betty is right.

I still, however, got none of the conqueror's satisfaction in watching these gents dragged up the gallows steps and dropped to oblivion.

I seem to have run out of filler at this stage but I have given you enough to keep you busy during a ride between a couple of campaign meetings so I guess we are even again. I see the stories on your opposition which does not appear dangerous unless my judgement is warped by too long an absence. In any case, I will be anxious to hear from you.

My best to Nancy, Florence and all of the boys.   M A R T I N

NOTES

1. In January, Hayden had been transferred to the Fifth Information and Historical Section of the Fifteenth Army, near Suippes; in February to Dinant, Belgium; and in April to Bad Neuenahr, Germany. "Diary of Martin S. Hayden," 189, 200, 220.

2. Marshall offered Hayden a position in the Historical Section.

3. The *Schutzstaffel* (protection squad), formed in 1933 as the personal body guard of Hitler and the elite corps of the National Socialist German Workers Party (Nazi Party), expanded to operate the concentration camps and to fight on all fronts; its defense of the Third Reich in the final years of the war significantly delayed Germany's defeat. See George H. Stein, *The Waffen SS: Hitler's Elite Guard at War, 1939-1945* (Ithaca, N.Y.: Cornell Univ. Press, 1966), 282-94.

4. The paramilitary underground forces in occupied France had united in 1943 under the National Resistance Council, a political coalition led by Georges Bidault.

Detroit. July 2, 1945
Edward J. Jeffries Jr. to John M. Carlisle

Dear Jack:

I was certainly glad to hear from you this morning, but you sounded plenty blue to me, my boy, and, while I don't blame you, it has been as hot as hell here, too. We aren't having as much fun as you think we are. We are just writing cheerful letters to you, hoping that it will pep you up. Incident for incident, you get more variety and more action, I am sure, than we do and, while it is certainly tough to be away from your near and dear ones, you know that you are coming back, and they will know what a guy you really are on account of they can remember when you weren't here.

I have been down in Chatham, Pennsylvania, about forty miles out of Philadelphia. It is the Maccabees old folks' home. Went down to Maccabees board meeting. It is a beautiful place, physically, but it is really depressing. It can happen to you in other places than the Philippines. Hell, you can be down there with nothing to look forward to but to die in those beautiful surroundings—quiet, peaceful, my God, you can hear yourself think. In fact, it was so quiet that I started to take up croquet again to prevent myself from going nuts.

Your articles and pictures, in fact your whole build-up, in my humble opinion, is improving. The papers give it a great spread, and I really and truly think that you are becoming a true local great shot.

We are opening campaign headquarters next Monday. We have them on the fifth floor of the Dime Building. Business is so good in town that we just couldn't get ground floor space anywhere down town that was at all suitable, except in the Free Press Building on the corner of Lafayette and Wayne, and all they wanted was $500 a month rent. Needless to say we didn't take that.

We have had a knock down and drag out fight over the Northwestern Airport site—that is, at Wyoming and Eight Mile Road. All the experts finally agreed that we shouldn't use [the] Eight Mile and Dequindre site, and after getting a verdict in the amount of $2,300,000 we have abandoned that. [Councilman Eugene I.] Van Antwerp is in the hospital with a broken leg. [Frank] Cody is in a very serious condition, and may not get well. George Edwards, as you know, is in the army. [Charles E.] Dorais, [William] Comstock and [William G.] Rogell opposed the Wyoming and Eight Mile Road site. [John C.] Lodge, [Fred C.] Castator and [Henry S.] Sweeney favored it. So it looked like a 3-3 tie. Off the record, behind the scenes I got Edwards back here, and he cast the deciding vote.[1]

If the Board of Commerce raises the money to purchase 704 acres, that's where Detroit's major airport will be.[2] If not, the problem remains.

Sincerely,   JEFF

NOTES

1. Edwards returned on a special leave from the army, arranged by the mayor. He then consulted with the Detroit Metropolitan Aviation Planning Authority and members of its engineering consultant firm, who agreed on the Eight Mile Road–Wyoming Avenue location; he also spoke with city engineers, who offered no "substantial objection" to the location. He voted with like-minded councilmen, disregarding those who wanted to see the formal reports of both the authority and the engineers before voting and who presented a telegram from the U.S. Department of Commerce urging caution in the site selection process. Never a political rubber stamp, Edwards backed Jeffries's position because he agreed with it in engineering and economic terms; he knew, of course, that Jeffries expected him to do nothing less than what was best for Detroit. The action was supported by many, including the editor of the *News.* See *News,* 19 June 1945, 1; 20 June 1945, 1-2; 21 June 1945, 20.

2. Contingent upon council approval of the northwest site, the Board of Commerce offered to raise the funds necessary to purchase the acreage and present it as a gift to the City of Detroit. See *News,* 19 June 1945, 2.

Detroit. July 11, 1945
Edward J. Jeffries Jr. to John M. Carlisle

Dear Jack:

We have officially opened campaign headquarters. I have made no radio speeches as yet, but my opponents, [Jimmy] Friel and [Richard T.] Frankensteen, have been on the radio once or twice a week for the last several weeks. So far they have drawn no blood whatsoever. Frankensteen accused the union of mobocracy. While the newspapers gave that a big play, the people he hoped to reach agreed with what he had to say but he made many union members as mad as hell. A few victories like that and the army is lost.

The apathy is disturbing. However, currently there is no upsurge to remove Jeffries, and that scares me because it's hard to rally my friends. I am sure the haters will be out and consequently I am worried. I have been working hard both day and night. Campaigning has removed me from the social whirl—even from golf. I have kept myself short in our own card game, however. I might tell you that they had a big party for [council candidate] Oakman the other night. All the newspaper boys were there and played at different tables. Only one lost—Leo Donovan. [Owen C.] Deatrick[1] said that that was due to lack of practice. Leo doesn't play regularly. The regular players, however, came into fresh money from strangers. We had a lot of fun distributing it among ourselves yesterday. Incidentally, Oakman had a big meeting. I am sure it was the biggest one of the primary campaign. I think his chances of election are excellent.

I saw John [S.] Bugas[2] the other day. He was hale and hearty and we swapped anecdotes about your past behavior. They were relatively favorable to you. I see Louis Colombo practically every time I play golf, and we take turns in telling how good your articles are and re-editing copy on them.

I haven't seen [Ace] Wilson in a couple of weeks, but I guess he is all right on the theory that no news is good news.

The more I think about it the more I think that my life recently has been quite uneventful–doing the same old thing in the same old way. I know that that sounds attractive to you, and we, incidentally, wish you were here to do it with us.

I have just written a letter to Gary, and told him how quiet our house is. The same relates to the city and the campaign. Without you it can never be quite like the last one. I think of you often enough so that I can feign a Carlisle stimulant. I suppose that synthetic as it is, it will work in about the same way.

Take good care of yourself.

Sincerely yours,   J E F F

NOTES

1. *Free Press* reporter.
2. FBI director in Detroit.

Dear Jefferson: *Molucca Islands, Dutch East Indies. 17 July 1945*
                                          John M. Carlisle to Edward J. Jeffries Jr.

I temporarily take back all my violent vociferation about how miserable you are to your friends. Your letter of July 2nd arrived today. It was just what The Great Doctor ordered. I was really a Sad Sack, as low mentally as I have ever been in this God-forsaken part of the world that only hard-shelled Baptist missionaries like in their efforts to put the beautifully-bodied Filipino maidens in un-beautiful Mother Hubbards.

So I was feeling like a well used dish rag when your letter came along with all the zip of a radio pin-up boy exulting over Wheaties. It was very nice of you, Jefferson. You must have read between the lines and projected yourself into the dark moods of this reporter. For last night it poured. In torrents. By bath tub fulls. Like a million shower baths running rampant. I am living with bomber boys at an air base. There were 16 in our old squad tent. It has holes in it. The rain just flowed in, as if someone with a nice pleasant temperament like Al Cobo had let the Mississippi in. I woke up, dazed, started to go into a crawl stroke. Half dreaming I thought I was down in the Pacific in a bomber. I was soaked. I took the dry blanket out from under my air mattress, put my rain coat over my mosquito bar, crawled back on my cot. No dice. The rain kept coming in. I got up four times, kept shifting the raincoat like a Chinese checker. No dice. More rain on me. In my face. On my feet. Coming in from the sides. The Big Moose, a bomber pilot who sleeps next to me and lets me wear his swanky dress hat when I go over to group command, The Big Moose said, "Oh to hell with it. If I have to sleep in a puddle, here I go." So I said, "To hell with it." I woke up cold and wet and shivering. All my gear was wet. I put on wet clothes, went outside in the rain; washed and shaved in the rain, slid on my prat in the mud. The last straw was when I dropped my only clean towel–in the mud. "Son-of-a-bitch," I said, "I'd like to shoot up that tent with a .45 pistol"–only you have to clean the automatic after you shoot. (Incidentally, I have learned to shoot that Bucking Broncho of an automatic.) It was raining when we went to mess. The food was lousy as usual. My mess kit slipped out of my hand and fell in the mud. "Oh, nuts," and anybody who ever calls bomber boys "the glamour boys" will get a good smack in the puss from me. Our camp is as comfortable as living in a wastepaper basket in a mud hole in the rain.

So you can imagine how I felt when in came the mail, two letters from the lovely Peggy, who writes with all that sweetness and spirituality that makes the eternal femininity so precious to guys like us; a letter from Doc [Glenn] Richards,[1] etc. So, now I feel better, and the sun is shining, and I have just bought 10 bottles of Aussie beer for $27, quarts. It is good beer, the finest in the world, with a 12 percent kick. I am throwing what the bomber boys call "A Push" tonight for a bomber crew of 10. I flew on a 14-hour combat mission with them over more than a thousand miles of Jap territory. The bomber sure pummeled the Japs that day. I never got such a kick out of anything in my life. I thought the Paris liberation was the biggest day of my life. To hell with that. I have been down at 50-foot level over the Japs now in a B-24, Jeff, that is the absolute epitome of excitement. So we are going to have a Push to celebrate–that we got back.

I also got a big kick out of going out on a 14-hour night patrol in a PT-boat, just hunting trouble, going right up to 200 yards of thousands of Japs and daring them to open up. That went on all night. It was a beautiful ride, and sometimes we layed doggo in the water and sometimes we went like the wind. We opened up once. My gosh, a PT boat really packs a wallop. Both those trips were real sport; going hunting for the Jap has anything in the world beat. I haven't told Peggy much about this and I haven't gotten around to writing about the trips yet. I didn't want The Sweetest Gal in the World to worry. But there are some things you have to do even though you don't want to do them. I admit I haven't got an iota as much guts as I like to think I have. Wholly Jesus, I go through the war in a constant state of fright. My pulse must be as fast as a P-38. Anyway, I finally got hep to the fact, which you recognized before I did, that the silly public wants its war correspondents to see and do things. Let me hear from you, Pal.

Faithfully,   J A C K

NOTE

1. DPW superintendent.

Detroit. July 30, 1945
Edward J. Jeffries Jr. to John M. Carlisle

Dear Jack:

I was very much interested in your letter describing the rain and the airplane experiences. I have always thought that the boys who flew the airplanes deserved even more credit than the boys who did the ground fighting. The reason I say that is, the boys who do the ground fighting do it all at once and then they are moved out and, more often than not, have nothing more to do. The boys who fly airplanes go in, get continually shot out and then go back to comparative safety, and then have to do it all over again time and time again. I am sure you agree with me that the anticipation of any struggle is even more fearful than the actual struggle. I have always thought that those boys who continually fly in over cities must have some rough minutes in anticipation of arriving at the destination.

Next week is primary day. Frankensteen has the same advertising firm that [Frank] FitzGerald[1] had. The cartoons and characters are even better. A couple of pamphlets being circulated call me simply "Junior." They have one showing [Councilmen] Rogell, Dorais and me in an old one-horse shay, with the allegation that that is the vintage of our transportation system. It is hard to tell what the outcome will be. As usual, the candidate is the most unreliable fellow you know. For sure some people are with me this time that were not last time. Whether I retain the same strength and will add to it, I will be able to report to you after the election. [Police Officer] Neil Boyle and I made five meetings and two picnics yesterday. It is just as hot here as in the Philippines—much drier though.

As you can imagine with the approach of the alleged zero hour I haven't been doing anything but work. I haven't even seen Ace Wilson for a couple of weeks. I have seen Doris [Wilson] a couple of times. They are apparently all right.

I got a swell letter from Martin Hayden the other day.[2] He is still in Germany and his observation of conditions there seems to be very good. He has got enough points to get out, but can't get anybody to discharge him. He is scared to death that he is going to be sent to the Orient.

Right at the present time Detroit seems to be in a state of suspense. Even the race situation is quieter than usual and apparently quieter than in any of the other big cities in the country. I am sure that more vacations are being taken this year than have been taken in the last few years. . . .

Charlie Oakman is conducting the most active campaign, certainly of any of the Councilmen, and sometimes I think even more active than mine. I think he has a fair chance. . . .

The Citizens' League endorsements[3] came out yesterday and approved Oakman and me. They left off Rogell and Van Antwerp.

We have had more argument and struggle over the proposed airport site than any other one thing that I know of with the exception of bi-racial housing. At the present time the Aviation Committee of the Board of Commerce is trying to raise money [$1,000,000] and purchase the land for the Wyoming–Eight and a Half Mile site. They had better be success-ful or the reputation of the Board of Commerce will be at a very low point for many years to come. . . . They have only a couple of days more to go, and I will let you know whether . . . they can raise it.

I read your letter to Florence, and steaks are hard to get even in this city. We have had quite an acute meat shortage. Things are loosening up a little. That steak idea is a good one. I wouldn't mind having one myself. I hear occasionally of someone's having one. I know they are around but I haven't recently had the enjoyment of sinking my teeth in one. . . . The only difference between us is that I think I will be able to make it and I am afraid you won't.

I have heard a lot of favorable comment on your broadcasts. I haven't heard one recently on account of I have been out trying to round up my constituents while you were talking to yours. Your stuff in the paper is frequently excellent.

I will write you a note immediately after the primaries and let you know what happened.

Keep your chin up. Just remember that it rains everywhere. Wherever you are it seems just as bad.

Best of Luck.

Sincerely,   JEFF

NOTES

1. FitzGerald lost the mayoral election to Jeffries in 1943.
2. See above, MSH to EJJ, 30 June 1945.
3. Originally organized in 1912 by Henry M. Leland, president of Cadillac, the Detroit Citizens League began as an upper-class Protestant effort to influence civic affairs during the Progressive Era. Among other undertakings, it interviewed can-didates for public office and evaluated their qualifications in the *Civic Searchlight*, essentially as endorsements to influence voters. Its most important officer was execu-tive secretary William P. Lovett, who served from 1917 to 1947 and supported Jeffries throughout his mayoralty. See Raymond R. Fragnoli, *Transformation of Reform: Pro-gressivism in Detroit–and After, 1912-1933* (New York: Garland, 1982), esp. 17-48.

Detroit. July 30, 1945
Dear Martin: *Edward J. Jeffries Jr. to Martin S. Hayden*

I can't tell you how much I enjoyed your last letter. It is the kind of information that we never get and, if we did, I wouldn't have the same confidence in it that I have in yours. You haven't lost your knack of writing. The fact of the matter is, as your experience has broadened, I think your technique has improved. It was thoroughly enjoyable.

The primaries will be a week from Tuesday and, of course, July and August are traditionally bad months for meetings—very hard to get to the people. However, it works the same for all the candidates, and I am hopeful that as usual I will be able to weather the strain.

The increase in gasoline has tremendously revived the summer picnics. In my humble opinion I will trade any of the vicissitudes of the military for Sunday picnics. But, like you, I am a good soldier and I am still fighting the flies, drinking that warm beer and being thankful to food rationing on account of it's hard to get food for summer picnics, thank God.

I got a letter from Jack Carlisle today and he has been riding airplanes on bombing missions, riding PT boats on search parties, sleeping in the rain and water, fighting prickly heat and, for the first time in his life, thoroughly enjoying an honest gripe and, with it all, writing some good stuff. As you no doubt know, he is in the Philippines or thereabouts.

I was a little disappointed that you didn't get home with all the rest of the boys. I am surprised that you don't get discharged. It certainly will be great to see you.

We are still fighting over an airport site. . . . The Board of Commerce promised 740 acres at the Wyoming and Eight and a Half Mile site if we could buy enough more land to make it three square miles. The Council divided 3-3. I got George Edwards back . . . to break the tie . . . [by voting for the Wyoming site]. That was immediately followed by a recommendation from a Board of Aviation Experts for a new site that nobody had ever thought of—Gulley Road and Warren Avenue. . . .[1] So we are really in a muddle now. But . . . if the Board of Commerce comes up with its 740 acres we will have an airport at Wyoming and Eight and a Half Mile Roads.

I am interested in hearing what your observations are, as well as those around you, on the recent elections in England. I think that the people in this country were genuinely and universally surprised. It seemed quite logical that with the terrific pounding the English have taken they would want to be free of everything and anything that reminds them of the six years of punishment they had to take.[2] But I don't know whether that is accurate or not.

Detroit has been in a kind of state of suspense recently. There have been quite a few cutbacks, employment in war factories is not at the high level it was in 43-44, but the service industries are still woefully short of man power. People are taking checks and enjoying the unemployment compensation, moving about in a very leisurely fashion to get reemployed. Even the race question is not so burning. The fact of the matter is, it seems to be quieter here than in most other big cities of the country. I suppose that this is just the calm before the storm. Brother [R.J.]

Thomas, the UAW babe, is predicting a wave of strikes. If he means it, they can certainly create them, but I am taking a grain of salt with the statement because, while we had a lot of labor trouble and no doubt will have more, the uncertainty in everybody's mind of the future must, of necessity, make them move cautiously. The economic upswing has reached into every nook and cranny of the country, and certainly the thinking people are not anxious to rock the boat, and must be a little worried about the inflationary possibilities and their effect on the economy of the nation.

Our health, generally speaking, is pretty good. I haven't been able to do much except work in the campaign lately. I am already looking avidly towards the latter part of August when there will be a temporary lull.

Let us hear from you more often. We all enjoy your letters. Best of Luck to you. Come on home.

Sincerely yours,   JEFF

NOTES

1. Near Hawthorne Valley Golf Club in present-day Dearborn Heights, eight or nine miles northeast of the Detroit Metropolitan Wayne County Airport.

2. With the surrender of Germany on 7 May 1945, many expected an end to Churchill's wartime coalition government. The prime minister himself opposed a return to party politics before defeating Japan, but Labourites and Liberals preferred a general election on 25 July. Churchill erred in abandoning his advantage as war leader and statesman to attack the opposition, particularly the Labour Party, as purveyors of socialism that would require some form of Gestapo. He misread the electorate's increasing acceptance of state planning, wrought by the war, which ironically his own party embraced to a degree; he stressed Japan's defeat, military demobilization, and postwar concerns, which voters thought much less important than Labour Party emphasis on bread-and-butter issues (especially housing). Churchill's defeat (Labour, 393 seats; Conservatives, 213 seats; Liberals, 12 seats) seemed incomprehensible to those who viewed him as a great war leader, but they failed to understand the leftward trend of British voters and the broadening class appeal of the Labour Party. Although Churchill understood the nation's need to win the war, Labourites realized the populace's need to win the peace. See Paul Addison, *The Road to 1945: British Politics and the Second World War* (London: Quartet Books, 1977), 252-69; Keith Robbins, *Churchill* (London: Longman House, 1992), 148.

                            Okinawa, Ryukyu Islands. 25 August 1945
Dear Jeff: *John M. Carlisle to Edward J. Jeffries Jr.*

My mail is all snafu, so I have yet to hear how you made out in the primary,[1] and since I always expected the best I shall continue to expect it. I think you should kick Uncle Ace [Wilson] in the posterior because he promised last April to cable the news to me but he apparently is inanimate with a cable. So there is not much I can say about something about which I have no news. It is surprising to me that someone in the Jeffries camp did not cable me. I must have been quickly forgotten.

I have been doing a Jeffries the last two weeks, trying to convince everyone who will listen that I should be one of the first war correspondents into Japan. At first there were about 150 correspondents trying to get in, and now a lot more have swarmed into these parts from Guam, Australia and the States, so that there must be about 300 all trying for the same thing and the Army, the Navy and the Marines are having their hands full of newspaper hornets. . . . But the Army has always been very rational on these things and has always been fair to me, and now I am of the opinion that I have gotten the fairest deal from the Army that one correspondent representing only one paper can get. The proof will be what time tells. However, I have done the best I can and I know that it is all I can do. But from knowing me, you will know I did my best. Goddamn it, this is the biggest story in the world today and there is so little I can do to help myself.

But that is why the newspaper business intrigues me so, there is never a time when a good story is not hard to get and I am not running uphill to get it. All I hope is that I get all the way uphill. Ah me, when I get depressed at all the strife and turmoil of this trade, I sometimes think that I was cut out to be a soda jerker.

Well, Okinawa is a very nice place. It is cool, few mosquitoes, and the landscape is rolling, with deep little valleys and tall little hills, and our camp is on a picturesque hillside. The sunset tonight was beautiful, like a display on canvas in the Art Museum [Detroit Art Institute], or like a Negro blood-and-thunder evangelist's conception of heaven. Just a blanket of gold through the white clouds, with the sun hidden, and a backdrop of azure sky and green, pine tree studded hills. Ah me, if I could do this in oils, which I cannot (since neither you nor I are much good with oil) I could portray this scene for you.

Here on Okinawa, the GI's are singing, "I am dreaming of a White Mistress." My jeep driver today in an early driving rainstorm was a former New York adagio dancer called Honey Bee. I bought six bottles of Detroit beer for sixty cents and had them cooled in the mess sergeant's reefer. You guessed it: He is from Detroit. I traded two ounces of Scotch whiskey for six pairs of wool socks which I haven't gotten yet. A carton of cigarettes costs 53 cents at the post exchange. Wrist watches are repaired at the ordnance depot. The Flipos on Luzon are manufacturing phony Jap battle flags for the tourist trade. A bottle of bourbon costs $1.25 through the Army—when you can get it. I have had two bottles since I have been overseas. The army special service on this island has a circulating library of several thousand current books. Runs a portable library out of a big tent. Surprising, too, how much the GI's read. All of us take our poncho's to the outdoor movies, and they have the movies every night. It always rains for some reason. A bulldozer ran over the radio cable today and the radio glamour boys were scarlet since they were off the air all day. I wonder if their public suffered? A guy who was a first class news-paper man in New York is the head of a motor pool; and a gent who sold magazine subscriptions is a public relations officer for an army unit. For an Army guard of honor going into Japan eventually, the soldiers were measured by a tape measure. Had to be six feet tall. Ouch! [Bandleader] Kay Kyser has been wowing the GI's on this island, four performances a day. But the best entertainment I heard was in the East Indies from some Harlem male & provocative high yaller gal singers. Very good.

Well, Jefferson, all my love to your little verbal hatchet and your ascending disposition, and let me hear your analysis of the primary, whatever it may be, with best regards to Florence.

Faithfully,   J A C K

NOTE

1. In the mayoral primary of 7 August, Jeffries (68,754) placed second behind Richard T. Frankensteen (82,936) and ahead of Jimmy Friel (35,720). See *Chronicle*, 11 Aug. 1945, 1.

Detroit. October 16, 1945
Edward J. Jeffries Jr. to John M. Carlisle (telegram)

Dear Stinky, Welcome back. How's the third honeymoon?[1] The shoot-ing may be stopped in far Pacific but it's still going on here.

NOTE

1. Returning from assignment in Europe the previous year, Carlisle had referred to the reunion with his wife as a second honeymoon.

Yokosuka, Japan. 31 October 1945
Dear Friends: *Harold J. Schachern to Dear Friends*

Tomorrow will be November 1, and if the atomic bomb hadn't ended the war ahead of schedule, it would be D-Day in Japan.[1] And instead of sitting in my stocking feet idly pecking at a typewriter, I'd be as nervous and busy as a midshipman on watch. Frankly, I'm awfully glad they in-vented the atomic bomb.

That Fighting Lady who never got to war, the U.S.S. *Puget Sound,* is back at anchor in Tokyo Bay after covering the Eighth Army landings at Matsayuma and Nagoya, some mention of which you may have seen in the local press.

I am at a loss to explain our military value there, for it was like covering the landing of a Kiwanis picnic at Bob-Lo.[2] We just launched our planes, they flew over the beach, impressed the natives, took pictures and came home.

We had only one mishap. One of our torpedo bombers had engine trouble near Nagoya and the pilot made a wheels up, water landing. He and his two-man crew got ducked but were picked up shortly by a minesweeper. . . .

The pictures showed the usual wrecked buildings and that's about all. There were, however, a surprising number of undamaged Jap aircraft parked about. But that isn't surprising, for a friend of mine, fairly high in Marine Third Division circles, told me . . . that they had 8,000 planes, all rigged for Kamikaze [suicidal] attack, and 10 divisions that we didn't even know about, drawn up on Kyushu ready to smack us when we went in there. It was his studied opinion that we might even have lost that one.

I had the pleasure . . . of talking with a man who witnessed the explosion of the Hiroshima atom bomb. He is Father Rudolph Schmidt, a German Catholic priest on the staff of the University of Tokyo.

"It was a beautiful morning," he said, "and I was walking along the street in the outskirts of the city. There was no air raid warning, nobody where I was noticed the plane which dropped the bomb. We were perhaps seven miles from where it hit in the center of town, but all of a sudden there was a terrific roar and a terrifying, burning wind which flattened and seared everything in its path. Houses, trees, bushes, grass, men, women and children went down in front of it."

Father Schmidt's arms still bear the scabs of frightful burns. I have had another unusual, although scarcely savory, experience since writing you the last time. I drew shore patrol duty, and with my crew of seamen, was assigned to the geisha[3] and red light district, at least that part of it that is not out of bounds.

I fear I have to report that the American serviceman isn't being a very good boy in Japan. The Navy, steeped in tradition, has divided the houses under government supervision into three classes: one for officers, one for chief petty officers and one for crew.

It was our job to keep order in the ranks lined up in front of the enlisted men's establishment, to see that they kept single file, did not push, shove or get boisterous in ranks and did not cut in ahead of their shipmates. . . . The line was a good, big city block long and stayed that way throughout most of the day.

A crew of pharmacist mates and a Navy doctor were on duty in the lobby who, without help, forced every customer to take the proper precautions. Also in the lobby was a sort of cashier, probably a civil service man, who rang up the yen on a cash register and passed out numbered checks to the clients so that everyone would be taken care of in his proper turn.

The place boasted 140 "beautiful geishas." They weren't beautiful, but I'm sure the 140 was correct. I also must admit the place was efficient. It was a model of mass production.

True to the act of Congress which made me a gentleman and mindful of OCS, I wouldn't believe such a situation existed in the house reserved for officers until I, purely in the line of duty, took a turn through there. Here I found a much smaller line, a mere 20 or 25, but then, there aren't nearly as many officers.

One of the minor mysteries around Tokyo at the present is the fate of the Imperial Palace. The place is guarded closer than Fort Knox by members of the Second Cavalry Division, who are the biggest men in the world. Nobody, except the highest ranking members of the occupation forces, have been permitted to see it.

A shipmate of mine, however, who spent considerable time in Japan before the war, visited friends at the Swiss Legation yesterday and they told him the reason nobody is allowed to see it is that it is no longer there. They claim it was 90 percent destroyed by bombs and fire, and that his Imperial Majesty is now living with his family in one of the outbuildings.

I can't understand why they are keeping it a secret. My only reaction to the news was, "too bad," but maybe they think the Japs would kick up a fuss if they knew the Emperor was practically in the street, and winter coming on.

Yankee business acumen is showing itself here and it bodes ill for Japanese economic structure. The shore-based boys are getting rich off the inflated Japanese Yen. American cigarettes, candy bars and soap, bought at overseas prices, bring as high as a 50 to 1 profit. It is getting so bad that on some stations they have stopped selling the men these items, and now they are out trading souvenirs for cigarettes with the men coming ashore from ships.

A sailor I struck up a conversation with in Yokosuka boasted: "I've sent home over a thousand bucks and I haven't been here a month. These monkeys will pay anything for smokes. Right now I'm building up a stock of shoes. When winter really sets in, they'll pay anything for a pair of shoes to keep their feet warm. If you're smart, you'll do the same."

I purposely didn't get his name, for if I had, a letter like this would probably land him in Portsmouth.[4] Come to think of it, maybe that isn't such a bad idea.

Most of the ship-based sailors and marines, like myself, are principally interested in souvenirs, samurai swords and rifles being the most avidly sought after. So far I haven't been successful, for whiskey is the chief bartering tender, and I never could hang onto whiskey long enough to barter with it.

When we first arrived here two weeks ago, the asking price for a good sword was $400.00. Since then . . . the army has loosened up with them and you can now trade even for a bottle of Schenley's Black Label. . . .

There has been a standard saying throughout the Marine Corps during the war to the effect that "the army has everything." It never was truer than here and now. I've walked the streets of Tokyo for hours, practically begging for one of the above-mentioned items, but without success. Yesterday I stood in front of Second Division HQ and watched them unloading truck loads of both, but a burly dogface sergeant just grinned and said: "Sorry, lootenant, but these are for the army. You'll have to get your own."

And so I did. Getting several Marines for support, we braved the headquarters of the great man himself, General Douglas MacArthur, known as God, Jr., to Marines in this theatre. There we found a Navy officer, a sort of liaison man between the army and navy, and to him we told our sad tale. The upshot of it was that he arranged for two trucks and a landing barge to haul more than a thousand rifles, one for every man on our ship, and 100 sabers, one for each of our officers. It was just like getting a news story. You gotta go to headquarters and ask the most important man you can find.

This may seem like a foolhardy way to dispose of firearms, but they are of bastard caliber and there won't be a cartridge in the United States that will fit them. What they don't get rid of in this way, they plan to burn.

Another favorite item is the parachute. The large cargo type contain over 1,000 feet of the finest Japanese silk and they come in various colors. My roommate came back to the ship last night loaded down with one of a beautiful pastel blue. His wife, he said, has long had an ambition to own a stock of real silk sheets. She is going to get them, and anything else she can fashion out of the stuff.

There are caves in the hills surrounding Yokosuka and American servicemen are permitted to cart away just about anything they find. The ones containing gasoline and explosives are closely guarded, but the others are wide open. Many of them haven't been explored by anyone, and there is no telling what they may hold. Everyone I've talked to who has been there has neglected to take along a flashlight, so their foraging has been confined to the mouths of the caves.

- November 1 -

A bad storm blew in on us last night and I had to stop writing to help secure various pieces of gear which were adrift on the flight deck. By the way, the boat that went after our swords and rifles got caught in the same storm and had to put back to shore, so we still don't know if they got any booty.

Our ship has received tentative orders to "magic carpet" duty, which is the Navy designation for ferrying duty. A repair ship is to come alongside and install five-tier bunks on our hangar deck for the 1,000 or more soldiers who will make the trip back with us. Scuttlebutt has it that we will leave here about 5 November, headed for San Diego or San Francisco.

Scuttlebutt further has it that the 250 Marines aboard will be taken off the ship once we hit the U.S. There really isn't much sense keeping them aboard, for they are all attached to the air department, and a carrier converted to a transport has little use for such.

I believe I told you before that I am one of two Marine fighter director officers aboard. Our duties, though interesting to the layman, are still kept under wraps by Navy regulations.

My supplementary duties include editing the ship's newspaper, ship's historian and, of all things, ship's bandmaster. I have a 16-piece dance band that I wouldn't hesitate to take into the Graystone [theater] tomorrow night. Most of the men were professional musicians in civilian life and use this means to keep in practice.

One of the boys who helps me with the paper worked for INS [International News Service] in Washington before joining the Navy. I suspect he was an office boy, but he has a lot of talent and I would advise INS to hire him back. His name is P.D. Malkie.

I have met but one Detroiter in Japan. He is Lt. (junior grade) Garnet Griffin, who went to Assumption College with me, and who worked as a reporter in Detroit before going to the NLRB [National Labor Relations Board] as a public relations man and then into the Navy. He is gunnery officer aboard the U.S.S. *Chevalier* . . . which has been swinging around its hook in Tokyo Bay since the occupation began.

All of us noticed a big change in Tokyo since we were here last. The Army seems to have a better grip on things and its presence is much more noticeable. You see more sentries about town, more MP's and more service personnel apparently on official business, rather than Kimona hunts.

There is a lot more repair work going on now than there was two weeks ago. Many of the burned out office buildings, and there are scarcely any other kind, have had new window glass installed, and plasterers and painters can be seen putting the interiors in order. I don't think our occupation leaders are particularly concerned whether the Japanese repair their cities or not. I believe they are letting their reconstruction plans entirely up to themselves.

This is probably the wisest course, but the people don't seem to be doing much about it. I have never seen such wholesale idleness. The streets are jammed with people with apparently nothing to do but walk the streets and grin at the antics of the odd Americans. Except for a few surly army veterans, they are all friendly, anxious to please and be of service. But they seem incapable of helping themselves. Even the businessmen of the country have shown no initiative. The Tokyo area is jammed with service men armed with millions of dollars which they will spend on anything, yet they've done nothing to fix up their stores or secure attractive merchandise which I am told can be bought dirt cheap in the interior and sold at a tremendous profit here.

A pharmacist's mate on another ship showed me a very interesting document coming out from the beach the other afternoon. It was a letter written by a Japanese girl to an American army private who had been a prisoner of war in a camp adjoining her family's farm. I would have liked a copy of it, but we were in a pitching whale boat at the time and it was impossible to write, even if we had the materials.

Apparently this soldier had enjoyed some liberties about the camp, for he had become well acquainted with the entire family and they all sent their deepest affection to him. The girl, obviously, had fallen in love with him, for much of the letter was in the "Poor Butterfly," "Never the twain shall meet" vein. She promised to cherish his memory forever and one line which struck me particularly, went like this:

"Through knowing you, I feel that I have come to understand America and Americans. Although you were a great, strong man, you had the soft, kind heart of a girl. This is something we never understood about you people, but which is being brought home to us now."

She went on to explain that the family had been forced to leave the farm for the city and that while the future seemed bleak and uncertain, she, her family, and she hoped, all Japanese, were prepared to climb out of the terrible circumstances into which they had brought themselves.

The sailor who had the letter said the girl had approached him shyly in a Tokyo department store and asked if he would mail the letter from someplace in the United States, explaining that the Japanese are not permitted to post foreign mail. She spoke and wrote passable English, although neither she nor the letter explained where she learned to do so.

The two or three newspapers I have seen in the last month have made much of the fact that the Japanese are doing everything to cooperate with the occupation forces, especially the absence of armed resistance. This is perfectly true of the seacoast cities where our forces are present in any strength, but there is some doubt about the interior, and I give you this second-hand experience as an example.

Four of our pilots hitch-hiked and walked some thirty miles to an interior town to visit some army friends who are quartered there. They were met at the outskirts of the town by soldiers armed to the teeth, who were aghast at these foolhardy Marine pilots who had ventured there without even a sidearm to protect themselves.

"We've been sniped at constantly," they said. "We've had hand grenades thrown at us and they have attempted to dynamite our barracks in the night. You are lucky to get here alive."

They came back to the ship in an army truck guarded by soldiers with rifles at the ready.

There has, however, been only one shooting incident in the Tokyo area and a Jap was on the receiving end. He was a motorist who either failed to understand or refused to heed a sentry's challenge, and got a slug from a Garand through the head.

To return to the relations between Japanese women and American servicemen, romance here has not been entirely commercial. At any time of day you can see soldiers, sailors and marines strolling arm in arm with Japanese girls in the public parks, or petting under the trees. Kissing has never been a popular pastime in Japan, or so I'm told, but as you know, they are great imitators and seem to take to the practice. As a race they are physically unattractive, but before passing censor [*sic*], you must consider that they are probably the fairest, blondest creatures many of these boys have seen in months, and in some cases, years.

- November 2 -

I mentioned in my last letter the hatred the Japanese bear for the United States Marine Corps. It is worse than I thought. Our line troops were the first to give them a setback in the war. I refer to Guadalcanal and the other Solomons campaigns.[5] Our pilots were the first to beat them in the air, excluding [Col. Claire] Chen[n]ault and the Flying Tigers.[6] Apparently there was a terrific propaganda campaign in Japan as a result of these and future actions, aimed principally at Marines. This was so successful that the term Yankee Marine is practically a synonym for beast or barbarian. While walking shore patrol duty, I stopped to kibitz on a conversation between two Marine Sergeants and a pretty Japanese girl. She spoke in stilted school room English and gestured where her English vocabulary failed her. She asked what they were and they replied that they were American Marines.

"No, no, you are bad, bad," she said.

Grinning from ear to ear, they quickly assured her that this was a mistake; that they were nice, East Coast Marines, and that she must be referring to some lowborn West Coast gyrenes.[7] She went for it, for when I left she was smiling and jabbering: "You Johnny, you pretty boy. Hokay, Bob, you pretty boy too."

We had bad news this morning, or at least I thought it was bad news. We received a dispatch transferring us from the 5th to the 7th Fleet and we are leaving here November 15 for Shanghai, so the "magic carpet" deal is off. This reduces my chance of getting an early discharge, for as long as I am aboard this ship, there is some justification for keeping me in the service, for the Marine Corps has only a handful of officers trained for this ship-based duty and none of them are regulars. I'd like to see China, but I'd much rather see Detroit.

Of course it is only conjecture, but some think we may have to give the Marines a little air support if they get in trouble keeping Chinese national troops and communist forces from one another's throats in Northern China.[8] Otherwise, there doesn't seem to be much justification for us going there. One thought is consoling. The 7th Fleet can release us for ferrying duty just as well as the 5th Fleet could. In fact, I'm rather counting on it.

I've just thought of one more anecdote which may help you understand the inscrutable Japanese character. A group of us cornered a Jap interpreter and were asking him questions. Someone asked if the Japanese were glad the war was over. He hesitated, then said that, in general, everyone was. Someone asked if the Kamikaze pilots, for example, were glad or relieved that it had ended.

He hesitated for a long time on this one, hemmed and hawed for a while longer, then said that he didn't think they were. The reason, he thought, was that they had a divine mission to perform and were disappointed because those alive had not been able to complete it. Asked what he thought of the practice of hara-kiri,[9] he replied that he, as a civilian, would not consider it. (Whenever the Japanese mention hara-kiri, they go through the stomach cutting motions.) But, he hastened to add, he would expect any soldier to do it and that he, if he were a soldier, would not hesitate. When asked why, he merely shrugged and said that it was an old and an honorable tradition.

As for me, I'm glad the war is over, I'm not on a divine mission and I want to get the hell out of here.

Yours,   HAROLD

NOTES

1. Had the war continued, U.S. plans called for a two-stage invasion of Japan: Operation Olympic under Gen. MacArthur was scheduled to commence on 1 November 1945 and establish a foothold on Kyushu island; Operation Coronet under Adm. Chester W. Nimitz was to follow through on 1 March 1946 and deliver the decisive blow at Honshu island, which included Tokyo, in what would have been the largest amphibious landing of the war. U.S. commanders expected stiff resistance and very high casualties. See John Ray Skates, *The Invasion of Japan: Alternative to the Bomb* (Charleston: Univ. of South Carolina Press, 1994).

2. A Canadian island located in the Detroit River and leased by Detroit-Windsor Ferry, which supervised the popular recreation area and transported passengers to it. The company's refusal to permit blacks on the island resulted in a legal suit that dragged on for over two years and ended with Recorder's Court Judge John J. Maher fining it $25 for having violated the Michigan Civil Rights Act (1937). The case involved a Detroit citizen, the local NAACP, and the Mayor's Interracial Committee and, despite the small fine, proved symbolically significant for the future of race relations in the city. See *Detroit Tribune,* 30 June 1943, 1-2; *Chronicle,* 24 Nov. 1945, 1, 4.

3. In the Japanese society of this era, women were divided into three categories: nurturers (wives and mothers), knowers (creative artists, especially writers), and temptresses (geishas, entertainers, prostitutes) with clearly defined, institutionalized roles. The temptress provided "seductive pleasures of atmosphere, artistic performance, conversation, or personal service." See Robert Jay Lifton, *History and Human Survival: Essays on the Young and Old, Survivors and the Dead, Peace and War, and on Contemporary Psychohistory* (New York: Vintage, 1971), 261-65.

4. U.S. Navy prison in Virginia.

5. On 7 August the U.S. Marines landed on Guadalcanal to challenge Japanese advances in the Solomons and begin a six-month struggle for the island, which marked the first Allied offensive and a turningpoint in the Pacific theater of war.

6. Partially deaf and coming out of retirement in 1941, Chennault led the American Volunteer Group, 100 pilots from all three services who flew planes out of China for salaries provided by the U.S. government. The Flying Tigers, as the unit became popularly known, drew greater support as the war progressed, largely because of the interest of President Roosevelt. See Perret, *There's a War to Be Won,* 284, 288-89.

7. Slang for members of the U.S. Marine Corps.

8. The Kuomintang of Chiang Kai-shek and the Red Army of Mao Tse-tung were engaged in a civil war for control of China while they fought as U.S. allies against the Japanese. Mao Tse-tung's Communist forces eventually forced Chang Kai-shek and his supporters into exile on the island of Taiwan.

9. Hara-kiri, the colloquial term for *seppuku,* is the ritual suicide by disembowelment of traditional samurai who had dishonored themselves or their shogun warlords; it was so painful that an assistant decapitated the disgraced warrior soon after he slashed himself. Nevertheless, the concept of taking one's life in defeat or for victory carried over into the Japanese military class of World War II. As the war progressed and defeat loomed, however, many Japanese officers and soldiers set the practice aside. See Takeda Izumo, Miyoshi Shoraku, and Namiki Senryu, *Chushingura: A Puppet Play,* trans. Donald Keene (New York: Columbia Univ. Press, 1971), for a fictionalized drama of the samurai code; Meirion and Susie Harries, *Soldiers of the Sun: The Rise and Fall of the Imperial Japanese Army* (New York: Random House, 1991), 423-25, 459-60.

Detroit. November 12, 1945
Edward J. Jeffries Jr. to Harold J. Schachern

Dear Harold:

Your letter gave us a better account of present conditions in Japan than anything we have read. We all read our copies avidly. Then along came your telegram today.[1] Thank you.

It doesn't sound as though you would be back in the immediate future, but we hope that it won't be too long. Martin is here on the beat. He returned a few weeks ago and did not miss the thick of our local battle.[2] John Carlisle is still in California, but he is coming home by easy stages. Mrs. Carlisle met him in California and they are having a kind of celebration.

The mayoralty campaign was a nasty one.[3] It was the most bitter municipal campaign in the city's history. We were optimistic when election day dawned bright and warm. Heavy voting began immediately. More than 510,000 voters turned out. My opponent received about 215,552 and I received about 269,915 when 1,126 out of the city's 1,136 [precincts] had been counted.

As you probably know, George Edwards was elected President of the Council.[4] He is in Manila or thereabouts now. He is needed here to help us occupy Detroit rather than help occupy Japan or other parts of the Pacific. Charlie Oakman ran sixth in the [council] race—making him Henry Sweeney's successor. Helen Bryant ran tenth. John Lodge ran second, Frank Cody third, Bill Rogell fourth.

[*Times* reporter] Jim Inglis has been back for several weeks. He looks fine and is glad to be here. You probably know that Charles Weber is now with the *Free Press* and replaced Leo [Donovan] on this beat. Leo has the automotive world column. . . .

Eddie Rickenbacker[5] has invited me to go as one of the guests of the Eastern Airlines on the inaugural trip between Detroit and Miami. We'll be gone for three days. I don't know that you'd call it purely business.

The United States Conference of Mayors will hold its annual meeting in New York City December 9. I plan to be present.

I certainly wish you well at Christmas time and hope that the New Year will be entirely to your liking.

Sincerely yours,   JEFF

NOTES

1. Schachern had congratulated the mayor for his election victoty over Richard T. Frankensteen: HJS telegram to EJJ, 12 Nov. 1945, Box 3, Mayor's Papers.

2. Hayden had returned to Detroit in early October and covered the mayoral campaign for the *News*.

3. In a more intense replay of the 1943 election between Jeffries and Frank Fitz-Gerald, both sides engaged in name-calling, and neither candidate embraced the explosive issue of integrated housing. Jeffries's supporters seemed the more culpable: some called Episcopalian Frankensteen "a Jew and a nigger lover," and others labeled him an anti-Semite; Jeffries himself linked the UAW vice-president and CIO Political Action Committee director, his union supporters, and Communists in a conspiracy to undermine democratic rule in Detroit. Jeffries won 274,435 to 216,917 by collecting most of the votes that had been cast for Friel in the primary. See Conot, *American Odyssey*, 392-94; *News*, 7 Nov. 1945, 1.

4. Edwards secured the council presidency by 3,738 votes, placing highest–241,253–among the nine councilmanic candidates voted into office in the general election. He had completed OCS in March and reported to Camp Maxey, Texas, for combat training before being ordered to the Philippines in August, where he joined the War Crimes Division. Meanwhile, Peggy Edwards and their friends ran his Detroit campaign.

5. Well-known aviator (in both world wars) and airline executive.

Dear Friends: *Honshu, Japan. 16 November 1945*
                                 Harold J. Schachern to Dear Friends

It is not my intent to deluge you with a lot of information about occupied Japan, for I'm sure any efforts of mine would only confuse you. I merely thought that you and some of your confreres, your lives narrowed by the confines of Grand Boulevard and the Detroit River, might enjoy a look at some of the scenes here through the eyes of an amateur Burton Holmes.[1]

You might say it is a little late for me to be writing about Japan, for we pulled up anchor just two hours ago and are on our way to Saipan, mission unknown. We had expected to go to China and saw some justification for that, inasmuch as the Marines in North China seem very apt to get caught in the cross fire between Chinese Nationalists and Communists.

We could protect some American life and property there, but whom and from what we are going to protect in Saipan seems a little vague at the moment.

We made our last few liberties in Yokohama and Kamakura, accent on the "ma." We can dispose of Yokohama in very few words, for it, or what is left of it, isn't greatly unlike western cities.

It got a much worse pasting from our bombers than Tokyo. Block after block lays in absolute ruins, with the remaining buildings either burned out or badly damaged. Despite this, it is obvious that the city was far more modern and westernized than Tokyo.

The reason for this, it appears, is that Yokohama was more completely destroyed by the 1923 earthquake and its business section was almost entirely replanned and rebuilt. The Detroit City Plan Commission will appreciate the convenience of this. Besides the modern buildings, the city boasts wide streets and numerous parks.

Kamakura, I believe, is far more interesting. It is a quaint little shrine town about halfway between Yokohama and Yokosuka and is reached by a 40-minute train ride out of either city. The train is an electric one, almost identical with "el" [elevated] trains in Chicago, Boston and New York, except that it is crowded night and day, every day and every night, with the smelliest humanity on earth.

A word about Jap smells. They are a noted bath-taking people, but they don't follow through on it. They are complete strangers to dry cleaning and pressing and seldom take the trouble, I suspect, to launder their clothes. The result is that whenever you get in an area as congested as the Tokyo-Yokosuka Line, the air is soon permeated with a mixture of body odor and ripe fish, the latter being carried unwrapped and spread upon the faces of the passengers.

The suburban commuter runs pretty much to type wherever you find him. In Detroit he follows his wife's instructions by stopping at Sanders or Awrey's for some fresh dinner rolls or a cake before catching the 5:20 at the foot of Brush street for Birmingham, Bloomfield or Pontiac. In Yokohama he pauses before a peddler squatting beside the curb, brushes aside the flies to select a fragrant mackerel, then sprints for the station. Both men, in time, become accomplished sprinters.

As often as not, you and your companions are the only Americans aboard. This makes the trips somewhat harrowing the first time, inasmuch as the train goes through frequent long, dark tunnels. In time, however, you become convinced of the Japs' docility.

Across the street from the Kamakura station is a little shack, headquarters for a row of waiting rickshas. If you shout long and loud enough, a couple of skinny, ragged Japs will come running out, smiling their dirty, stained little smiles, and bobbing their heads.

We had come, primarily, to see the famous Kamakura Buddha, one of the largest, oldest and most renowned in the Orient, being built by imperial order in 1252. We were armed with only one word to help us find it, "daibutsu," which is Japanese for Buddha. So the three of us climbed into as many rickshas, shouted "daibutsu" and waived [waved] ahead.

They caught on immediately, and straining against the inertia of our American avoirdupois, they started off. The average Jap ricksha boy isn't very big. Mine was about five feet tall and would weigh, I judge, an even 110 pounds. He is used to pulling people his own size, so that when he starts doing business with Americans, (my 165 pounds made me the runt of the three) he finds the going pretty rough. He just isn't used to beef on the hoof that size.

Once underway, they settled down to a shuffling, apparently tireless gait, their split-toed sneakers padding silently along. If there is anything that will give you a more lordly feeling than being towed through crowded streets by a sweating little Jap, I should like to experience it. Believe me, this lad from the sticks knows what it feels like to be the High Poobah, if only for a day.

Despite the luxurious feeling, this mode of transportation could scarcely be called efficient. On one trip we found only two rickshas for three men. The third man agreed to hoof it, with the understanding that we would swap off with him when he became tired. We found, however, that by maintaining a brisk American stride, he could run these boys into the ground.

Stretched in single file like [P.T.] Barnum's elephants we set off down the pleasantly shaded, well paved street, past men in rumpled suits and women in baggy kimonas, neither of whom paid us the slightest heed. Not so with the children, however. Japanese children are pretty much like any others, so we soon found ourselves making surprised replies to children's choruses of "hello" and "goodbye," both words being accented on the first syllable and repeated twice in rapid succession.

We reached the shrine grounds in about 30 minutes. Over the entrance was an Oriental arch hung with signs in Japanese and flanked on either side by a 10-foot-high statue of a fearsome Jap monster wearing the traditional war costume, an upraised Samurai sword and an expression of diabolical fury. It was, we surmised, a warning to unbelievers to stay out of the sacred grounds.

Led by one who had braved such awesome portals as the Detroit Club and the DAC [Detroit Athletic Club], we barged in. Following a rustic path, we could see the towering head of the idol peering from the distance through the now leafless branches of cherry trees.

Meeting a strange god in his own bailiwick is an experience not to be dealt with too lightly. We had seen a good deal of Japan, but through the eyes which automatically compared what they saw with things similar in America. [Rudyard] Kipling's "blinkin' idol"[2] suddenly became a powerful force which has influenced the destiny of a large part of the world's population, and it was something we couldn't dismiss with "we have one bigger and better in Kansas City." People chase a lot of false gods in America, but they aren't 27 physical feet across the shoulders and 37 feet from buttocks to pate.

"Big", said one of my companions simply.

At the rear of the all-bronze statue we discovered a low opening into its hollow interior. Two window-like openings high on the idol's back revealed a staircase which we mounted to a platform level with the eyes. There we found another deity, this one unidentified, facing aft toward us.

In the interests of writing the story "up," I would like to say that it was of solid gold. That would add the proper Oriental, exotic touch, but I suspect it was only gilded.

Back in front of the Buddha we watched Japanese women accompanied by children making visits to the shrine. They all went through a regular routine which consisted of clapping their hands twice, kneeling, pressing their palms together in the conventional manner of the Christian communicant and uttering a silent prayer. This they followed by throwing a few coins into a corrugated tin box and selecting a stick of incense from a container, which they lighted at a shielded candle and stuck into a pot half filled with sand.

When we had the place all to ourselves, we picked up a piece of the votive incense and made an exaggerated to-do when we discovered it was ordinary punk, which we used to buy for a penny a stick to light our 4th of July firecrackers. This, we agreed, was the outstanding discovery of the day.

Returning to the gate we found our ricksha boys waiting for us, and by much gesturing conveyed to them we wanted to see Kamakura's second best attraction, its reputedly ancient and world famous wood carving industry. I say it is world famous, but I must admit I never heard of it until two weeks ago.

They took us to several shops which had large stocks of these objects d'art for sale. They turned out to be such functional items as cigarette and cigar boxes, fruit bowls, trays, bon bon dishes and salad plates. All are beautiful and, next to their lacquer work, about the best workmanship we found in Japan. They are hand carved from solid pieces of either cherry or poplar and are stained a beautiful mahogany shade. We purchased a few pieces at 10 times their pre-war price. My selection was a fancy cigarette box, while one of my companions spent his last yen for a large fruit bowl carved from the heart of a Kamakura cherry tree. I made my purchase small, for I already need Bill Malloy[5] and a small truck to get me and the junk I have accumulated off this ship.

On the way back to the station we had our chop-chop boys detour onto some of the unpaved residential streets. Those were lined on both sides by high board fences surrounding the homes of well-to-do Japanese suburbanites. For all of our neck craning, all we could see were the sloping roofs of the houses. The Jap is a stickler for privacy in his home.

At one busy intersection we saw two Japanese women squatting amid a crowd, openly nursing their babies. There was much thighslapping and tittering when they noticed our surprised looks. Even my chop-chop boy turned and grinned at our Yankee naivete.

We experienced some difficulty when it came time to pay off our ricksha boys. Their gestures and flood of Japanese meant nothing to us, so as a feeler I handed my boy a five-yen note. The effect was catastrophic, for he started to wail and complain in a mounting torrent of Japanese and it looked like he was going to cry. I don't much like tears, even from a Jap, so I hurriedly gave him another five yen.

That must have been union scale for the job, for he immediately was all smiles, bows and dirty yellow teeth, saying over and over again, "arigato, arigato", which is Japanese for "thank you."

Inside the station we saw what to a sympathetic eye would be a pitiful sight. It was a draft of the dirtiest, raggedest, most cadaverous Jap soldiers you could imagine, all awaiting transportation home after starving, fighting and suffering for as much as four years on various Pacific islands. I didn't see the German army in defeat, but I'm sure it couldn't have been as tattered, starved and dejected as these scarecrows.

An English-speaking Jap explained to us that none of them had heard from or of their families, and that their families had heard nothing of them since they left home.

"They speak of nothing else except getting home and finding whether the home still exists," he said.

"Poor devils," said the same companion who had thought the Buddha merely "big."

Kamakura was particularly interesting because it was completely untouched by bombs and its streets are practically free of Allied servicemen, who now are beginning to crowd other towns I have visited. I believe that life there is about as near pre-war normal as you could find it anywhere in the empire.

By then it was train time and Japanese trains run on time, so we were soon carried aboard by the rush of Jap travelers. The train was filled with the same people and the same smells. We do a lot of beefing about our ship, but it was with strictly pleasant anticipation that I thought of its clean interior and the hot chow that awaited us. Moreover, I made up my mind, then and there, that, water rationing or no water rationing, I would revel that night in a long, hot shower.

This may sound like a vacationing stenographer's account of her travels, but I really don't have anything much better to do to while away long night watches.

Our skipper has been discharging people from the ship as soon as they have sufficient points. Already, however, we find ourselves down to a skeleton crew, and he now says it is going to be very, very tough to get off. This isn't particularly encouraging news to a guy who dreams of a white Christmas. Besides, Saipan seems a hell of a long ways from Woodward Avenue.

By the way, is Jerry Pettit[4] running his "Bundles for Servicemen" this year?

Yours,   HAROLD

NOTES

1. A travelogue writer.
2. British poet and novelist (1865-1936), who wrote of empire and imperialism. His poem "Mandalay" provided Schachern's reference: "Bloomin' idol made o' mud – / Wot they called the Great Gawd Budd–." See T.S. Eliot, ed., *A Choice of Kipling's Verse* (Garden City, N.Y.: Doubleday, 1962), 196.
3. *Times* reporter.
4. *Times* reporter.

[Saipan, Mariana Islands]. 27 November 1945
Harold J. Schachern to Dear Friends

Dear Friends:

I have no way of telling whether the saga of Captain Oba, commander of Imperial Japanese forces on Saipan, has reached the civilian press. If not, I think it worth the telling.

Oba has been in command of an estimated force of from 65 to 100 Japanese soldiers who have been holding out guerrilla fashion for 16 months since Saipan was secured by soldiers and Marines in July, 1944.

Nothing is known of him except his name and the fact that he is an extremely foxy agent, for his feat is little short of miraculous, considering the fact that Saipan is but 12 miles long by five wide, with a good percentage of it covered by open air strips and Army, Navy and Marine warehouses and camp sites.

The Fifth Marine Battalion, a provisional outfit of crack jungle fighters, is stationed there. Its patrols have combed the island relentlessly, explored every cave, prodded every woodchuck hole, but the elusive Captain Oba and his stubborn riflemen have always been able to scamper away.

They have seen them from a distance a number of times but have never been able to catch them. They are positive of one thing and I think it highly interesting, they have four women with them. In that respect, I shall always maintain that Japanese military leaders are more enterprising than ours. Marine friends of mine who went into Kwajalein[1] found not only women there, but ration books on the prisoners. No "C" books were found. Everyone, apparently, regardless of rank, drew a basic "A" book.[2]

As late as last month, Oba's men killed four Americans, including a naval ensign, two seamen and a marine enlisted man. In the case of the marine, he was being lowered into a cave in the side of a cliff, by rope, to look for souvenirs when he was hit with a spurt from a machine gun, coming from the mouth of the cave.

The ensign and two seamen, armed with rifles, were also looking for souvenirs when they were ambushed. The marine was also armed. It appears that only those who are armed are fired on. Since those two incidents, they have tightened down on restrictions, and personnel going ashore are limited to a few recreation and working areas. In addition to these occurrences, personnel are still frequently injured by booby traps that have weathered the storms of 16 months.

When we arrived here last week, I learned from Lieut. Col. R.F. Scott, commander of the 5th Marines, that the Island Commander, Rear Admiral F.E.M. Whiting, in desperation, had imported three platoons of Samoan scouts, whom he was having trained to ferret out Oba and his crew.

Before they could be put into action, however, a Marine patrol was surprised four days ago by a Japanese enlisted man who stepped out from behind a tree with his hands in the air and demanded to be taken to the commander of the Allied forces on the island.

This boy was dressed for a general's inspection. He was wearing a brand new uniform, he had a fresh haircut, manicure and shave and his trousers were pressed to a razor sharp crease. His dress shoes sparkled in the sun.

When taken to Admiral Whiting, he said that rumor had reached his superior, Captain Oba, to the effect that the Imperial Japanese Government had capitulated. If this were true, he was willing, even anxious, to surrender his command. But, he cautioned, he must have absolute proof that it was true.

"I'm willing to give him all the proof he needs," Whiting is quoted as saying. So he loaded him down with copies of *Time, Life, Newsweek,* The *New York Times* and copies of other American publications which showed American servicemen in familiar Japanese surroundings, and sent him back into the brush to confer with Oba.

He returned with the message that "Captain Oba thought this all very interesting, but that he demanded that he be permitted to speak with the highest ranking Japanese prisoner on the island."

The best they could do was a Jap lieutenant commander who was let out of the stockade and sent to Oba with the soldier. They returned, this time the soldier bringing the message that:

"Captain Oba thinks what the lieutenant commander has to say is also very interesting, but he demands as further proof a signed statement from the highest ranking Japanese officer in the area that the surrender has actually taken place."

So Admiral Whiting broke out a plane and had one of his staff fly to Pagan Island where a Japanese general is still in command. We haven't occupied Pagan, but have removed its 3,600 defenders and left the general 65 men to keep house for him.

The general willingly wrote out a statement in his own hand and signed it. When the Jap soldier had taken this to Oba, he returned with the following message:

"Captain Oba is now convinced that Imperial Japan has actually surrendered and he is willing to surrender his command, but he demands the following terms of surrender: That he and his men be accorded full military honors, and that they be given preferential treatment, which includes being segregated from our countrymen who have succumbed to earlier surrender demands."

Admiral Whiting said nothing doing, that they would have to surrender unconditionally or not at all. The messenger took this back to his chief, and Admiral Whiting and his staff settled back to await developments.

While they were waiting, word arrived which pretty near blew up the negotiations. Some souvenir hunters who had slipped by the M.P. lines had flushed and wounded two of Oba's men. Naturally, the Admiral was furious. Oba had been a thorn in his side ever since he has been here, and he was anxious to have him out of the way.

Hourly since then there has been an announcement on the Saipan radio warning personnel to keep out of restricted areas and to fire at Japanese only in self defense. Today the following story appeared on page one of the *Saipan Beacon*:

> The Island Command, Saipan, is conducting negotiations with Captain Oba, Japanese army officer, in regard to the surrender of Japanese military and civilian personnel under his control who are still hiding out in the hills.
>
> Two Japanese were wounded Sunday, apparently by souvenir hunters who ignored an Island Command order to avoid restricted areas while the surrender negotiations are underway.
>
> Captain Oba is apparently endeavoring by all his means to disarm and assemble all men under his command. All personnel must keep out of restricted areas until the surrender takes place, probably about December 1.
>
> Military police have been directed to arrest any personnel found entering a restricted area.
>
> Rear Admiral F.E.M. Whiting, Island Commander, estimates that there are still between 65 and 100 well-armed Japanese still at large.

I learned most of this story while riding around the island on a sightseeing tour with Colonel Scott. We had parked our jeep at the top of a hill and he was pointing out spots where highlights of the battle for the island took place. A jeep pulled up and two of Scott's subordinates got out to talk to him. In the back seat were the enlisted Jap soldier and that lieutenant commander. They were then on one of the several trips they made to Oba's hideout.

I met Scott through a friend of mine, Major Joe Quilty, air-ground liaison officer for the Third Marine Division, whose brother is a shipmate of mine. When Joe flew up from Guam the other day to visit his brother, he brought with him a little wizened up Marine warrant gunner who is rounding out his 30 years in the corps.

He loves the corps with an amazing passion, but is convinced its glories are all in the past.

A veteran of Soissons, the Argonne and Nicaragua,[3] he remembers when marines went into battle with nothing but a pack, canteen, a campaign hat and a rifle. Now they use such fancy folderol as airplanes, flame throwers, artillery and tanks. Sometimes, and he blushes at the thought, they even get a ride in a truck or a jeep on their way to battle.

One night on Iwo Jima,[4] Joe sent him with a radio gang up ahead of the lines, their mission being to seek out stubborn points of resistance and call down carrier planes to bomb and strafe them at daybreak. Their route was a small river . . . and they slogged their tortuous way up its course, waist deep in water and muck, all night long. They slipped and fell and floundered on, Japs all around them in the inky blackness, and death a probability at any minute.

All this time, the Gunner was packing a 50-pound radio and a Garand rifle on his head to keep them dry. They reached their objective, however, had successful results, and when the rifle companies had moved up to take over, trudged all the way back.

When they got back to their command post, the whole patrol dropped in their tracks from sheer exhaustion; all but the Gunner.

"By God, Major," he said, "That's the most fun I've had in years. Why it was just like fightin' with the old corps. We oughta do that more often."

Although jungle growth has reclaimed and recovered most of the scars of war, there are still many grim reminders of war on Saipan. The beaches still are littered with helmets, both American and Japanese issue, cartridge belts, ammunition, canteens, knives, bayonets and rifles. General Sherman tanks and GM-made "ducks" [DUWK amphibious vehicles] stand at crazy angles in the surf, shell holes still showing in their now rusted sides.

At one place, a huge hole has been dug and into it dumped at least 200 mechanized vehicles. Caves right within the recreation area are paved with bleached skulls and bones of Jap defenders.

Our ship is anchored right off what was once the village of Garipan. It is there no longer. A naval supply base has taken its place. Above it rises Garipan Hill, where so many soldiers and marines died trying to dislodge the Jap artillery which was sweeping the beaches.

On the wall of the officers club bar is a large sign which reads: "The spot on which this club is built was secured by the Second Marine Division, 3 July, 1944."

I cannot quite describe the mixed feeling which occurs when you hit a beach like this in a marine uniform with nothing more pressing on your mind than a bourbon and water.

Yours,   HAROLD

NOTES

1. One of the Marshall Islands captured on 6 February 1944. U.S. forces found numerous laborers, mostly Koreans and some Okinawans, indicating the source of the women; Japanese soldiers from the Philippines and elsewhere account for the ration

books. See Kent Roberts Greenfield, gen. ed., *United States Army in World War II. The History of the War in the Pacific,* 11 vols. (Washington, D.C.: U.S. Government Printing Office, 1955), vol. 6: *Seizure of the Gilberts and Marshalls,* by Philip A. Crowl and Edmund G. Love, 209-12, 216, 225, 301.

2. Books for A and C field rations, respectively the food served in a mobile kitchen (4,300 calories per day) and in individual cans (3,400 calories per day). See Lee Kennett, *G.I.: The American Soldier in World War II* (New York: Scribner, 1987), 98-100.

3. The Marine veteran had participated in the closing battles of World War I (1918) and had served in Nicaragua with the intervention forces that protected United States canal and economic interests (1912-33).

4. On 19 February 1945, U.S. Marines landed on Iwo Jima, one of the Volcano Islands in the western Pacific, 750 miles from Tokyo, which provided strategic bases from which to bomb and blockade Japan. Hence the Japanese fought fiercely to keep the island, which fell five weeks later on March 16 at a cost 24,891 casualties. See Vincent J. Esposito, ed., 5th ed., *The West Point Atlas of American Wars,* vol. 2, *1900-1953* (New York: Praeger, 1972), Map 162.

> *Manila, Philippine Islands. 12 December 1945*
> *George C. Edwards to Assorted Friends*[1]

STANDARD OPERATIONAL LETTER X

I. THE BEACH HEAD THAT WASN'T THERE. On August 8, at Camp Maxey, I got orders to report to a West Coast station for shipment overseas.[2] It wasn't difficult to guess what was involved, for I was a qualified Infantry Combat Platoon leader with four months of troop duty, and everybody knew the land invasion of Japan was scheduled for the near future. I and fifty other looies [lieutenants] like me thought to ourselves "at long last, this is the why . . . of all the uniforms and marching and training and shooting and teaching. Finally here we go and on schedule!"

The war had ended; but we were still on the same schedule when . . . 300 of us . . . arrived at the 24th Replacement Depot, 60 miles north of Manila, P.I. The 24th had been scheduled to follow the invasion into Japan and [provide] replacements for the replacements who fell a bit farther on.

And believe . . . me, the plans were well laid. Never have I seen the shipping, the stock piles of food, and equipment, and munitions, and the men . . . waiting there all ready to go. . . . I reckon the Army planning section had provided for every contingency known to man that could happen. . . . The Japs just couldn't do anything that hadn't been accounted for well in advance. But they did. *They quit* and the resulting confusion was indescribable. Apparently there wasn't a plan for that.

For weeks and months after V-J day, men and supplies . . . continued to arrive at this invasion base to supply and reinforce the beach head that wasn't there. The impromptu planning that had to be done as to where to park the food, trucks, guns and shells and what to do with the men must have been a G-3's [operation officer's] nightmare.

Give the devil his due! The tide is being turned and a reasonable facsimile of order is being wrought out of chaos. The incoming troops and supplies have finally dwindled to a trickle and the outgoing ships have sailed for home with the high point combat men aboard. And as for me—two weeks after D day, in place of being with my platoon somewhere on the coast of Japan, I found myself seated at a desk in a burned out office building in Manila, surrounded by the atrocity files that told the story of the backwash of war.

II. 23 DAYS ON A TROOPER. First something about the trip over. We sailed from the Port of Los Angeles aboard an 8,000 ton converted Dutch freighter named *Kota Baroe*, which we were told was Malayan for "Beautiful Town." Again—could be! The crew also affectionately referred to her as "The Greyhound of the Pacific." Again—could be! All I know is that we were 23 days aboard her and 21 days out of sight of land and that the first two weeks of that time were the most miserable two weeks of my [physical] existence. . . . There must have been many, many longer, more crowded, more insufferable trooper crossings than ours, but to date I haven't seen any detailed description of one. . . .

We had roughly 300 officers and 1200 enlisted men aboard a converted freighter which had passenger accommodations for about 50. For those 50 of our high ranking brass it should have been a pleasure cruise. They had topside state rooms (crowded I grant, but with *air*), and they ate excellently prepared, excellently served meals off table cloths in the comfortable ward room of the ship. The rest of us (officers and enlisted men) were berthed in the holds and fed in a mess hall. . . . I was in the bottom hold of the ship, immediately below the mess hall. We slept in relatively comfortable four-tiered bunks, but the lack of air and the indescribable stench completely discounted that. I am not now speaking of good healthy body odor, or the smell of unwashed feet. Those things you get used to in the Army. What got me was the smell of stale food, dirty dish water and garbage which descended upon us like a cloud from the mess hall above—and the stench of the aged cold storage eggs in a refrigeration unit in our hold.

The first two weeks of the voyage I spent the nights wandering . . . to try to sleep on the steel deck drenched by rain or spray from frequently heavy seas. And . . . when I have trouble sleeping, something is wrong.

But even this wasn't the worst feature of the trip to me. In addition . . . *I couldn't eat.* And when that happens, something is really wrong! I would be the last to assert that I am a good sailor, but on the whole trip I was never actually ill and I was almost always hungry. . . . The food was the worst prepared—the mess hall the worst run of any I've ever encountered. The only decently prepared food we got . . . was provided by a couple of volunteer bakers who turned out some excellent bread and pastries toward the end of the voyage when the complaining reached such a pitch that the bakerless mess sergeant called for volunteers. Would that they had called for volunteers for the whole mess crew. There was actually only one meal served aboard to which I would not have preferred eating K rations[3] on deck if we could have got 'em.

The first four days of the trip it really took a hardy soul to buck that mess line. With room (and air) enough for about 200, the *Kota Baroe* "gulp and git" fed 1300 men standing on both sides of narrow tables. With the lurching of the ship occasionally sending trays and garbage and diners flying across the hold, and with the K.P.'s (the real heroes of the trip!) alternately ladling out food and vomiting in a handy bucket, there was little incentive to linger over dinner. I suddenly discovered that all my life I had depended on being able to kill the better part of three hours every day very satisfactorily—just eating. That discovery I made just as you are awakened on a summer night by the noise that the fan doesn't make when it stops.

Our course from Los Angeles was laid for the San Bernardino Straits, 6456 miles away along the great circle route. It took us 900 miles north of Hawaii, and 100 miles south of Iwo Jima and no where near any other land. Enroute I learned for the first time that Tokyo is somewhere around 2000 miles closer to the United States than Manila and that the Pacific Ocean is a helluva big place.

The last week of our trip was almost as pleasant (aside from chow!) as the first part was unpleasant. By then we had headed south out of fog and rain and heavy seas. The sea turned smooth as an inland lake. The sunsets were the most spectacularly beautiful that I have ever seen. The rich golds and purples of the sunset and the dramatic white masses of clouds suspended over the deep blue of the Pacific made unforgettable scenery. And best of all the nights were clear and starlit, perfect for sleeping on deck. You have no idea what a comfortable bed a steel deck can be.

On the 21st night we made our land fall, and at dawn we awoke in the inland waterway that leads through the San Bernardino Strait and the Sibuyan Sea, 400 miles to Manila Bay. For two days we traveled in sight of picture book islands—coral beaches with green clad mountains rising steeply above them with coconut palms outlined on the crests. Here and there along the shore were thatched (nipa) huts; and bancas with colored sails coasted along the shore. In the distance we could see the Mayon volcano, one of the few still active in the Philippines, with a plume of smoke trailing downwind from its cloud clustered crest.

In these straits just a few months before was fought a part of one of the greatest naval battles of history.[4] There were no signs of it visible.

III. MANILA, THE PEARL OF THE ORIENT. In the list of utterly destroyed cities in the world, they seem to have omitted Manila. It would be hard for me to say why. Before the war Manila was a beautiful city with broad boulevards, wide bridges and hundreds of modern business and public buildings which would have done credit to any large American city. Out along [George] Dewey & [William H.] Taft Blvds.[5] were dozens of luxurious skyscraper apartments looking out over Manila Bay. Of all these buildings there is not a one that is not substantially damaged by the storm of fire, shell and demolition that swept through Manila last February. And there are only about 3 which, by peace time terms would not have been called completely destroyed—one apartment building, the . . . custom house, and the Trade & Commerce Bldg. where I work—damaged by fire and minor demolitions but saved by our engineers from the great explosive charge the Japs had planted in her elevator shaft.

On the north side of the Pasig River, the pattern was set by the Japs— every building burned, every fourth one wrecked by demolition. Some of the results are fantastic. One concrete and steel structure, 5 stories high, was literally plucked out of its roots, moved bodily some dozen feet where it leans precariously at a 70% slant against a burned-out neighbor. Another modern movie theatre has a 20 foot bomb crater where its orchestra pit used to be and its concrete and steel frame . . . is cracked and bulged out into an egg shape by the explosion.

South of the Pasig River, our arms can lay claim to. Here a couple of weeks after General MacArthur had proclaimed the taking of Manila, American infantry, armor and artillery literally blew the city down on top of . . . Jap naval and merchant sailors organized into provisional Marine battalions. The desperate fury of that last stand of the Japs in Manila was matched only by the utter barbarity of their rape and massacre of the Filipino civilians trapped with them in the Intramuros and South Manila section.

In instance after instance in the fight for Intramuros and South Manila our heavy artillery and tanks were lined up side-by-side to pour pointblank fire at some massive building that the Japs had fortified until it finally just collapsed on their heads. Far be it from me to criticize that practice. An infantry attack without terrific artillery superiority . . . would have been suicidal. The Spaniards had built a wall 20 or 30 feet high and 40 to 50 feet thick all around the old city of Manila, and it was this the Japs elected to defend.

It was a fight to the finish and the old City of Manila is now a pile of rubble. Strangely enough the wall that gave Intramuros its name . . . is more nearly intact than any structure inside it.

I can't forget the ruins of Santo Tomas University. . . .[6] At the base of a crumbling pillar was an unmarred bronze tablet proclaiming "The University of Santo Tomas—Founded 1611 the Oldest University under the American Flag." Beyond lay the university—a twisted mass of stone and steel and tile and ashes. I could see some foliage within that looked like there had been a courtyard, and . . . the garden of the main building of the old University. The regular pattern of flower beds and urns and trees and fountain could still be discerned, though the trees were torn and stunted, the urns overturned and broken, and the flowers choked by the luxuriant weeds of this tropical climate. There were two other people in the garden, . . . an old woman digging for roots . . . as if her life depended on it (it probably did!) and a brown-skinned naked urchin taking a bath in the water that flowed from the broken pipe that had once fed the fountain.

The most appalling ruin in Manila is the Philippine Legislative Building where the Japs fought one of their last battles and where American heavy artillery blew it apart pillar-by-pillar and stone-by-stone. The result has about the same resemblance to its former architectural dignity as a man's face . . . to a human countenance after a half pound chunk of a shrapnel had smashed into it.

Manila–the Pearl of the Orient. It will be a long time before she regains the proud title. Now her streets are paths pushed by bull dozers through ashes and rubble. . . . Her homes are make-shift sheet-iron shacks or patchwork apartments in burned-out shattered buildings. Her commerce is largely black market trade in the 20% of Army supplies which are estimated to be diverted before reaching their G.I. destination. Her food, at least for the poorer people who seem to be the great majority, is either black market . . . at fantastic prices (a fair meal–15 pesos or $7.50) or . . . G.I. field rations or the garbage from Army mess halls . . . [aboard] the great army barge that pulled into the presidential dock shortly after Manila's capture. . . . Her water supply has only been listed as safe for drinking for a month now.

Some progress is being made at rebuilding and each area that the steam shovels clear reminds you all over again of Manila's tragedy. From almost every mound of ruins that the shovels open comes the smell of death and decay, and twisted steel and brick and ashes and bones are loaded indiscriminately on the G.I. trucks.

Even the nights remind you of what war brought to Manila for rebuilding operations go on 24 hours a day to the tune of heavy trucks and shovels and hammers and saws. And the almost nightly carbine firing in the streets shows that the chaos is not only wrecked buildings and roads and machinery.

In the midst of all this we live very comfortably, billeted in a burned-out department store, messing in a burned-out newspaper office. You can get used to anything. In fact you rapidly get so you don't even see these things. The chief . . . comment on Manila is an irritated complaint against the Filipinos that the City is so messed up!

IV. IN RE WAR CRIMES. In February 1945, the American Press reported the dramatic liberation of 2146 American internees from the Los Banos Internment Camp–at that time still 30 miles behind Japanese lines.

On 24 February 1945 the Associated Press reported:

> . . . Manila–Striking with quick precision from the sky by land and over water deep into enemy territory at dawn yesterday, American troops and Filipino guerrillas brought . . . freedom to 2,146 allied and co-belligerent captives in the civilian internment camp at Los Banos, 30 miles south of Manila. . . .

The attack was opened when the paratroopers . . . dropped directly on the camp, surprising the Japanese garrison. . . . At the same time, the guerrilla forces . . . attacked by land.

By the time the Japanese commander, his staff and 243 guards had been killed, amphibious troops reached the nearby beaches of Laguna de Bay, and . . . [evacuated] the internees. . . .

At the same time, Homer Bigart of the *N. Y. Herald Tribune* wrote a feature on the most hated man in the Camp!

"The Story of Lieut. Konishi"

. . . Los Banos, Luzon, Feb. 23. . . . Behind the guardhouse . . . sprawled a young Japanese lieutenant disemboweled by a grenade. It was . . . [Sadaaki] Konishi, overseer of the camp, a little man with golden buck teeth and a nerve paralysis that twisted his face into a permanent leer.

In his handling of the 2,100 internees Konishi had followed a policy of slow, deliberate malnutrition. Coming to Los Banos last July, he immediately cut the food ration in two and forbade trading with natives. . . .

The surrounding countryside was rich in produce. . . . In December . . . Rev. Constant Jergens, a Netherlands priest . . . went to Konishi:

"We do not ask the impossible" said . . . Jergens, "but if we could only have a few coconuts."

"But there are no coconuts" replied Konishi blandly. He turned to an aide and said in Japanese: "Let the bastards starve!"

When I first reported to the War Crimes Investigating Detachment, I was assigned the Los Banos Internment Camp case.[7] Since a couple of hundred affidavits substantiated . . . the fate of the Jap guards, my assignment was simply to write the story of the camp for use in the trials of the high ranking Japanese who had charge of internment camp policies. . . .

Los Banos is a little town on the Southern shore of . . . a big lake called Laguna de Bay about 40 miles south of Manila. The camp itself was located on the grounds of the Agricultural College of the University of the Philippines and a more desirable setting as to scenic beauty, climate and food supplies would have been hard to find. The area surrounding it was a tropical rain forest and one of the most productive in the world in coconuts, bananas, and camotes . . . which can be seen growing in profusion from the camp site. Yet in January and February 1945 all of the 2146 internees were on the bare edge of starvation, and existing from day-to-day on . . . a handful of unhusked rice and at least 20 of them died directly from starvation or from disease induced by starvation.

In addition . . . two Americans had been killed at the camp . . . [returning] after a dangerous foray to try to get food for themselves and their starving companions. One was killed outright by a guard. Another was wounded . . . [and soon] executed by order of the camp commander.

The further I went into the case, however, the more it appeared that the worst Japanese deeds had been visited on the Filipino residents. . . . For the great majority of the internees, the liberation provided a happy ending to three years of misery. Not so the Filipinos.

Overjoyed at the coming of the Americans and apparently with no thoughts of the possible retribution, the Filipino guerrillas had turned out somewhere near 1000 strong to aid the attack . . . [on the internment camp]. But when the evacuation had been accomplished, the Americans embarked (as indeed they had to) in their amphibious trucks and departed for the American lines.

Perforce the Filipinos stayed—and so did the Japs.

Three nights later the first blow fell. The guerrillas had elected to try to hold the college grounds and for two days they succeeded. By the end of that time they were tired and disorganized and when the Japs came in force from the nearby town of Los Banos, they promptly withdrew to the hills. . . .

The non-combatants, old men, teachers at the college, their wives and children and the inhabitants of two small barrios close [by] . . . had gathered in the Church of the College. The young men were with the guerrillas. The rest thought the guerrillas would protect them, thought the Japs might respect the church, thought the Japs wouldn't harm old men and women and children.

. . . at around 2 A.M. on February 17th, the Japs . . . called all the Filipinos to come out and some did—only to be promptly bayonetted or shot. Then an attempt was made to break down the door . . . and a boy in the church tower threw a hand grenade. The Japs retaliated by opening fire on the church with a machine gun. Then they set to fire it, and waited outside to see that no one escaped. The priests who were captured . . . before the burning, were found the next morning, one hanging from a tree . . . [and] the other bayonetted to death at his feet.

Approximately 100 people were killed that night in the church and near it—the great majority of them were women and children. But the story does not end there. This same pattern was repeated 5 times in different barrios of Los Banos during . . . February and March. 486 Filipino residents of Los Banos paid for the liberation of the Los Banos Camp and their pro-American sympathies with their lives.

My job . . . was to identify the persons who had done it and if they were still alive, find them.

Two things made the job difficult. The survivors never knew the names of their persecutors or their Army units and usually added, "All Japs look alike to me." And the staff and guard at the Los Banos Internment Camp were all dead (or were they?), and the deadest of 'em all was Konishi (or was he?)

My first inclination to doubt the interne affidavits and the published stories of the fate of the camp staff, came when I could get no indication that it had ever totalled more than 80. How then had we killed 243 of 'em? Also how had it been possible even with complete surprise to kill 243 enemy soldiers, rescue 2146 internees and withdraw within 4 hours with no casualties. Also among the several who had personally killed Konishi in various ways, which one was right.

Then I ran across . . . Filipino witnesses who swore that a week after the liberation, Konishi was in Los Banos and in charge of the Japanese detail which murdered 29 Chinese civilians.

Then I ran across Pete Miles, the American internee who escaped from Los Banos—made his way through the Jap lines to meet the 11th Air Borne and help plan the rescue. On the morning of the liberation, Pete had come into the camp with the reconnaissance team and the guerrillas 15 minutes before the Paratroopers and amphi tracks and . . . [he] said, "243, Nuts! I went all through the camp. I saw a few dead Japs and there wasn't one . . . officer. If there were a dozen killed I'd be surprised."

As it turned out even Pete exaggerated. . . . In place of 243 there were 3 Jap privates killed. The much-killed Konishi was (and is) very much alive. All of the officers and 70 some . . . enlisted men took off for Mt. McKilling the very moment they saw the first parachute. Konishi . . . was almost too slow. By the time he left the barracks the Americans were already in possession of all the roads and Konishi and a dozen men . . . hid in a ravine beside the camp hospital within 200 yards of the field where the 2146 internees were loaded on . . . trucks.

Konishi proved to be the key to the whole Los Banos case. For once we became convinced he survived the liberation, we started looking for him among the 70,000 Japanese prisoners of war scattered in some 2 dozen prison camps on Luzon. We found . . . a Jap who saw him surrender—then another . . . in the squad that Konishi took with him . . . when he joined the Japanese Battalion . . . garrisoning Los Banos. Then a Jap who had seen Konishi in a certain company at Luzon, Prisoner of War Camp #1. And finally in a . . . work camp in Manila (engaged in re-building the Wack Wack golf course) we found Warrant Officer Sadaaki Konishi, former Quartermaster of the Los Banos Internment Camp, gold teeth, buck teeth, leering grin and all, and I can authoritatively report that he hadn't been disemboweled.

From there on the case fell apart like jack straws when the key stick is pulled out. From the Konishi squad we learned the identities and fates of all the camp staff and guard. From them we learned also the regiment, the Battalion, the Companies, and the key officers and non-commissioned officers involved in the church massacre and the other killings in Los Banos. And one by one we traced them down until we had proof of their deaths or we had them identified, located and transferred to a War Criminal stockade to await trial. These last I can't write about, since their trials are still to come. The rest of the story above was related publicly by various of the Los Banos case witnesses who testified in the [Lt. Gen. Tomoyuki] Yamashita[8] trial.

At this point I can hear some of my friends saying "Just how naive has this guy gotten? Doesn't he know that atrocities are part of war? How about Hiroshima? Doesn't he know that International Law is a farce once war starts?"

Yep, I know. There is no real body of International Law that deals with war crimes. There is no International Court with jurisdiction to try war criminals and this is pretty much victor's justice—that we are meting out.

There is no doubt that the sympathies of the Filipinos were pro-American, and that with the landings at Lingayen Gulf that sympathy became much more active and more likely to be expressed in knife thrusts and rifle fire. By the humane rules of land warfare[9] . . . even the people of an invaded and occupied country . . . must avoid such guerrilla activities or be subject to summary trial and execution if caught.

To the Japs the Geneva Convention was silly.[10] They didn't bother with trials nor try to distinguish between possible guerrillas and obvious non-combatants like women and children.

When Jap soldiers were fired on, they just killed everybody in the barrio and toward the end . . . openly expressed the opinion that all Filipinos were against them and all should die. Maybe they never . . . knew how right they were—for the Colonel uttering his opinion uttered it to the pro Jap Mayor of Los Banos who was also head of the pro Jap Ganap party—[and] . . . a long standing member of the guerrillas.

Still I guess that the murder of women and children where there is no apparent [military] reason . . . for their deaths and where there is a good chance to distinguish between them and the combatants . . . is sufficient reason for figuring that the perpetrators should be indicted and tried.

. . . One of the *very* disturbing factors is just who dunnit.

1) Was it the general who probably said, "Colonel I'm damn tired of all the guerrilla trouble in your area—clean it up and quick and I don't care how you do it!"?

2) The Colonel who said, "Kill all guerrillas, men, women and children"?

3) The Battalion Commander who repeated these orders with relish and executed them with the same relish?

4) The Company Commanders who . . . executed the orders, but apparently didn't enjoy the job?

5) The Non-Coms and privates who killed with rifle, bayonet, or torch, 486 men, women and children?

The Japanese Army discipline is terrific.[11] From childhood each kid is trained to obey a military command as the highest duty. . . . You never saw such saluting in any American Army camp as the Jap prisoners do in the P.W. [Prisoner of War] camps to American and Jap officers alike. Their officers are still waited on hand and foot and obeyed automatically while the new American masters are obeyed with even greater (if possible) meekness, good humor and efficiency. And in most instances the Japanese involved in these massacres talk quite freely of their roles and excuse themselves completely of any moral guilt for the worst deeds that you can think of by simply stating "Those were my orders."

From all the above . . . [I] discern two conclusions. . . . 1. Such discipline as the Japanese Army exemplified is near the ideal for any military organization (don't think some of the U.S. Army's high brass wouldn't like it)—and is very dangerous for any democratic nation and for the world. 2. The crude attempt at creating a body of international law and defining international crimes and setting up an international court . . . here and at Nuremberg, is still one of the hopeful efforts being made in the world—whether it succeeds or not. For the very attempt implies that there must be a body of world wide law, a standard of world ethics and perforce a world organization to enforce them. I don't know whether Mr. [Henry A.] Wallace was right . . . when he proclaimed this the Century of the Common Man, but for certain, Mr. [Wendell L.] Willkie was when he called his [book] *One World*.[12] It will be either *One World* or None.

V. MY LAST MERRY CHRISTMAS FROM AN ARMY ADDRESS (I hope.)

I was strongly reminded just now that Christmas was nearby, the loud speaker in the A & R [amusement and recreation] tent blaring "I'm Dreaming of a White Christmas." At the moment I am figuratively and literally sweating out a boat-home, for it is a hot sticky day such [as] . . . only the Philippines provides. I'll never make it by Christmas, but far be it from me to complain, for my orders are out, and I am definitely on my way. And it is only 10,000 miles by slow freighter back home. Some 10 days after the Detroit election, I learned that I had been elected Council President. Peg's wireless of the day after the election had been garbled by an operator from "first" to "fifth"—which seemed reasonable enough to me.

The actual result left me very surprised, very pleased, and for once in my career quite humble. Any job in the Detroit City government is important—the Council Presidency even more so. I hope I'll be able to live up to what apparently a lot of Detroiters think I can do. All I am certain of is that I will work at it.

There must have been more friends than I have any idea of who worked for my election while I was addressing Japanese P.O.W.'s rather than Detroit voters. To all of them my deepest thanks.

And to one of them—one of the first to urge me to run for office, and one of the staunchest friends ever since—to Council President John Lodge, my very real gratitude for the most magnanimous post-election statement I have yet seen.

. . . to all of you, a very Merry Christmas and a happy New Year. I shan't be there to help celebrate either of them—but I should be seeing you soon thereafter.

Best regards & Seasons Greetings,   GEORGE EDWARDS

NOTES

1. Edwards airmailed this SOL to his wife on 12 December, intending it as a "Christmas & New Years greeting" to friends. He himself "sailed for home by slow transport"—yet arrived two months before the letter did. Hence he belatedly reproduced it and sent it out, as explained in GCE to Dear Friends, 7 March 1946, Box 2, Mayor's Papers.

2. Edwards completed OCS at Ft. Benning in March and received advanced leadership training at Camp Maxey, Texas, until ordered overseas in August.

3. K rations (emergency field rations) came in three small boxes containing a can of meat for each meal, biscuits, chocolate, bouillon, and so forth, which provided 3,100 to 3,400 calories per day. See Kennett, *G.I.*, 100.

4. The Battle of Leyte Gulf (23-25 October 1944), which actually occurred in Surigao Strait between Leyte and Mindanao, south of the San Bernardino Strait. See C. Van Woodward, *The Battle of Leyte Gulf* (New York: Macmillan, 1947).

5. Commodore Dewey defeated the Spanish fleet at the Battle of Manila Bay on 1 May 1898, opening the way for U.S. control of the Philippine Islands after the Spanish-American War; Taft served as president of the Philippine Commission (1900) and first civilian governor (1901-4) of the islands.

6. The original campus, Edwards noted, "not the new buildings in North Manila" that served as "an internment camp."

7. George C. Edwards, "Outline for Speech on Los Banos Rescue," c. 1960, pp. 1-5 (author's possession, courtesy of Edwards). See Edward M. Flanagan, Jr., *The Los Banos Raid: The 11th Airborne Jumps at Dawn* (Novato, Calif.: Presidio, 1986), 214-17, for Konishi's trial (23 November 1945–15 January 1947) and death by hanging (17 June 1947).

8. Japanese commander in the Philippine Islands.

9. The Geneva Convention on Prisoners of War, 1929.

10. Japan was a signatory at the Geneva Convention but neither ratified its proceedings nor incorporated them into the training of officers or soldiers. Not until February 1942 did the Japanese government indicate its willingness to apply the accords "whenever they were not in conflict with existing laws and regulations." And even then it gave little thought to a coherent policy until significant numbers of the enemy were captured. See Harries and Harries, *Soldiers of the Sun*, 479; Kennett, *G.I.*, 164, 184-90.

11. Discipline, like obedience, in the Imperial Japanese Army was very strict but depended on specific leaders, units, and circumstances. As officials needing greater numbers of men opened military ranks to less desirable recruits and as initial victories turned increasingly to defeat, soldiers became more undisciplined and brutal. See Harries and Harries, *Soldiers of the Sun*, 42-43, 458-59, 477-84.

12. Former Vice-President Wallace (1940-44) contended that the wise and moral application of technology to natural resources through worldwide agencies could abolish poverty and benefit common people globally; Republican presidential candidate Willkie (1940) argued that the future required thinking in terms of international collaboration that crossed "national, ethnic, and racial lines." See Edward L. and Frederick H. Schapsmeier, *Prophet in Politics: Henry A. Wallace and the War Years, 1940-1965* (Ames: Iowa Univ. Press, 1970), 35-37; Russell Lord, ed., *Henry A. Wallace: The Century of the Comman Man, Selected from Recent Public Papers* (New York: Reynal & Hitchcock, 1943); Howard Jones, "One World: An American Perspective," in *Wendell Willkie: Hoosier Internationalist*, ed. James H. Madison (Bloomington: Indiana

Univ. Press, 1992), 103-24; Wendell Willkie, *One World* (New York: Simon & Schuster, 1943).

At Sea. 11 January 1946

Harold J. Schachern to Dear Friends

Dear Friends:

. . . the last time I wrote you we were just about ready to pull up anchor at Saipan and proceed still further West. We spent the next two weeks en route to and operating in and around Lingayen Gulf, north of Manila.

We got ashore a couple of times for some Luzon local color and American beer, but the country around there was a little too primitive for any good liberty. Besides, the Philippines are in the midst of a vicious inflation, and beer at $1 Yankee a bottle made drinking the private vice of the rich.

The village of San Fernando proved interesting, I suspect, simply because it was the first Filipino native village we had seen. The people lived in semi-American houses of combined thatch and lumber; wore semi-American clothes, and lived the typical life of the poor the world around. We found them more reserved, less cordial than others of our "Little Brown Cousins," but, in comparison to the Japs, a very handsome people. We anchored . . . at the scene of the first American landings on Luzon.

About this time the admiral of our seven-ship task group got the brilliant idea of taking a vacation. He reasoned that as long as he had to keep between 4,000 and 5,000 unhappy, frustrated would-be civilians this far from home, he might just as well show them some of the orient.

So, on December 9, we sailed for Hong Kong, which was to be the first stop on an itinerary which included Shanghai, Singapore, Rangoon, Batavia and Sydney.

We had seven days ashore in Hong Kong and I can recommend the place highly. We had to be back for muster each morning, so it was impossible for us to take any trips into the interior. We did manage, however, to get over to the mainland to Kow Loon, but beyond there were only narrow trails winding into the mountains, and China is not yet a mechanized nation.

. . . Hong Kong is a British crown colony which was wrested from the Chinese in the Opium War of 1840. It is composed of the island of Hong Kong, where is located the City of Victoria, which is approximately the same size as Toledo, and the Kow Loon peninsula, site of the City of Kow Loon.

Hong Kong . . . suffered little from the war, although we heard many tales of Jap atrocities. What little bombing that was done was restricted to military targets, such as the navy yard on the outskirts of town and ships in the harbor. I believe the only time our planes struck there was last January when [Admiral William F.] Halsey's[1] carrier-based planes gave Jap shipping and harbor installations a working over.

American ships always get a rousing welcome in Chinese ports because it means big business, and does that make the British mad. Before we ever dropped our anchor, the ship was entirely surrounded by hundreds of junks, sampans and bum boats, all loaded with things to sell.

As usual, the medium of exchange was the American cigarette, and the trading was lively. Believe it or not, a large percentage of their stocks was in American watches, for which they were asking from two to three cartons of cigarettes each. God only knows where they got them, although a Chinese-American in Victoria said they were originally looted from Americans throughout China when the Japs took over, and taken away from the Japs by the Chinese when the tables were turned.

American-made flexible watch straps cost two packages of cigarettes; teakwood and camphor chests, two cartons; hand-carved figurines, six packs; and pornographic pictures, a package each.

American sailors for generations have headed first for one place upon going ashore in Hong Kong, the famous "Thieves Market" . . . . It is located in an alleyway connecting two of Victoria's main streets. Its curbs are lined with squatting Chinese, all hawking the most unrelated stock of merchandise imaginable.

Cloisonne vases and jade shared the same curbstone counters with Palmolive soap and Interwoven hosiery. There were the inevitable American and Swiss watches. . . . The ivory merchants and wood carvers were in the majority, however. Their work was beautifully done, but the subjects a little bizarre for my tastes.

After making a few minor purchases, we made a pleasant discovery here. While looking over the gaudy wares of a silk merchant, a smiling Chinese boy, looking for all the world like one of Charley Chan's movie sons, stuck his chin over my shoulder and said: "Look, lieutenant, this stuff is strictly for the birds. I can show you a guy who has the real goods."

And that's how I met Irving Ko. Irving is the 17-year-old son of a Philadelphia laundryman who was sent by his parents to their native Hong Kong in 1940 to learn Chinese and the custom of his people. Came the war and he was trapped here. He had his American citizenship papers beneath the floor in his uncle's home and sweated out the occupation, managing to keep body and soul together by working at odd jobs and stealing food from the Japanese army.

"You're the first gyrenes I've seen since I left Philly, and I'm sure glad to see you," he said. He straightway became our constant guide and companion during our stay there, showing us all the back street shops and coaching us in the Oriental science of bartering.

In China, bartering is not only a business and a science, it's a game, and Irving turned out to be an excellent teacher. The routine would be something like this. You pick out a silk kimono. You didn't admire it too much. That would be fatal. You acted as if it merely amused you. Then you casually asked the price.

"This number one, veway nice [*sic*], cost one hundred Hong Kong dollar" (about $25 American), the merchant would reply.

"Offer him ten," Irving would say out of the corner of his mouth.

Then the merchant would inevitably laugh, good naturedly, amusedly. You dropped the kimono and started to walk away. This would be his cue to ask:

"How much you pay?" Then you knew you had him. He was willing to dicker.

He would go to 90, you would raise to 14. After 30 minutes of this see-sawing your offer would amount to something like this: $30 Hong Kong, six packs of Camels, three Hershey bars, three Nestle bars and two packs of Juicy Fruit gum.

Then Irving would whisper over your shoulder: "He's weak, he's weak, you've got him on the ropes. Offer him one more Hershey bar and you've got him in your pocket."

It never failed. The bargain was always consummated when he said it would [be]. Personally, I never bought a kimono, for I know my wife would rapidly develop an allergy for crimson dragons on a purple background. Some of my friends did, however, and I offer you one of their experiences as an example.

We took the usual ricksha rides to the local points of interest; fashionable West Point, the Happy Valley race track and the most amusing sight of all, the Japanese Victory Monument. This is built of blocks of gleaming white stone and stands atop the highest and steepest mountain on the island.

The Japanese commander forced Chinese prisoners to drag and carry these huge blocks up . . . the mountain by hand. The British governor general is now going to make Jap prisoners of war carry them back down and with their own hands construct a public lavatory. Who said the British don't have a sense of humor?

Kow Loon was out of bounds to American servicemen, but on Irving's assurance that there were no MP's or Shore Patrol there, we boarded a ferry boat and went over. There the shops were fancier, the people more prosperous and the entire atmosphere quieter. We saw the finest Chinese objects d'art, amazing stocks of jade and semi-precious stones and shelves full of British woolens and Scotch whiskey, all prohibitively priced.

Here, as in Victoria, it was almost impossible to get a drink. Vat 59 was $35 a fifth; American beer $2 a bottle, and Hong Kong beer, $1. Hong Kong beer tastes like my Dad's first attempt at making home brew.

But Irving was enterprising. He got wind of a British officers club. Drinks in British clubs are always dirt cheap, but they're awfully hard to find. Irving found this one. As is customary in British officers clubs, however, the whiskey ran out 10 minutes after we got there; the brandy went in another 20 minutes, and then the gin and rum in rapid succession. When they got down to port wine, we threw in the towel.

Since the British have re-occupied Hong Kong, Irving has had to return to high school, which means he has to go to bed nights. So we had to find a night guide. We found him in that club and he was heaven sent. He was Captain H.L. Ozorio, a Chinese-Portuguese doctor in the British medical corps.

When the Japs took Hong Kong, he got his wife to Kunming, then returned as a counter-espionage agent. Towards the end of the war he became liaison man between the American Army Air Forces in China and the Chinese underground. Leading a cloak and dagger existence, he circulated as a combination spy-surgeon through dozens of hospitals in Jap-held China. He introduced us to some of his colleagues; hotel clerks, shop keepers, even ricksha boys.

"There aren't so many of them left," he explained. "Many were caught and beheaded."

You will begin to think there are no limits to this man's powers when I tell you he plays the piano just slightly better than Duke Ellington.[2] I have never heard a better piano player.

The most exotic spot he took us to was the Kan Ming Cafe, located in West Point, the Grosse Pointe[3] of Victoria. It is Hong Kong's most exclusive restaurant and the meal they served us defies description. Typical of the better Chinese restaurants, it was built on various levels.

The higher up you go, the fancier the appointments, the better the food and service and the more beautiful the waitresses. The Kan Ming has six floors and we didn't spare the elevator. The place was beautifully decorated, even by American standards, and the service supreme by any standards.

We had three waiters and three waitresses who alternated carrying in the strange dishes they served, lighting our cigarettes and keeping our glasses full of hot rice wine. In addition, we rated three of their "most beautiful" girls whose job it was to sit at the table and ladle out our portions of food from the steaming chafing dishes, demonstrate the proper use of chopsticks and provide conversation. The latter was a hopeless task, for they spoke little English, and we spoke no Chinese.

About midway in the meal, a three piece Chinese orchestra, playing native music on strange stringed instruments, came in to entertain us. One was a one-string, mandolin-type affair, while the second resembled the zither, except that it was played with small felt mallets. With them was a Chinese sing-song girl who sang the monotonous melodies in a pleasant enough voice.

. . . [After] a while [the music] began to make sense and we found ourselves humming it and enjoying it. It is rather primitive stuff, but not unlike the native folk music of Europe and our own American South. I am thinking particularly of our Negro spirituals. The big difference, Ozorio explained, lies in the fact that Chinese music is all written in major, they being entirely unfamiliar with minor chords.

The food itself was as strange as the surroundings. While none of us would care to go on a diet of it, we thought it delicious. Such dishes as steamed fish with sweet and sour sauce will never replace ham and eggs or porterhouse steak in the American taste, but we can recommend it on your night out. Those of you who frequent Tom Wong's[4] would feel at home there. I described Wong's dishes to Ozorio and he said: "Your Wong must come from North China, for that is Northern cooking."

We also had fried prawns with ginger sauce, chicken and nuts with cream, sweet corn soup, pig's shank with vegetables and many other dishes which passed in front of us so rapidly and in such profusion that I didn't get time to memorize their names.

The mention of hot rice wine probably doesn't make the average American mouth water, but it certainly sparked the meal, probably because it followed a quart of excellent Scotch whiskey lavishly provided by our guide. The wine was very dry and, served at room temperature, would have greatly resembled Sauterne. Frankly, we don't think the California wine industry will have to bank on the turns to beat it, but I'll remind you again that drinks are hard to get here.

A note of unreality . . . was struck by a row of leather-covered couches at one end of the room which were provided for patrons wishing to smoke after eating. And by smoking, they didn't mean Prince Albert. For some reason or other, however, they didn't ask us if we wished to sample the joys of opium.

When Ozorio learned I was ship's bandmaster, he insisted on a tour of Hong Kong's dance spots, at each of which he was greeted with loud acclaim. In each case he took over the band and immediately appointed me tenor saxophone player. I hadn't done that since my college vacation days when we would take a postman's night off and go sit in one another's bands.

Before he left us on our last night in Hong Kong, Ozorio told me his greatest ambition in life is to be an American, and he thinks he's going to make it as soon as his trick in the British Army is finished. I hope he does. I think we can use him.

The people of Hong Kong were sorry to see us go, for we brought the largest group of American sailors and the only marines they had seen since before the war, and American servicemen have always meant money in the bank to these people. We hadn't had any money-spending liberty since we left Pearl Harbor in October, so the boys poured ashore well heeled. There hadn't been so much business in Hong Kong in years. On the last day there wasn't a kimono or pair of silk pajamas left in town.

An officer fairly high in our Army Air Transport Command told us the local British authorities were more than a little angry because we had made them lose face with their subject Chinese. He made us a bet that our plans to visit other British ports would be cancelled . . . at the request of the British foreign office. He was right. . . .

We left Hong Kong on December 20 to spend Christmas in Manila, and it was there that we learned of our change in plans. We weren't terribly disappointed . . . [that] we would be heading East, in the general direction of the United States.

Manila was a keen disappointment, for it is no longer the beautiful city we remembered from pre-war newsreels. From end to end it is a bomb-wrecked ruin. The people seemed incredibly poor and here inflation was even more vicious than in San Fernando. Although food seemed fairly plentiful, prices were staggering; shoes were not to be had, except at black market prices.

Except for castoff or stolen American army uniforms, there seemed to be little clothing available. American GI beer, acquired through theft and, I fear, black market activities of American servicemen, sold openly for as high as $6 a bottle, and the shabbiest flop house hotel room rented for $15 a night.

Until we arrived, there were only two marines in Manila, a colonel and a major who are in charge of interpreters at the war crimes trials. Like Irving Ko, they were glad to see some gyrenes. "The army is OK," they said, "but you know how it is."

In typical tourist fashion, we toured all the rubberneck points of interest, spending a day . . . tramping around Corregidor,[5] and going through infamous Bilibid Prison and Santo Tomas University. These were all very interesting, but we got our biggest kick out of a day spent at the war crimes trials.

The principal trials, those of brigadier generals and above, are being held in the war-damaged governor general's mansion, while lesser lights are tried in a group of frame buildings which the army has thrown up on the mansion grounds.

We sat in on several of these while waiting for the main courtroom to open. One interesting case concerned a Japanese colonel who commanded the military police at Santiago, and who was charged with executing a number of Filipino civilians without a trial.

His defense counsel, an American army captain, sought to prove that the colonel was not the head of the military judiciary in the area, nor was he the reviewing authority. He maintained that the colonel, in carrying out the executions, was merely following the orders of a military tribunal. He couldn't seem to prove, however, that such a tribunal ever existed.

Although we never learned how he made out, I, for one, wouldn't have given a nickel for the Colonel's chances, for he was the perfect cartoonist's conception of a Jap military leader —bald head, mustache, buck teeth, round, dumpy figure and bowed legs. You've seen his caricature a thousand times in *Colliers, The New Yorker* and the Sunday comics. Lichty[6] does him especially well.

Lieut. General [Hikotara] Tajima was on trial in the main courtroom when we got there. He was commander of Japanese forces on Batan

Island, not to be confused with the Bataan to which Douglas MacArthur returned.[7] Tajima was charged with beheading a long list of prisoners of war, including three American fliers. His entire staff of some dozen officers and noncoms were also on trial with him.

We listened to the complete testimony of a young Filipino woman, sister of two of the victims. Tajima's American defense counsel sought to break down her story that her brothers and their associates were harmless civilians who were not engaged in guerilla activities.

He argued that the Filipinos in question were guerrilla troops, dressed as civilians, and were, therefore, not covered by the Geneva agreement governing the treatment of prisoners of war.[8] He also maintained they were engaged in espionage activities and thus were liable to the fate of apprehended spies.

The girl . . . stuck staunchly to her story.

"My brother told . . . [Tajima's aide] that he liked the Americans better than he liked the Japs, and he told him why. That is all they had against them," she said.

. . . I must admit that there was a great deal of hearsay and surmises in her testimony, which the defense counsel sought to have thrown out as evidence. But the four-man court, composed of two army brigadier generals and two colonels seemed out for Tajima's blood and denied every one of his objections.

We were all a little shocked at this, having seen judges throw this type of testimony out repeatedly in American courts, but after considering that this toothy, grinning little bastard had hacked the heads off three American pilots for pure spite, I, for one, didn't much care whether he got a break or not.[9]

One of our party summed up our feelings pretty accurately when he said: "Let's hang the whole damned gang right away so we can get over in time for the bar opening."

You'll have to consult the back issues of the paper to learn what ultimately happened to Tajima,[10] for although we promised ourselves to spend all our remaining time there, we sailed with the tide for Guam the following morning.

We spent . . . one day at Guam. There we loaded some surplus aircraft which they wanted transported to Pearl Harbor. Pearl Harbor seems as near home as Royal Oak[11] when you are that far away, so the news was received with relish. It was at least in the right direction.

We are still en route and are due to arrive there January 14. It has been a rough trip. For five straight days we bucked a head wind that ranged from 45 to 60 miles an hour. We lost the captain's gig [boat], most of our life rafts and all of our peace of mind. You should try it sometime. Even if you didn't get seasick, you would . . . develop a case of complete frustration, jangled nerves and bruised flesh.

After we get to Pearl Harbor there are three possibilities. . . . First, that we will [assist in the] . . . training [of] marine squadrons in carrier procedure; that we will return to the United States for yard availability, or go into aircraft transport duty. The latter seems likely, for the navy has thousands of planes scattered throughout the Pacific which can be used for training purposes. . . .

If we should do this, I would stand a good chance of getting . . . out of the service. If not, I've been had, for there aren't more than a dozen officers in the Marine Corps trained in this type of work, and all of them are reserves with as many points as I have. There would be no justification for keeping Marine fighter director officers aboard a transport, so that is my only hope. Once off the ship, I'm of no value to the Marine Corps until another war comes along, and I figure on being too old for the next one.

During this tour, try as I might, I haven't been able to avoid making like William L. Shirer[12] every time we hit a strange port, Hong Kong and Manila were no exceptions, so I soon found myself asking people what they thought about the United States, Britain and current questions.

About the only thing everybody agreed on in Hong Kong was an intense dislike for the British and admiration, born of amazement, for the United States. The job our air transport command did alone in India and China has made the British look like pretty small potatoes. A common expression among Orientals is: "Those crazy Yanks. They can do anything."

Everybody agrees that America's big hope for international trade in the years to come is China. In order to do this, they argue, we must invest in the industrialization of China, for a prosperous, industrial China will buy 10 times as much from us as a poverty-stricken, agrarian one. I believe history bears this argument out. They point out that Britain, and to a lesser degree the Netherlands, have every other market in the Orient bottled up, so we have no where else to go.

The man in the street in Manila, it may surprise you to learn, wants no part of independence. He's more interested in freedom, and he feels his best hope for that lies with the United States. The ones I talked to . . . said it is the rich landowner class which is stumping for independence. He fears that if they win it, it will then be a case of the rich getting richer and the poor poorer.

Another reason he wants to hang onto Uncle Sam is the fact that the country has been devastated by war, and he feels that America is the only one which can and will rebuild it for him. Everywhere I heard it said that enterprising Americans . . . connected with the construction industry—architects, lumbermen, contractors, will find this a promised land for some years to come.

The Filipino also is terribly concerned about the runaway inflation which is even now making it difficult for him to get enough to eat and wear. Only the backing of the United States Treasury and American legislation can defeat it, he feels.

I was shocked to hear American Army men belittle the Filipino's war effort. One infantry captain who had been there since D-Day said: "There were more pillaging, raping and murdering by Filipino guerrillas than by Japs. Since we arrived, all he's done is steal from us. We've lost better than 20 percent of all the millions of dollars worth of supplies and equipment we've landed here through theft."

The army and navy were making a determined effort to stop this theft when we were there, but this had resulted in almost open warfare. An army sergeant, brother of one of our pilots, told me: "When we stopped them from stealing, they got out their guns they had used against the Japs and started using them on us. Foraging parties raid our camp every night and we have pitched battles. . . . I guess they need the food and are willing to fight to get it."

A lieutenant of engineers on Corregidor told me: "We've tried hiring Filipinos to help us repair the island, but it's no good. They won't work, no matter how much we pay them. We have to put a guard over them every minute to keep them from stealing us blind. One Jap prisoner is worth 50 of them.

"The Jap prisoners are swell. They follow orders to the letter and work until you tell them to quit. When it comes time for them to be shipped home, they bawl like babies and beg to be allowed to stay. They say it is the happiest life they have ever known, the best food and the best treatment."

Now that you know all about the Philippines, I'll close, hoping the next thing I write for you will be on *Times* copy paper. I promise to keep it shorter.

Yours,   HAROLD

NOTES

1. U.S. Naval commander in the South Pacific.
2. Edward Kennedy Ellington, internationally renowned African American composer, pianist, and band leader of jazz music in the 1930s and 1940s.
3. A wealthy suburb east of Detroit.
4. A Detroit restaurateur.
5. Three days after the attack on Pearl Harbor, Japanese forces invaded Luzon in the Philippine Islands, forcing Gen. MacArthur to withdraw his forces to the Bataan peninsula and his headquarters to Corregidor island. MacArthur was ordered to the safety of Australia in March 1942, but U.S. and Filipino troops under Lt. Gen. Jonathan M. Wainwright held Bataan until April 9 and Corregidor until May 6; their determined defense slowed Japanese control of the archipelago and indicated vincibility, thus symbolizing Allied hope for the future. See Kent Roberts Greenfield, gen. ed., *United States Army in World War II. The War in the Pacific,* 11 vols. (Washington, D.C.: U.S. Government Printing Office, 1953), vol. 4: *The Fall of the Philippines,* by Louis Morton, 353-66, 454-67, 562-84.
6. George Maurice Lichtenstein graduated from the University of Michigan (1929) and returned to his native Chicago as a cartoonist for the *Chicago Times.* He created the comic strips *Sammy Swirt* and, beginning in 1932, the familiar *Grin and*

Bear It. See Martin Sheridan, *Classic Comics and Their Creators: Life Stories of American Cartoonists from the Golden Age* (Arcadia, Calif.: Post-Era Books, 1942, 1973), 253-55.

7. Bantan Island lies immediately north of the Philippines, approximately midway between Luzon and Taiwan. In contrast, the Bataan peninsula juts into Manila Bay on the west coast of Luzon (northernmost of the Philippine Islands), site of the allied surrender to Japanese forces in early 1942 and the ensuing "death march" of U.S. and Filipino prisoners that claimed more than 5,500 lives. MacArthur's triumphant returned to the Philippines occurred in February 1945. See Perret, *There's a War to Be Won,* 495-97.

8. See GCE, SOL X, 12 Dec. 1945, above.

9. Given the samurai tradition, which required soldiers to fight until disabled or killed and to commit ritual suicide if captured while wounded, many Japanese officers held prisoners of war in contempt. Moreover, they saw them as potential sources of information, requiring harsh interrogation methods. Rank-and-file soldiers considered prison guard duty almost as dishonorable as being captive themselves and treated POWS accordingly. See Perret, *There's a War to Be Won,* 495; Harries and Harries, *Soldiers of the Sun,* 476, 478.

10. Tajima was sentenced to death by hanging for having executed the aviators without a trial. See *New York Times,* 2 Feb. 1946, 3.

11. A suburb adjacent to northwest Detroit.

12. Widely known journalist who later wrote the best-selling *Rise and Fall of the Third Reich* (New York: Simon & Schuster, 1960).

SELECTED
BIBLIOGRAPHY

MANUSCRIPTS

The letters in this anthology come from three sources, two of which are rich depositories of primary sources for the history of Detroit.

The Burton Historical Collection of the Detroit Public Library holds the Mayor's Papers (1939-47) of Edward J. Jeffries Jr., which contain most of the correspondence from Martin S. Hayden, Harold J. Schachern, and Walton Stoddard White. Here, too, are many of George C. Edwards's personal letters to the mayor and some of his Standard Operational Letters (SOLs). Together they indicate anew Jeffries's significance as a major political figure for local and national urban studies during the Great Depression and World War II.

The Archives of Labor and Urban Affairs of the Walter P. Reuther Library, Detroit, house the George C. Edwards Collection, which includes his military, political, and private wartime correspondence: most of his SOLs, and his more personal letters to and from servicemen, civilian friends, and political associates. Those from James P. Simpson, John J. McElhone, and Joseph P. Lash are most valuable for this book, but many others provide insights into the lives of Edwards and his wife, and their important contributions to the city and its liberal forces.

Finally, family members and relatives of the letter writers have lent the author some of the correspondence and other priceless materials in their possession, such as the "Diary of Martin S. Hayden: October 1943–August 1945," which records Hayden's experience overseas; and "World War II: June 1944–October 1945," a compilation of John M. Carlisle's stories from the European and Pacific fronts.

BOOKS AND ARTICLES

Berthelot, Helen Washburn. *Win Some, Lose Some: G. Mennen Williams and the New Democrats.* Detroit: Wayne State Univ. Press, 1995.

Capeci, Dominic J., Jr. *Race Relations in Wartime Detroit: The Sojourner Truth Housing Controversy of 1942.* Philadelphia: Temple Univ. Press, 1984.

Capeci, Dominic J., Jr., and Martha Wilkerson. "The Detroit Rioters of 1943: A Reinterpretation." *Michigan Historical Review* 16 (Spring 1990): 49-72.

———. *Layered Violence: The Detroit Rioters of 1943*. Jackson: Univ. Press of Mississippi, 1991.

Carlisle, John M. *Red Arrow Men: Stories about the 32nd Division on the Villa Verde*. Detroit: Arnold-Powers, 1945.

Clive, Alan. *State of War: Michigan in World War II*. Ann Arbor: Univ. of Michigan Press, 1979.

Conot, Robert. *American Odyssey*. New York: William Morrow, 1974.

Darden, Joe, Richard Child Hill, June Thomas, and Richard Thomas. *Detroit: Race and Uneven Development*. Philadelphia: Temple Univ. Press, 1987.

Edwards, George. *Pioneer-at-Law: A Legacy in the Pursuit of Justice*. New York: Norton, 1974.

Ephron, Nora. *Scribble, Scribble: Notes on the Media*. New York: Knopf, 1978.

Esposito, Vincent J., ed. *The West Point Atlas of American Wars,* vol 2, *1900-1953*. 5th ed. New York: Praeger, 1972.

Fine, Sidney. *Frank Murphy: The Detroit Years*. Ann Arbor: Univ. of Michigan Press, 1975.

———. *Frank Murphy: The Washington Years*. Ann Arbor:Univ. of Michigan Press, 1984.

———. *Violence in the Model City: The Cavanagh Administration, Race Relations, and the Detroit Riot of 1967*. Ann Arbor: Univ. of Michigan Press, 1989.

Fragnoli, Raymond R. *Transformation of Reform: Progressivism in Detroit— and After, 1912-1933*. New York: Garland, 1982.

Funigiello, Philip J. *The Challenge to Urban Liberalism: Federal-City Relations during World War II*. Knoxville: Univ. of Tennessee Press, 1978.

Gelfand, Mark I. *A Nation of Cities: The Federal Government and Urban America, 1933-1945*. New York: Oxford Univ. Press, 1975.

Kennett, Lee. *G.I.: The American Solider in World War II*. New York: Scribner, 1987.

Lash, Joseph P. *Eleanor Roosevelt: A Friend's Memoir*. Garden City, N.Y.: Doubleday, 1964.

Lingeman, Richard R. *Don't You Know There's a War On? The American Home Front, 1941-1945*. New York: Putnam, 1970.

Litoff, Judy Barrett, David C. Smith, Barbara Wooddall Taylor, and Charles E. Taylor. *Miss You: The World War II Letters of Barbara Woodall Taylor and Charles E. Taylor*. Athens: Univ. of Georgia Press, 1990.

———, eds. *Since You Went Away: World War II Letters from American Women on the Home Front*. New York: Oxford Univ. Press, 1991.

———, eds. *We're in This War, Too: World War II Letters from American Women in Uniform*. New York: Oxford Univ. Press, 1994.

Meier, August, and Elliott Rudwick. *Black Detroit and the Rise of the UAW*. New York: Oxford Univ. Press, 1979.

Morris, Richard B., ed. *Encyclopedia of American History*. New York: Harper, 1953.

Perret, Geoffrey. *There's a War to Be Won: The United States Army in World War II*. New York: Random House, 1991.

Polmar, Norman, ed. *World War II: America at War, 1941-1945*. New York: Random House, 1991.

Rich, Wilbur C. *Coleman Young and Detroit Politics: From Social Activist to Power Broker*. Detroit: Wayne State Univ. Press, 1989.

Shogan, Robert, and Tom Craig. *The Detroit Race Riot: A Study in Violence*. New York: Chilton, 1964.

Sitkoff, Harvard. "The Detroit Race Riot of 1943." *Michigan History* 53 (Fall 1969): 183-206.

Terkel, Studs. *"The Good War": An Oral History of World War Two*. New York: Pantheon, 1984.

Tillery, Tyrone. *The Conscience of a City: A Commemorative History of the Detroit Human Rights Commission and Department, 1943-1983*. Detroit: Wayne State Univ. Center for Urban Studies, 1983.

Vexler, Robert I., comp. and ed. *Detroit: A Chronological and Documentary History, 1701-1976*. Dobbs Ferry, N.Y.: Oceana, 1977.

INDEX